Selectivity

Selectivity

The Theory and Method of Fly Fishing for Fussy Trout, Salmon, and Steelhead

Matt Supinski
Foreword by Al Caucci

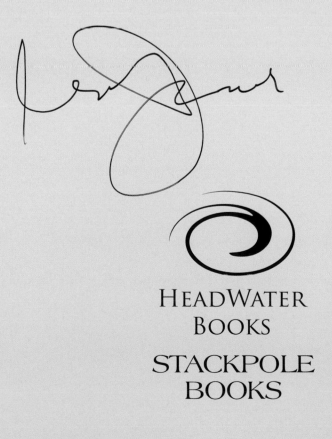

HeadWater
BOOKS

STACKPOLE
BOOKS

Published by
STACKPOLE BOOKS
5067 Ritter Road
Mechanicsburg, PA 17055
www.stackpolebooks.com

Printed in the United States of America

10 9 8 7 6 5 4 3 2 1

FIRST EDITION

Library of Congress Cataloging-in-Publication Data

Supinski, Matthew, author.
 Selectivity : the theory and method of fly fishing for fussy trout, salmon, and steelhead / Matt Supinski ; Foreword by Al Caucci. — First edition.
   pages cm
 Includes bibliographical references.
 ISBN 978-0-8117-1101-2
1. Fly fishing. I. Caucci, Al, writer of supplementary textual content. II. Title.
 SH456.S87 2014
 799.12'4—dc23
                        2013037089

Contents

Foreword vii

Acknowledgments xi

Introduction: Some Notes for Nonbelievers 1

Selectivity: The Phases 7

Trout: An Overview 19

Trout: Habitat, Behavior, and Tactics 37

The Selective/Reflective Trout 61

The Aggressive/Active Trout 97

Steelhead 123

Atlantic Salmon 171

Fly Plate Recipes 207

Index 254

Foreword

Al Caucci

In June 1962, after reading an article in *Field and Stream*, I became fascinated with the possibility of fly fishing for wild brook trout in the Mount Katahdin area of Maine. My amazing wife of one year, Betti, sensed my obsession with this fly-fishing thing and booked a Maine trip so that I could learn how to fly fish for trout. Previous fishing days had been spent with bait and spinning rods casting for bass, walleye, and even channel cats in the local lakes and the tide-water Delaware River between Trenton, New Jersey, and Philadelphia, as well as surf fishing for stripers off the Jersey Shore, an hour's drive from my house. The fly-fishing world was a million miles away from the culture of my Italian neighborhood in Bristol, Pennsylvania, a northern burb of Philly.

A few weeks later, in mid-June, Betti and I embarked on the two-day drive, which included a four-hour slog on a dirt logging road, to Mount Katahdin and Lake Sordahunk. I had a newly acquired Shakespeare Wonder Rod and Pfleuger Medalist reel with an HCH line recommended by George, the owner of the lodge that we had booked. He promised to teach me how to fly cast (there were no fly-fishing schools in those days). George assigned us to a log cabin that included access to a boat and outboard and then proceeded to give me a lesson in fly casting: "Just go like this and go like that," he said. "It takes a long time to become a fly fisherman, just keep practicing. See ya later."

"George, what about the flies?" I protested. "We only use Parmachene Belles and Hornberg Specials here," he said, and he gave me a small box of the big flies, size 6 and 8 as I recall.

We took the boat out on this beautiful lake just before sunset. Trout were rising all over the place. It was an awesome sight for this city boy, and I cast at those fussy devils until dark without hooking a single one. Something was wrong, and I couldn't figure out what! It was probably my casting. Or maybe George had given me the wrong flies. I explained the problem at dinner and he said that I was being too impatient: "You've got to keep practicing, it takes a long time to become a fly fisher."

I didn't get much sleep that night. At six o'clock in the morning I elbowed Betti, who was sound asleep. "Time to go fishing," I said. "No, no it's still dark," she said sleepily, but one look at me and she knew it was hopeless to argue. After boating through the mist, we pulled into a cove where the trout were rising just like they had the night before. We started casting with the same flies and the same results. "Something is wrong here, Betti. Hand me that fly box," I said. I dumped the flies from the box and used it as a scoop to collect the insects caught in the water's surface film. Then I started the motor and sped back to the lodge.

I rang the bell in the office, and when George showed I said, "George, I need flies that match these little dark flies, please let me see what you have." George mumbled "pain in the ass" (or something to that effect) as he handed me a cigar box of snarled-up flies. I picked some small darkish dries, size 16s, and searched around for some tippet material thinner than the 10-pound test he had given me the day before. When I got back to the cove I tied on a dark size 16 Black Gnat, and bingo. I hooked and landed my first trout and caught my limit in about an hour (no one had heard of catch-and-release in those days). Betti also landed a number of those 12-inch beauties.

I learned an important lesson that first day about selective trout (even with supposedly dumb brookies) and it became a credo for the rest of my fly-fishing life. From that day forward, whenever I approached a trout stream, river, or pond, I became obsessed with the insects that were on and under the water's surface. I searched under rocks for insects before the hatch and skimmed the surface during the hatch. I'd also comb the leaves of bushes and trees for the adult insects. Casting to fish was not a priority until I figured out what bugs were on the water and determined the fly I needed to match them. I spent most of my time observing the bugs on the water and formulating the strategy I needed to hook feeding trout without spooking them.

Throughout the sixties I transformed into a fly-fishing maniac, taking weekend trips to the mountain rivers of the Poconos, Catskills, and Adirondacks. I couldn't get enough fly fishing. Betti initially joined me on these trips but eventually tired of those long days when I left the stream only reluctantly at dark. She hinted that my surf-fishing cousin might be interested in fly fishing, and he soon became my first fly-fishing buddy!

It was great to be a fly fisher in those days. There was a fly-fishing revolution going on with books, new technology in equipment, and a greater awareness of the environment. All of this inspired me not only to fish, but also to experiment and develop a better fly-fishing strategy. My mechanical engineering background gave me the tools and the ability to analyze and solve problems, which I applied to my fishing research. I read every entomology and fly-fishing book I could get my hands on: Charlie Fox's *This Wonderful World of Trout*, Vince Marinaro's *A Modern Dry-Fly Code* and *In the Ring of the Rise*, Art Flick's *Streamside Guide*, Ernie Schwiebert's *Matching the Hatch*, James George Needham's *Biology of Mayflies*, and many more.

Betti and I soon bought a property in the Poconos, and we scrimped and saved enough to build a modest cabin on a small "trib" of the upper Lehigh River. It was close to a half dozen of my favorite steams in the Poconos and southern Catskills, including Brodhead and Bushkill Creeks and the Lehigh and Beaverkill Rivers. I also made trips to the spring creeks of the Cumberland and Lehigh Valleys and to the famous central Pennsylvania streams. During this period I worked my engineering job in the Philly area on weekdays and pursued my passion for fly fishing on weekend and vacation jaunts to the cabin. Every Friday, Betti and I would load the station wagon with our three kids, a dog, a cat, and a parakeet, and return on Sunday night.

By 1965 I was experimenting with tying flies and redesigning standard flies to catch fussy browns. Although I used Catskill dries, I found they were not effective on persnickety trout, especially wild browns and 'bows. Observations of the insects in the small aquariums that I kept at the cabin revealed that most of the insects, especially the mayflies, would struggle in the surface film when evacuating their shucks, and many didn't make it through the meniscus, remaining crippled throughout the process. Those that made it had a hard time getting up on their legs because their bodies were stuck in the surface film. This was also true on the rivers I fished, especially in the long, smooth pools. Hackled flies with hackle fibertail clumps, found in the Catskill ties and Wulff patterns of that time, kept the fly's body out of the surface film, giving the impression of evasiveness, rather than the vulnerability that I saw in my aquariums and on the rivers.

This observation led to my creation of the Compara-dun dry fly in 1966. Due to the absence of hackle, the body of the Compara-dun stuck in the surface film, matching the vulnerability of the emerging insects that trout key on. The hollow fibers of the deer-hair wing and pontoon tail fibers of the Compara-dun kept the fly afloat better than the Catskill and Wulff patterns. The fly was rugged and lasted many chewings. I also experimented with deer hair for emerger and caddis wings and perfected these later with Bob Nastasi.

I met Bob Nastasi in 1970. He visited with a neighbor and mutual friend, Otto Barz, to check out my cabin and have a few drinks. A recent convert to fly fishing, Bob's eyes lit up when he saw my fly-tying equipment, flies, and aquariums. We became fast friends and talked until the wee hours about trout and insects. Bob, a partner in a New York City advertising firm, was creative, enthusiastic, and a brilliant graphic artist and photographer with an amazing sense of color. He was also bonkers about "match the hatch" fishing. We had similar backgrounds: he came from a tough neighborhood in Brooklyn, and had moved to New Jersey recently with his wife and three kids. My neighbor, Otto Barz, was an executive at an NYC textbook publishing house.

Within a few weeks I received a call, and an invitation, to join them in a publishing venture on angling/entomology books. I would provide the planning, stream research, and the writing; Bob would do the artwork and photography and assist me in the stream research and fly pattern development; and Otto would handle the publishing, editing, and business end. It was an ideal combination, one that turned my life in a new direction. We formed Comparahatch Limited, and published *Compara-hatch* (1973), *Hatches* (1975), *Flytyers Color Guide* (1978), and *Instant Mayfly ID Guide* (1983). We also produced fly-tying materials and trout flies. (Nick Lyons published *Hatches II* in 1986 and my 2012 streamside guide *The Mayfly Guide* was recently published through The Lyons Press.) We kept our day jobs and invested the profits from Comparahatch into new projects. My friendship with Bob lasted a lifetime until he passed away in 2004. We were like brothers and I miss him dearly.

Every twenty or thirty years a fishing book comes along that is so much better than the rest that it becomes a must-read, a bible for all serious anglers. Matt Supinski's *Selectivity* is one such book. He emailed me a draft in the middle of the Delaware Hendrickson season (my kids and grandkids are forbidden to even marry during this time). I was glued to my computer screen reading it nights and mornings, days on end, when I wasn't fishing. And then I reread it as if I didn't believe the first read. Its pages are loaded with original information and thought-provoking theories, not just the evolutionary reshuffling and regurgitated stuff that is found in many fly-fishing books these days.

Selectivity is a great read—current, refreshing, entertaining, and reverent with a good dose of plain speak. Supinski's sense of angling history and tradition is extraordinary for this day and age. His rapport with the writers (both old and new), photographers, top guides, and world-renowned lodge owners is obvious, and amazing photos and quotes from fly-fishing elites and newcomers are generously distributed throughout the book.

Hundreds, maybe thousands, of books have been written on the subject of trout, salmon, and steelhead, yet Matt covers his subject matter thoughtfully and cleverly in one efficient, expertly written volume. Supinski organizes his subjects into the Aggressive/ Active (A/A), Selective/Reflective (S/R), and Passive/Dormant (P/D) behavior patterns. Each phase dictates the qualities and nuances a fish will display when operating in each mode so that an angler can make calculated adjustments in his approach to match fly size, silhouette, style, color, tippet size, and presentation. I have long used a similar technique on my rivers, studying the different riseforms to determine what phase of insect the trout were eating and what style of fly to use—emerger, dun, cripple, or spinner—and ultimately how to present my imitation to those selective trout. Supinski takes it to another level with his diagnostics, not just for trout, but for the moody steelhead and the wacky personality of the Atlantic salmon. It's mind-boggling stuff! Each of Supinski's phases bears important subchapters addressing different species (browns, rainbows, brook trout, and others), river ecosystems, chemical makeup, evolutionary history, intimidating conundrums for prey and predator, spring creeks, freestone rivers, tailwaters, and a lot more. Each subchapter has even more headings, focusing on tactics, rise types, specialized equipment, water temps, trophy fish, and ethics. All of this is done in an engrossing, entertaining, and humorous style.

Supinski is as interesting as his book. He has undertaken extensive angling adventures in all the coveted fly-fishing venues of Europe, Russia, Patagonia, New Zealand, Alaska, British Columbia, and Canada's Gaspé Peninsula. He has experience on the prolific spring creeks, freestone streams, and tailwaters of the United States, including the Delaware, Missouri, Bighorn, Beaverhead, San Juan, Clinch, Frying Pan, Silver, and Armstrong. He logs mega days on the Muskegon and other famous Michigan rivers.

Lodge owner, guide, teacher, video star, writer, and fly fisherman, Matt Supinski spends three hundred days per year guiding and chasing trout, steelhead, and salmon—a real fly-fishing maniac! He holds the world record for landlocked Atlantic salmon, and like most pioneers, is in constant pursuit of perfection on the waters that he fishes. He started his career as a chef out of the Culinary Institute of America and did an apprenticeship in Rome, Italy, before moving to Washington, DC, to pursue a career in the hotel and food business. Supinski feels equally at home with a sauté pan and a wine decanter, or clipping a handcrafted cigar, as he does with a fly rod. My kind of guy!

I can't wait to hold a finished copy of *Selectivity* in my hand so I can read it yet again and pass out copies to my fly-fishing friends. A better compliment would be tough to come by.

Acknowledgments

I have been humbled and blessed to have had so many of the world's best and brightest fly-fishing talents and legends be part of my passionate subject. Writers, guides, fly tiers, photographers, lodge owners, and the brightest ichthyologists and minds in the world of fly fishing for trout, steelhead, and Atlantic salmon—all have been vital to this book. I can't thank all of you enough!

Many thanks to John G. Miller of West Branch Resort in the Catskills (www.westbranchresort.com) for his outstanding trout photography, macro insect images, and a guiding mind that understands selectivity to its limits. Thanks also go to the master of Atlantic salmon and trout, Arni Baldursson of Lax-Á Angling Club (www.lax-a.net) in Iceland, and to Jean-Guy Béliveau of Québec, who dives into the underwater world to study *Salmo salar*; both men provided outstanding photography, fly patterns, and insight on Atlantic salmon behavior. Thank you to Stacy Niedzwiecki (www.stacyn.com) for her stunning photography of flies and fly plates. Thanks to Greg Senyo (www.steelheadalleyoutfitters.com) for his fly patterns and relentless innovations; to Roman Moser, the European legend from Austria, for his fly patterns and insight; and to the doctor of brown trout and Atlantic salmon, Dr. Bror Johnsson, author of *Ecology of Atlantic Salmon and Brown Trout*, for his contribution to this book. Thanks also to Jason Jagger of Colorado for his fantastic photography examining how trout view surface prey.

For great insight, comments, fly patterns, and photography from different fisheries around the world, I would like to thank Peter Christensen, Denmark; Luka Hojnick, Slovenia; Wojtek Gibinski, Poland; Paul Marriner and David Bishop, Canada; Gordie Pecheur, Canada; Scott Howell, Oregon; Pat Dorsey, Colorado; Thomas Woelfle, Germany; Mike Schmidt, Ohio; Josh Greenburg, Gates Au Sable Lodge, Michigan; Mike Bone, Clinch River, Tennessee; April Vokey, Brian Chan, and Pierce Clegg, British Columbia; Brian Kraft, Sportsman's Lodge, Alaska; and Tony Hayes, Tongariro Lodge, New Zealand.

Thank you to all the amazing photographers who were kind enough to share their magnificent work: Jeff Bright (California, www.jeffbright.com), Ken Takata (Montana, www.kentakataphotography.com), Jim Klug (Montana, www.yellowdogflyfishing.com), John Sherman (California, www.johngsherman.com), Albert Pesendorfer (Austria), Terry Lawton (England, www.terrylawton.co.uk), Terry Matthews (England), Andy Grace (England, wurzelsweb.co.uk), Hakan Stenlund (Iceland), Colin Monahan and Ross Purnell (Pennsylvania), Chris Kayler (Virginia, www.chriskaylerphotography.com), Jim Krul and the Catskill Museum of Fly Fishing (New York, www.cffcm.net), Jeff Cole, Rich Felber, and Tommy Lynch (Michigan), Giuseppe Saitta (Idaho), Mick Hall (Australia), Brian Trow (Virginia, www.mossycreekflyfishing.com), Melanie Morrett (Ohio) for her pastel watercolor of the Letort, Grzegorz Radtke and Rafal Bartels (Poland), Clark Smyth (Wyoming), Lucas Carroll (New York), Ulf Sil (Sweden), Greg Thomas of *Fly Rod & Reel* magazine, Zach Matthews (Georgia), Anders Sorensson (Sweden), Mark Adams (Colorado), Ben Heine (Belgium), Steve Morrow (British Columbia), John Flaherty (Illinois), Andrew Bennet and Philippe Jugie (France), John Murphy (Michigan), Dave Martin (England), Daniela Beveliqua and Mauro Misteli (Switzerland), Bill Greiner (Massachusetts), Nick Sawyer (England), John Pierson, Tom Murray, Gudhmunder Geir (Iceland), Gerard Visser (Holland), Andrew Martin (England), Miguel Casalinuovo (Tierra Del Fuego, Argentina), Henrik Larsson (Sweden), Tom Harman (Minnesota), and Alex Lafkas (Michigan).

Thanks also to all the amazing fly tiers: Vidar Egilsson (Iceland), Rob White (Scotland), Pat Cohen (New York), Claes Johansson (J:son Sweden), Ken Morrish (Oregon); Piotr Michna (Poland), Oliver Edwards and the late Frank Sawyer (England), and Cecil Guidry (Indiana); Mike Batcke, Leonard Halladay, Pete Humphreys, Rich Merlino (Michigan), Jeff Andrews (Michigan), Bob Bemmer (Michigan), Jeff Bacon (Michigan), Phil Pantano (Connecticut), Ed Shenk (Pennsylvania), Paul Weamer (Pennsylvania), Mark Sturtevant (Pennsylvania), Herb Weigl (Pennsylvania), Tom Baltz (Pennsylvania), John Nagy (Pennsylvania), Jan Nemec (Nevada), Joe Shafer and Will Sands (Colorado), the late Fran Betters (New York), Harry Murray (Virginia), Marc LeBlanc (Canada), Austin Clark (Canada), and Scott Smith (Canada).

I am also grateful to my late, great fly-fishing mentors: Vince Marinaro, Carl Richards, and my Polish dad Antoni. May your souls find you on a perfect river in heaven filled with rising trout.

Thank you to all the great legends and icons of our sport who gave *Selectivity* such nice comments: Dick Pobst, Al Caucci, Doug Swisher, Bill McMillan, Trey Combs, John Randolph, Ed Shenk, and Dave Hughes.

Thanks to my wife, Laurie, a wonderful photographer and fly fisher, and to my son, Peter, who endured years of me painstakingly writing and editing this project.

Thank you to my thousands of wonderful clients and readers of my books and articles that have allowed me to live the dream-come-true lifestyle of a fly-fishing guide and author.

And finally, thank you to my editor, Jay Nichols, who is a master extraordinaire at what he does, and who took this monster project and tamed it for you to read and enjoy.

Vince's Meadow in Letort Spring Run, PA. MELANIE MORRETT

See facing page: It is a magical moment when a trout perceives a floating mayfly on the surface, whether a natural or an imitation. All of its lifelong learning experiences with ambushing prey and watching its biological world unfold daily will all boil down to just a few seconds as it decides to accept or reject the fly. The selectivity phases in this book will better help you understand what is going through the trout's mind in these breathtaking moments. JASON JAGGER

Introduction: Some Notes for Nonbelievers

The selectivity of trout has always been the most difficult and challenging of the numerous problems that confront the fly fisherman. Now and in the future, with fishing pressure increasing at a tremendous rate, the problem will become even more acute. With the advent of special fishing regulations and an increase in the number of no-kill areas, trout that are caught more than once become even more selective and leader shy.

Doug Swisher and Carl Richards, *Selective Trout* (1971)

G. E. M. Skues, the heretical nymph angler, once said, "one must separate the dead knowledge from the live knowledge." He was referring to the dead knowledge and writings of the grand pontificators who sat behind their bureaucratic desks smoking their pipes and writing about their fishing trips years ago and about conditions or techniques that no longer applied. The live knowledge comes from the passionate angler/guide who is out there every day on all types of rivers, putting probing hands under rocks looking for bugs and trout food, doing stomach sample analysis, watching trout rise, and observing migrating salmon and steelhead slide into their river holding lies.

G. E. M. Skues was the master of the English chalkstreams in the early 1900s. The first proponent of the nymph, Skues's thoughts about trout behavior prompted myself and many before me to delve into the mysterious world of selective trout. "If I did not believe that the trout took the artificial fly not only as food but as food of the kind on which he is feeding, the real interest of trout fishing would be gone, so far as I am concerned," Skues wrote in *The Way of a Trout with a Fly* (1921). TERRY LAWTON

Fly anglers have many different opinions about selectivity, a term I use in this book both generally to describe the overall mood of the fish and specifically as a particular mood, or phase, in which the fish is extremely discerning and difficult to catch. Some agnostics claim that calling a fish "discerning" or "wise" or "educated" is nothing more than a concept invented by overly enthusiastic authors, guides, and other angling fanatics. Selectivity agnostics believe that any fly will do as long as it is the right size, a drag-free float is all one needs for a successful presentation, tippet size does not really matter, and trout and salmon are simple creatures that do not make behavioral corrections like humans do. They believe selectivity is creating a mountain out of a molehill.

But, in my humble opinion, as a passionate guide and angler who spends up to three hundred days a year on the water, the more time a fly angler spends on the water on different ecosystems and fishing for different trout, steelhead, and Atlantic salmon species around the world, both wild and stocked, in the fishes' most feral state or in urban environments, the more they will conclude that selectivity is not a hoax.

I have way too many stories about my experiences with selectivity. Some I will share throughout the book, but I want to share three examples right now, which to me illustrate some of the different "faces" of selective trout. The first is a story about how fishing pressure can make trout wise; the second is about how not only fishing pressure but also continued and prolonged exposure to a food source can make fish selective and discriminating. The final story illustrates how, through the course of a hatch (not a hatch in a day, but a period of the same hatch), as fish become more exposed and used to certain foods, as well as increased fishing pressure, there is often a predictable progression from Active/Aggressive (A/A) to Selective/Reflective (S/R) to Passive/Dormant (P/D) and that no one of these phases is cut-and-dry; they are always merging into one another.

Despite our best attempts, we'll never know it all. As philosophers, scientists, and theologians have all pondered the mysteries of life, religion, and the universe, so goes the study of selectivity. At times it seems so simple, yet it can be so complex and enigmatic that it forever keeps us in awe. We are captivated by the perpetual search for the right fly, the perfect presentation, the right answers, just as we forever seek the universal meaning of life—who we are, where we are going, and how god and our behaviors as mortals fit into this universal journey. The beauty of selectivity is that despite the immense cerebral capacity we possess as thinking beings, we are constantly humbled and often embarrassed by a pea-brained trout or salmon; this is why the British founding fathers of fly fishing were so fascinated by the ways of the trout.

When fish are caught and released they become much harder to fool and catch. Some species such as brown trout and Atlantic salmon have a greater propensity for these learned behaviors. These coy and wary traits can be linked to their long evolutionary history and exposure to civilization as both humans and trout evolved fifty to seventy million years ago. On my first trip to the River Test in England back in the 1980s, I asked the gillie/guide which fly I should use, and I had a lot to choose from: "Sir, put on any

The chalkstreams of England like the Rivers Test and Itchen have been exclusive private playgrounds for the wealthy and the nobility. Here on the waters where Halford and Skues had the famous battle between what is proper for the sporting gentleman—the dry fly or the nymph—the trout were raised in side-channel hatcheries and were released at large sizes. They were vulnerable to any well-presented fly they saw. Things have changed there with more catch-and-release and wild trout management. KEN TAKATA

dry fly that fancies you, as long as it's between a size 12 and a 14."

Bingo! I put on a size 14 Quill Gordon, a Catskill fly created to imitate a host of dark mayflies, and I caught two large browns on two casts. What I thought would be selective spring creek browns like we had in Pennsylvania or Montana were instead almost as dumb as just-released hatchery trout. Well, by George, that's just what they were!

English chalkstreams have channelized water from the main streams, known as carriers, where browns are raised on floating pellets to encourage surface feeding. The 16- to 20-inch, wild-looking fish I was catching had been released just two days before and would take twigs, leaves, or popcorn from the surface if you threw it at them. The English also wanted you to kill your brace of two fish, after which you were done and off to the cleaning station and the pub. Catch-and-release had no place here; it would only make for browns that were tough to catch.

When we went to the River Itchen days later, which was managed for wild brown trout and catch-and-release, refusals even to perfectly tied Pennsylvania and Montana spring creek flies were common and we were humbled—lucky to catch one trout. Returning to the Test after two days of beat fishing, we bribed the gillie on the Timsbury water with a few Yank Benjamins to let us catch-and-release all day long. My partner and I, in our youthful greed, caught perhaps sixty-plus big fat browns. The gillie wrote us months later and said that the beat was "worthless once you Yanks left. Nobody could get those fish to take a fly and they shut the beat down for the rest of the season mate . . . shame on you lads!"

In the stark wilderness of Russia's Kamchatka and in the Iliamna of Alaska, the magnificent wild rainbows receive light pressure early in the season, have zillions of spawning salmon eggs on which to feed, and can be caught by the dozens on the same egg or fly. But by the end of the season, the catch rates drop

Catch-and-release practices and heavily pressured flies-only waters are selectivity's incubators. Sometimes just walking into other less-fished waters on the same stream will see a drastic change in the temperament of the trout, some of which haven't been caught before or haven't seen multiple fly presentations. RICH FELBER

because the rainbows become selective to the egg's hue, size, and translucency, becoming just as finicky as a midge-eating trout! You see guides painting all kinds of fingernail polish hues and tones on their bead eggs as the new egg-eating connoisseurs become downright stubborn and tenacious in their preference for exacting imitations. The rainbows will even refuse exact salmon egg naturals altogether.

I learned about fishing pressure and the complex interaction it has with discriminating trout early in life, on a beautiful little spring-fed, cow-country freestone river named Wiscoy Creek, located in New York's Southern Tier, where finding finicky and impossible—or easy—trout was a matter of walking a short distance. With several stretches of heavily trafficked fly-fishing-only, catch-and-release water, the Wiscoy's wary and coy wild brown trout are notoriously hard to catch. One July morning while fishing the no-kill fly water, as tiny Trico mayflies filled the air and spinners landed on the water, I could not buy a trout. Even the most exacting Trico spinner imitations and 7X brought refusals.

Though I would now ask for permission, in the brashness of my youth I walked upstream and under a barbed wire gate onto posted farm property. My first cast, sloppy as it was, produced a gorgeous 19-inch

brown. The hooking and catching as I walked upstream never stopped. But after losing a box of my good flies after bending over so many times to let fish go, I was devastated when my last good fly imitation that was catching so many trout was finally lost in a tree. I was forced to put on a large, gaudy, and ugly size 10 Cahill nymph with red thread, which I plucked from a rusty box I hadn't used in years. As I dropped down to 3X tippet, I fished it down and across and couldn't get the fish to stay away from my junk fly. It was sheer madness. A downstream wet-fly swing never worked on these Wiscoy fish! Why now? Did I stumble on a chance hatch encounter? Or was it that the fish saw no pressure?

After catching and releasing dozens of wild browns in the 9- to 17-inch range, I returned to that stretch of creek several more times. Each time the fishing became tougher until it just simply shut off with perpetual refusals and oblivious fish. The fishing became just as difficult, if not worse than, the no-kill fly water, despite the large burrowing mayflies still hatching nightly and my perfecting daily my adult and wiggle nymph imitations to exact duplicates.

Here was a situation where my fishing pressure and the timing of a particular mayfly hatch combined to make the fish ultraselective, even close to not taking flies at all. My experience, and many will concur, is that trout—especially stocked fish—that are unpressured will take a wide array of flies and presentations. But the wild browns of the Wiscoy soon compounded pressure and an exact hatch situation and became much harder to catch. It only took one angler—me—who was dangerous enough to know the game to make these fish that way. Was my big, ugly, whitish-cream rusted nymph an example of dumb, untainted, and aggressive trout willing to take anything that somehow corresponded to food and the hatch just starting up? Initially I believed so. Or, did I perchance stumble onto something else, something more complex and difficult to understand?

Two years later when the book *Selective Trout* by Doug Swisher and Carl Richards came out, I learned about the burrowing giant white *Ephemera* and *Hexagenia* mayflies. It turned out that the upper stretch of the Wiscoy and nearby East Koy had populations of both, and as I swung the big grayish-white and rusty nymph to shore in early July, I was imitating the burrowing nymphs' migration toward the shore. The reason the trout were taking my imitation was now clear. I was matching the hatch and taking aggressive fish, which soon turned ultrapicky and became nontakers because of my fishing pressure—despite my perfect fly imitations and presentations.

Later in the season, the Tricos were still on the water in my little posted paradise, but the wild browns refused them completely, instead rising to almost invisible no-see-um midges. It wasn't until a brown size 24 flying ant got stuck in my eye did I figure out that the trout had switched and were feeding on them. But as soon as I determined that ant preference the trout soon switched back to Tricos. The chase was always there and never did I have a comfort zone; this is how pressure and prey diversity constantly present themselves in an elusive juggling act to the angler. Here again was where repeated fishing pressure and the wild trout's elusive and finicky habituation to hatch and prey diversity caused a conundrum for the angler.

I learned that perpetual beatings of the water to death with the same patterns and techniques like on today's heavily trafficked special regulation waters will eventually send tough-to-catch fish into a P/D state until they are allowed to feed comfortably. The solution is to fish other water that might not be as highly regarded but often has greater rewards—marginal trout waters often yield some of the largest trout.

An extremely selective trout, such as a Wiscoy Creek or New Zealand brown (above), can be stalked and sight-nymphed with extreme focus while watching the fish's every move, quiver, refusal, and overall disposition to the fly, a method used by Danish fly master Mikkel Poppelhoj. PETER CHRISTENSEN

Here trout biomass is less and thus there is more food for the few fish that hunt there.

When their quest goes awry, anglers look for explanations, reconfigure fly patterns, and change presentations. When a wary fish is caught after a series of strategic decisions, that process becomes addictive. Understanding the actions and reactions of fish is the key to unveiling selectivity and catching more fish. One of the biggest impediments to catching tough fish is our own ego. We often impose preconceived notions of trout behavior, hatches, and killer fly patterns that should work, but quite often don't work when trout are being selective. Guides are notoriously stubborn and set in their ways when it comes to fly patterns and tactics that have proven successful in the past. They bullishly stick to them; I am speaking from experience, mind you. How many times I have said "Nice fly, try it!" as I was trying to be polite and supportive to a client. I believed in the back of my mind that there was no way in hell that fly would catch fish . . . and bingo! The client catches a huge fish on the first cast, much to my amazement and confusion. The fish's habituation and aversion to imitative fly patterns and all-too-common presentations that lack creative precision is a big part of understanding and cracking the selectivity code. Beyond basic proficiency with casting and other skills, having an open mind is the next most important attribute that I want my clients to have. You should question everything.

My forty-seven years of fly fishing for trout have given me the joy or fits of dealing with fussy fish. I have since had thousands of interesting and eye-opening encounters. These incidents shattered my preconceptions, my absolute knowledge and certainty of how fish will behave (or should behave), and what they should take. Eating humble pie as a fly angler will bring you more satisfaction and eventual conquest than the everyday ease and comfort of the sport. For those anglers who choose to fish with blinders on, the selectivity agnostics, I say may you forever fish your familiar patterns, your favorite and maybe only pool,

and catch the good fish on occasion. But I assure you, the "on occasion" will become less frequent.

Because I have learned so much through observation over the years, I encourage all serious anglers to take notes (using diaries, smartphones, or whatever else that works) about every fish encounter. Some will say that this is "old-school," but you will see patterns emerge and behavior repeat. Sometimes the complete bewilderment that you will record will amaze you when reading it in hindsight. We should approach every trout and salmon refusal to a fly and those fish-less days as insight and opportunities for future success. Hardship ultimately brings angling peace and satisfaction.

One final note. Throughout this book, the reader may be taken aback by my romantic tendency to anthropomorphize the three species' behavioral quirks and complexities, often relating them in human behavioral terms. Some might say that "They are only fish with a pea brain!" I beg you to indulge me and expand your mind; consider the fact that our quarry are highly intelligent, evolved species that must be treated with extreme respect if one is to consistently catch them. I realize intelligence is a human attribute and animals have instinct, opportunity, and learned and innate responses. But when you are humbled to tears and are frustrated in your fly-angling encounters time and time again by a "pea-brained organism," you will be able to more readily associate the word "intelligence" with fussy fish.

Facing page: Whether on England's River Test or on Colorado's South Platte, understanding the selectivity phases—Aggressive/Active, Selective/Reflective, Passive/Dormant—will provide anglers with the productivity, imagination, and improvisation needed to create the right approach for fussy trout and salmon. KEN TAKATA

Selectivity: The Phases

Interactions between fish and angler go far beyond the normal obstacles a fish encounters in the savage yet simple natural world. Because of the methods, techniques, and technology a cerebrally gifted and tactful predator like man can employ—cunning and calculating skills of mimicry and deception when imitating a trout's food with a perfect replica of an artificial fly, or antagonizing the steelhead/salmon's aggressive/predator strike response by irritating the aggressive salmonids' optic/hormonal system with the bright colors found in a Willie Gunn tube fly— the fly angler becomes the apex hunter with no equal. The angling arts have developed over the centuries with one sole intent—to conquer a fish's pea-sized brain—and this high level of predator sophistication is not all that common in the natural world.

Despite our cunning and technological advances, we continue to be humbled by our quarry, especially on the highly pressured, catch-and-release waters of public rivers and streams that most of us fish. Fish are constantly changing their behavior in response to factors such as man-induced fishing pressure, changing environmental conditions, evolving ecosystems, the various types of river systems and their fertility, and the innate personalities of each salmonid species.

The Letort brown trout is a beautiful fusion of the German Black Forest and Scottish Loch Leven strains. Its Teutonic red dots and white circles, along with its blue parr marks, blend with the more pronounced large oval circles of the Celtic trout. Letort trout continually refuse even natural insects, let alone imitations. MATT SUPINSKI

Through the trout and salmon's innate and learned behavioral process of filtering and dissecting information and potential threats, fish continually baffle anglers no matter how perfectly their Blue-Winged Olive fly pattern replicates the natural. But that is also what drives us to pursue them.

My notion of "selectivity" attempts to address what I call the fish's "split personality." Why at times they can be ferocious predators and kill artists exercising extreme precision, but with a selective and precise demeanor. Or why they can be downright impossible to catch, either being extremely fussy and elusive or completely despondent.

These bipolar behavioral phases of selectivity have taunted anglers for as long as people have been fly fishing. When Dame Juliana Berners penned the first annuals of fly fishing in 1496 along the banks of the River Avon in England with her *Treatise of Fly Fishing with an Angle,* she was already addressing fly selectivity issues with trout and salmon. Describing how an Atlantic salmon takes the fly, she wrote, "The salmon does not bite on the bottom but at the float. You may sometimes take him, but it happens seldom." These powerful words still echo how Atlantic

salmon—and most of the fish species that we pursue, for that matter—are viewed today.

We have all been humbled by a fish that scorns our fly, whether that is a wild brown trout rising to a heavy hatch of mayflies or hundreds of pooled-up Atlantic salmon or steelhead holding in plain sight. These fish may give our flies a look, perhaps a chase, but unfortunately no take, thus leaving us confused, dejected, and constantly searching for answers to this enigmatic conundrum. It is this puzzle that I attempt to solve in this book.

The Selectivity Phases

The first step to solving the puzzle is to identify the nuances of the term "selectivity." My theory of selectivity deals with three phases or situations in which the angler can find the trout, steelhead, or salmon to be in at one time or another at any point in their lives:

- the Aggressive/Active phase (A/A)
- the Selective/Reflective phase (S/R)
- the Passive/Dormant phase (P/D)

In each of these stages, the fish behave (and respond to your flies) quite differently. Each encounter

Selectivity Phases

AGGRESSIVE/ACTIVE (A/A)

- Primal hunter instinct (kill artist)
- Sexually dominant behavior
- Triggered by the sudden onset of an abundant food source
- Determined and resolute feeding spree

SELECTIVE/REFLECTIVE (S/R)

- Extremely fussy, discriminating, and cautious in feeding
- High degree of awareness of both food and environment
- Many refusals to fly imitations and even natural food forms
- Often a result of an overabundant and diverse food source
- Usually a result of fishing pressure

PASSIVE/DORMANT (P/D)

- Listless, dour, or sulking behavior, often in a comalike trance
- No interest in typical daily feeding or dominant behavioral displays
- Often a result of extreme or poor conditions, overfeeding, or a focus on nocturnal feeding
- Result of persistent predator advances or extreme angling pressure

the angler has with the fish is unique, and effective anglers must successfully identify the appropriate state of selectivity and choose the proper tactics and presentations to ensure success. By understanding the phases, an angler can make calculated adjustments and modifications to his or her presentation, such as selecting the appropriate fly size, silhouette, and style, appropriate tippet and length, and correct presentation and approach. It all boils down to this: the better you understand your quarry by studying and exploring the subtle nuances of the fish's behavior and the often intricate presentation techniques necessary to fool them, the better able you are to catch them, even when faced with frustrating angling situations that trout, steelhead, and Atlantic salmon are highly touted and noted for. Many guides call it paying your dues through time on the water. The three stages—shortened to A/A, S/R, and P/D in this book—all have

unique, yet consistent, behaviors, and each salmonid species' behavior in these selectivity phases is influenced by its environments, evolution, and innate and learned behavioral experiences.

Aggressive/Active

In the **Aggressive/Active (A/A) phase**, the fish is on the prowl like a shark hunting its prey. It is aggressively targeting either specific or multiple forms of prey in an opportunistic fashion, like in a huge mayfly emergence where emergers, duns, spinners, and cripples can be so abundant that fish feed ravenously and without caution.

Much of the selective process of trout, steelhead, and salmon is born out of the instinctive response to arousal, aggression, and comfort. In the A/A state, a fish will strike in a rhythmic aggressive pattern: for

Norwegian salmon, like this one from the Alta River, are in the extreme A/A phase as they hunt for prey in the Atlantic.
ARNI BALDURSSON/LAX-Á

Left: A magnificent fresh-run silver Atlantic salmon that crushed a Green Highlander fly in an A/A display. MATT SUPINSKI

instance, trout feeding indiscriminately during a heavy caddis egg-laying flight. The examination process of the natural and imitation fly is quick and concentrated, not picky or fussy like in the S/R state. Only a predator alarm, a rapid degradation of ecosystem conditions, or a diminishing hatch will throw off the constant hunt-and-destroy gorging.

A/A phases are also common to trout in fast-flowing, high-gradient freestone streams that remain cold all season. Within the heavy boulder-strewn rapids and pocket waters, all offerings must be quickly devoured and captured, since the trout's window of interception is small, and opportunity comes infrequently. It is interesting to stomach-pump a fish and investigate the ingestion process of high-gradient freestone stream trout. Often twigs, plastic/rubber bands, and gravel might be found alongside aquatic vertebrates and invertebrates. The trout's need to quickly intercept and capture food far outweighs the selective process.

Brown trout have perhaps the longest relationship with nature and civilization, having been around for seventy million years. Though they are the same fish no matter what type of river in which they are found, their behavior is modified to their ecosystem. Here on Michigan's Pere Marquette, where the first stocking of German-strain trout took place in North America in the 1800s, the browns have retained the colorful red spots of the Black Forest *Forellen*. The perfect freestone/spring creek fusion of this river makes the browns wary because they have to share the river with migrating salmon and steelhead. This fish took a Roman Moser sculpin in an A/A fashion. MATT SUPINSKI

The A/A behavior in steelhead and salmon is usually manifested in fresh-run fish that come up in higher water. Until they adjust to their newfound riverine environment and become cautious, these sea- or lake-going fish are still in a pattern of being constantly on the prowl and hunting for prey. Here the search-and-destroy mechanism is fully intact. When a fresh-arriving fish is greeted with ideal water flows and temperatures, the aggressive "big bite" will be unleashed to its ultimate potential. A fresh, dime-bright Atlantic salmon on Québec's Gaspé rivers in the first week of June, when water flows are strong and cold, will take a large Lady Amherst or Green Highlander with a reckless abandonment not common to the snotty mannerisms of late-season salmon.

As fish carry out their spawning rituals, vying for hierarchical dominance and jousting for alpha positioning, they also become aggressive and will frequently attack your flies as they do each other. This attack-and-destroy behavior accounts for many trophy trout and salmon being caught during the spawning periods despite their normally wise and aloof old-fish demeanor. Biologists set aside sanctuary waters and mandated closed seasons to protect the fish from anglers during this vulnerable period.

While spawning aggression in the spring and fall is a seasonal component of the A/A behavioral mode for trout, it is not as pronounced as in the migratory steelhead and Atlantic salmon runs. However, stripping large flies invokes an A/A response from large trophy trout that feed on large baitfish; this tactic invades the fish's space and triggers an aggressive strike out of dominance.

A/A fish can often be easier to catch because they are feeding with reckless abandon and can become oblivious to your presence. However, catching a fish in this stage may not be as easy most anglers think it should be, and at times the phase must be deciphered and interpreted correctly. Trout could be rising with a heated frenzy to a heavy early season mayfly hatch of Hendricksons, but only targeting the most abundant stillborn emergers—thus making your adult Compara-dun go totally unnoticed.

A/A behavior can also occur when there is a total change of environmental conditions, such as an unusual influx of food, changing water conditions, or both. An excellent example of this takes place, albeit infrequently, on the Delaware River in New York and Pennsylvania, and something similar occurs on other tailwaters such as the Clinch River in Tennessee and White River in Arkansas. Under normal, clear flows and in the serene placid pools and eddies common to tailwater fisheries, the wild browns and rainbows can be downright impossible to seduce with the fly.

In the hot El Niño summer of 2001, a heavy flood born out of heat-induced thunderstorms dumped feet of rain on the Delaware River watershed, which the Downsville and Pepacton Reservoirs in New York could not hold. As a result of being at full capacity, the top-spill of the dams was flowing into the high, heavily muddied West and East Branches. Out came thousands of alewives and shad baitfish. The wild trout went on

Good fly anglers go to extremes for a stealthy approach: crouching, kneeling, or crawling on the belly are needed to keep a low profile against hyperselective trout in clear waters where the fish can see every shadow and movement. Here on the Tomlinka River in Slovenia, the vision of the trout is enhanced by the ultraclear emerald waters. LUKA HOJNIK

a crazed piranhalike feeding frenzy, hunting down every crippled baitfish in the tall shoregrass eddies and backwaters. Stripping large shad and baitfish patterns turned huge 22-inch-plus browns, which were rendered stupid and clumsy compared to their cautious and selective daily regimens where a streamer would scare the living daylights out of the fish. In one day of floating with West Branch guide John Miller, we landed eleven browns between 20 and 27 inches on streamer techniques. The Harvard-educated Delaware fish became junkyard dogs feeding off a slop wagon.

In the **Selective/Reflective (S/R) phase**, the fish behaves with an extreme awareness, inspects everything to the minutest detail, and acts with a cautious discernment. It is reflective of its food and surroundings and does nothing hastily when feeding or assimilating to its new ecosystem, as would be the case when freshly migrating steelhead and salmon are ascending their natal rivers from the big ocean and lake environments. This can be embodied by a large Atlantic salmon clearly seen in a pool on the Grand Cascapedia River in Québec, quivering its fins and examining and poking at your dry-fly bomber presentation for the twelfth time, yet with no firm commitment to take it. This stage is perhaps the most complex and beguiling since it has complicated fish behaviors that can drive an angler insane, and it's for this reason that I spend

the most time on it in this book. The fish can go from sometimes taking your fly to often refusing it, perhaps looking at it for long durations and then refusing it, or finally to playing with your fly or the natural in a cheeky, jovial manner the way a porpoise doing tricks at a Sea World aquarium show would. This stage is different from the trout in the A/A phase we saw rising with a heated frenzy to a heavy early season mayfly hatch of Hendricksons, but only targeting the most abundant stillborn emergers. Here it has a specific target—the emerger.

Often in the S/R mode, there are no set rules, no push-button solutions, but only series of fish behavioral patterns, codes, and peculiarities that an angler must decipher through observation, eventually leading to success with these highly observant S/R fish. Here the utmost perseverance, experimentation with presentation and fly, and critical observation can mean the difference between an angler's success and failure. Sometimes the angler might stumble on dumb luck with an unorthodox fly and presentation, which though a welcome surprise, is rare. The wise fly angler won't bet on dumb luck providing consistent success in this stage.

S/R fish are typical of certain conditions, often found in spring creeks and tailwaters. First, the river or lake ecosystems must be stable. This includes ideal

It was on the spring creek waters of the Wieprza River, which ran through my dad's farm in northern Poland by the Baltic Sea, that I first observed all three phases of selectivity. I grew up there, observing fish behavior from a tree house "laboratory" my cousins and I built over one of the river's many pools. Here, its magnificently colored native browns were ultra S/R to the Blue-Winged Olive mayfly body's color variations—my old Iron Blue English dry flies were too big and the wrong tone, and the patterns didn't fool them. The river's seasonal runs of sea trout and Atlantic salmon allowed me to observe the way they slipped in and out of the three selectivity phases on a daily basis. Later in life, when I fished Pennsylvania's limestone spring creeks, my boyhood observations helped me to better understand the ultra S/R spring creek trout behavior. RAFAL BARTELS

flows that are normal and stable for a given period of time (no drastic fluctuations, floods, or droughts). Second, water temperature should be ideal or as close to it as possible for the given salmonid species' preference range. In these conditions the fish are functioning at peak metabolic performance, they are not super hungry, they have an extreme abundance of food opportunities, and they have placid conditions in which they can carefully examine the natural food choices and an angler's fly. Because of this, S/R fish are harder to fool with artificials, and can even refuse naturals.

Just as the river environment is crucial, so is where in the river the fish reside, including the taking, feeding, or examining lie they choose. All salmonids feed or take the fly in either a receptive stationary state or in the hunting mobility of predation. Perfect taking lies exist when all of the salmonid's needs are met. These include security and escapement to cover; the luxury and leisure of optimal flows, which carry the prey/food offerings of naturals and their imitating flies into the fish's ideal window of opportunity, opening the door for the fish to strike its prey or examine it further; and a fulcrum point of total awareness, allow-

ing 360-degree vision and other sensory awareness by the fish in all the optic and sound vibration fields—vertical, horizontal and from above and below. All these conditions must be met to elicit the ultimate S/R behavior.

A pool in a gentle-flowing spring creek or tailwater can provide a series of feeding opportunities, from a short-lived and sparse hatch of Blue-Winged Olives and midges to the occasional flying ants and terrestrials, occasional large mayfly, or a regular and strong (but compact in time) hatch like the Tricos. Due to the variety and infrequency of food forms from the minutiae to the large mayfly, the fish must change its degree of finicky discretion with each new element of the biological drift. The trout is reflecting on each new and ever-changing food opportunity, and it must make decisions based on past experiences with that food form/color/silhouette and what worked or didn't work, perhaps as recently as an hour ago. This is unlike one giant massive hatch, where the feeding signal is strong, constant, and assured.

For sea- or lake-run fish such as steelhead, Atlantic salmon, and sea- and lake-run trout, which have

The large, glacial-cut holding pools on Atlantic salmon rivers like the White House pool in the Gaspé are a sort of mini ocean. As much as twenty feet deep, they are cold, well-oxygenated, and have shelves, ledges, and boulders of volcanic rock and limestone. Here, the larger salmon have all the security in the world from predators. On the stable, smooth surface of the pools, each cast brings alarm and gives the trout a perfect window through which to view its prime predator—man. JEAN GUY BÉLIVEAU

procreation as their primary drive, S/R states come into play when a fish has time to be aware of its surroundings and the food in the river that recalls its imprinted behaviors of chasing aquatic insects and baitfish when it was a small river parr or smolt, as well as recently learned experiences with ocean and lake food forms as an adult. This creates strong urges in the fish, ones not necessarily born out of hunger. The urge will eventually elicit a take, as the fish will strike a fly fisher's offering even though it doesn't have to feed once it has migrated upriver. For the Atlantic salmon and steelhead, which eagerly take flies, this reflective process of past feeding experiences is the reason they provide such highly sought-after and consistent sport to the fly fisher, as challenging as it may be.

The S/R behavior is most ideally displayed by Atlantic salmon when they are holding and suspended in pools during the summer and early fall prior to spawning. Take the world-famous wild Atlantics of Québec's Gaspé Peninsula. For millions of years the peninsula's pristine, crystal-clear rivers have been spawning grounds of genetically superior Atlantics of up to 60 pounds, and the waters still offer the fly fisher's dream of hooking an Atlantic that can be willingly reactive to the fly or downright stubborn and impossible. *Salmo salar*, known as the ultimate "thousand cast" fish, displays the reflective behavioral mode more consistently over a larger period of time than does any other salmonid.

Reflective behavior in the salmon on the fertile rivers of the Gaspé's south shore is a result of streams with high populations of aquatic vertebrates and invertebrates and a rich food source in the Bay of Chaleur, a place loaded with pelagic baitfish, crustaceans, squid, and eels. Since the Atlantic salmon parr spend up to three years in these fertile waters before smolting and migrating to their hunting grounds off the coast of Greenland, their natal imprinting to food forms is more extreme compared with that of their cousins on the more sterile and cold spate rivers. The S/R behavior of adults in large pools emerges from their upstream migration—which begins as early as May—when they have plenty of time to become aware of food forms in the water, are subjected to angling pressure, and other variables.

The S/R response is also highly shaped by man and other creatures: natural predators, farm animals, and other fish. There is no question that salmonids, once having been caught and feeling the steel of a hook, or caught and having gone through the fight-or-flight battle—or combination of the two—have gone through a traumatic, life-threatening experience. There are also dangerous encounters with ospreys, kingfishers, eagles, herons, cormorants, and other birds that prey on the fish. These encounters ultimately produce wary and large trout and salmonids for the angler to pursue.

Finally, the **Passive/Dormant (P/D) phase** can find the fish in a disposition of complete obstinance and refusing to take your fly. This phase can be the most dejecting to the fly angler. There is a distinct difference between a fish that is extremely hard to catch and a fish that is uncatchable because it has completely shut down its desire for food.

A P/D fish will be in a state of trance or hibernation; its vital signs are functioning but there is zero acknowledgement or interaction with the fish's natural world. It is for the most part as if the fish were asleep with its eyes wide open, swimming in a listless catatonic state. The fish may be hiding in cover or fully exposed in the streambed. It shows no interest or acknowledgment of the angler or the fly presentation. Its body language may often seem odd, such as facing downstream in a back eddy on the bottom or performing a monotone finning in the current, totally oblivious to the surroundings.

P/D behavior in all salmonids is usually provoked by external conditions such as extreme water temperatures and water levels. However, it can also be caused by overfeeding or satiation, habituation to certain routine fly presentations and angler intrusions, or a biologically induced comalike trance, resulting in total passivity to its external world.

The P/D response is a self-regulating behavior. When a trout on a freestone stream such as the Beaverkill in the Catskill Mountains of New York encounters extremely warm and low water levels due to a heat wave and drought, it will seek out deep spring-fed holes and cold tributary creek seeps. Here it will forgo all feeding activity because doing so involves the expulsion of energy; the fish instead goes into the P/D phase in order to survive. Here it lowers all its vital functions to the minimum level and lives on stored body fat until conditions cool down below 70 degrees Fahrenheit. Feeding may resume slowly over time.

The same holds true for perhaps this same trout in winter. Catskill Mountain winters can be extremely harsh with subzero temperatures. Rivers may be choked with shelf and anchor ice, which can be lethal to trout getting locked up in it. In the extreme cold, a trout's metabolism would shut down to baseline low levels; however, it will still feed in tiny spurts throughout the winter. Its feeding behavioral need is low and usually peaks with a one- or two-degree warming on a winter's afternoon; thus, you should concentrate your angling on the warmest part of the day. The same holds true for winter steelhead and wintering-over lake- and sea-run browns and Atlantic salmon. Pacific salmon die after their late-summer/fall spawning cycle.

Water conditions can also make a salmonid P/D. A sudden sediment load from a flood or erosion, which turns the river muddy and clogs the trout's field of vision and gills, will quickly turn a salmonid dormant. Heavy flood flows will do the same and cause a hunkering-down, dormant-behavior response in which the fish stays in its chosen habitat lie or holding pool.

Predation, including fishing pressure, is another common cause of P/D behavior. Fleeing predators like eagles, kingfishers, herons, otters, sea lions, and orcas will cause this passive behavior and force the fish into seclusion, hiding, and extreme down states of being. Massive schools of salmon and steelhead at sea will become extremely passive and dormant when being hunted by predators like orcas and sea lions and will lie near the bottom or tight against deep structure to avoid detection since predator hunting revolves around sensory vibrations through the lateral line. Where trout and salmon see heavy catch-and-release pressure, they can become chronic nontakers since their wariness is on hyperalert. Pressured fish in the S/R phase will shut down for short periods. When they see extreme catch-and-release pressure they can become totally neurotic and refuse to eat even naturals, sometimes even starving to death in the extreme P/D phase.

Atlantic salmon spend more time in this phase than other fish—they do not need to feed when they enter the river. The P/D fish differ from that extremely cautious fish in that their entire psyche/behavior/metabolism almost becomes oblivious to the fish's external world. When wading you can step on these fish by accident, and they are often not spooked by your close presence like a cautious fish would be. P/D behavior usually stems from less-than-ideal water and ecosystem conditions, as well as from transition metabolic functioning, such as a salmon's body going through an extreme metamorphosis as it develops huge sperm and egg organs for reproduction. This transition slows the salmon's arousal to predation/aggression and normal daily behaviors. Cautious fish will seek shelter or act coy and deceptive, and perhaps cloak themselves by being dour, but this state will quickly change given ideal predatory conditions. P/D fish can go into a funk for considerable periods until substantial changes in the environment or physiology are met. P/D behavior is nature's way of slowing down the fish for survival, just as humans feel like they have been hit by a train when they get the flu—it allows the body to rest and the immune system to do its work.

Low-water drought conditions, heat waves, and lethally warm water temperatures have the most profound effect on the P/D behavior since they have severe negative physiological implications. Conversely, floods and high water can also trigger dormancy, as can discolored water. Though brown trout have been known to eat themselves to death, a satiation factor normally kicks in and causes the trout to stop feeding until the hunger drive returns. Spawning trout can also flip-flop between bipolar selectivity phases, going from P/D to A/A behavior based on each fish's own personality and aggression or lack thereof. P/D trout are perhaps the easiest nut to crack since they cannot stay away from feeding too long or they will die—unlike migrating steelhead and salmon.

The P/D phase often puts a huge damper on your fishing trip, whether it's a day outing to your favorite stream or a much worse scenario in which you travel halfway around the world on a destination trip. You get to the lodge and find out the fish have completely shut off and the fishing is terrible. Though fishing prospects are bleak, all hope is not lost here for the angler. This state can be turned around for success by learning how to identify its peculiarities and the various approaches and methods of presentation that will make the fish become a fly taker. Fortunately for the fly angler, the trout cannot afford to spend too much time in this state for fear of starvation and death—whereas the steelhead and Atlantic salmon may go a

Pooled-up salmon and steelhead will have S/R or P/D demeanor and can be very difficult to catch. Often they focus on the tight protocol hierarchical spacing, as seen here, and are totally immersed in the mentality of aggressively protecting their lie and pod status. MATT SUPINSKI

Pooled-up Atlantic salmon on Québec's Grand Pabos. When they are in the P/D phase, they won't take flies and will remain in a uniform listless state of spatial separation based on hierarchical dominance. They can become "takers" when the right presentation or conditions change their demeanor. Unorthodox flies and presentations usually turn the trick. MATT SUPINSKI

year without eating and live off of stored body fat reserves.

There is an unknown component to P/D behavior where fish have been known to snap out of this selectivity phase by a quirky and unusual stimuli—perhaps by an otter swimming through a pool, or by a fly presentation that triggered some innate primordial behavioral response. One technique for Atlantic salmon and brown trout that seems to work quite often is taking a large fly/bomber/streamer and just stripping it over a pool of dour fish, creating such a ruckus that even the dourest of fish can't refuse. If you think of the extreme and bizarre in presentation, you might have luck with P/D fish. But this technique would only make cautious fish even more so—there is the difference.

Habituation

Habituation and assimilation behaviors are important components of my theories of selectivity. In psychological terms, it is the gradual decline of a response to a stimulus resulting from repeated exposure to the stimulus and labeling it as nonthreatening and part of a normal environment. Once the threat (or perceived threat) is evaluated and qualified as a potential threat or not a threat, the opportune behavioral regime eventually adjusts and becomes the new normal, until another threat is perceived and evaluated.

Take for instance the wild trout that inhabit the lovely limestone spring creeks in Pennsylvania's Cumberland Valley. In the mid- to late twentieth century, cows and riparian grazing were rampant in this region. Livestock were allowed to freely graze up and down the stream, degrading banks, defecating in the stream, and in general doing what most would think would destroy a trout stream. Aside from the bovine fecal matter, which actually adds some nutrient value (Vince Marinaro once said, "The best thing that can happen to a trout stream is for a cow to take a big dump in it!"), grazing also added silt, a life-threatening danger to trout. When the Falling Spring Run was at its pinnacle, its wild Shasta-strain rainbows and brown trout developed a complicated S/R feeding pattern.

Riparian grazing on farm meadows is synonymous with spring creeks all over the world, such as this pastoral chalkstream in England. Cows, sheep, and horses all flock to the lush grass watered by the seeps. Today, trout habitat for spawning and cover, which grazing destroys, is protected by bank stabilization. The crude but effective wicker shown here fences out the grazing livestock. KEN TAKATA

Primary to the habituation process were the free-grazing cows that would parade through the streams each day on their way back to the barn.

Initially, the young trout, fingerling, parr, and yearlings were startled when they experienced this intrusion. Yet eventually they adjusted their "fear meter" to low levels once they were assured the livestock posed no threat to their level of security and balance. Once the fish mature (reach 6 to 10 inches and larger) the wild trout seek opportunity from intrusion. Many a day while I was fishing Falling Spring, Letort Spring Run, and similar spring creeks in Wisconsin, Minnesota, and Montana, I witnessed trout that eventually realized the timing of cattle stomping through a creek at certain times of the day by either sound vibration or photo light level, only to take advantage of the spring creek San Juan Shuffle. For those not acquainted with this somewhat egregious display by glory-seeking anglers on the San Juan River, they try to chum up the biological drifts of midges and tiny olives by stomping boots in the stream bottom in order to create a feeding frenzy by the "habituated" trout. It is an example of the Pavlovian Dog, or conditioned reflex, concept (Pavlov's dog salivated when a bell was rung, as it associated the sound with food). The trout began to anticipate food was on its way every time the cows got nearer. Here, the trout are habituated to the initially perceived predator, and that intruder becomes an ally or accomplice in the feeding and comfort of the fish. When you have a symbiotic relationship of mutual advantage from predator/prey (for example, a shark and a remora) selectivity to habituation can act in favor of the prey.

Facing page: Brook trout in stillwaters, like Hebgen Lake in Montana, can be ultraselective when feeding on chironomid midges. Trout that sip midges on lakes and beaver ponds are called "gulpers." MICK HALL

Trout: An Overview

[The trout] is a kill-artist whose hunter skills are cultivated and refined from babyhood; without them he would die. His relentless pursuit of a victim is a startling study in concentrated deadlines. His way of life is a perpetual search-and-destroy mission.

Vince Marinaro, *In the Ring of the Rise* (1974)

Fly fishing for trout encompasses all three phases of selectivity, which interchange frequently. This is due to diverse feeding situations, varying types of river habitat and their ecosystem components, and species-specific behaviors exhibited by trout all over the world. Interpreting these phases entails many diverse fly presentations and patterns and an in-depth understanding of how the selectivity phases manifest themselves in diverse ecosystems. Only then can the angler crack the code for success.

Trout selectivity issues differ from those of steelhead and salmon because the latter are primarily fly fished for in the natal rivers of birth or stocking, or on their spawning return from ocean

The brown trout, *Salmo trutta*, has been around for seventy million years and is closely related to the Atlantic salmon. While it is surface oriented and will take a dry fly, it is incredibly wary and selective. RICHARD FELBER

All the details of the fly presentation must be perfect to imitate the natural mayfly—body silhouette, wing profile, size, color tone, and translucency—and of course, the drift must be exact for a trout feeding in the S/R mode. JASON JAGGER

Left: A large tailwater brown trout like this one on Michigan's Muskegon River can slip into all three selectivity phases in one day. This wise leviathan became A/A during an early American March Brown hatch that commenced and abated quickly, causing an A/A sense of urgency. MATT SUPINSKI

or lake—not in their principal hunting grounds like the trout in a river, lake, or stream. There are exceptions, of course, particularly in the spring when salmonids are targeting baitfish along the ice-out shorelines, or when steelhead and salmon congregate off low river-mouth estuaries. These fly fishing opportunities are limited.

The steelhead and salmon for the most part don't "eat" on these migrations to their natal waters, with exceptions occurring in the freshwater-to-freshwater potamodromous Great Lakes fisheries. There the lack of renal system issues saltwater fish have in regulating salinity doesn't play a role, thus prolonging the feeding behavior. In general, triggering a steelhead or Atlantic salmon to take a fly involves exploiting an imprint to adult and natal foods as well as aggression

related to spawning, not just normal feeding behavior as with trout fishing.

The trout can be in any selective phase anytime on any given day, and can, at times, flip-flop between these phases. It can be in a highly aggressive mode from daily hunting and feeding, from asserting territorial sexual dominance during spawning, or from choosing and competing for prime feeding and holding lies. Or it may be extremely demanding and selective due to unlimited food choices, or from the fact it has been fooled and hooked before, thus requiring more focused evaluations and presentations by the angler. Bring into this mix the P/D mode caused by fear and flight from predators, dangerous water temperatures, and overall poor stream conditions like floods and droughts, and figuring out how to catch the trout can become complex.

Selectivity by Species:
A Closer Look

> "To the dry fly fishermen, the Brown trout is the wariest, wiliest, most fascinating, challenging, respected and best-loved trout of all!"
>
> Cecil E. Heacox,
> *The Complete Brown Trout* (1974)

In the trout world, each species has developed a survival strategy based on its evolutionary history, preferred habitat, and choice of prey. These three critical factors dictate that innate behavioral codes are transmitted from each generation and that the cost/benefit outcomes of a fish's feeding selectivity are efficiently measured. The overall personality and behavior of each trout species is stereotyped but has great variation.

Selectivity in trout species can closely correlate to the species' long history and exposure to civilization and ecosystem threats and encroachment. Brown trout have coexisted with man for the longest time; the Eastern brook trout holds a strong second. The rainbow has a short time span of interaction with human civilization. It has been thoroughly domesticated through the hatchery systems due to its gregarious and eager-to-bite personality, making it perfect for put-and-take fisheries. Generally, wild trout will exhibit the widest range of the three selectivity phases, which is why indigenous and wild strains are so important to protect. But stocked fingerling and holdover trout in perfect habitats containing abundant and diverse food sources will become just as S/R as their wild cousins.

Trout Selectivity

A/A

Necessity to feed opportunistically with short window for maximum caloric intake (as in fast freestone rivers)

Frenzied feeding during a hatch with resolute and efficient simple rises (can be discriminating to specific emergence phase)

Result of a new and abundant food source (cicadas, grasshoppers, baitfish spilling from reservoir)

Night feeding

Trout less discriminating to fly design; more tolerant to larger tippet sizes and sloppy presentations

S/R

Typical of spring creeks, tailwaters, and catch-and-release waters

Leisurely yet precise feeding with a high degree of inspection of every detail

Compound and complex rises, refusals

Abundant and diverse food sources; preoccupation with minutiae

Cautious and stealthy approach required; rest fish often

Fly presentation must be perfect—drag free or with movement, fine tippets, sparse fly designs, and often repetitive

P/D

Overfeeding/satiation

Change in weather

Spawning (not pre- or post-)

Excessive pressure ■

The brown trout has been around perhaps longer than civilization itself. Like the dog, it has learned to be comfortable with mankind's intrusions and has the uncanny ability to deceive, arouse, and become reclusive at will. MATT SUPINSKI

The relationship between guide and angler is priceless. Carefully stalking your trout, making a perfect presentation, and choosing (and often changing) the right fly is the key. Thinking "outside the box" and doing what it takes to provoke a strike response is often necessary. A feisty Tierra del Fuego sea-run trout can have mood swings that only a guide knows. JOHN SHERMAN/THE FLY SHOP

Brown Trout

From the early writings of the English chalkstream school to the New World mecca of the Catskills' hallowed waters to the new frontier of Montana, the brown trout is the "holy grail" for fly fishers that love hard-to-catch fish. A brown trout probably spends more time in the S/R phase than most trout do. This is a result of its extreme caution and discernment of all things in its ecosystem, and its great and diverse appetite, which allows it to prey freely and discriminately. Even though habitat shapes a fish's behavior, the brown trout's stubborn attitude prevails wherever it is found.

Low light levels bring out brown trout to feed, regardless of whether there is a hatch, and most large browns are caught in the evenings and through the night on mouse patterns, big streamers, *Hexagenia* mayflies, and large stoneflies. On my home Michigan waters, where the ratio of browns to rainbows is about even, sunny days always produce more rainbows; cloudy, rainy days produce browns. Results are similar on the Delaware River and other tailwaters throughout the country.

Enduring water up to 80 degrees—and able to function metabolically in waters in the low 70s—the brown trout prefers slower-moving waters where S/R feeding behavior is the fish's desired phase. It also is extremely surface oriented, as its diet can comprise up to 90 percent aquatic insects.

At first, the introduction of the German brown trout to North America was not favorably looked upon because the browns were much harder to catch than the brook trout they displaced. However, the detailed and sleek new fly designs by Theodore Gordon, Edward Hewitt, and others soon gave fly fishers an edge. Browns are not always super selective. Brown trout become aggressive and active during prolific hatches, influxes of baitfish, hatches of cicadas and terrestrials, and seasonally and cyclically abundant food opportunities like the mouse hatch in New Zealand. Continued carnivorous predation also triggers A/A behavior. This is *Salmo trutta*'s darker killer side that makes it so successful in the A/A mode.

Brown trout are the oldest known living members of the trout family, dating back to seventy million years of evolution. Many strains are found throughout their native range but they all have one thing in common—their wary, fussy attitude, even in the A/A phase. JOHN MILLER

Right: Patagonia brown trout. Brown trout have tremendous vision and shun light more than other salmonid species, preferring cover such as logs, boulders, bridges, deep pools, mill dams, and undercut banks for holding lies in rivers and streams. JIM KLUG/YELLOW DOG TRAVEL

It is a phantom that appears in fisheries that were long lost and thought to be void of trout. Its extreme reclusiveness is a factor that the angler must always take into consideration. The brown's extreme curiosity and urge to venture into somewhat undesirable ecosystems makes it kind of a junkyard dog of the trout world. Some of the best trophy brown trout waters of major rivers are near sewage treatment plants, heavily polluted hatchery effluent, suburban artesian wells and waste discharges, and other urban environments. For some odd practical purpose, the brown trout, though a lover of pristine waters, can also wear the hat of a slumlord. It has learned over the millennia that high nutrient loads of pollution usually entail a fertile ecosystem with many A/A prey opportunities.

Pennsylvania's Big Spring Run, formerly the site of a massive hatchery, was an organic-polluted spring creek when the hatchery was dumping fish fecal matter into the stream. Its insect life suffered along with its indigenous wild brook trout. Here monster browns ate "honey bugs," a fly tied out of cream chenille or fox fur that imitated clumps of hatchery sewage coming out of the concrete holding ponds, which were loaded with midge larvae.

Dozens of unique brown trout strains evolved over millions of years from Europe, Asia, and North Africa. Some, like the closely related Marble and Hucho trout, have approached river-monster status. These strains have ferocious A/A feeding tendencies and attract anglers from all over the world. (See page 34.)

SEA- AND LAKE-RUN BROWNS

Somewhere in their evolutionary journey, brown trout eventually found their way to the seas and oceans, similar to rainbow trout becoming steelhead. These sea-run browns are found in their native range from Iceland to the United Kingdom to the European Baltic theater. But nowhere can they approach such amazing sizes like they do at the "end of the world"—Tierra del Fuego. This "Land of Fire" is at the southernmost tip

Due to a brown trout's slower attack speed compared with steelhead and salmon, Tierra del Fuego browns pursue a variety of food forms the ocean gives them. They are not picky and anything that swims is a meal. But once hooked, they can become fussy S/R beasts. ANDREW MARTIN

of the earth in Argentina, the last land mass before you get to Antarctica. Its long cool summers and wet moderate winters create the perfect environment for *Salmo trutta* to ascend the region's big rivers like the Rio Grande and Gallegos. Here the coastlines between the Atlantic and Pacific Oceans funnel a massive nutrient load and biodiversity of food forms and pelagic baitfish like no other place in the world. The region's oceangoing brown trout roam the deep waters near shore, predating upon everything they find—shrimp, squid, and every baitfish known to both oceans—thus becoming enormous in size. The Rio Grande boasts a run of approximately 75,000 fish that average 12 pounds or more.

The brown trout of Tierra del Fuego often hit the 20-pound mark. Fish of 30 pounds are not unusual, and some heavier than that have been captured. Since the region's rivers are in low-lying tundra estuaries, they are nondescript. Swinging flies like big black uglies with rubber legs—and using two-handed Spey rods to help combat the wind—is the way to go here.

The two-hand rod swinging technique here is less of a broadside approach than a jigging and upstream lifting, which slowly entices the big fish to strike your fly. Remember, these A/A fish aren't used to having to work hard for their food and will nail a creepy black

rubber-legged stonefly or a Woolly Bugger on demand. Slow down your presentations here for success. Once the big brute browns have been in the rivers for some time and have seen angling pressure, they will adopt more S/R behaviors. Switching flies constantly is the trick to keeping them A/A.

One of the main reasons a sea- or lake-run brown trout remains so A/A is the fact that it spends a considerable amount of time in big, oceanlike environments where its food supply is plentiful. Due to its more solitary roaming tendencies, a function of *Salmo trutta*'s personality and nature, it is not hunted by predators to the degree that the more packlike Atlantic salmon is hunted. From Sweden's Mörrum River to Poland's Baltic coast, sea trout will enter almost any coldwater river or stream to spawn. They are not far-ranging ocean navigators like the Atlantic salmon they resemble, instead intent on pursuing the extreme bounty of the eutrophic waters close to the coastline. Here they prey on crabs, crustaceans, squid, capelin, and herring. This garbage feeding makes them A/A in their predatory behavior. Rarely are they selective, which can occur even in the A/A phase. They are great fighters and extremely sought out due to their ease of catching, unlike large land-based browns. On the Mörrum in Sweden, sea-run brown trout reach massive sizes and are often caught with the same fly-swinging techniques used for the Atlantic salmon that also run the river. Due to their nature of predatorial feeding, the browns are lovers of the more gaudy flies with motion and movement; leeches and buggers, as well as baitfish patterns, can be devastating. The Truttanator Sculpin is lethal on sea- and lake-run browns (see page 117 for pattern).

The Great Lakes offer some of the best sea- and lake-run brown trout fly-fishing opportunities in the world. The region's latest world-record fish came from Lake Michigan, near the mouth of the Manistee River on the Wisconsin shoreline. The Great Lakes salmonid revolution blossomed in the early 1970s, wilder than any biologist could have imagined. It began when Pacific coho and chinook salmon were introduced in Lake Michigan, and the Great Lakes states and the province of Ontario began to plant domestic and Seeforellen-strain brown trout in their waters in large numbers. The "Pacific salmon experiment" Michigan embarked upon in the late 1960s was an attempt to find an apex predator able to devour the overpopulated alewife pelagic baitfish that had invaded from the Atlantic Ocean when the Welland Canal opened for freighter traffic. The baitfish were becoming a nuisance species, fouling up beaches with their dead carcasses. The browns being introduced at the same time found this food source impossible to resist.

In the fall of 2009, a new chapter of the Great Lakes tale took place on the Big Manistee River in Michigan. Joe Healy, fishing for chinook salmon on a warm, clear, sunny day, latched into a "brown trout from hell," landing a 41-pound, 7-ounce leviathan that became the new world record. The fish had stayed in the lake for years chowing down on baitfish and finally decided to come upriver and spawn. For all practical purposes, this will most likely be a Seeforellen (German alpine) strain, a type which has been used to stock the Great Lakes and is known to attain leviathan sizes. The Michigan record was shattered in 2012 when the new world-record fish, weighing 43 pounds, was landed on the Wisconsin shoreline.

The opportunistic and wide-ranging feeding tendencies of sea- and lake-run browns have found them eating shoreline mice, small chickling ducks, eels, and anything else that swims. The Great Lakes are the

Great Lakes–run brown trout and those found in the Baltic Sea from Scandinavia to Poland have a reputation as voracious feeders that will stop at nothing to get a good meal. The old sayings that "a brown will eat anything that doesn't eat it," or "a brown trout would eat its tail," cannot be more true. HENRIK LARSSON

Left: Great Lakes–run browns will take a fly, any type of fly, anytime, anywhere, and often more than once! But once it has been caught and released, the brown trout is one of the most cunning, elusive, and wary salmonids ever to evolve. That is what accounts for their huge sizes. Combine these "Dr. Jekyll and Mr. Hyde" qualities, and you have one hell of a game fish on the fly rod. COLIN MONAHAN

Releasing a chrome-bright sea-run brown in Tierra Del Fuego's harsh windy and cold conditions. JOHN SHERMAN

perfect "soup bowl" of food for this predator. The browns are also fond of nocturnal hunting. They slowly cruise the shorelines and harbors of the Great Lakes, preferring 60- to 63-degree waters—too warm for Pacific salmon and steelhead.

As the Great Lakes continue to change due to invasive species like the zebra and quagga mussels, Asian carp, and exotic Mediterranean crustaceans, the lake-run browns are poised to become the species that will most likely capitalize on these food chain fluctuations. A Great Lakes Pacific salmon's diet is about 80 percent to 90 percent alewife baitfish. These pelagic baitfish have seen such drastic population swings from year to year that in some cases they have become almost nonexistent, as is the case in Lake Huron.

Since the Great Lakes have an incredibly diverse prey food chain that includes alewives, smelt, emerald shiners, deepwater sculpin, gobies, sticklebacks, and shrimp, the brown will eat every one of these wholeheartedly. Along with native indigenous species like yellow and white perch and walleye, these prey fish populations fluctuate drastically in both raw numbers and in their percentage of the overall prey population.

Since the A/A lake-run brown does not discriminate it can adjust to the most abundant entrée.

The browns are fond of harbors and warmwater discharges from power and nuclear plants, sewage purification stations, and other areas that are usually home to high plankton and nutrient loads, which feed pelagic baitfish and other smaller prey species. Recently, all the Great Lakes have become infested with the giant *Hexagenia limbata* mayfly, as a result of much cleaner habitat. When these large, size 4 mayflies hatch in July, they cover the roads like confetti, disrupting everything from night baseball games to shoreline airports. Lake browns become ferocious topwater sippers when this hatch goes on for weeks on end thanks to the extreme water clarity brought about by the filtering zebra mussels, and the giant native mayfly has become a stable food source for brown trout and steelhead alike, especially in the shallow-water environment of Lake Erie.

Rainbow Trout

Depending on its environment, the rainbow can be as easy to catch as the brookie or as ultraselective as the brown trout. It doesn't shun light or seek concealment like the brown; it does not need pristine, icy water like the brook trout. Having evolved in the high altitudes of the Continental Divide has made the rainbow used to its sunny environment. Rainbows thrive in all water types and have a high tolerance for water temperature up to 80 degrees.

For this adaptability and general propensity to eat everything from Velveeta cheese balls to worms or crickets to size 28 midges, the rainbow is a popular stocked fish. But even among wild fish, its gluttonous behavior will force it to adapt to highly challenging and selective river venues if it is forced to do so. It will compete with the most fussy and wary brook and brown trout, gulp for gulp, when given the ideal habitat for its A/A behavior to dominate. But pure wild strains, which have a tremendous exposure to different foods and river ecosystems, are extremely intelligent, wary, and have incredibly acute vision.

New Zealand is a mystical place and its rainbows, due to the ultraclear waters, can be very S/R. The country's world-famous rivers like the Tongariro, Owen, Ngaruroro, and Rangitaiki, are surrounded by glacial rock and lush, cascading waters that form perfect gravel. These stone rivers run gin-clear and are a turquoise color. With areas like Lake Taupo acting like

Perhaps no other trout has done more for the sport of trout fishing in general than this western American native. Indigenous to the Pacific Rim, from Southern California to Alaska to the Kamchatka region of Russia, it is perhaps the most vibrant thriving and reproducing trout of all. Its natural beauty is unparalleled. JOHN MILLER

Right: In the Patagonia region of South America, rainbows grow large in the high Andes lakes and become voracious feeders. JOHN MILLER

an ocean for the California-transplanted rainbow trout and steelhead that can run up its river tributary, you have a home for enormous migrating and resident rainbows. These wilderness fish are often as S/R as brown trout since the larger specimens are targeted by the trophy-hunting clients and guides. Holding in long, slow pools and in small spring creeks, they are extremely wary of your advances; they must be stalked individually and extremely carefully, with a stealthlike approach. Often natural insects are refused due to the acute selective demeanor of these rainbows in such pristine water environments. The migrating steelhead-like rainbows of the Tongariro go from A/A to S/R phases incredibly fast due to the river's clarity, food supply, and the fact that the fish retain the urge to eat on their spawning runs, much like the Great Lakes freshwater steelhead. Residents of other rivers grow large and selective as a result of concentrated

The trout mecca of New Zealand is an enchanted land of primordial forests, waterfalls, and clear turquoise waters and spring creeks. It is pure wildernesses akin to that present at the dawn of man. TONGARIRO LODGE

Left: Iliamna rainbow trout are some of the hardest-fighting fish in the world. These fish will strike your fly and get you into your backing in seconds. These big salmon egg-eating wild rainbows stretch your fly line up and down the river, and fishing for them becomes addicting. JIM KLUG/YELLOW DOG

daily pressure from guides and lodges and pristine, clear water, making a stealth approach and perfect cast essential.

Every selective trout has a breaking point, a time when it will act stupid and attack a hard-to-resist food source. When the twenty or more species of cicadas are in season, or the mouse hatch is in full bloom during bumper years of beech tree seedlings, the largest trout can be caught—but they still exhibit great caution, even when in A/A phases.

When massive food events precede a cold, harsh winter, trout will instinctively tune their cost/benefit computer to the A/A selective feeding mode. If there is one thing that rainbows have learned in their transmitted genetic code of learned conduct over the millennia, it is how to A/A binge feed on salmon eggs. The rainbows evolved on the heels of the massive runs of Pacific salmon and they are epicurean egg eaters. Any-

where rainbows are stocked for put-and-take fisheries from Arkansas to California you will find riverside grocery stores selling canned corn, jars of salmon eggs, and small cheese balls—all capitalizing on the penchant rainbows have for salmon eggs. Nowhere is this gluttonous A/A feeding more pronounced than on Alaska's rivers and the Lake Iliamna system.

Iliamna is the eighth-largest lake in the United States. Its system includes the Kvichak River, which drains the lake into Bristol Bay. It is a wild land of unparalleled beauty. The lake is 77 miles long, 22 miles wide, and comprises 1,000 square miles. Sockeye and king salmon migrate through it from Bristol Bay. It is also home to native grayling and lake trout. But it is best known for its magnificent, brilliant-colored rainbow trout that grow to steelhead size and can be ultrapicky and selective when the salmon egg hatch starts. Brian Kraft, owner of Alaska Sportsman's Lodge, knows these rainbows better than anyone else, and has lived the Alaskan dream for many years. He speaks passionately about his rainbows: "The wild native rainbow of the Iliamna drainage is a different genetic strain than other rainbow trout," Kraft says. "These fish also have a tremendous amount of protein to feed on. The largest salmon run in the world makes it to the tributaries of Lake Iliamna via the Kvichak River. This run typically is over two million sockeye alone and the other four Pacific salmon species also

make it to the drainage. These rainbows act like steelhead by transitioning throughout the system in search of the egg feast."

Kvichak River rainbows embody energetic A/A feeding, taking advantage of every day the salmon are moving to the system. They will take dry flies, salmon flesh flies, leeches, and sculpin. They also love mouse patterns. Once they get on the egg-eating binge, they become extremely A/A, yet remain discerning about pattern.

One popular tactic is using 6 and 8 mm plastic TroutBeads pegged an inch above the hook; each guide has his preference of colors. Salmon egg imitations are an art form here. Guides will spend days coloring eggs with nail polish and paint to imitate the various embryonic development stages that the rainbows key on. Each species of salmon has a unique egg color, from pink to orange to red and all hues in between. As soon as the eggs hit the water (and before they are fully embedded in the gravel), they will change to a pale cream color, and can later turn blue when in their final stages of decay. The rainbow trout can vary their preference from day to day and from week to week.

New and exciting egg imitations have been developed by Walt Mueller of Colorado. Called the Soft Milking Otter Egg, these are made of a translucent plastic material in dozens of colors and look exactly

Otter Eggs and trout beads come in a vast array of translucent and opaque colors—the trout don't stand a chance here! Use threading needles and small red/orange beads to peg the eggs. Once the tippet material is placed through the eye of the needle, pierce the egg and slide it up the leader. Add a tiny red bead below it, and then the hook. The micro red bead acts as the egg's nucleus and prevents it from sliding over the hook. MATT SUPINSKI

like the real deal. By using a tiny red ceramic craft bead for the embryo, the imitation can be pegged up just like the hard plastic ones. After the rainbows have been hooked dozens of times, they still remain aggressive, but they become more selective. The Otter Egg's realistic hue and translucency is usually the only way that the huge rainbows of up to 30 inches will succumb to light fluorocarbon tippets. Once the salmon start to die, flesh flies tied with creamy pink rabbit strips do the job as the rainbows turn their ravenous A/A search to the next most abundant progression of the Alaskan smorgasbord. Also the fish's selectivity will be much lower as the waters chill and winter approaches.

Brook Trout

Our North American native trout is a member of the char family. Its colors span the visual rainbow. Particularly during spawning, the brook trout's colors live up to its Celtic name of "charr," meaning a blood-red color. Evolving nearly thirty million years ago in the Oligocene Epoch as the North American glaciers retreated, the brook trout invaded all the ponds, lakes, rivers, and brooks that were cold, clear, and highly oxygenated.

John Goddard and Brian Clarke wrote, "the Brook trout is a Brook trout, no matter where you find them!" But a highly selective spring creek brook trout of Pennsylvania's Big Spring or Wisconsin's Timber Coulee, which provide abundant food and stable water flows, is no comparison to a food-deprived brookie of a cascading, sterile mountain stream, where it must take what and when of such food it can get. The latter's ferocious appetite for cold, pure clear water, filled with oxygen—surging rapids, waterfalls, and swift, boulder-strewn rivers—is not conducive to selective appraisals of each ingestion of food. Being exposed to extremes of water flow and temperature, anchor ice, and all the other harsh elements of a free-stone mountain stream, it must take what it can get, when it can get it.

If the brown trout is the rock star of the selective trout world, the North American brook trout would be an Elite or Ford modeling agency's example of beauty and perfection. Perhaps there is not a more beautiful fish that swims the planet. In my experience, the brook trout of Big Spring Creek are more S/R than the fat rainbows or brown trout. This brook's preference was a steady diet of gray-black and cream size 28 midges, with tiny red bloodworm larvae. MATT SUPINSKI

A dammed stream can create an ideal situation for the brook trout. The pond that is formed by the dam, such as a beaver dam, becomes rich in slow-moving food organisms like scuds, sow bugs, baitfish, and water beetles, as well as aquatic insects like midges, caddis, and some silt-burrowing mayflies. Due to the stagnant flow, vegetation will build up and nutrients like plankton will accumulate. This vast amount of food allows the brook trout to move about in a slow, introspective fashion, allowing for S/R feeding and a pace and lifestyle it is not used to in the faster-flowing brooks and freestone streams; in this respect, beaver ponds act somewhat like a large spring creek pool. The trout's awareness and fussy attributes are enhanced, and it will take its time in feeding. If the incoming stream is fertile, the water will eventually enhance the food population of the pond on a cyclical basis through biological drift and insect mating flights. Most importantly, the incoming stream must have cool, gravel-laden waters in which the brook trout can migrate and spawn successfully. When the beaver is

startled by an angler or predator's intrusion, it sounds an alarm by slapping its tail on the water surface, which becomes the "stop feeding" signal to a brook trout. This creates a perfect "got your back" relationship that favors the trout.

When approaching beaver pond brook trout, treat them like those found in spring creeks. Use long, fine leaders and tippets, make a low, stealthy, and quiet profile, and make a delicate presentation. The trout will predominantly feed on midges and tiny Blue-Winged Olives, which love this type of habitat. But there are large burrowing mayflies that hatch cyclically here and are relished by the trout, along with flying ants and other terrestrials. Timing is everything for the bigger mayflies, which have a short hatch cycle. An overcast day is a real plus. Pay close attention for back-and-tail bulging trout feeding in the meniscus.

COASTERS

Primeval wilderness environments, a tremendous food supply, and abundant pure cold water combine to

Below: When you target big brookies, whether in Québec, Labrador, or Nipigon, bring your monster streamer box and load up with lots of big white rabbit strip flies. Use heavy tippets and short leaders with T8 and 11 sinking heads and single-handed rods that can cast big streamers. If you get bored catching fish on streamers, wake huge foam terrestrials through the pools. MATT SUPINSKI

Coaster brook trout are extreme carnivores and anyone who ever fished a white streamer knows how effective it can be for these A/A predators. A small white Muddler Minnow was always deadly for me when I fished the Allegheny freestoner brookies of my youth and it continues to work no matter where brook trout are found. White rabbit strip Matukas even drove the wild S/R brookies, like this one from the Cypress River, Lake Superior, absolutely crazy. SCOTT SMITH

make for aggressive coastal sea- and lake-run brook trout like those in the Great Lakes, Labrador, or even Patagonia. I had a chance to experience these oversize brookies, known as coasters, along the north shore of Lake Superior. In the Nipigon district, these monsters can approach 20 pounds. The cold, deep water of Lake Superior, when combined with high-elevation forests and feeder rivers and stream habitat that is loaded with gravel and insect life, becomes the ideal wonderland for brook trout parr to grow impressively large and smolt successfully. The current world-record brook trout of 14 pounds was caught on the Nipigon River.

My baptism of coaster brook trout came on a day late in August, after heavy rains had swollen the Cypress River. "We're going to hit it just right!" Scott Smith said, beaming from ear to ear. We hiked several miles along a steep, rocky ridge and canyon filled with black bears. When we got to the pool, fish were boiling and porpoising like it was Marine World. I've never seen anything like it. Rigging up a Teeny 300 sink-tip, and putting one of Scott's Green Butt Monkeys on, my first cast and strip had 5 pounds of

coaster brook trout shaking its head with the streamer firmly implanted in its mouth. This was way too easy, but I loved it! I would often have two or three brook trout chase my streamer right to my feet as I waded the bank and streamer-stripped my arm off. Timing is everything. In our case, the combination of several days of cold rain after a hot summer, onshore winds on big Lake Superior bringing in cold water, and fishing a few days before the season closed, made for prime conditions. It doesn't get any better than this. After about twenty or more hookups, with several fish going close to 8 pounds, my camera and its roll of slide film were exhausted.

"Do these fish ever become selective and complacent?" I asked Scott.

"Never. They just get meaner with time as spawning aggression takes place," Scott said. "This is a special place. It only exists because it's unique wilderness. It's like we're here hundreds of thousands of years ago. Pretty cool, eh?"

The Char Family

Arctic char (*Salvelinus alpinus*) are similar in color to the Dolly Varden and are present in North America, Europe, and the Asian Arctic, mainly in South Arctic and alpine lake systems. This is the only species of freshwater fish found close to the Arctic region. It subsists on a diet of krill and baitfish, which gives its flesh a deep red color and makes it highly valued as food. The red, blue, and white circle spotting, along with the char's rich red sapphire belly, is breathtaking.

In the high Canadian Arctic, Nunavut's Tree River produces some spectacular arctic char for the fly fisher. Their arrogance is on display in their fearless invasions into shallow waters and shoreline feeding areas. Here they become extremely alarmed by your presence and a bad cast will put them down. The sheer abundance and diversity of food preferences of arctic char dictate their extreme selectivity and predator makeup. Fond of chironomids, crustaceans, and any aquatic food form, they have a diversified hunting nature similar to that of a spring creek trout. When feeding on salmon eggs, they become just as A/A as Alaskan rainbows, but in this phase are fussy to color translucency and opaqueness with great detail. Peter Christensen, the famed Danish fishing DVD star, has traveled all over the world in search of arctic char. He describes their A/A finicky nature:

Arctic char grow to large sizes because of their voracious appetites, but can feed in the S/R mode when not spawning and hunt their prey close to shore. PETER CHRISTENSEN

Lake trout (above) are constantly in the A/A mode and on the hunt for all sizes of pelagic baitfish prey. PETER CHRISTENSEN

In my experience char can be picky and selective when they are in fact looking for food in the A/A mode. There is a lot of good char fishing going on outside the spawning season, where the fishing situation can be compared to classic brown trout fishing with small dry flies, nymphs, midges, and so on. My own char fishing has been focused on the spawning runs that enter rivers across the Arctic from June and onwards.

Lake trout (*Salvelinus namaychus*) are native to North America and the Arctic region lakes, including the vast Great Lakes system. In the Great Lakes and in the Canadian lake regions of northern Ontario they hunt alewives, chubs, herring, smelt, gobies, sculpins, sticklebacks, and other trout and salmon. They are gluttonous eating machines approaching weights of near 100 pounds as they feed aggressively in the deep, light-void environments of the big lakes. On occasion they become S/R, especially during large chironomid midge matches and while cruising shorelines for crustaceans, but that selectivity mode is mostly foreign to them.

Bull trout (*Salvelinus conflentus*) are similar to Dolly Varden in appearance and inhabit the Pacific Northwest. They are extreme piscivore predators, and when they grow larger they can obliterate other trout populations. Until about the 12-inch range, they are ravenous feeders on all insect and crustacean life. But soon after, they are often found chasing and eating a fly fisher's smaller caught trout, and they can provide the surprise of a lifetime when they inhale your caught fish. They are highly pursued by Western streamer fishermen.

Marble and Huchen

Slovenia is an enchanting land of jagged, snowcapped mountain peaks shrouded in dense fog and lush green forests. Its rolling foothills and pastures are filled with cows and sheep, and farmers' horse-drawn carts clap alongside the road just as they did hundreds of years ago. The rivers are home to the native grayling, brown trout, and pike species. But it's the marble brown trout (*Salmo trutta marmoratus*) and the giant Hucho hucho, a relative of the monstrous Mongolian taimen,

Marble trout, a strain of brown trout unique to the rivers of the Adriatic Sea and native to the Balkan ranges, are one of the largest stream-dwelling trout in the world. They can approach weights of nearly 55 pounds. They have the appearance of a sexually mature adult Atlantic salmon, with their deep marble color spotting that sometimes resembles that of a lake trout. LUKA HOJNIK

that have lived here for millions of years. On crystal-clear rivers like the Soca and Unica, the eutrophic waters contain massive mayfly populations. These include the *Ephemera danica*, a giant (size 8 or larger) yellow and white mayfly that hatches in mind-boggling populations. Sometimes the spinners are so thick farmers shovel them into pens to feed chickens and pigs. If you could be there to witness this hatch, you would see A/A trout feeding behavior like you have never seen before. Here is where the marble trout, primarily a meat-eating piscivore, will come up and feed aggressively until it is completely satiated.

The marbles prey on almost any food form that they can swallow—smaller trout, perch, baitfish, and sculpins, as well as mice, snakes, small birds, and ducks. When you target marble trout, you are fishing big "roadkill" streamers, targeting deep holes in the undercuts of limestone rock ledges. This is trophy fishing at its finest. Fishing streamer patterns that look like young grayling, which the streams are full of, is your best place to start.

Since the valleys are narrow, the heavy rainfall from a passing storm in the mountains will discolor the water with a milky hue. This is the time to hunt marble trout and its cousin the Hucho just like you would other brown trout around the world. Night fishing is also productive where legal. Luka Hojnik is a Slovenian marble trout specialist and lives and breathes these magnificent beasts. Luka's approach with these A/A creatures on the Soca River, like with all big brown trout hunting, is to fish on rising, colored water after a good rainfall. He uses large streamers and covers the color spectrum using short, stout leaders and tippet. Since marble trout and big browns are A/A apex predators hunting other fish, early dawn can find them just about anywhere in the stream, from shallow runs to the near-shore areas where they hold their nightly foraging escapades. In addition to the marble trout, Hucho hucho, or Danube taimen, are found here mainly on the larger rivers and chalkstreams of the Sava and Croatia's Krka. A record specimen weighing 115 pounds was once caught. They are ravenous in their meat-eating tendencies and are referred to by the locals as the "River Wolf." They have been known to target muskrats, squirrels, snipes, and ducks. Any river trout of any size is fair game for the Hucho.

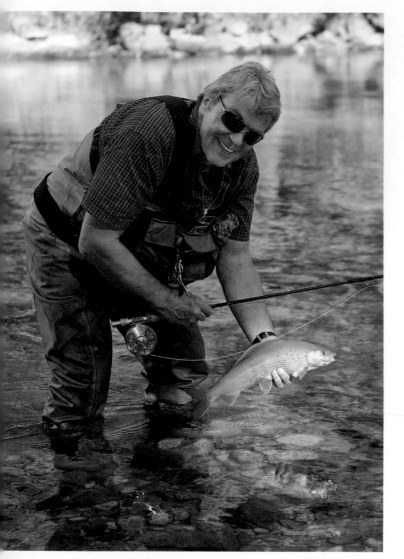

The "queen of the waters," the grayling, is a magnificent fish that thrives in all the alpine and low-lying valley streams of Europe. Though known to be prolific feeders and willing to take the fly, they can be extremely fussy when operating in the S/R mode. ALBERT PESENDORFER

Grayling

Thymallus thymallus is an amazingly beautiful fish of the salmonid family that lives across the entire upper northern latitudes in both hemispheres. Graylings prefer clean, cold-running rivers but also inhabit lakes and brackish waters. The Baltic Sea has great populations of this fish in its estuaries and feeder lake systems.

Grayling are extremely competitive and can out-reproduce trout populations where found. They are lovers of freshwater scuds, nymphs, and larvae, which they take with their downturned mouths, but they will come up and take dry flies with uncanny S/R dispositions. Wojtek Gibinski, the modern dean of Poland's San River of trout and grayling fame, is mesmerized by how selective they can be. He uses Czech and Polish nymphs and dries, which have all sorts of sprigs of color in their abdomens, to pique the interest of these selective "ladies of the stream." Wojtek elaborates:

Nothing in the world, not even a bad wife or husband, can be as fussy as a grayling. I have spent hours standing over big fish and not catching, and see them rise to dries or take nymphs. But in a massive hatch, when the water is covered with flies I've seen them refuse at the last moment natural and fly imitations, because it wasn't perfectly well presented or something with the natural was just not right. One of my mentors in fly fishing used to react on the occasion when all his flies were being ignored by a fussy grayling by saying, "If you don't like my fly Mr. Grayling, tie yourself a better one!"

Facing page: Whether you're in England's Hampshire, Pennsylvania's Cumberland Valley, Virginia's Shenandoah Valley, or the Driftless Area from Wisconsin and Minnesota to Montana's Paradise Valley and Idaho's Sun Valley, all have one thing in common—extremely Selective/Reflective spring creek trout. Here a River Itchen brown in England is on full S/R alert. ANDY GRACE

Trout: Habitat, Behavior, and Tactics

Trout selectivity is directly related to habitat, food abundance and diversity, water fertility and temperatures, and the relative ease—or difficulty—a trout will encounter when pursuing its prey. Since I cannot possibly cover all situations and behaviors, I will focus on the best examples of how these habitat variables directly dictate trout selectivity in addition to the influences of each species-specific, innate genetic behavioral code.

Habitats can be macro environments like freestone or tailwater rivers, or they can be more defined microhabitat environments such as trout lies that are associated with dam and mill pools, bridges, undercut banks, woody debris, beaver ponds, and boulders. These environments dictate the selectivity phase the trout will operate in most frequently and determine our tactics for catching them.

This is where the common denominators of selectivity comes into play—adaptability and refinement. If a Galapagos Island woodpecker finch learns to use a stick as a tool for displacing worms from a tree branch, does it mean the finches in my Michigan backyard can do the same? Probably not! An organism will adapt and refine its behavior to fit a specific environment.

Spring creeks, limestoners, chalkstreams—no matter what they are called and where you find them, they are special places with ideal water temperatures and food supplies. Here the author probes Hot Creek in California during a Trico hatch. LAURIE SUPINSKI

Trophic concepts classify ecosystems by nutrient richness and productivity, which are vital for rivers to produce character and life. An environment's character dictates how the prey and predator relationships of its biological food chain will respond and behave on a daily basis. *Oligotrophic* systems are poor in nutrients and their overall food chain is rather low in productivity. Such systems typically emanate from rock and calcium-carbonate caverns and headwaters. *Eutrophic* rivers are the complete opposite. They are rich in nutrients such as plankton and have a great diversity of benthic invertebrates and vertebrates for the trout to feed on. *Dystrophic* rivers emanate from heavily forested regions that pump organic hummic acids into the system. A peat-stained color and high acidity usually characterize these river and peat bog systems.

The key is to find rivers that have a combination of all these three factors. When you do, you have the ideal trout and salmon systems. Oligotrophic waters are pure, cold, and clean. Even though they are sterile, they are ideal for trout reproduction due to their clean, cold gravel environments. Eutrophic waters have the nutrient load for a healthy trout ecosystem.

Dystrophic waters have the tinted stain often conducive for gregarious trout feeding and cloaking behavior for security, along with producing certain food forms that prefer the acidity, such as stoneflies. Dystrophic rivers also have much wooded debris like sweepers, stumps, and log jams, which are ideal cover for lunker alpha trout. Thus when we find a unique balance of these factors, we find perfect habitat.

Spring Creeks

Limestoners, or chalkstreams as they are known in England, percolate from the exposed subterranean caverns lying at the bottoms of mountains and valley ranges where volcanic rock upheavals took place. They gush from the valley floors at a perfect water temperature of 48 to 55 degrees and remain that way year round, despite heat waves, subzero winter temperatures, droughts, and floods. Limestone spring creeks are loaded with alkaline calcium carbonate ($CaCO_2$). This along with other nutrients is a powerful stimulant that starts the whole food chain process, beginning with aquatic vegetation like elodea, duckwort, chara, and watercress. These plants cause plankton growth and create habitat for aquatic insects and other benthic invertebrates.

The biodiversity of food forms in a small spring creek is unparalleled. Mayflies, scuds, sow bugs, crayfish, and sculpins are all found here. In spring creek pastures, the infusion of terrestrial bug food forms like cicadas, beetles, ants, and grasshoppers is only a plop and a gulp away. Field mice, small snakes, and other rodents all become available.

Trout anglers know these little ditchlike jewels from Pennsylvania's Cumberland Valley, Virginia's Shenandoah Valley, Wisconsin and Minnesota's cow country, and the spring creeks of Montana. The headwaters of Michigan rivers like the Pere Marquette and Au Sable, just to mention a couple, provide this type of habitat. But nearly every state and continent has spring creek waters, which are more staggering in scope than early fly-fishing pioneers like Marinaro, Halford, and Skues originally thought. France, Germany, Iceland, Slovenia, Argentina, and Chile are loaded with spring creeks

In these clear and cold waters, trout are often S/R and will humble and torment even the most accomplished angler. These tiny creeks provide perfect concealment for trout under their tall undercut grassy banks, and their soft meadow soils transmit vibrations to the trout that announce anglers as they approach the creek. Sight-nymphing is the predominant technique for trout on spring creeks, and it is very much a hunting pursuit where stealth, precision casting, and fly presentation reveals the true soul and spirit of the trout as an angler observes it feeding, taking, or refusing the fly in plain view.

There is an age-old battle between approach philosophies, dating back to the English chalkstream methodology. It was common practice to fish a dry fly only upstream to rising fish. As more and more large spring creek waters were discovered—such as Silver Creek in Idaho, and spring creeks in Montana, Europe, and New Zealand—it was found that the larger waters were best suited to the use of downstream fly presentations, like the down-and-across reach cast. Long 12- to 16-foot leaders with fine 5- to 7-foot tippets could be presented to the highly selective fish, so the fly comes into the trout's window first, before its leader. Drag is eliminated and reduced by long drifts, especially when combined with a puddle cast and downstream stack mending.

However, this complex issue is a double-edged sword. Approaching from the downstream position

Freshwater scuds such as *Hyalella* and *Gammarus* are very abundant in the weed-filled habitats of spring creeks. They are the trout's staple "bread-and-butter" food source year round, and the fish will become hyper S/R to their exact fly imitations. JAY NICHOLS

allows the angler to be cloaked as the fish faces upstream. If the angler adopts the coming from upstream, fishing downstream approach, part of his or her body or fly rod will penetrate the bending refractive window of the S/R trout's vision, thus sending alarm.

Regardless of which approach you desire, a low, stealthy profile is the key. Walking softly, sometimes crawling around on elbows and knees, is required for easliy spooked wild trout. Having good knees and patience is required, and kneepads under your waders also help. When Ed Shenk of Pennsylvania's Letort fame fished upstream from the Bonny Brook Bridge, he did it on his knees, and would only use short rods so as to not to cast a shadow on the water and be able to poke into tight spaces along the undercut banks and weed channels.

Primary lies for large trout include gravelly riffles, weed channels with clear sandy patches, and undercut banks. Many anglers focus on deeper runs and pools, which do not always hold large S/R trout; feeding lies are more closely associated with abundance of prey and insect life. In these prime spring creek lies the weeds and watercress oxygenate the water and add depth and displacement, in addition to providing forage for plankton and crustaceans. The aquatic vegetation shields the current's flow and filters out silt, creating clear, sandy patches that are essential for a trout's surveillance. Various aquatic insects such as chironomids, *Baetis*, *Tricorythodes*, and *Simulium* midges all favor these areas. An undercut bank allows the large trout to survey and pursue the current's biological drift while having a roof to hide under.

Spring Creek Leaders

These leaders are meant to taper down quickly. They have a heavy butt section where needed, since the leader often lays on aquatic weed beds after the cast lands. It is also helpful when fighting fish, as the leaders will often accumulate vegetation as the fish dive into it. The 4 to 6 feet of supple tippet is necessary for the compound/complex spring creek rises, long drag-free floats, puddle casts, and upstream modified reach casts. These tippets also employ a convex "kicker" midsection that gives an extra push when roll casting or when casting into tight situations among willow trees and brush. It is also effective for the meadow grass situations encountered on small, medium, and large spring creeks. For the butt sections use Maxima Chameleon or Ultra Green, Rio Powerflex, Climax, or Orvis Super Strong Mono. Note that at the thicker butts I use .022/.021 diameters since each company has different specs here. For the final 4X-5X-6X through 12X, use supple fluorocarbon like Varivas Super Tippet Fluorocarbon, Rio Fluoroflex Plus, Mirage, and others that are similar. For tiny midge presentations, Varivas Super Tippet Midge is strong and supple from 8X through 12X. Use 4X for larger mayflies and hoppers.

Ten-foot Spring Creek Leader

For use on the tight, small meadow pasture creeks like those in the Driftless Area of Wisconsin and Minnesota or on upper Letort and Falling Springs Runs in Pennsylvania.

.022/.021	14"
.020/.019	10"
.017	8"
.015	8"
.017	10"
.013	6"
.010-1X	6"
.008-3X	6"
.007-4X	6"

Tippet: Use 4 feet of 4X through 10X fluorocarbon tippet. If you are nymphing, start the fluorocarbon at the 1X sections. All knots should be three-turn blood knots except when you get to the X attachments, which should be four-turn blood knots. The large to small diameter attachment, from .017 to .013, should be triple surgeon's knots. The fly knot should be an improved Duncan Loop/Uni Knot, which is run through the eye twice. Use lots of saliva when tightening the loop down to the fly and make sure the knot turns three-quarters in a circular fashion once tightened.

Fifteen-foot Spring Creek Leader

For larger open waters like Montana's Armstrong and Nelson's Creeks, California's Hot Creek, Virginia's Mossy Creek, and the open waters of Pennsylvania's lower Letort Spring Run.

.022/.021	18"
.020/.019	14"
.017	12"
.015	8"
.017	12"
.013	10"
.010-1X	8"
.008-3X	8"
.007-4X	8"

Tippet: Use 6 feet of 4X through 10X. When connecting large variances in leader diameter size, use a triple surgeon's knot. When connecting slight variances, use a nail knot with four to five turns on each side to seal the knot. ■

Take long breaks on small pieces of water. Spend more time observing than fishing. Blend into the water and meadow like a great blue heron. On spring creeks, slow everything down, keep your movements to a minimum, and visualize your presentation before you cast. On bigger waters like Silver Creek or Henry's Fork it might take a good fifteen minutes before you get into a position to make a down-and-across cast so that you don't create a wake and scare the fish. KEN TAKATA

Spring creeks tend to favor the delicate clinging mayflies and the larger silt-burrowing species, since gravel is usually confined to specific areas of gradient in faster flows. Spring creeks' hydrological problem of slow, low-lying minimal gradients is a benefit to those species of aquatic insects mentioned above. Because the tremendous eutrophic nutrient load gives vegetation and decaying detritus strongholds along banks and river channels, the Blue-Winged Olive species, Sulphurs, Ephemeridae, and chironomids are the best bets for the surface hatch-matching fly fishers. Some stonefly activity is present, mainly the small black and yellow stoneflies, which are early spring emergers. Caddis also do exist, but prefer slightly warmer water conditions. When a large trout is surface feeding and a hatch is in progress, anglers should target several clear weed channels adjacent to each other or a place for a

Blue-Winged Olive *Baetis* nymphs love the clinging vegetation that spring creeks and tailwaters provide. JOHN MILLER

trout to escape, such as undercut banks or wooded deadfalls.

Many spring creeks throughout the world, such as Spring Creek in State College, Pennsylvania, have small private or government fish hatcheries on them. The red chironomid bloodworm larvae is in good supply on spring creeks where this activity takes place since the worms feed on trout fecal matter, and small patterns imitating bloodworms work extremely well.

S/R surface-feeding fish in spring creeks have short windows of opportunity for feeding, but once the fish senses no alarm or intrusion as you patiently and quietly remain still and in position to cast, you are close to victory. If you have timed your arrival with the peak of the hatch emergence, the fish may begin to get sloppy and clumsy, which is a nice rarity of an encounter. But timing is everything. If you wait too long, that drizzle of rain and clouds might give way to sun and that short BWO hatch will be over. Blue-Winged Olives of all types—*Baetis*, *Drunella*, and *Pseudocloeon*—are fond of low-light conditions coupled with a light rain or drizzle. These hatches occur all year on spring creeks and tailwaters, especially in the mid- to late winter and on fall afternoons. The key is to be there at the optimum time when the fish are most adventurous and feeding steadily. When things start to wind down, you won't see as many surface-feeding fish, even though bugs may still be on the water, and the fish are easily alarmed. At this time, nymphing scuds, sow bugs, and Pheasant Tails is a good choice, even if you see some Blue-Winged Olives left on the water. Fish feel more comfortable feeding below the surface.

Dry fly presentation on spring creeks can be tricky. The placid water is deceiving since the weed channels send undulating currents to the surface and create all sorts of back swirls, eddies, and unnatural hydrodynamic movements that affect your fly. On spring creeks, the channels between the vegetation are often

narrow (except during winter weed die-offs) so the trout's feeding and viewing window is also limited. That your window of presentation may be only a few feet, with your main leader butt falling on the aquatic grasses near the feeding channel, or eventually being dragged there, complicates things immensely. Your cast must be precise at the get-go since you might not be allowed a second chance. Throwing a puddle cast, or sweeping to the left or right with a reach cast mend, which gives you a somewhat downstream reach cast, can buy you a little time for a drag-free presentation.

A down-and-across reach cast is usually the only way to go for selective spring creek trout on larger waters. In this situation, the fly comes into the fish's window first, before the tippet material, and so the trout will focus all of its effort on scrutinizing the imitation and less time scrutinizing, or "being disappointed" as Marinaro put it, by a dragging fly, even though drag might be almost imperceptible. On big spring creeks like Armstrong, Nelson's, and Silver Creek, and a host of others in Patagonia and New Zealand, you could get out and wade and move into position slowly. On the limestoners of Pennsylvania, Wisconsin, and Minnesota you have to hide behind trees, shrubbery, or other obstacles to shield your advances from upstream as you descend on a fussy trout.

A common scenario on spring creeks around the world—from Idaho's Silver Creek to Falling Spring Run to the Test—is for trout to hold in reverse current eddies and backwaters sipping spent spinners and other insects. On Idaho's Silver Creek, which supports one of the highest possible densities of insect life and

Do browns grow large because they live in tricky, hard-to-cast-to areas, or do large browns intentionally seek impossible, shelter-driven lies? The verdict will never be out on the subject matter, due to the fact that they coincide. JOHN MILLER

Patagonia's Coyhaique region in Chile is loaded with tiny spring creeks that have perfect brown trout habitat. There are hundreds upon hundreds of these often-tiny creeks—some never explored—and many hold leviathan browns. When working any small spring creek, you must be on your elbows and knees. But due to the fact big rivers get all the fishing attention from the lodges and drift boats, the small creeks get little pressure. JIM KLUG/YELLOWDOG

trout in a stream, large rainbows and browns will sip and gulp on the surface in the backwater sloughs just like they do on Armstrong's and Nelson's spring creeks of Paradise Valley in Montana. The Trico hatch is massive here. Every day from summer until late fall, the hatch and spinner fall occur from dawn until the high noon sun. It is structured and regimented, and the fish population attends to its feeding needs daily. Pods of rainbow and brown trout will take position in small schools on the shallow runs, waiting for the spinner flights to fall and the orgy to begin. Dominant fish jockey for position and try to protect the prime feeding lanes. An occasional big brown bully will crash the orgy and push out all the submissive rainbows.

The biggest rainbows and browns here seem to be the most reclusive feeders. They feed by intercepting the prime mother lodes of backwashed spent spinners in the sloughs, where each alpha fish dominates its own private piece of Idaho real estate. In the reverse-spiraling sloughs, the heavy accumulation of spent spinners and lack of current flows makes these big bruiser trout nearly impossible to catch. The slightest intrusion of your fly and leader on these currentless waters casts a warning signal.

These backwater, reverse-current-eddy, sipping hogs can be found from Falling Spring Run in Pennsylvania to the River Test in England. The first step in cracking the code is to approach these fish from the upstream position and stay low. Make a downstream puddle cast into the feeding lane since the current is going back upstream in a clockwise spiraling motion. To be successful with these fish, try double or triple spinner patterns. On a size 16, long-shank hook, I tied two female and one male spinners, with clear bodies with peacock thoraxes or all-black bodies to imitate the male and female couplings. Organza was used for the wing material. I increased the natural bend of the hook to imitate the burnt-up and spent form of the fly. Be patient through many refusals and looks.

You'll be spending a lot of time on proper fly selection, silhouettes, size, and color, but the single-most important delivery item is the leader. Spring creek

Silver Creek, running through land owned by the Nature Conservancy, is an oasis in the vast arid desert of Sun Valley. Among the big sky and grasses between the mountains, the valley below scrapes the top of huge subterranean aquifers to create a high-altitude spring creek like no other in the world. GUISEPPIE SAITA

leader tapers must have a firm and heavy butt section to punch casts into wide-open windy valleys. The tapered section, from main butt to the long fine tippet section, must be a series of quick short tapers. When you hook a fish on 7X tippet and it dives into a heavily weeded vegetation bank or channel, the middle part of your leader better be heavy and strong with good knot strength or you will never land the fish. Five to seven feet of tippet—primarily fluorocarbon—allows for slack puddle casts and stack mending to get long drag-free drifts to complex feeding trout in swirling surface currents.

Tailwaters

Cold water from reservoirs makes tailwaters the perfect (unnatural) trout ecosystems. Deeper reservoirs like the Navajo Dam on the San Juan, the Cannonsville and Pepacton Reservoirs on the Delaware, the reservoirs on the Bighorn and Missouri, the White, and the Clinch and Holston Reservoirs in Tennessee hold cold, well-oxygenated, nutrient-rich waters. The deeper the bottom draws from these reservoirs, the colder the water. It is common during water releases on the West Branch of the Delaware to have river temperatures near 40 degrees even when air temperatures are hovering near 100 degrees in July. To see super Sulphur hatches in the middle of a sweltering-hot July day on these systems is a miracle of the tailwater.

These tailwaters are for the most part low-gradient, flat, stable, slow-flowing waters, with pools and flats that allow the trout to roam and pursue their food carefully. Since tailwaters embody all river types and characteristics, they host some of the most complex food chains from all the four major insect groups—mayflies, stoneflies, caddis, and midges. Reservoirs are usually rich in *Daphnia* and plankton, which supports *Mysis* shrimp, sow bugs, chironomids, caddis larvae, stoneflies, and mayflies. These highly sought-after food items are favored by the trout. This abundance of insect varieties—sometimes all hatching at the same time—plus catch-and-release regulations, create ultraselective trout. On waters like the Delaware, even an 8-inch wild brown trout will give you refusal fits.

Wild rainbows, sipping the surface on ultra-rich ecosystem tailwaters like those of the Bighorn, Missouri, and San Juan of the West, and the Delaware and Muskegon of the East—can become extremely fussy S/R feeders. Their acute vision can tolerate brighter sunlight, allowing them to pick out the finer details of fly presentation when minutiae and Sulphur/PHD hatches are on the water. They also can better detect shadows and sloppy casts, causing havoc for an angler. JOHN FLAHERTY

No matter where in the world they are found, tailwaters are synonymous with multibrood Sulphur hatches that create extreme S/R behavior. The clinging and detritus feeding (decaying vegetation) *Ephemerella* of the Sulphur family—most notably the invarias, dorothea, and pale morning dun infrequens—love tailwater rivers. Cold water flows and prolific vegetation make tailwaters their playground. They have no photophobic preference, unlike the Blue-Winged Olives, which prefer low-light rainy days. When the Sulphurs hatch, their emergences are heavy and prolonged. Heavy angling pressure on catch-and-release tailwaters will force the fish to inspect every natural and fly imitation to the last detail. The wild trout megasystems of the New York–Pennsylvania border waters of the Delaware and the South Holston and Clinch Rivers of Tennessee have perhaps some of the strongest super Sulphur hatches in the east. Montana's Bighorn, with its prolific Pale Morning Dun (Sulphur) hatches, is the West's crown jewel.

The West Branch Delaware's multibrood Sulphur hatch lasts for at least four months. Invaria, dorothea, and rotunda, as well as September's *Heptagenia hebe*, a mottled winged Sulphur, account for daily heavy surface feeding. The Delaware's June and July hatches are most prolific when cold water is being released in hot summer conditions, with flows averaging anywhere from 400 to 1,000 CFS. Water temperatures are generally in the low 40-degree range in the morning, but as noon approaches, they warm up to near 48 to 50 degrees, which is the magic Sulphur number. It's "banker's hours" gentlemanly fishing, which a true dry fly purist likes.

Morning fog and steam on the water allows you to sleep in and enjoy a leisurely breakfast. The onslaught of drifting adult duns starts around noon in the upper river at the "gentleman's club" section near Stilesville, New York. Due to the cold water, the duns float upright, sideways and stillborn, for long periods before taking flight; it looks like Creamsicle-colored confetti sprinkles coat the river as far as the eye could see.

Cracking the Code: Garbage Feeding

It was a warm early September afternoon on the Delaware River's Stockport pool (aka "big bird pool"). This is a long flat pool of even depth, from knee deep to chest deep, where the flows are perfect and cold when the release is on. Here the wild rainbows of the Delaware cruise all day and evening picking up everything in the surface soupy mix: *Heptagenia* Sulphurs, Blue-Winged Olives from size 18 to 26, tiny Trico size 24 spinners, flying ants, and the occasional large *Isonychia* or *Potamanthus* giant dry fly. They will also take any terrestrial that could possibly blow into the water, and those damn tiny cream midges of fall in size 28s. Given this pool's smooth flow, these fish garbage feed slowly and cautiously.

On that particular afternoon, I had this pool to myself—a rarity. My beloved wife, who was not yet into fly fishing, sat patiently and read a book in her lawn chair along the bank. I subjected this woman to almost five hours of the madness of my failed pursuit to hook a large and obstinate 24-inch rainbow that was holding in a V-shaped slot above a current slicer. The midstream boulder allowed the fish to comfortably sit and examine food as it came by him in a leisurely fashion.

The water looked like a buggy version of minestrone soup. While I rested the fish for what seemed like an eternity (in reality, only fifteen minutes), I watched her come up to the surface more than two dozen times and take *Heptagenia* Sulphur, several

The old slogan, "if you can't stand the heat, get out of the kitchen," is perfectly applied here when fishing to wild main stem Delaware rainbows. They are especially hyper S/R in the fall, when the fish have seen it all and been pricked or caught dozens of times. They basically dictate their own pace. MATT SUPINSKI

This perfect scenario makes the river's wild browns and rainbows take the surface parade in compound and complex inspections of both the natural and imitation. Here they often target the half-sunken emerger and stillborn nymphs. The most effective way to fish these conditions is with a CDC or snowshoe rabbit emerger and Pheasant Tail Nymph dropper on 6X tippet. You have a good chance of fooling a 25-inch brown with such a system. A CDC Compara-emerger with brown Z-Lon tail shuck is at the top of the list for super Delaware guide Johnny Miller. He calls it "trout crack."

When there is an abundance of a single food source that the trout become fixated on, you must have perfect fly designs and presentations. Two examples of such fisheries come to mind. On Colorado's

sizes of Blue-Winged Olive, flying ants, a large *Isonychia*, a large *Potamanthus*, a small twig, a half shuck of a brown stonefly, a ladybug, a couple small Trico spinners, and something tan I could not discern—it looked like a leaf particle. Unlike the masking hatch where the fish is keying in on one particular but undetectable food form, this was the epitome of the garbage feeder.

After five hours of throwing all of the above-mentioned items—except for the shuck and the leaf/twig, which I had no imitation for—I received seventeen refusals, countless not-interested-ins, and many, "get that thing away from me!" responses from my nemesis trout. My mind started to churn and think of memories past. My thoughts took me to September in Pennsylvania on the Yellow Breeches flat water above the dam at the Allenberry Resort. Here the water was still, with floating autumn leaves dotting its surface, and trout were taking tiny size 28 to 32 white midges and cruising around right in front of my face. There was one last-ditch fly that always seemed to work for me there, despite how hyperselective these fish were: a size 20 bright orange ant with grizzly hackle. This was the ticket, and my last-gasp version of Pickett's Charge.

Despite the warm weather, I was shaking as I tied on the little orange ant for my last shot at glory. To further complicate things, I went to 7X, which could have been a stupid move because these wild 'bows fought and jumped like steelhead, but it was a long shot worth taking. My first cast was slightly off the feeding lane target, but the fish perked up its fins and noticed the fly immediately. "Yes," I said in my head, "something's changing here." That was the hardest look at my fly I had seen yet. I might be onto something. Waiting as you would with an Atlantic salmon refusal, I let the big rainbow think about it for a while. After several minutes, which seemed like an eternity, I glanced back at the bank to see my wife packing up

her chair and getting ready to bolt! "One last cast," I screamed as I loosened up my reel's drag. I knew that if I caught the fish, we would have one hell of a battle on that 7X. I delivered the cast perfectly to the left side of the foam line. The fish noticed it immediately, started to rise slowly, put its head over the fly, and took it down. I waited for a second and a half, set the hook slightly, gave it slack, and then we were off to the races! I screamed at the top of my lungs, running downstream a hundred miles an hour as my drag system was screaming. "Fish on!" Almost one hundred yards downstream at the tailout of the Stockport pool I finally eased this magnificent-colored, silver-bodied rainbow—which had fought like a steelhead—next to shore, where I put my small net over it. I couldn't believe this thing wanted that orange ant so badly. There were no orange ants here; red ones are present on rare occasions. I got a great picture of the biggest rainbow I ever caught, and felt like I was king of the world!

The next day, trying to find selectivity closure, I went back to the fields near the Stockport water and I looked for ants. I found black ones, brown ones, and one red one that was sort of a dull burgundy. I stuck it in some water in a glass and let it sit around for a day. Guess what color it turned the next day: orange! So often when you have the proverbial, "dumb-luck fly" that they should not take but cracks the garbage-feeding code, there sometimes is an underlying selectivity component at work that is actually mimicking the natural. Or can it be the hot orange color or total novelty in the fly that caught the trout's interest. So when all else fails, go to the orange ant. They must taste like truffles to a trout. Or was it the aggressive color of orange that got the fish's attention, just like often you get strikes to your orange foam strike indicator? For complete closure to this case, we must ask the trout. An open mind and luck is the ticket to S/R garbage feeding. ■

Frying Pan and South Platte Rivers, it is *Mysis* shrimp, and on Michigan's Muskegon, it's the caddis. These tailwater reservoirs have a common relished food source for their prey: *Daphnia* zooplankton and phytoplankton. Their amazing *Mysis* shrimp populations and caddis larvae prey on the plankton and sustain the growth rates of super trout. Without these two-year-long available food sources, the trout would

spread their foraging by seasonal availability and opportunity to diverse food.

Below Ruedi Dam on the Frying Pan and Cheesman Canyon on the South Platte, the water flows clear and cold. Red sandstone cliffs covered with a pine/fir mix provide a gorgeous backdrop. The rivers' leviathan trout are stalked by a ravenous cadre of trophy-trout hunting fly fishers. The dam's bottom draw sucks out

Mysis shrimp are a delicacy for trout and salmon around the world wherever they are found in excellent numbers. Note the shrimp's translucency. GUDMUNDUR GEIR

The releases on tailwaters like the Tennessee's Clinch (shown here) and the world-famous White River system in Arkansas can average anywhere from a base flow of 95 CFS to really cranking levels of 3,000 to 5,000 CFS. Those are wild fluctuations capable of catapulting trout into any of the three selectivity phases. ZACH MATTHEWS

the *Mysis* and has the shrimp available for the trout waiting in the tailwaters below. Live *Mysis* shrimp are translucent. Fishing these patterns dead drifted with subtle movement can account for large trout right near the bottom draw itself. But as the *Mysis* wane and die off, they turn white from light exposure farther downriver. You must have both patterns.

The *Mysis* shrimp drift is subtle and so drag-free presentations are paramount, though at times Pat Dorsey, in his book *Fly Fishing Tailwaters*, recommends swinging and twitching the patterns. Sight-nymphing is your best bet, since the large white opening mouths of these huge S/R trout are easily detected at considerable depths in these clear-water situations. Needless to say, it is important to have the best polarized sunglasses money can buy. On the finicky Muskegon River in Michigan, my home guiding river, *Hydropsyche* caddis are the S/R trout's bread and butter. Cinnamon and little green caddis (*Hydropsyche bifida* and *Cheumatopsyche speciosa*) build nests along the rocks and are available year round; they hatch from May through October. The caddis, as with the *Mysis* shrimp, are ravenous zooplankton and phytoplankton eaters. Their larvae, anchored on the rocks, can withstand strong fluctuations in flow, which makes them perfect for the fluctuating flows and

Fish in pressured waters such as Cheesman Canyon on the South Platte in Colorado can be extremely difficult to catch. Because of the extreme water clarity and abundant biodiversity of scuds, small mayflies, and midges, the fish consume vast quantities of minutiae to grow to leviathan sizes. Their habituation to anglers and extreme concentration on specific food forms makes them selectivity's ideal ambassadors. MARK ADAMS

temperatures of tailwater habitats. When the Muskegon trout are on the caddis, I've seen many so-called experts get their butts handed to them.

Why such extreme selectivity for *Mysis* and caddis-eating trout? The age-old concept of cost/benefit enters in. For these trout to grow large and advantageously fat, they must consume hundreds of these food items a day. They meticulously feed by setting up proper feeding lanes to intercept their prey. The trout focus totally on the steps of selection in trout vision: shape, silhouette, size, color, and behavior.

For caddis, fly behavior is critical. The emerging pupae dead drift, gyrate, or pulse, all in one drift. The adult pops through the pupae cuticle quickly. When the females come back to oviposit their eggs, they do so by bouncing on the surface or diving under the water to deposit them on the rocks below. A

My ascending caddis pupa is lethal during a super caddis hatch. It serves the dual purpose of imitating either an ascending pupa or a diving adult female caddis returning to the surface after laying her eggs on the bottom. Fish it with upstream and downstream mends to pulsate and stutter the fly. MATT SUPINSKI

Muskegon S/R trout could have as many as five hundred pupae, larvae, or adult caddis in its stomach at any given time, all of which had to meet the selectivity profile of the natural. So if that doesn't sound complicated enough, you must be prepared to imitate all six phases of this hatch in one session on the water.

Gentle sipping rises occur to spent caddis or floating crippled pupae that have just turned into adults. JOHN MILLER

My friends Carl Richards and Gary LaFontaine came up with some highly specialized imitations. In these heavy caddis-infested rivers—another being the Missouri tailwater—exactness matters. An Elk-hair Caddis often won't cut it. When the trout key in on a specific phase like the pupa, which comprises 75 percent of the feeding during this hatch, dead drifting or twitch-and-go drifting pupa will give you many looks and often rejections. But when the hatch is on heavy," sheer numbers of naturals is the key. Eventually the trout make mistakes in these situations after you have consistently and monotonously presented your fly over and over to the same fish. It might take dozens of casts, but you should stick with one good fish despite refusals. Observing its behavior will pay off. A mid-depth suspended trout jittering from side to side usually indicates feeding to ascending pupae or drifting larvae rises. Quick slashing rises usually indicate feeding on emerging pupae or ovipositing females that climbed underwater to lay eggs and are now swimming back to the surface. Often trout will leap completely or partially in the air when A/A attacking egg-laying females.

Sight-Nymphing

When I am nymphing crystal-clear water, common in tailwaters and spring creeks, I approach slowly and cautiously, dividing each piece of the river into small parts. Our tendency on rivers is to roam and wade till

we're blue in the face and fishless; always thinking there is a monster lurking around the next bend is not the appropriate way to fish. Here, each piece of water can hold a large trout—in habitat-rich spring creeks and tailwaters, the sheer amount of fish lying in total disguise is amazing. There are hundreds of fish among all the weed growth, undercut banks, and dark channels. You often walk past sections of a fertile habitat and trout lies while looking for the honey hole. On one of my favorite spring creeks in Wisconsin, it took an electroshocking fish survey to teach me this lesson. The biologists came downstream and shocked a section of river I thought was fishless—16- to 24-inch browns appeared out of nowhere, leaving me completely baffled.

Sight-nymphing is hunting, plain and simple. Bilateral and extremely acute vision is required. Stalking at a low profile out of the sun's shadow is a must. And having the patience to study the patterns and behavior of a large S/R trout nymphing is paramount to success.

Tips for Trophy Fish

Timing is everything here. The power of cloudy days with light rain is amazing on these rivers, which are broad and wide open without shade. Often when you fish them on sunny days (the Delaware is one example) you could swear there isn't a trout to be had. Big and selective tailwater trout are always on the hunt for food, comfort, and feeding handouts and they go through all the selectivity phases in direct correlation with the conditions. They can traverse many miles of river in several weeks due to the stable hydrodynamics and flat river terrain. For the most part this dictates their mobility, and so the angler must be also mobile.

If you're a hatch-matching dry fly nut like me, it's critical that you know a stream's aquatic insect hatches as well as the percentage of mayfly, caddis, stoneflies, chironomids, and midges that make up each hatch, so that you have a basis for fly selection. No two tailwaters have the same emergence schedule; the hatches are dictated by climate zones and seasons. Some tailwaters, such as the San Juan River, will have many year-round emergence schedules, with concentrations of midges and tiny Blue-Winged Olives occurring daily.

During a hatch, I recommend fishing upstream of the fish, so that you can present the fly with a down-and-across reach cast. The greater distance you can keep from the fish the better. Be careful not to produce

Frank Sawyer nymphing on his beloved Avon in Hampshire, England. Sawyer wrote in *Nymphs and the Trout* that "Nymph fishing, if you are to be successful, is indeed a matter of being careful. It is not just the business of throwing a nymph at all the likely places and hoping the fish will take it. You turn yourself Into a hunter and, with all the keenness of a stalker after a stag, figure wits and your eyesight against the facilities and faculties of the wild fish who are on the feed and continually on the lookout for nymphs moving in the water or below."
TERRY LAWTON

An original Sawyer Pheasant Tail Nymph. If I had to fish one fly pattern in the world, the Pheasant Tail Nymph would be it. Created to mimic the *Baetis* Blue-Winged Olive nymphs, it is a general pattern that imitates a host of mayflies, particularly Sulphurs. Like all of Sawyer's nymphs, this simple design is highly effective for S/R trout when all other nymphs fail. It has no legs since the *Baetis* is a quick swimmer and its legs are tucked in. TERRY LAWTON

wakes, which will quickly shut down the fish. Long leaders of up to eighteen feet allow you to fish five to seven feet of tippet material, which can allow for extremely long drag-free float.

CHECK OUT THE SHALLOWS.

It was a bright sunny day in July, with a heat index near 100 degrees. The water temperature was in the mid-50s and nothing much was on the surface. "You'll be amazed at the water these fish are holding in—inches!" said John Miller. "They are holding in the tight rocky riffles and tailouts right by your feet!" he said. When big, selective browns and rainbows have optimal water conditions, their highly driven meta-bolic engines are in overdrive and they will hunt

insects in areas where the nymphs concentrate before the hatch. They find islands that have shallow riffles and gradient structures. They position themselves close to the shoreline for crawling and swimming nymphs. John cited two big browns in the mid-20-inch range, right in spots that were shin deep. Developing a keen eye for the body silhouette, tail, and white mouth is the key to spotting these fish. Both of the fish ate our *Isonychia* wiggle nymphs like

I learned the New Zealand–style approach to trophy-hunting nymphing from the Zen yogi trout hunter and guide Johnny Miller on the wild, selective-trout-filled Delaware. JOHN MILLER

candy, though in the bright daylight they were reluctant to move far outside of their feeding lanes for them. Make sure your nymph imitation is presented well above the fish and turn it broadside just before it enters the fish's window.

Too many anglers fish out of the comfort of a drift boat even during low water flows. This will spook the trout with your high profile. It is often, but not always, better to get out and wade slowly into position. LAURIE SUPINSKI

KNOW THE TEMPS

On tailwaters across the country, optimal conditions are not always where the water is the coldest. Often bottom-released water at dams is too cold and sterile and it isn't until the water warms to a more agreeable range (between 50 to 65 degrees) and the food becomes more diverse that you begin to see larger, selective trout. For instance, on the Neversink, another Catskill tailwater, the steep canyon walls of the mountains on the upper East and West branches of the Neversink above the reservoir trap underground spring and rain runoff water, causing the river's acidity to rise. The Neversink's diminishing mayfly and caddis life and increase in acid-tolerant stoneflies has been documented by USGS surveys. By these systems feeding the reservoir, what comes out of the bottom draw is extremely cold, clear dystrophic water lacking fertility. It isn't until the water warms up and receives oxygen and sunlight that fertile habitat, like vegetation and deep pools, forms in the lower valley. The river then starts to hold large wild S/R browns many

Laurie Supinski probes the Neversink tailwater, which looks like a giant spring creek. Its enormous rock- and boulder-lined pools, which run for more than one hundred yards, can reach depths of eight to ten feet. These are the huge winter holding pools that do not accumulate anchor ice and allow for large trout and young of the year parr to survive the harsh Catskill winters. MATT SUPINSKI

miles downstream. Trout in tailwater systems can, and do, travel great distances in search of ideal habitat.

Freestones

Freestone rivers are synonymous with trout and salmon fishing. They were the ideal primordial forest environments with cold, clear waters when the fish evolved 70 to 30 million years ago. The birthplace of European fly fishing in the Dinaric Alps of Macedonia, the "ground zero" of the American fly-fishing school in the hallowed Catskills, and the home of the new age of Western fly fishing on the Madison in Montana—all are freestone rivers. The sounds of waterfalls and rapids cascading through rocky volcanic boulders and the sight of spring brook tributaries winding through dense green forests are things of beauty. But if spring creeks embody stability, freestone rivers facilitate chaos. Freestone trout must master fast river flows for food detection, tolerate droughts and floods, and constantly be aware of predators that often go undetected due to the volatile and fast-flowing surface water that distorts the trout's vision.

Freestone rivers are a complex capillary system of multiple mountain springs, creeks, rivulets, and spate runoff water that channelized through geologic time. Rock in all forms—andesite, basalt, carbonite, granite, dolomite, shale—is carved and molded into various-sized boulders, stones, and gravel, which shows the power and patience water has with time. Freestone river environments change constantly, and each river system in the world is unique, which is what makes fly fishing fascinating. Most freestone rivers start off oligotrophic, as sterile but extremely pure water emanating from underground caverns void of oxygen. As they hit the forest, tundra, or river valleys, light, oxygen, and organic matter start to add eutrophic fertility, and so begins the food chain.

Austria's Roman Moser, a world-famous fly fisher, fly tier, and author, knows freestone rivers, particularly his alpine models, better than anyone. He describes freestoners simply: "On the freestoner, the annual temperature ranges and the varying currents

Mountain freestone rivers, from the Alps to North America's Appalachians and Rockies, are the ideal cold and oxygenated waters for trout spawning and holding habitat. They also contain incredible diverse populations of mayflies, stoneflies, caddis, and midges necessary for trout growth. Indigenous marble brown trout and Hucho are highly sought after on the oligotrophic clean waters of Slovenia's Soca River. LUKA HOJNIK

Left: Trout fisheries of the lower river systems that are deemed marginal waters are often undervalued for their trophy trout potential on streamers. Due to the lack of angling pressure while most fly fisherman search out blue-ribbon heaven, these big brown trout beasts often are not pursued, and are usually caught by bass or other warm-water anglers by mistake. Anglers all over the world know waters that fit this description. MIKE SCHMIDT

affect the [trout's] feeding behavior and its selectivity. Fish in such waters cannot afford to be fussy. In those times when lots of food is present, they must put on reserves of fat in order to provide energy during lean times (floods, periods of heat, or winter). Here the rule is: the faster the current, the less selective the fish can be."

Though Moser is concise and accurate in his description, and freestone trout streams are often synonymous with A/A trout always in search of a meal, they can also have selective fish if there is abundant food and good habitat like big pools, boulders, log jams, fast riffled gradients, long slow valley stretches, and deep eddy pools. Longer seasons and influence of

Freestone trout can be tough to fool, especially if there is a heavy hatch with multiple stages of the insect on the water, but most take what they can get when they can get it due to the highly fluctuating flows. Here a wild brown trout nailed a large Wulff fly in the Patagonia region of Chile. JOHN MILLER

predation (e.g., lots of catch-and-release angling or invading birds of prey) can also make the fish harder to catch.

Trout species of a large freestone river will find their own habitat niche. Freestone trout probably spend more time in all three selectivity phases than their watershed relatives. Vast, cold, cascading headwaters are usually preferred by brook trout, charrs, and grayling. Food is scarcer in these environments so trout, mostly brook trout, will be extremely A/A in nature except during extreme winter and heat-induced droughts, which rarely affect the high-elevation cascading waters. Freeze-up does not occur in water of this type. Fed by spring seeps and shaded by the dense mountain forests, temperatures in the creeks remain low even in extreme heat. Trout reproduction is usually high here, and stunting of growth in the fish population can occur due to extreme competition for food supply.

As freestone rivers broaden and nutrient loads and water temperatures increase, so too does the S/R behavior. These midsection waters often become the domain of brown and rainbow trout. But the truly large S/R brown trout lurk in the low-lying, slow-moving lower valley sections, which can be the most fertile in stable waters, and which are at the higher limit of the trout's temperature tolerance range. These areas are usually seen as marginal trout water; however, they often hold the largest fish. The larger S/R trout in these stretches are known to migrate great distances based on conditions.

Big-boulder water is a magnet for trout on freestoners. It allows them metabolic comfort, and the different current configurations caused by the swirling and undulating of the currents around the rocks allows them to selectively examine their prey. Stoneflies are significant to acidic mountain freestone trout rivers and boulder habitat all over the world. They gather organic debris between the stones and woody debris for food and are relished by trout for their meaty qualities and size. When trout are on the hunt for these crawling nymphs and become connoisseurs of them, they will focus on the insects' movements and species-specific behaviors, despite the roiling water. The most

The Catoctin Creek Conundrum:
When Mountain Freestone Trout Behave like Spring Creek Sophisticates

Most think fast-flowing freestone trout should be the least selective since they have to be opportunistic feeders, where color and extreme proficiency in vision have no significance. Even Vince Marinaro had somewhat similar views, which he later in life refuted. I was headed in that same direction until I was humbled by some wild mountain freestone brown trout decades ago on Maryland's Big Hunting Creek on the enchanting Catoctin Mountain, part of the Appalachian Ridge.

It had all the classic American freestone hatches—March Browns, Green Drakes, Sulphurs, olives, stoneflies, and everything else. During this summer's heat of the mid-Atlantic, its waters still stayed cool, but low. Long pool eddies would develop in areas where the waters were normally flowing at a racecar pace. It had wild brook trout in its upper reaches above Cunningham Falls, along with large stocked rainbows that were put in by the state to make things a little less difficult.

A wild cunning brown trout of Big Hunting Creek above the lower gorge. An extremely careful hands-and-knees approach, long, thin, gentle tippets, and an exact imitation and a "plop" of the fly were necessary to fool these finicky little German aristocrats. MATT SUPINSKI

But it was the resident wild browns, scattered throughout the creek system, that were elusive and downright impossible to catch—they haunted and vexed my deepest dreams. Even though the state and federal fish commissions said the standing populations were hundreds of pounds per acre, I'd be damned if I could catch them at any given time. They were perhaps easiest in the spring when the waters were fast and cold, when a heavily weighted March Brown nymph or hare's ears dredged up the occasional 8- to 10-incher, not much compared to the browns of up to 20 inches that were often found during electrofishing surveys. But in the summer, when the pools were still, green inchworms, ants, beetles, and other terrestrials would plop into the water and create easy prey for the trout. In these placid pools, the browns' vision was impeccable and almost instantaneous refusals occurred. What impressed me the most was the immediacy of the refusals from the wild browns. In spring creeks, you would see long inspections, maybe even refusals and comebacks for a second look. But not here. The browns here seemed to have superpowers and could detect a fraud almost immediately.

Trout have a fixed-shape lens system that focuses in and out like a camera lens. Visible light is composed of a wide range of wavelengths, violet being the shortest and red being the longest. Water absorbs the red lengths much quicker than the blue lengths. The shallower the fish's lies are, the greater focusing sensitivity to light it will possess. So a wild brown trout living in the faster, shallower waters of Big Hunting Creek will have a sensitivity level peaking between 450 and 625 nanometers. A deep-dwelling lake trout in 100 feet of water might be lucky to hit a sensitivity level of 390 nanometers. Overall the eye of the fish is similar to the human eye, except that it has no tear ducts or eyelids. The fish's vision also has a reflective index (light-bending ability) of 1.65, which is higher than any group of vertebrates.

I have a theory that a trout eventually perfects and enhances its vision over time based on degree of vision difficulty and the fact that freestone trout vision

Big Hunting Creek cascades through a series of densely forested gorges and canyons over large proterozoic greenstone and white quartz boulders. Its waters can run fast and raging after rains and spring snow thaw. CHRIS KAYLER

is superior to that in trout from gentle-flowing spring creeks and tailwaters. Vision is a function of light. The shallow freestone environments, with their cascading waters that distort the surface window, provide a visual cloaking shield that hides the fish from predators. The trout can hold in skinny water where light is prevalent. But on the negative side, the fast-moving waters and distorted, rippled surface require the trout to make quick interceptions of food forms. Here the fish's vision must be impeccable and hyperaccelerated in its accuracy. I realize that I am making a bold statement here that may be controversial. In the grand scheme of selectivity to optic enhancements, freestone trout have a much tougher road to survival. Since the spring creek or tailwater trout has a relatively relaxed environment (except for when dams are flooded or are generating electricity) to inspect its food and prey, these fish have the great luxury of being S/R. This may in fact make them optically lazy, especially the large spring creek trout that Frank Sawyer mentioned; these trout were easy to catch on his Avon River in England due to their love of dark undercut cover, pref-

erence for hunting at night by sound, and general preference for slow water. The photophobic shunning of light by big brown trout can have a negative impact on their optic development that can result in poor vision.

Scientists know that human vision can be improved with daily use and practice on focusing. Vision degeneration can be hereditary or a result of injury, poor nutrition, constant low-light exposure, or lack of use. My theory is that the consistent use and focusing required in shallow-water mediums, like small fast-flowing mountain streams with plenty of light, allows selectively superior wild freestone trout to exercise their vision to the point of extreme accuracy and depth penetration. Could these wild brown trout possess superior vision because of the brutal fast-flows and limited vision windows of their natural environments? I believe so. So the next time you think freestone trout are so opportunistic and gullible, think again. These are violent environments that demand the vision of an eagle. ◾

effective way to fish this type of water is with a tight line nymphing technique and heavily weighted flies.

For consistent big-trout action on freestone rivers, learn to read the boulder-strewn pocket water. Big trout will often use the undercut grooves behind rock bottoms, even in faster midstream sections, as prime taking positions. These areas will usually accumulate the water currents carrying the biological drift in a suction vortex, often spiraling backward and depositing nymphs and food. Big selective trout like these places since they are usually dark, have choppy water and undersurface currents to shield them from predators, and provide many avenues for escape.

On smaller mountain freestone streams, creeping up from downstream at a low profile is the best way to avoid detection, since elevation drops can enhance your profile in the fish's window. This holds true for whether you fish a tiny Smoky Mountain brook trout stream, a high alpine river, or one of the upper headwaters of an Arizona mountain Apache trout stream. Learn two single-handed Spey casts—the double Spey

and snap—to avoid the tight brush. Leaders should have short butt sections allowing for longer tippets, to provide extra drag-free floats and room for puddle, slingshot, and sidearm casts and mends. Climbing behind a boulder for concealment and "dapping" is a perfect way to go unnoticed. High-sticking is necessary to keep as much fly line off the water as possible, since this is where your drag comes from in the small-pool, fast-cascading environments. Once you encounter more wide-open, midsized sections as the valleys broaden out with less gradient—similar to the water on north-central Pennsylvania's Pine, Kettle, and Slate Run Creeks—longer leaders and down-and-across reach casts for dry-fly fishing can be made.

As for nymphing, which is perhaps the deadliest day-in and day-out, season-by-season technique on freestone rivers, the high-stick indicator method is most popular. Use weighted flies (pre-molded bodies, wraps of silver or copper, or bead heads) to help get the fly down quickly. Tungsten shot (where allowed) above or below the flies allows your strike indicator to

Since my aunt and uncle lived in Salzburg, Austria, I was able to fish the Salzach River and its stonefly hatch. Here Daniela Bevilacqua, noted Swiss master fly fisher, is pictured on the same river with her prize. DANIELA BEVILACQUA/MAURO MISTELI

The beauty of New Zealand's topography, its people, and its food, coupled with some of the biggest, most beautiful, selective trout on the planet, makes you want to live there forever. For anglers who love tough trout, the Tongariro and its trout offer paradise on earth.
TONGARIRO LODGE

periodically bounce up and down to let you know your nymphs are in the strike zone. Estimate your flies to be set from your indicator about one and a half times the depth of the area you are fishing. I personally prefer the "crappie nymph rig," where the lead is below two tandem dropper nymphs. Czech/Polish nymphing with a tight-lining, bottom-bouncing approach is also deadly, though if you need to cast long distances, you're better off with the strike indicator or wet fly swing technique. When nymphing, longer rods such as the new 11/12-foot switch rods/two-handers allow you to mend farther and more efficiently.

Deep, ultraclear pool habitat is another perfect micro-environment for a discerning trout. The trout can maximize their vision perception along vertical feeding lies that allow them to target the complete insect emergence cycle at a convenient S/R pace. Larger prey items are also more easily detected since there is not much cover in the wide-open spaces of the pools.

On New Zealand's broad rivers, where large rainbows and browns take up territorial dominance in the slow areas of the deep clear pools, the trout become selective feeding machines that use their acute vision and learned behavior to drive anglers mad. Here, your gillie, who has the eyes of a hawk, carefully stands on the high ground above the pool watching your target as you stealthily move into position. You are constantly changing flies, offering different silhouettes and fly designs with each cast, and offering perfect presentations. Here S/R fish will rise to the fly and refuse it on dozens of occasions before they are fooled. Thanks to their having been caught and released countless times, and the region's wilderness environment and perfect climactic conditions that are conducive to long life, New Zealand trout can become the poster children for S/R trout.

When the trout take up feeding positions, they do so in the comfort of the mid-depths. These are the most difficult fish to catch in any river system due to the fact that they fine-tune their window of vision to both extremes—the distant and the up-close. If they lay on the bottom or close to the surface they would compromise their vision. Only an extremely selective

During the cicada season, you can rest assured that every fly fisher and gillie combination is throwing large cicadas in all colors, sizes, and profiles of fly designs. Every gillie has his or her own "dope and dynamite" pattern in his or her fly box. Here is where "thinking outside the box" comes into play. TONGARIRO LODGE

and intelligent trout selects this mid-depth lie, which is optimal for capturing anything emerging in the bottom or floating on top. Many gillies will admit to their clients that some fish are downright impossible, since they have been hooked so many times and have accumulated such learned behavior. But here, the fly angler takes on the pursuit and hunting as 90 percent of the gig. The extreme acute perception of the fish is especially apparent with cicadas and other terrestrials with very pronounced appendages. The trout exhibits complex/compound rises to the surface, floating directly vertical with the imitation or natural, and then turns downstream, only to return to its former lie; then, at the last minute, it chases the natural or imitation downstream for a second or third time before refusing or taking it.

Though your gillie may profess to know it all—and for the most part, he does, at least about his rivers and their fish—daily work makes creatures of habit in any profession. If you experience consistent refusals in the mid-depth pools of these big New Zealand rivers, or on any river pool on the globe for that matter, show the trout something different (sometimes radically different). Often a tiny translucent green beetle, a tiny ant, or a big Royal Wulff, which looks nothing like the natural, will cause "the lord of the pool" S/R trout to make a pivotal mistake and take your fly. I can't tell you how many times this has happened, especially with wild New Zealand rainbows. The fish's demeanor can, and often does, change through repetitive forced presentations. Remember, curiosity killed the cat!

Facing page: When massive hatches of mayflies and caddis occur, like this one on an Alpine tailwater, thousands of adults float helplessly and trout will often be seen rising everywhere in a "bulging back and tail" form. The adults will mask the true food source of stillborn nymphs or pupae in the meniscus, which far outnumber them, leading to incorrect imitation in this S/R conundrum. Here, Roman Moser scouts for "backs instead of heads" to fish a Pheasant Tail nymph for that one trophy catch. ALBERT PESENDORFER

The Selective/ Reflective Trout

Trout spend more time in the S/R phase than in any other. For the past two centuries, fly-fishing writers from the British chalkstream masters G. E. M Skues and Frank Sawyer to today's modern fly-fishing writers and thinkers have pondered over perplexing selectivity issues. Evolution has made trout an extremely finicky, wary, and intelligent fish species, even though instinct, acute senses, and innate genetic programming are what trout possess, rather than humanlike intelligence.

Stable conditions and optimal feeding lies are required for S/R trout. Nowhere are these criteria better met than on a spring creek such as the Letort or Silver Creek. Stream flows are stable, as are water temperatures; in a stream such as the Letort, there is a constant flow of food in the form of mayflies, terrestrials, sow bugs, and shrimp, among other things. Amid the wide-open pasture spaces typical of many spring creeks, the trout can see shadows bouncing off fly fishers' bodies, rods, lines, and sloppy casts—all of which signal caution to the fish. Combine these characteristics with catch-and-release practices and you get some of the most selective trout in the world.

Similar to a spring creek, a tailwater has long, flat pools and eddies, cold reservoir-fed waters, and selective trout. Wide-open spaces and large pools and runs allow trout the ability to migrate in search of food to fill their ravenous bellies. A trout sipping tiny Blue-Winged Olives on a long, flat pool will be put down by a bad cast, a sloppy drift boat, a long shadow, or a fly that doesn't match the natural. The cold water, availability of diverse food items, long, slow pools that make it easy for trout to see the surface, combined with catch-and-release regulations, create wary and selective trout.

There are thousands of S/R examples that I can cite. But doing so would take volumes due to their extremely varied nature. In this chapter I will only deal with the most significant examples and attributes of trout selectivity and how they affect the fly-fishing experience around the world. I will provide the reader and fly angler a foundation to identify the phase and its complexity and give solutions for cracking the code to angling success.

The Checklist: All Systems Go

At times trout feed with a reckless abandon and allow anglers to get quite close to them and make repeated casts without spooking the fish, but this is rare. Most of the time a fish is on high alert because of its incredible sensory perception, particularly its vision. A trout's acute vision is closely associated with how it takes a natural fly or imitation, in addition to influencing how it perceives its prey, its predators, and its environment.

Marinaro's descriptions of simple, compound, and complex riseforms are helpful in describing some of the trout's behaviors to a surface natural or fly. During a consistent and somewhat frequent emergence of Blue-Winged Olives or Sulphurs, the A/A or S/R trout will set up at the most advantageous feeding station—usually in or near the bubble/foam line, which concentrates the current's flow. The trout takes adults, emergers, and spinners in a simple riseform as the steady supply of naturals is funneled and accumulated. The trout's confidence in the abundant food source elicits

Vince Marinaro described his photos as "an attempt to penetrate the trout's secret world." His groundbreaking close-up photography of a brown taking surface flies in his *In the Ring of the Rise* was the hallmark photo essay on the subject until Jason Jagger, the master of Colorado's rivers, came along. JASON JAGGER

no red-flag signals of alarm for something amiss or awry (like a sloppy cast or an unnatural-looking dragging artificial), making this simple rise an efficient and opportunistic way for the trout to consume as many naturals as possible.

This simple riseform also is common in fast freestone streams, since the trout has no time for a careful inspection of its food and must react quickly. Here the trout makes a brief vertical ascent to the surface at an angle of 10 or 11 o'clock, allowing for simple intercept and ingestion of the aquatic insect or terrestrial.

If the fish has lots of time to inspect its food, such as in a long, flat run or pool, or slow feeding lane, common on wider creeks and rivers, compound rises are more common, especially during sparse hatches or to the occasional terrestrial insect. Here caution and uncertainty of the surface prey enters the equation. This riseform usually sees the trout ascending slowly and less deliberately; it suspends itself directly vertical from head to tail below the natural or artificial fly for a few seconds, or it makes a prolonged vertical drift in the flow as its nose edges up to the fly before it eventually decides to take or refuse it. Refusals can result from the drag on a dead-drifting mayfly, the lack of movement of an artificial fly (which is needed with a twitching, skipping caddis egg-layer), a tippet that's too large, or something else that just didn't seem right.

Here the natural and artificial fly must have all the proper characteristics that the trout is looking for based on its past experience. Fly size, wing and tail

silhouette and style (an upright or folded profile with or without speckled mottling), body proportions/segmentations, and color hue all are examined quickly as they come into viewing range. Compound rises usually exist when the trout has been hooked before, has received substantial angling pressure on catch-and-release waters, or there is a combination of phases in

Top: Upon closer inspection, the shape, form, and density of the body in the meniscus all become very obvious. Mayflies, midges, stoneflies, and caddis all have their peculiarities with even more pronounced shapes for a S/R trout to discern. **Middle:** All insects behave uniquely. Mayflies twitch on occasion, stoneflies flutter, and caddis hop and gyrate as they lay eggs and emerge. Terrestrials often panic when they move from terra firma to an aquatic surface, and behave like struggling victims with frenzied appendages and erratic quivers. Even though a trout's mouth may be ready to engulf its prey as it approaches the surface, a refusal can occur at the last microsecond. **Bottom:** Finally, the breathtaking moment of acceptance. A quick hook set is necessary, especially for hyper S/R trout who can spit out a fly in an instant. The mouth expels an air bubble during the gulp, which helps anglers determine how big the head might be, and if the pursuit of a trophy on the dry fly is worth the time—and often frustration—of the chase.
JASON JAGGER

the hatch activity (like during caddis, mayfly, and midge hatches when emergers, adults, and spinners are all on the surface at the same time or many different types of insect species on the water at the same time). The S/R fish's indecision to take the surface offering creates complex riseforms that are frustrating both to the angler and to the trout itself. These rises occur to naturals and to the fly fisher's imitation equally.

The compound rise turns complex as the vertically suspended trout floats under the insect and then turns downstream in pursuit, usually only to refuse it or elicit a take. Many times it will make the downstream pursuit only to abandon the chase and return to its former pre-rise position; then, at the last second it will make a bold downstream dash to take the offering that proved too irresistible to refuse. When this occurs (this also happens with steelhead and salmon) rest the fish before the next cast and let it think about its decision not to take. This usually makes its heart grow fonder and results in an "I got to have it" acceptance on the next fly presentation.

Complex rises usually occur to larger mayflies that just started emerging in the spring (Quill Gordons, for instance) since the trout hasn't seen anything that big since last spring and is somewhat confused and surprised. It quickly and opportunistically learns to relish the new prey. These rises also occur to quickly moving caddis and stoneflies, and to large terrestrial objects like grasshoppers and cicadas.

S/R trout—usually larger ones—tend to look for a few discerning characteristics to seal the deal. If you impart a simple twitch or quiver at the right time, or apply a side-swimming motion to the fly, you can flip the attack switch on a cautious and highly speculative trout. This natural quiver or twitch is common with mayflies unraveling their nymphal shucks and drying their wings. The cross-current swimming and struggling is common with stoneflies and large swimming mayfly nymphs moving toward shore. Hoppers and other terrestrials also skitter toward the shore.

An S/R trout will often weed out the "real deal" fly from a good duplicate through the process of elimination. The S/R trout will accept or refuse the fly offering or natural based on calculated steps. And extreme S/R trout will often make refusals to naturals, when the balance of the checklist items didn't add up.

Let's go through an example of an S/R trout's systematic checklist regarding a surface fly. In our example, the fish will be feeding in a spring creek or long pool in a tailwater. This fish has all the time in the world for discernment. It is well fed, and thus has no need to make rash decisions like a freestone trout.

CHECK NO. 1: WINGS

As the surface fly approaches the trout's outer window, the wings take shape through the refraction of light bending around corners.

Perhaps no one spent more time thinking about how trout see than the master of the Letort Spring Run, Vince Marinaro, whom I was fortunate to have as a mentor before he died. He was fascinated by how a trout sees its natural world. Not until his works and those of the English duo of Goddard and Clarke did we really have a clear grasp on what, and perhaps more importantly when, a trout sees what it does.

Marinaro delved deep into the underwater world of what the trout sees. His "Felix the trout" character in his images for *In the Ring of the Rise* made the complex vision of a trout understandable. The trout's window of vision is an inverted pyramid; the deeper the trout lies, the wider and broader the vision window becomes. As the trout approaches the surface, the window diminishes considerably and is less sharp in focus.

Marinaro constructed slant boxes with a built-in mirror, through which he was able to see how the surface fly came into the trout's window of vision. Most flies and naturals looked like white spikes in the film, the natural obtaining this effect from its legs, the manufactured dry fly from its hackle fibers.

As the fly approached the trout's window, the tall wings of a dry fly or an adult mayfly were the first ascertainable parts to the trout. At the 10-degree angle, the silhouette of the fly became more apparent as refraction allowed the trout to see around corners. It was not until the fly reached the main window that its details, body color, hackle, and wings all became perfectly clear.

Because of refraction and the trout's ability to "see around corners," the wing profile, along with the upward-curved two or three tails of the mayfly, comes into view first—whether the mayfly is facing downstream or not. During days with lots of sun, the wings' dark silhouette will show up against the light background of the sky. On cloudy days the S/R trout will be even more finicky with wings since it can pick up all the mottling or clear details.

The sailboat wing profile of mayflies is hard to mistake for the adults, as is the case with the folded

Though most mayflies will normally ride facing upstream or downstream, depending on how they hatch, they also will sometimes ride sideways when in their stillborn emerging state, flipped over in awkward positions. JASON JAGGER

and fluttering flat wings of caddis, stoneflies, and midges. Rarely are these latter wings motionless like those of the mayfly; the fluttering wings are best imitated by CDC in clumps that appear to flutter.

CHECK NO. 2: SHAPE AND BODY SIZE

As a trout nears the surface and its vision becomes more acute due to greater light levels—including sunlight, moonlight, and even starlight—fly shape, body size, silhouette, and other discernible traits like legs and tails are checked.

The natural food form's body shape can take on countless dozens of forms from all the various mayfly, stonefly, caddis, and midge species, not to mention all the wild-looking shapes and forms of terrestrials.

Mayflies can be slender or meaty, with body shapes that can be tubular, rotund, or trapezoidal. Mayflies have distinct posterolateral spinal bandings and segments in the lower two-thirds of their abdomens. They are typically floating flush in the film because the leg tarsus usually lifts the upper thorax off the water, the same as an artificial fly's hackle points do. S/R trout will hone in on these details.

Body length is one of the easier details for a trout to discern, and so the right body-to-wing proportion is critical. Keep in mind that caddis and midges have sparse bodies that are shorter than (at least two-thirds or half) the total length of their folded, tent-shaped wings. Most fly tiers make bodies too bulky and thick.

Quill/biot bodies or just thread and a touch of dubbing works best for smaller mayflies. For the larger species, gradually taper the bodies thicker from the abdomen toward the thorax with deer hair and foam. These can be made into nice tubular bandings or spinal plates with tying threads or by using the new synthetic tubular bodies from J:son Sweden, Montana Fly, and Rainy's and coloring them with markers.

CHECK NO. 3: COLOR, TRANSLUCENCY, AND HUE

As the body of the fly floats flush in the more defined trout window, the body segmentations and color can be easily perceived.

Marinaro's aquarium images revealed that when a mayfly spinner is in the surface film its body size and color are fully exposed. Flies that rode high on the surface, like palmered skaters or hackled Catskill-style dries, showed only a few surface piercings of the feet or hackle barbules.

But insects on placid waters usually rode flush in the film, revealing their true color. If the trout's inquisition as to whether the fly is fake or real starts at the refractive angles upstream of its lie yet too far outside its more defined vision window, the vertical wings on the dry are first to come into the fish's mirror focus. So it makes sense to make sure your fly's wings are the perfect color, mottling, and silhouette. As the body of the fly floats flush in the more defined trout window, the body segmentations and color are easily perceived by the trout.

Trout and salmon perceive three aspects of color: color itself, translucency, and hue. Keep in mind two things play a huge role in the fish's perception: light or the lack thereof, and the fish's color vision imprinting based on recent or current ecosystem habitat and hormonally driven perceptions. Strong daylight actually makes color less important since the sun's rays can scatter color perception and change the way color is perceived. When fishing on sunny days we often see dark Blue-Winged Olive adults flying in the air as whitish or cream-colored bugs. A newly migrated steelhead or salmon fresh from the ocean, sea, or lake has its rods and cones fixated on blue and green tones and gradually comes to prefer the dark black/red/copper spectrum as its river life unfolds. To a spawning salmonid, the bright red/orange/pink colors strike the eye with a vengeance; I believe this reflects the fish's spawning color preference and may fuel the hormonally driven aggression.

Cracking the Code: Wiggle Nymphs

Big mayfly hatches are known to bring out aggressive fish that chase large floating duns. But sometimes the presumed behavior of what the trout "should do" takes an unexpected turn. The East Branch, an icy-cold tailwater with temperatures in the 40- to 50-degree range, brings a slug of cold water into the warmer Beaverkill during the summer. A perfect scenario is created for the river's trout to prey in several pools below the confluence, where water temperatures mix and hover in the upper 50s to mid-60s.

Before the East Branch spills into the "Kill," there is a large pondlike pool with heavy silt and boulders where large burrowing mayflies tend to accumulate. On one particular overcast night there was a good caddis emergence and trout of all sizes were working the surface. After I caught several 8- to 10-inch beautifully colored brown trout and one rainbow, I had about a half hour remaining before dark. While looking downstream at two large boulders I saw a riseform that looked like a beaver rolling its tail. Wading downstream, I saw the first of several large yellow-orange *Potamanthus distinctus* emerging; these huge size 8 Yellow Drake summer mayflies probably hatched in the silted and rocky bottom of the lower section of the East Branch. These mayflies are gorgeous specimens, and are a big mouthful for large, fussy trout. As I watched the water, their numbers increased. When you see a dozen or more of these mayflies, that's a huge hatch. Usually you see one here and another over there.

Near the top of the run by the largest boulder, I saw the big brown trout, and I was stunned by its size—this was truly the largest Catskill brown trout I'd seen. I selected a snowshoe rabbit's foot hair and yellow-body size 8 *Potamanthus* emergers from my box and nervously began to tie one on as dusk set in. The fish was at the head portion of the V slot created by the boulder and was rising steadily, so I had a 1-foot drift lane for my target. After several drifts and seeing naturals refused, I myself was confused. "This toad can't be ignoring the easy meat buffet of adults," I thought.

Again the back and tail rise came to nothing on the surface. "The fish must be taking emerging nymphs, it has to be!" I thought to myself. I had in the box one crudely tied *Hexagenia* wiggle nymph that I use for Michigan steelhead. It was somewhat rusted out, but it was the closest thing I had to a large yellow-bodied nymph. Tied on 3X tippet, this wiggle nymph would be my best bet. After two dead drifts, with a greased-up leader as an indicator, I decided to twitch the nymph to the surface before it hit the boulder. Wham! That toad nailed the thing!

My drag system went into overdrive shock. After wrapping me around two rocks, which sent me in over my waders to unravel the first snag, the big brown ran me into a fast channel where I fell. Water filled up my waders and soaked my fly boxes, and the fall made me lose my Polaroid sunglasses and my good fishing hat and drenched my camera. After all this I finally beached the toad. Luckily the camera still worked and I got a snapshot of the magnificent 25-inch beast of a brown trout. As I removed the hook, the rusted gape snapped off. That was a close call!

A day later I visited one of the fly shops in Roscoe, where I saw several *Potamanthus* adult fly patterns all labeled "the hot fly!" Nowhere did I see a wiggle nymph. That morning I tied a half dozen more realistic imitations. For a week I slayed the big Catskill browns.

It seemed like a no-brainer that the trout would eat adults off the surface, but the nymphs were struggling in the colder water and so the fish targeted them. On most sections of freestoners where large *Ephemera* emerge, water temperatures are in the 60s. Here big bugs have a quicker emergence and are airborne; an adult is usually targeted since the nymphs are moving and swimming fast. When confronted with large

When Carl Richards wrote his book *Emergers*, his focus was on the wiggling, undulating movements of big burrowing mayflies as they emerge. Now I know why that fish took my poor articulated version. Everyone else was flogging it with the adult pattern, or "the hot fly" of the fly shop. Need I say more? This fly catches fish all year long due to its meaty appearance and the swimming motion. It can be fished down-and-across and is an excellent searching pattern when nothing is happening hatchwise on freestone and tailwater rivers. MATT SUPINSKI

mayflies like the drakes, *Isonychia*, and *Hexagenia*, concentrate in the upper meniscus using wiggle or crippled nymphs to attract selective trout. The flies have to look pretty. Just have the suggestion of wiggling and movement as they emerge. You won't be disappointed!

ISOCAINE WIGGLE

(Author)

Back hook:	Daiichi 1260; break hook in vise once tied
Thread:	Brown 6/0 UNI
Tail:	Gadwall feathers
Rib:	Copper Ultra Wire (medium)
Body:	Mahogany-dyed ostrich
Back:	Pearlescent Hareline flat tinsel
Front hook:	Daiichi X120
Tail:	Hungarian partridge palmered
Body:	Mahogany-dyed ostrich
Wing case:	Pearl Hareline flat tinsel
Legs:	Brown or orange flake Hareline Crazy Legs

Notes: The fast-swimming motion of the emerging *Isonychia* nymph is a strong trigger for trout and even drop-back steelhead, as the wiggle articulation gives the nymph irresistible appeal. Swing and twitch the fly down and across, wet-fly style, and be prepared for violent takes. You can also fish them dead-drifted by pulsing and jigging the fly as it comes into the trout's window. When nothing is hatching this is an excellent searching fly that can be quartered down and across to move trout when nothing else will.

FISHING THE WIGGLE NYMPH

I guide on my Michigan rivers and fish the Catskills on my vacations. Both environments are loaded with large burrowing and fast-swimming mayflies, which has given me a real appreciation and perspective on the importance of adding movement to large mayfly nymphs. This makes them deadly to trout and steelhead that are on the hunt for big, juicy nymphs and emergers, an idea

Carl Richards introduced on my home waters back in the 1980s. These nymphs have long, segmented bodies, with pulsing gill plates and fast-wiggling swimming motions, and so the articulated two-section nymphs can be manipulated by the angler for arm-jolting strikes.

Hexagenia, *Isonychia*, *Potamanthus*, Gray/Green/Brown Drakes, and Black Quills all move rather quickly and quirkily, like minnows. The first Gray Drake nymphs found by John Miller—discovered by flashlight in a backwater slough on the massive Gray Drake–rich waters of the Muskegon at three o'clock in the morning—were first thought to be minnows. They were tough to net for aquarium observation. No one had witnessed them hatching before because they crawl on shore to hatch.

Fishing wiggle nymphs is like fishing wets or streamers in a down-and-across style. Position yourself upstream of the target area, cast quartering downstream, and swing and twitch the wiggle nymphs with a quick jigging of the rod tip as you hold the rod tip close to the surface to create tension and drag. The articulated monofilament connection on the nymphs should be loose and light to allow for maximum movement. When your fly approaches the strike zone, accelerate the swing and twitching by lowering the rod tip. Then allow a dead-drift pause, repeating the twitching and jigging in intervals. Most strikes occur as the nymph is swimming downstream away from the fish. Let the fish set the hook itself and avoid striking, just as you would in riffle-hitching for Atlantic salmon. The tension and the current dragging the line will set the hook for you as the fish strike these flies hard. Wiggle nymphs are also great searching flies on big tailwaters when there is no perceived hatch because you can cover lots of water. ■

Add lifelike qualities to your Wiggle Nymph by using materials like ostrich herl, which makes a pulsating motion similar to that of gills. A tungsten bead head will allow you to swim, dip, and jig the imitation for more realistic movement. MATT SUPINSKI

Spring creeks, with their abundant food sources and complicated weed-filled channels, offer up challenging ultraselective trout. The PMD's color is an important key when designing nymph and emerger patterns, since the trout has plenty of time to inspect the pattern on slow-moving spring creeks. You will have frustrating days whether you are on the Henry's Fork of the Snake or here on Nelson's Spring Creek in Montana. MATT SUPINSKI/HARMAN

Translucent insect bodies and wings allow light to pass through them, which is usually the case with the lighter mayflies like Tricos, Cahills, and Sulphurs. The opaque bodies and wings of the darker mayflies do not transfer light through them and have deeper tones. But hue plays a significant role in all aquatic and terrestrial insect bodies and physical parts because water and light combine to give the insect a multitoned hue. The *Isonychia* mayfly is a perfect example of this. Its body looks purplish/brown/mahogany and exhibits a multihued appearance. Salmonids pick up on these details. Thus the various dubbing blends have increasingly focused on hue, with new UV materials being added to the catalogs each year. Caucci and Nastasi's work with body color and vision took the whole hue perception to another level and led to their Spectrumized Dubbing, which imparts the different color hues of the insects and looks impeccably real when wet. This effect can only come about when various colors are fused together and one sees how they react with water and light.

When the body of the fly is flush in the film, like a spinner, emerger, or stillborn nymph would be, all the details available for the trout's inspection come into play. Based on my personal experience, I find that for tough, selective trout on today's pressure waters, even the color of the thread and hook matter.

CHECK NO. 4: BEHAVIOR

Here the trout detects movement (caddis, stonefly) or lack thereof (mayfly dun).

Let's take a trout in a fast, free-flowing river. Its food highway is moving at an alarming rate. It is sort of like being in the helmet camera of an Indianapolis 500 driver going 230 miles an hour. Playing a video game as such, you'll find yourself crashing into the wall many times. Under these conditions, it's a minor miracle when the trout intercepts a real piece of food. It is no surprise that a freestone trout's stomach sample contains twigs, plastic, and all types of non-food forms. Details are critical to a trout's discerning whether something is food or not. Sometimes, when food is moving at high speeds on a fast-moving free-stoner right past the trout's underwater field of vision, the decision to take will often rest on qualities other than body segmentation, perfect salute, and minute details. Prey movement, such as ascent, swimming motion, gyrating, and diving, becomes a key detail for a S/R trout. Such movements immediately make a piece of food come alive and separate the natural from the imitation.

Drag-free is only one type of presentation. Yes, it does constitute the majority of surface presentations, and one who masters the down-and-across reach cast with a long drag-free surface float will catch a lot of fish. But there are plenty of situations where insects are skittering, waking, jumping, and gyrating. S/R trout look for that movement to be completely convinced. Even if the mayfly appears to be drifting drag-free, often it will twitch ever so slightly.

One technique I use for this difficult hop-and-skip caddis ovipositing is called the "Statue of Liberty" cast and mend. As soon as your fly lands on the water, raise your casting arm up high, armpit exposed, like the Statue of Liberty. This lifts and hops the elk- or deer-hair caddis skyward and drops it as you continue these exaggerated mends to show the fish the popcorn style of caddis egg laying. I use this for hopper fishing also.

Just as the S/R trout discerns a dragging mayfly imitation and says no, the underwater world has nymphs, larvae, scuds, sow bugs, and sculpins, all moving in various directions and speeds—an unlimited universe of things always occurring in the biological drift. The late great British nymph master Frank Sawyer was the first to demonstrate the value of imparting motion when he twitched and lifted his Pheasant Tail Nymphs with deadly success.

When I was fishing the wild brown trout streams of New York's southern tier during my youth, a certain elderly gentleman who had tremors in his hands from Parkinson's disease was the area's deadliest wet-fly swinger and nymph fisherman because his flies were always moving, twitching, and shaking, just by circumstance of his affliction. We could never figure out why he was such a deadly troutsman until I stopped to talk to him and watched the constant trembling of the rod.

This last step, Check No. 4 (behavior), will be used against the angler in conjunction with Check No. 3 (color/translucency/hue) in the trout's ultimate decision. Thus, I believe these two steps to be the

final juggling act for hooking an extremely S/R trout, which may go through a series of Marinaro-esque complex rises: following the fly, turning back to its original lie, following it again, and finally taking it as it slips off the lip of a tailout pool.

A Sprig of Color

Sometimes just having a color variation or a fly with subtle color change can make all the difference. Simply changing to a Pheasant Tail with a sprig of yellow or orange dubbing in the thorax instead of a regular pheasant tail during Sulphur and Pale Morning Dun hatches has made a difference.

Since much of my S/R trout discussion revolves around the dry fly, let's take the sprig of Sulphur color to the underwater world. Since color is a function of light penetration, its relevance may be less appreciated deep down on the bottom of the pool. Many Czech nymphs feature a sprig of color or "hot spot" tied into them under or in the middle of the larva and nymph patterns, making them effective. On a hot June afternoon on New York's Beaverkill River, two humongous brown trout gave me a glimpse of their ability to perceive color in deep water.

I was fishing the heavily pressured catch-and-release Horton Brook pool by the iron bridge, standing with at least fifteen or so other anglers on both sides of the river. Everyone was nymphing with intense concentration but no one was hooking up. I was using a foam indicator and nymphing Sawyer Pheasant Tail Nymphs with no success. The various Sulphur species were hatching, and their deep Creamsicle-orange body colors should have made for strong color imprinting by the feeding trout. Since the water temperatures were rising from the heat, the fish were taking positions in well-oxygenated deeper pools near springs.

I began exploring my nymph box as the crowds started to thin because of the tough fishing. Scratching their heads and wiping sweat from their eyebrows, the other ardent avid Catskill nymph fishermen were changing flies constantly hoping for one last hook-up. A pheasant tail with a deep-orange thorax and wood duck legs caught my attention in my fly box. After what seemed like hours, my bright orange indicator went down, and I was into a real good fish. I thought I had hooked a huge carp. After a dogged battle, a nearby angler was kind enough to grab my net and help me land the enormous brown. My hands began to tremble as I taped it at 25 inches. The other anglers

Master guide John Miller caught this fat and gorgeous "farm pool" West Branch Delaware wild brown that couldn't resist a Sulphur emerger. MATT SUPINSKI

standing around me were as astonished as I was. You usually don't catch a Catskill brown trout like that at noon on a hot June morning.

I photographed my catch on Kodachrome slide film and sat down to take a brief break, smoking a cigar and enjoying a beer in celebration. Anglers poured around me asking, "What the heck did you catch that thing on?" "A pheasant tail!" I humbly answered, as I zipped my mouth shut and felt like I was king.

After a long break, I proceeded again, knowing full well the fishing was long past the prime stage. The water temperature was in the mid-60s and a steady rain had started, which drove the rest of the anglers into their cars and away. Because I wanted to try and learn something, I experimented with different thorax body colors—olive, red, purple—to no avail. Before calling it quits I put on the hot orange thorax fly again. Three drifts and the indicator vanished and kept going downstream. Another huge 20-inch-plus brown jumped and was going toward my backing, running downstream to the East Branch. The only guy left on the river was my new friend who had netted my previous fish . . . he was shocked to say the least!

In hindsight, it seems that certain extremely selective fish associate certain colors—both on the surface and underwater—with specific hatches. It seems the power of suggestion, as minimal as a sprig of color, has a profound effect.

Tips for Tricking S/R Trout

SLOW DOWN AND BLEND IN

When a trout seems oblivious to an angler's advances and relentless casting, it's often because the fish has been habituated to your presence (see page 17 for more on habituation). A S/R trout on the Beaverkill's Cairn pool, which has twenty guys standing in it every day, eventually assimilates to two wader-clad legs next to it while it feeds.

From a guide's perspective, I can tell you how important it is to slow down and blend in, to create a quiet time when trout perceive all is calm and natural. The old-timer sitting on the rocks and smoking his pipe as trout sip tiny Blue-Winged Olives on a long Ausable River pool in New York's Adirondacks is a classic example of this time-tested tactic. Bright-colored clothing is for magazine covers only! As the fly fisher stays motionless or near motionless, he will become part of what is "normal" for the trout.

Trout can become gluttonous and indulgent quickly, or they can be put down. Timing is everything. Once comfortable with your wading or your drift boat's position, your trout, if it is put down, will resume its rhythmic feeding when all conditions are "go."

LET IT RAIN

Raindrops on the water are a blessing and a curse. When sight-nymphing, it makes discerning the trout's movement and feeding pattern hard for the angler. For the trout, rain gives it more feeding comfort from predators as its surface window is distorted. However, distinguishing surface insects for identification makes for a tougher game for the trout. In these situations, even poor fly presentation and imitations can be accepted by even the most S/R trout. I recall a day filled with rain on the Delaware tailwater at the Junction pool, whose trout are known throughout the world as being the most selective. They took my Blue-Winged Olive emergers with a reckless abandon during a rainstorm; such careless behavior never happens on the Junction pool. The same ideas apply to the distorting ripples created by waves and wind, which have the same effect both on prey and predator.

REDUCE RIPPLES

The sound and vibration an angler gives off is also important but does not have as powerful or long-lasting influence on the trout as vision detection does.

On broad, calm, and flat rivers, every cast, shadow, and reflection must be controlled by the angler. Selective fish are extremely alert. Selection and survival have allowed the true ultrafussy salmonid specimens to genetically pass on their acute sensory perception to future generations. ALBERT PESENDORFER

The detection of sound by fish is linked through two sensory systems: the inner ear and mechanosensory lateral line. Given that the fish evolved in dark environments with less than optimal light, hearing and vibration sensation played a more important role than vision. The approaching wading fly fisher should walk slowly to prevent foot vibrations, especially in soggy spring creek environments, get in the water as little as possible, and cast carefully so the line doesn't create a lot of disturbance on the water.

CAREFUL BOATWORK

The obvious benefit of a boat is that you cover so much more water and can anchor in the pools wading anglers can't get to. However, you need to keep some things in mind when fishing from a boat. An angler's casting creates lots of reflections, and your profile is increased from the height of a drift boat. When the trout is looking up at the high floating wings of the mayfly as they come into its vision window, your head and body will also be highly visible on the edge of the bent refraction window. If you can

get out of a drift boat and approach selective trout by wading at a lower profile, do so. Always look at which direction the sun is to your profile and limit the shadows.

Dropping anchors and clanging the bottom sends massive vibrations. Oars hitting the surface or the side of the bow create vibrations and ripples. Your feet stomping on the boat's bottom can also scare fish. Be careful when lowering the anchor—do it slowly!

Often when your boat is anchored, it creates temporary hydrodynamic flows and feeding lanes. A wading angler or an anchored drift boat acts like a big boulder or obstruction in the stream, deflecting surface and underwater flows and setting up different currents and feeding lies that would not exist were you not there. The S/R trout quickly detect this change in hydrodynamics. They will either adapt to it and form new feeding lies as it accumulates the biological drift, or they will leave the lie. If there is a decent insect emergence, the trout will always adapt. The long, flat eddys and placid pools of the tailwaters are affected most by this change in hydrodynamics.

A Sweet 16: Naturals and Important Considerations

1 EMERGING SULPHUR

Emerging Sulphur (*invaria, infrequens, dorothea*). JOHN MILLER

It wasn't until the publication of *Selective Trout* and *Hatches I* and *II* that the word "emerger" played a significant role in fly tying and hatch matching for the troutsman. Thanks to the amazing streamside nymph gathering and countless days of observing aquatic insects by hatch-matching geniuses Carl Richards and Al Caucci, we now know more about how trout key in on these helpless and easy targets during a hatch.

Sulphur emergers are of vast importance, especially on the smooth surface meniscus of long, flat pool and eddy waters. These mayfly crawlers like weed, gravel, and detritus habitats, and they are fond of ice-cold tailwaters and spring creeks where the slow, cold waters also hinder their emergence.

S/R trout are emerger connoisseurs. In an emerger situation, the short, cropped budding wings and trailing nymphal shuck stick out like sore thumbs. Slanted emerging wings can be duplicated with deer hair, CDC, Z-Lon, hackle tips, and other material. The trailing shuck is best tied with the proper-colored Z-Lon or Antron; the abdomen of the dun is colored with a brown Sharpie.

Caucci's Compara-emerger, developed in the late 1960s, was the first realistic pattern to break into this fascinating new frontier of dry-fly fishing. His CDC Compara-emerger (early 1990s) with Z-Lon shuck was the forerunner of the CDC age. Al tied it on a heavier,

curved scud hook to push the emerger a little deeper into the surface film, and he tied in an exaggerated CDC wing so he could see the size 20-24 *Pseudocloeon* pattern on the water. Due to its success he expanded the pattern to all the species of mayflies carried in his fly shop at the time.

2 GRAY DRAKE DUN

Gray Drake dun (*Siphlonurus*) emerging. JOHN MILLER

Though most mayflies emerge from the water, Gray Drakes (*Siphlonurus*) and some, but not all, *Isonychia* see their nymphs migrating to the shoreline to emerge on weeds, logs, and sticks in calm backwater eddies. The Gray Drake spinner is the only stage the angler needs to be concerned with since the trout almost never see the adult subimago and crawling nymph. The spinnerfalls include multiple coupling, with several males targeting a specific female. They hook up and copulate in mid-air and then fall to the surface. The larger S/R trout will target the double and triple patterns and naturals that are bigger than a single spinner. Due to *Siphlonurus*'s slender abdomen, they wither and curl quickly upon mortem. Always make your spinners slender and with a slight curve to the body of the hook.

3 ISONYCHIA SWIMMING NYMPH

An *Isonychia* swimming nymph. JOHN MILLER

These mayflies are a trout's porterhouse steak. They hatch in late spring, summer, and fall, when water temperatures are warmer, and they can be quick emergers on ice-cold tailwaters like the Delaware. They float as duns for considerable distances and are easily picked off by trout and swallows. But some of the most A/A trout feeding takes place just below the surface as the fast-swimming, minnowlike nymphs move down and across with the current, wiggling their wide torsos for speed. An Isocaine Wiggle nymph swung down and across while being jigged and twitched brings fierce takes from trout. Target the riffles and pocket water and swing and work the nymph into the beginnings of the flat pool sections and at tailouts. Make sure you are using the strongest tippet appropriate for the fly since everything—fly and fish—is moving fast and takes are powerful.

4 CALLIBAETIS ADULT

These gorgeous speckled mayflies are a prominent western hatch. Like BWOs, they have multi-broods and love the slow, weedy, long flats and back sloughs of tailwaters and spring creeks such as the Missouri, Henry's Fork, Delaware, and the Muskegon. They are also found in great numbers in ponds and reservoirs. The nymphs scurry and cling prior to emergence in the backwaters as trout hunt them aggressively; a speckled soft-hackle pattern twitched and stripped can bring good takes. The ovipositing imagoes tend to ride the surface for a considerable time, and here the S/R trout closely key in on wing mottling and a wide two-tail spread since the flies ride upright before spreading spent. The spinner flights feature a distinct up-and-down suspended vertical dance like that of the BWO. This movement catches the trout's attention before the fall. Nymph, emerger, adult, and spinner can all be present at the same time in the right conditions.

5 HEXAGENIA LIMBATA

Hexagenia limbata. JOHN MILLER

A *Callibaetis* adult. JOHN MILLER

The giant *Hexagenia limbata* is the largest mayfly in the world and is prominent in North America. This hatch has a broad importance since trout, steelhead, and Atlantic salmon all find the flies highly desirable.

In *Hexagenia limbata*'s initial hatching phase, the fish are super aggressive and target emergers and spinners because the mayflies' caloric value is so high. Emergence is quick due to the warm water and air temps in June and July when they emerge. Several nights into the hatch, the satiated trout become more selective and prefer stillborn emergers. Fishing pressure has already set in by this time, but slightly different fly presentation usually fools the now fussy and finicky lunker trout. Finally, P/D behavior sets in as complete gorging and satiation makes the fish lethargic, sometimes to the point of shutting down. As the hatch wanes, the fish become more aggressive toward a diminishing resource.

The hex has a prominent place in Great Lakes steelhead hatch matching since the rivers and lakes harbor large numbers of hex. The nymphs will leave their silted burrows up to a dozen times starting in winter, exposing themselves to waiting steelhead.

6 ACRONEURIA/ALLOPERLA/ ISOPERLA STONEFLY NYMPH

Acroneuria/Alloperla/Isoperla stonefly nymph. JOHN MILLER

Stoneflies, the first food chain shredders, are another huge source of calories for trout, steelhead, and salmon, especially on acidic mountain freestone streams. They love fast, cascading waters that are pure. *Plecoptera* nymphs swim, bounce, and crawl toward the shoreline to hatch on land, bridges, and rocks. The A/A trout usually position themselves near shore and wait in the undulating pocket water. Fish can key in on the stonefly nymphs' swimming and crawling movements, along with the detailed body segmentation. Steelhead on Great Lakes and Pacific Rim rivers are fond of stoneflies. Rivers that have good populations, such as the North Umpqua and the Dean, also have excellent dry-fly opportunities with some spectacular A/A surface feeding.

7 BLUE-WINGED OLIVE

Blue-Winged Olive. *Baetis, Drunella, Pseudocloeon.* JOHN MILLER

Olives emerge year round with multi-broods and are extremely important to trout. These fast-darting and swimming nymphs like vegetation habitat and range from sizes 14 to 26. They vary dramatically in body hue and wing color. Colors can be anywhere in the spectrum, from bright apple green to a deep forest green for the bodies and light dun to dark coal for the wings. The spinners are a rusty brown or dark olive color.

S/R trout are keen to the particular body colors, but it is the slow emergence and prolonged floating of the duns and emergers that the trout really relish. The BWOs hatch often in fall, winter, and spring in vast numbers on ice-cold tailwaters and spring creeks. Here the S/R trout are particular to the emerger stage. BWOs are photophobic in nature, and spinnerfalls occur in the evenings or mornings or on overcast light drizzle days. Prior to the hatch, A/A trout will target the many ascending nymphs. Frank Sawyer's Pheasant Tail perfectly imitates the little swimmers. Since there is such a tremendous size difference between species, make sure your fly is the right size and you use sparse ties, especially with the tiny spinners. A slight twitch now and then to the adult or emerger can sway a stubborn trout to take. Long-drag free floats with fine tippets are often required.

8 CADDIS HYDROPSYCHIDAE PUPA

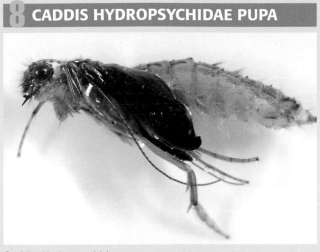

Caddis *Hydropsychidae* pupa. JOHN MILLER

Ever since Leonard Wright wrote *Fishing the Dry Fly as a Living Insect* and Gary LaFontaine, Carl Richards, and Dick Pobst produced their major works on caddis, fly fishers have had a better understanding of the caddis hatch; however, caddis hatches can still baffle anglers. There is a stretch on my Muskegon River I named the "House of Pain." Decades ago, when everyone was trying to figure out the complex and perplexing surface behavior of its ultrafussy trout, you could switch patterns dozens of times in a single night with hundreds of trout rising and have not a single fish to show for it. I seriously believe if you can catch trout successfully and consistently during caddis hatches, you can catch the most ultra S/R trout anywhere in the world!

As the pupae ascend to the surface, they pulsate, gyrate, drift, and twitch, sending S/R trout into fits trying to establish a rhythmic pattern off which to feed. During the hatching there is egg laying both on the surface and under water, as females dive to lay their eggs on the bottom or in near-shore areas. The caddis pupae are a meaty source of food and I have pumped hundreds of pupae out of a trout's stomach after a single night's feeding.

Trout targeting caddis pupae show individual preferences. Some like them gyrating, pulsating, or twitching, some like them dead-drifted, and some will switch their preferences between both styles on command. Pupae usually emerge at the surface quickly and the riseforms are explosive. Position yourself upstream of a good fish and start with a down-and-across reach cast

with the dead-drifted pupa. As you tight-mend upstream clockwise or counterclockwise (depending on which side of the stream you are on) give it pulsating and stuttering movements. Or, position yourself downstream and lift, twitch, and curl (perform a quick wrist roll mend) to imitate the pupa's natural movement as it ascends in front of the fish. Be prepared for many refusals and compound/complex rises and follows since each trout has its own comfort zone of feeding—some like the motion and movement, while others like them dead drifted. Use long leaders and tippets down to 6X-8X, with a minimum of four to seven feet of tippet. Key characteristics for selective trout include the dark-side wing pads and pronounced body segmentations.

9 DIPTERA MIDGE ADULT

Diptera midge adult (Chironomid/Simulium). JOHN MILLER

Midge hatches are the world's most prolific aquatic insect hatches. On Iceland's Lake Myvatn (Midge), located at the upper source of the Big Laxa River, the entire food chain lives off the massive Diptera swarms. Birds, trout, salmon, and other animals are sustained by the vast blizzard hatches. Since they are in such abundance and hatch year round in multiple broods, they are important in the chironomid and *Simulium* forms. On trout lakes and still waters they can be as large as a size 16, but in general you are dealing with fly sizes in the 22 to 32 range and even smaller.

When I fished the Letort and the Yellow Breeches in the late summer and fall as a Marinaro apprentice, we used size 28-32 white midge hatches and imported 8X and 9X tippet from Tortue in France. Midging trout are complex feeders because they target the emerging and wiggling larva on the sandy and gravel bottoms. They sip the ascending and surface pupae and target the floating adults all at the same time and with tremendous ease and delicacy, since these bugs are slow emergers. Toward evening they will concentrate on the backwater eddies where the spent spinners accumulate.

For those that refuse to fish size 28s (which I don't blame them), try using size 20-22 cluster midges, which imitate surface clusters or mating midges that get the larger trout's attention. The Griffith's Gnat and Gulper Special are two examples. Midge larvae come in red, green, gray, copper, and black colors. The adults are either at the dark spectrum (olive, gray, black) or they are cream white. Tying in a small pinch of orange foam or yarn at the head helps you see the fly better. Fish all midges dead-drift only.

When you are spring creek midging, fish a pupa below a hackled adult, since the fish will be feeding on a 50/50 mix of both. Use the hackled adult as a strike indicator. Chironomid midges hatch year round and tend to be on the small side, size 24-28. Their larvae exist in the vegetation, but also more prominently in the clear sandy patches found in the main stem and along backwater sloughs of spring creek bottoms. In these situations 7X and 8X fluorocarbon is a must.

The Green Drake is by far one of the most important and exciting big fly hatches to the eastern North America fly fisher. Similar to England's *danica* mayfly, it creates amazing A/A behavior even in the most sophisticated trout of heavily pressured tailwaters and spring creeks like the Delaware and Penn's Creek. On mountain freestoners in May where their numbers are few, each hatching dun is ruthlessly targeted in A/A fashion. But where these silt burrowers litter the water, like at Poe Paddy on Penn's Creek (an English chalkstream) or on the Delaware system, the trout follow the typical traffic-light pattern: green (A/A), yellow (S/R), red (P/D)—the same pattern as with *Hexagenia* (see page 119).

On colder tailwaters and spring creeks the duns ride the surface for extended periods. Imparting a slight twitch to the artificial can help sway the trout's decision, especially in full-view daylight hours. At dusk the fish's sense of feeding urgency becomes more intense so scouting out one good trout and sticking with it is important. You need to see the trout's rising intervals and determine if it is targeting adults or spinners, which are often on the water at the same time. A Compara-dun-style pattern with fully spread horizontal half-circle wings of CDC or deer hair (I always spec-color them with a marker) will often imitate the dun and spinner simultaneously. At times, it is important to imitate the natural's mottled wings.

10 GREEN DRAKE

Green Drake (*Ephemera guttulata*). JOHN MILLER

11 TRICORYTHODES SPINNER

Tricorythodes spinner.

COLIN MONAHAN

Tricorythodes hatches are some of the most dependable daily minutiae hatches and can last from July through October, creating some very challenging feeding for discerning trout. These tiny mayfly crawler nymphs are found on all types of rivers, especially waters with vegetation and detritus. They hatch in blizzard numbers each morning before noon and on cloudy days. The complete metamorphosis from nymph to dun to spinner happens in a few hours. The spinner is the most favored by S/R trout due to its mind-boggling numbers.

Tiny size 22-24 spinners with 7X are the norm on Eastern streams and large trout can ingest hundreds of spinners in a morning's feeding. Double patterns are tied on larger size 16 hooks to imitate the clusters often targeted by the more opportunistic and larger feeding trout. On bigger freestone streams and tailwaters, position yourself upstream for long, down-reach casts; on small spring creeks an approach from downstream is required. Look for some of the largest feeding trout in the shoreline sloughs and backwater eddies. One must time the feeding interval of a specific fish since the supply of floating spinners is constant. Don't cast immediately after a riseform—wait. Expect refusals and tie your patterns sparse, tying thread-only bodies with a tinge of dubbing for the thorax. Hook set should be slow and down toward the

water to allow the current to tighten the hook. A wide, slightly turned-out gap on the hook, like those on the Partridge Vince Marinaro Midge hooks and the Daiichi specialty wide-gap models, is preferred.

12 MAYFLY TAIL PROFILE AND BAETIS BWO SILHOUETTE

Mayfly tail profile and *Baetis* BWO silhouette. JOHN MILLER

Mayflies usually, but not always, float downstream, as emergers turn into duns and float considerable distances depending on river type, species, and water temperature. The trout's refractive vision window will pick up the wing profile and slightly bent-upward tails, as seen in the amazing John Miller image of a *Baetis* Blue-Winged Olive. *Baetis* have three tails, and to a S/R trout this may be a discernible factor in the heavily fished, fly-only, catch-and-release waters of the Delaware, Silver Creek, and Henry's Fork. Either way the adult comes into the window—front or back—the tails and wings are first on the trout's S/R checklist and must be properly imitated. This includes wing mottling, shape, and silhouette, along with proper tails. Some mayfly tails are short and stubby, others long and wispy.

13 GREEN EASTERN STONEFLY

Green Eastern Stonefly (Chloroperlidae/Utaperla). TOM MURRAY

The Eastern Green Stonefly has major significance to the Atlantic salmon of New Brunswick and Québec. The dean of *Salmo salar*, Lee Wulff, was the first to signal the importance of the large green stone. His Wulff's Surface Stone is the year-round go-to fly on Gaspé rivers like the Grande Riviere, the York, and the St. Jean, all of which have excellent stonefly populations. The river's salmon fry, parr, and smolts imprint heavily to this fly during their residency and downstream migrations. The fly is also effective on freshrun salmon, which have a strong A/A tendency toward the green/blue color spectrum when fresh from the ocean and seas. Tied parachute style with folded wings of deer hair, the pattern will wake and push water or swing down and across just under the surface. The bright green color is also effective in dead-drifted bomber dry-fly imitations.

14 BURROWING MAYFLIES

Burrowing mayflies (*Ephemera/Hexagenia/Potamanthus/Ephoron*). JOHN MILLER

Trout and steelhead can't resist these large and chunky nymphs that burrow in silt and marl. The nymphs will leave their U-shaped burrows before emerging, making them vulnerable prey. When in full emergence, their strong wagging and swimming bodies create motion that the fish target. These nymphs are ideal for the articulated wiggle nymph versions and should be tied and fished with a down-and-across swinging and twitching movement. My late friend Carl Richards detailed their behavior in his classic book *Emergers*.

The floating wiggle nymph like the one I detailed in the example of the Beaverkill *Potamanthus* hatch (see page 66) is a deadly technique because the flies quiver and float on the surface before fully emerging into adults. This fishing method is effective for S/R trout in the second hatch phase when adults tend to be scorned in favor of these meaty stillborn nymphs. Adding some CDC to the wiggle nymph (see fly plates) will give the imitation just enough buoyancy to float helplessly in the meniscus.

15 GREEN ROCK WORM CADDIS LARVA

Green Rock Worm caddis larva (*Rhyacophila/Cheumatopsyche*). JOHN MILLER

Besides being delectable food items for both trout and steelhead, the larvae's bright green color with black dark plates behind the nymph head is easily seen and targeted by both A/A and S/R fish in many fly patterns (chartreuse green is especially effective on steelhead rainbows). The larger *Rhyacophila* are free swimming, whereas the tiny greens are net- and case-spinning as larvae. You will see trout picking them off the gravel and rocks all day long before a hatch. In the spring, when female steelhead dig gravel redds for spawning, they dislodge countless green larvae. Trout and steelhead lie in wait behind the redd-building female.

You should fish these caddis dead-drifted and bouncing along the bottom, with a strike indicator one and a half times the depth of the water from the fly. Where legal, a two-fly nymph rig with a green caddis and scud or stonefly nymph is a deadly spring rigging technique for both fish. We use 5-weight rods, 5X and 6X tippets, and tiny size 16-18 green caddis and scud/midge/stoneflies during winter trout fishing in Michigan, and we constantly pick up large steelhead feeding like resident trout. I have also taken extremely S/R Atlantic salmon in fast pocket water in Québec while swinging and dead drifting large size 2-4 Chloroperlidae/Utaperla nymphs when nothing else is working. Remember that nymphing Atlantics is not considered "cricket" and appropriate because if not done properly and with caution it may foul-hook fish, especially in congested conditions. Here you are best to hunt and target individual fish in the riffles and pocket water and sight-nymph them individually.

This mayfly group is a fascinating mix of early to late-season hatches that has a special place in the hearts of eastern fly fishers. My first experience with them was on New York's southern tier waters of East Koy Creek. An amazing Gray Fox hatch had me mesmerized and so excited that I tied on a Light Cahill pattern poorly and a large brown broke it off when it jumped. I cried for days!

The American March Brown and the Gray Fox, along with Quill Gordons, are some of the biggest first flies of spring. The later Cahill emerge all summer into early fall and have a daily influence on trout streams. When the waters are cold they are slow hatchers so emerger patterns work well. But in warmer temperatures they pop quickly. Swinging Light Cahill–style soft hackles is effective in these hatches. Use generous amounts of wood duck in the patterns since the nymphs have a prominent spotting. The Ithaca Cahills have a bright luminescent orange body when turning to a spinner state, making the Fran Betters Usual pattern a great imitation.

The clinging flat, fat-bodied nymphs can tolerate fast water and diverse habitats and water temperatures. Prior to the hatch, the nymphs will collect in the backwater eddies and side channel flows and trout will feed on them there. ■

16 STENONEMA FAMILY

Stenonema family (*vicarium, fuscum, ithaca*). JOHN MILLER

Cracking the Code: The Drive-By

Johnny Miller is a top Delaware River guide who develops new techniques every year. Many anglers on this and other tailwaters get out of the drift boat and wade slowly into position so as to not spook fish. This works most of the time, but the wild S/R trout here have caught on to the game and can detect the most delicate footsteps or feel the slightest wake and vibration coming at them. Since most guides' anglers use the drift boat to get from point A to point B, rarely do they cast to rising trout while moving. "It's called the 'drive-by.'" says Miller, "It smokes fish!" After fishing the Big D system for decades, I was skeptical of his technique until I experienced it firsthand. "Cast out to well above the last rise you saw and keep mending and let the fly drift for a hundred feet as I float by," Miller told me. "It doesn't matter how close I get." "You're mad, dude!" I said, but I tried it. With the long drag-free drifts I was picking off S/R 20-inch browns a rod's length from the boat. I never would have believed it! The hyperlong drag-free drifts to compound rising trout were one key to the technique's success. But I went on to further theorize that the trout have become so used to the drift boats that they feed right next to them and actually feel more secure when a drift boat lifts anchor and moves. Perhaps the moving boat is a signal to safely feed—at least that's my theory. ■

Slow-emerging adult mayfly duns like Hendricksons, Blue-Winged Olives, or Sulphurs will collect in the backwater created by wading anglers. The drift boat bow also points to these backwater scenes and usually creates deposit areas for stillborn duns and spent spinners. If you sit in your drift boat quietly without casting for a long time, you will notice what I am saying. You'll observe the shift in trout feeding lanes as they adjust to your presence. They will eventually feed close to your wading position or below your drift boat bow anchor position. Here is where letting your caddis pupa, swinging soft-hackle or wiggle nymphs, and wet flies hang for a good period of time will bring arm-jolting strikes.

SUBSURFACE PRESENTATIONS

In all clear water, sight-nymphing is an essential part of being able to consistently catch fish on nymphs. It's accurate to say that 90 percent of the trout's food is eaten below the surface, and for an S/R trout that number might approach the 98 percent mark. Older, wiser trout become more photophobic and cautious, preferring to feed deep on nymphs, larvae, scuds, sow bugs, sculpins, dace, darters, and other small trout fry and chubs.

Sight-nymphing was perfected by Skues and Sawyer on the British chalkstreams, which had relatively shallow crystal-clear waters that allowed for observation of feeding trout. Thus sight-nymphing became the preferred method and minimalism in nymph design the tonic for stubborn S/R trout. I have realized and witnessed, as did Skues, that despite a visual hatch (Blue-Winged Olives, for instance), 70 percent of the activity of feeding fish was taking place down below.

Using stark-profile patterns like Sawyer's Pheasant Tails and Oliver Edwards's designs gives you the greatest success in stealthy presentations. Adding weight to the fly design with copper wire and tungsten heads and wraps allows you to forgo split shot, which spooks S/R trout.

In the S/R mode, trout in tailwaters and long, slow pools do not aggressively chase bugs but rather wait for the river to bring food to them. When they are actively feeding, they will not move more than a few inches and will closely scrutinize any fly drifting through their area. Casts and drifts must be precise to take this type of fish. Most often smaller flies and smaller tippets are needed and must be presented at the right depth.

There are three phases of sight-nymphing—deep, mid-water, and surface nymphing to bulging and tailing trout. In the deep presentation it is important to get your nymph down well in advance of the trout's lie of interception. This can be done by weighting the nymph, using a green tungsten split shot a foot or so above the fly, or by tying weight in the form of a bead head or copper ribbing into the fly itself. Nymphs are presented dead-drifted, twitched ever so slightly, or raised and twitched in a Leisenring lift, slowly swinging toward the surface to imitate the rising emerging nymph. Most trout will use a small feeding window or lane of six inches to a foot. An extremely selective nymphing trout won't move far to take the fly. On a rare occasion you will see them move more than a

The ability to see trout is an acquired discipline since they will mask their appearance to the habitat they occupy. Here is a brown trout that blends into the bottom vegetation of an English chalkstream. The white mouth is one of the key discernible components in the sight game that master nymphers pick up on.
TERRY MATHEWS

A magnificent brown trout on the West Branch Delaware caught during the Sulphur hatch. The Sulphur takes its time emerging, especially on cold tailwaters and spring creeks. During a hatch, emergers and crippled nymphs mask the obvious yellow dun sailboats with rusty leftover spinners from the previous night, or in this case, morning. JOHN MILLER

foot, but the waters must be crystal clear, and the offering rather large, like a big stonefly.

If you have good vision, you can see your nymph, or guesstimate where it is in the drift. With bilateral vision, you can watch the nymph and the trout at the same time. A taking or interested trout will do several things to alert you that it is interested. Initially, it will make a slight movement toward the imitation once spotted. Its ventral and pectoral fins will start pulsating and beating slightly. And of course, your focus should be on the white mouth as it opens for a take. Be warned that sometimes a trout's mouth will open near the insect imitation, only to refuse the fly. One mistake nymph fishermen make is to set the hook too early, thus pulling it out of the fish's mouth. A slight delay when you see the mouth open will be to your advantage. Set the hook down and to the downstream side so it is secure in the side of the trout's mouth.

In those instances where the hatch becomes prolific and the trout do begin to feed on the surface, there is still a great number of shy fish that remain nymphing in the middle water column. Here the dry/dropper nymph rig pays big dividends on tailwaters. Casts must be deliberate and on target, and drifts must be drag free. The fly selected must closely match the natural in color, size, and movement, be it deaddrifted or twitched. The angler must also be able to tell from the rise if the fish is actually feeding on surface dries or if it is taking emergers just below the sur-

face with the backtail bulging rises, as this will dictate both fly selection and presentation.

Masking Hatch

Swisher and Richards were the first to elaborate on the masking hatch, even though Frank Sawyer was the first to identify it. In a masking hatch, many species of insects can be on the water at the same time and at peak emergence, yet the trout focus almost exclusively on an insect that is not clearly identified or is not the most logical option to match the hatch, thus baffling the angler.

During the masking hatch, when different stages of the insect are on the water at the same time, a trout will generally focus on the most abundant food form of the day in a cost-benefit appraisal of metabolic conservation and minimal energy expenditure. However, given the feeding luxury of a heavy hatch, an S/R trout in particular, with its advanced and evolved curiosity, will add improvisational feeding into the structured behavioral programming based on its own unique personality and preferences. I tend to believe that no two trout, or two rivers, are alike in the shaping of feeding personalities. The best tactic against a masking hatch is observation and, when possible, fishing multiple flies.

During a masking hatch involving midges and tiny mayflies, it is often extremely difficult to ascertain with any degree of accuracy what the trout are feeding on since their riseforms and takes are so subtle, unlike when they are taking a giant *Isonychia* off the surface. Add to this the inherent difficulties of fishing small flies and you have challenging fishing. Masking hatches are notorious on rivers where several forms of the insects can be on the water at the same time. New Mexico's San Juan is one such example.

Biologists have recorded almost 4,000 trout per acre from the San Juan's "Texas Hole" down to the sloughs and braided channels where the water splits its stream course. This heavy congestion of S/R rainbows and browns can create specific individual feeding preferences during a masking hatch since competition for space is extreme in such a tight area.

There are two issues that can make the trout here ultra S/R. First, they get absolutely hammered by fishermen from all over the world in the catch-and-release areas. Next, the San Juan's massive food supply and its cold and slow, weedy waters create the ultimate slow and careful inspections of the natural and imitation fly by the trout. The trout's metabolism is in full operation, with S/R behavior constituting almost all of the trout behavior here. The best days here are usually cloudy days as Blue-Winged Olives emerge, mostly *Baetis* and *Pseudocloeon* hatches in sizes 18 to 26. When the adults emerge in the cold waters, they take forever to dry their wings. They float for a long period of time, twitching occasionally on the surface. Trout key in on the "twitching," and that is the S/R fish's hint that it's alive and not just another dead-drift artificial. Some of the adults will be taken on top. The majority are taken at the emerging, stillborn nymph stage below the surface meniscus and at mid-depths. The classic back-and-tail bulging rise is an S/R hallmark of the San Juan's broad-shouldered rainbows and browns. Here every fly pattern under the sun is thrown at these fish and refusals are the norm.

Midges will emerge at the same time as the Blue-Winged Olive hatch. This creates total confusion as to what hatch stage the fish are keying on and wreaks havoc on your selections. Some fish will be feeding exclusively on the olive nymph or emerger, some almost exclusively to the midge pupae. Here is how to crack this minutiae conundrum wherever you find it.

When chasing back- and tail-bulging fish during a Blue-Winged Olive *Baetis* emergence, use six to eight feet of 6X to 7X tippet. The top fly should be a CDC or snowshoe rabbit Blue-Winged Olive emerger, sparsely tied in sizes 18 to 22. Only the top of the emerger budding wings should be greased with floatant so the body hangs in or below the meniscus. For CDC, use House of Harrop cul de canard duck rump oil. The second bottom fly on this two-fly rig is a sparse stillborn Blue-Winged Olive nymph. Its main body is nothing more than stripped peacock herl to form segmentation, and a small thorax of peacock Hareline Ice Dub—that's it! When presenting this to bulging trout, the fish will take either the top emerger or the bottom stillborn nymph; the top emerger will be your strike indicator.

If you are uncertain as to which hatch the fish is feeding on, try using the peacock herl *Baetis* nymph and a chironomid larva in olive, brown, or black with micro silver ribbing as your tandem rig. Grease the leader to about three or four feet from the flies. If the leader goes down, you have a strike! Avoid strike indicators when fishing in this bulging arena. These fish are way too ultra S/R and indicators will spook them. Strike indicators can be used when the fish are feeding in deeper water. I prefer white to match the foam line, or clear.

The problem most anglers have in these multiple-hatch situations is that they move from fish to fish. Don't do that! Pick one good fish and stay with it. Find its steady rhythm and any peculiarities you can. Does it prefer taking a fly to a certain eye or on a certain side? Is it a quick or slow riser? Does it compound/complex rise? Which of its fins quiver first when it takes a fly? What is the take-to-refusal ratio? Some fish are just more refusers than takers; skip these fish if possible.

Favorite S/R Trout Flies

QUILL GORDON

(Author)

Thread:	Brown 6/0 UNI
Hook:	Daiichi D1182
Tail:	Gray hackle (rooster)
Body:	Peacock herl, stripped and varnished
Wings:	Wood-duck flank
Hackle:	Brown or dark dun rooster Grade 1

Notes: The introduction of wary, surface-feeding, S/R German browns wreaked havoc on Catskill anglers' ability to catch fish at the turn of the twentieth century, since the native brook trout seemed to take any fly and color. The Quill Gordon filled the void and met the need for a more exact duplicate with wing profile and body segmentation.

Designed by founding father Theodore Gordon for use on the Neversink River in the Catskills, this pattern set the standard for modern dry flies, breaking from the British school of generalized impressionistic patterns. The body segments and wing profile imitate myriad darker mayflies in the spring. During high flows of spring the pattern is unsinkable yet maintains a sparse silhouette. When floating, the backward-slanted wing profile replicates the natural. It is the standard for dry-fly imitations of the new era.

LETORT CRESSTACIA

(Author)

Thread:	Olive 8/0 UNI
Hook:	Daiichi D1120 scud or X Point 120
Tail/Back:	Rust or bronze Antron or Darlon
Eyes:	Burnt 3X Maxima Chamcleon
Body:	Mix of 40 percent gray, 40 percent light olive, and 20 percent yellow Hareline sow/scud; pluck out into oval shape and trim

Notes: This lethal spring creek fly imitates both *Mancasellus* sow bugs and *Hyalella* scuds. This fly doesn't look like much dry, but when wet its translucency is impeccable. S/R spring creek trout love sow bugs and scuds. On Pennsylvania's Big Spring, a large 20-inch brown that we often watched and nicknamed "The Juggler," would pick the sow bugs off the *Elodea* and *Chara* vegetation and bring them up with its nose, only to turn around and intercept them as they went downstream with the flow. The back blood vein and spine, as well as the translucency, are important characteristics. By plucking out the fibers with a needle in an oval fashion, it imitates sow bugs.

Blue-Wing Olives

Trout Crack
BWO

Reversed
Parachute BWO

Polish-Woven
BWO

BWO Traditional
Parachute

Trout Crack BWO
Emerger

San Juan Micro BWO
Stillborn Nymph

Bead Head BWO
Emerger

Cluster BWO

Bubble BWO
Emerger

Rusty Bronze
Spinner

BWO Parachute
VIZ

Pseudocloeon
Dun

P. T. Stillborn
BWO Nymph

Compara-
emerger

Spring Creek
BWO

Polish-Woven
Light BWO

TROUT CRACK (T.C) SULPHUR EMERGER

(Author; inspired by Al Caucci, Catskills)

Hook: Daiichi D1160
Thread: Yellow 6/0 UNI
Tail: Brown Betts' Z-Lon
Body: Yellow/orange blend Hareline rabbit dubbing
Wing: Light dun CDC

Notes: Al Caucci and others on the Delaware were the first to realize the importance of the trailing Z-Lon shuck during a mayfly emergence. The importance of a brown tail shuck imitating the adult shedding the nymph is imperative for finicky tailwater trout that see heavy fishing pressure. Johnny Miller, one of Al's guides, soon used the tail and a Sharpie for every mayfly. When combined with Al's amazing new patterns, the result was the "crack" a wild Delaware S/R trout couldn't resist. A brown Sharpie can also be used to color the lower quarter of the body.

SPRING CREEK BWO

(Author)

Hook: Daiichi D1182
Thread: Dark olive 6/0 UNI
Tail: Olive Microfibbets and dun hackle
Body: Dark olive 6/0 UNI

Wing: Gray hackle tips stripped and inverted in sailboat fashion
Parachute: Dark dun hackle

Notes: This pattern's sleek silhouette and realistic, minimal design is key when finicky trout feed on Olive adults on spring creeks and tailwaters. The trout hone in on the slightest twitch and movement of the adult, along with the slim profile. Olives often hatch in inclement weather during winter or on cold rainy days, and take their time leaving the water. Trout can examine the fly carefully, so all details must be perfect in order to fool a wise spring creek trout. The reversed hackle tip creates the ideal shape for mayfly wings.

GRAY DRAKE SPINNER

(Author)

Hook: Daiichi 1222, bent slightly
Thread: Gray 6/0 UNI
Tail: Moose mane
Body: Strands of stripped dun, gray, and grizzly hackle quills in bands; soak in water to prevent cracking when tied; may be lacquered lightly once tied
Wings: Sparkle Hareline Organza, light dun hackle palmered and clipped bottom and top

Notes: Most Gray Drake hatches in Michigan go on for at least a month, allowing the fish to become hyper S/R. As a result of S/R feeding to spinnerfalls and many refusals, I attempted to design the perfect mayfly spinner for my tailwater's Gray Drake hatch. The slim gray-and-white banding of the body is the key with *Siphlonurus*; remember that the fly is flush in the meniscus and has total visibility to the trout. Light and dark contrast in body banding is one of the most easily detected parts of the fly. Trout will also key in on the bent/curved body profile of a spent spinner (bend hook gently while it is in vise). Not all fish demand this but the true trophy trout that have seen tons of naturals and imitations will be choosy, particularly during this hatch.

Sulphur

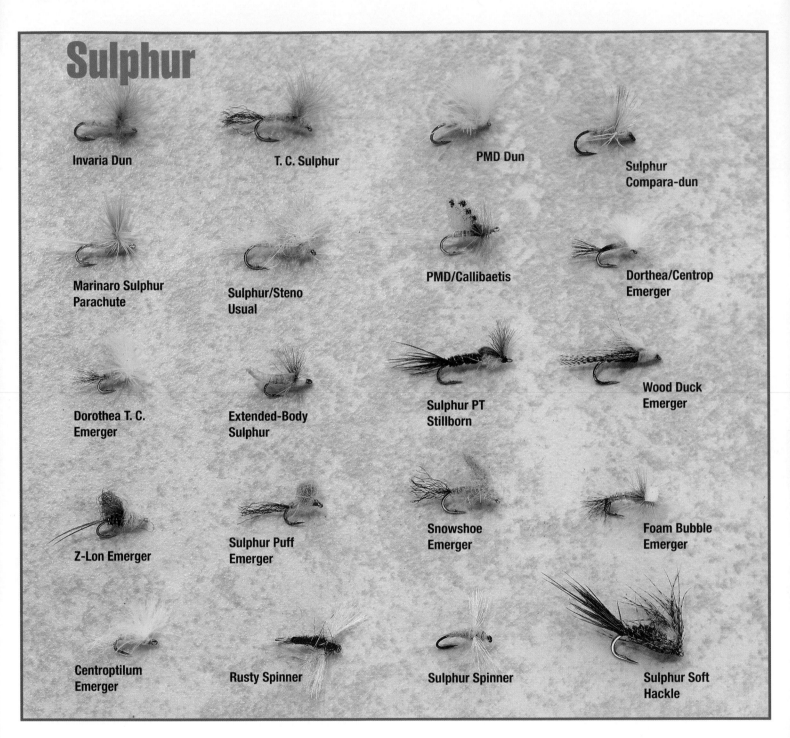

Invaria Dun

T. C. Sulphur

PMD Dun

Sulphur
Compara-dun

Marinaro Sulphur
Parachute

Sulphur/Steno
Usual

PMD/Callibaetis

Dorthea/Centrop
Emerger

Dorothea T. C.
Emerger

Extended-Body
Sulphur

Sulphur PT
Stillborn

Wood Duck
Emerger

Z-Lon Emerger

Sulphur Puff
Emerger

Snowshoe
Emerger

Foam Bubble
Emerger

Centroptilum
Emerger

Rusty Spinner

Sulphur Spinner

Sulphur Soft
Hackle

SULPHUR CRIPPLE EMERGER

(Author)

Hook:	Daiichi D1560
Thread:	Brown 6/0 UNI
Body:	Pheasant tail strands
Rib:	Copper Ultra Wire (extra small)
Thorax:	Yellow Wapsi Rabbit Dubbing

Wing case/Emerging shuck: Light dun CDC

Notes: This pattern is a day-saver when refusals are the norm during heavy Sulphur hatches, no matter where you find them. In cold water, nymphs struggle to emerge and many don't make it. When we filmed the *Selectivity* DVD on the Delaware, the Sulphur hatch was so thick that the largest trout were only concerned with the stillborn nymphs barely showing their wings.

HOT ORANGE ANT (TRADITIONAL AND MCMURRAY)

(Author)

TRADITIONAL

Hook:	Daiichi D1182
Thread:	Orange 8/0 UNI
Back abdomen:	Hot orange Hareline Dubbin
Thorax:	Grizzly hackle
Head:	Hot orange Hareline Dubbin

MCMURRAY ANT (ED SUTRYN)

(Author)

Hook:	Daiichi 1182
Thread:	Brown 8/0 UNI
Ant back/Front:	Balsa joined by thin mono, superglued, and inserted with needle. Paint red or orange.
Thorax:	Brown hackle

Notes: Often a bizarre color is enough to get a strike and this fly has done the trick for me when all else failed. The Royal Coachman, for instance, doesn't resemble anything and yet it is a killer fly. This hot orange ant is no exception. Most ants are black, brown, or dull red, so bright orange is not the color that comes to mind when tying ants. To increase the visibility of the McMurray Ant, you can mark the balsa with fluorescent paint.

PIOTR'S POLISH-WOVEN MAYFLY

(Piotr Michna, Poland)

Hook:	Dohiku HDG 644/8
Thread:	Orange UNI-Stretch
Body:	Orange and brown UNI-Stretch woven
Rib:	Yellow Hareline Micro Midge hollow tube
Wing case:	Light dun CDC puff
Head:	Tungsten nickel
Hot spot:	UV Orange Hareline Ice Dub

Notes: The Poles and the Czechs started turning heads when they kept winning international fly-fishing competitions with their effective, fast-penetrating weighted nymphs, which imitated caddis larvae and mayfly and stonefly nymphs. These nymphs were ideal in shape and silhouette and offered A/A trout and grayling in fast alpine rivers a longer view of the fly as it drifted slower than the speed of the current in the fast rock- and boulder-choked waters. This realistic larva/nymph often includes a "hot spot," a tuft of fluorescent in the thorax, to draw more notice. The flashy bead heads are deadly without split shot, which would hamper the fly's natural drift.

Crustacean

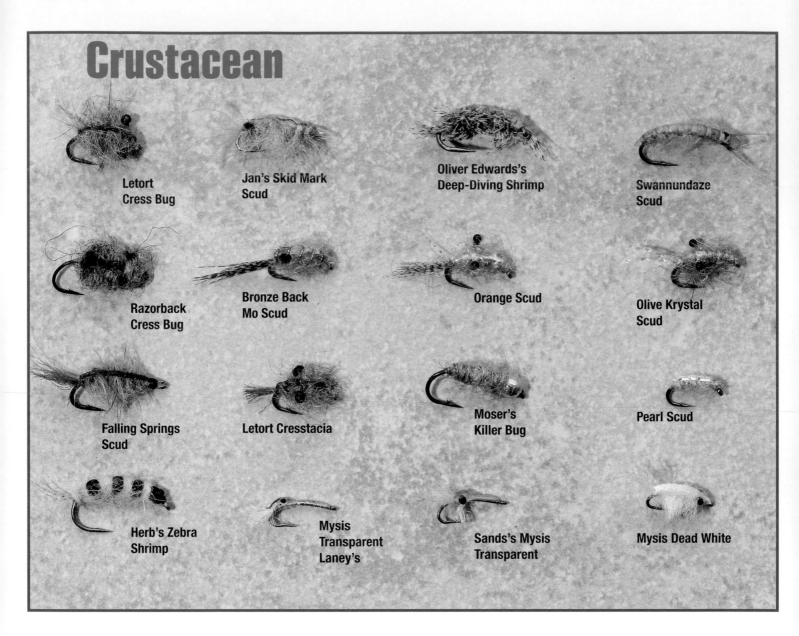

Letort Cress Bug

Jan's Skid Mark Scud

Oliver Edwards's Deep-Diving Shrimp

Swannundaze Scud

Razorback Cress Bug

Bronze Back Mo Scud

Orange Scud

Olive Krystal Scud

Falling Springs Scud

Letort Cresstacia

Moser's Killer Bug

Pearl Scud

Herb's Zebra Shrimp

Mysis Transparent Laney's

Sands's Mysis Transparent

Mysis Dead White

CAJUN LATEX AMBER STONEFLY

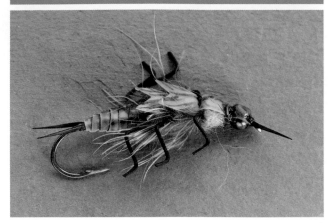

(Cecil Guidry, Indiana)

Hook: Daiichi 1730
Bead: Gold
Thread: Brown 3/0 UNI
Tail: Amber goose biots
Body: Yellow or cream latex glove or Hareline Dura Skin
Thorax: UV Lavender Hareline Ice Dub mixed with gold stone nymph Dave Whitlock SLF dubbing with dark dun CDC strands
Legs: Black rubber legs melted slightly for V shape or J:son silicon stonefly legs (medium or large). The J:son legs add width to the body.
Wing cases: Two V-cut latex strips marked—one long to cover bead and form first and second gill plate (separated by thread), and a second, shorter one for third gill plate down; use a brown Sharpie for slanted wing pad markings
Antennae: Amber goose biots

Notes: This realistic stonefly imitates the Perla and *Acroneuria* giant stoneflies found on high-quality freestone rivers from the Alps to Montana. Body segmentation is everything in large nymphs because their detail is more obvious underwater. On the Salzach River in Austria I had A/A trout target this fly while using the weighted potshotting method in which lead wrap or split shot would dip and dive the pattern between rocks and boulders. The trout waited for the up-and-down, zigzag motion of the stonefly in the fast currents as the stones tried to swim to shore and hatch.

For the body, cut the latex into strands of various thickness based on size of fly; wrap in bands up the hook, starting with smaller bands in back and becoming progressively thicker. The top of the nymph is mottled with brown marker. Overlap latex to add the wide, V-shaped body; use the old Partridge double-polygon shank nymph hooks if you can still find them, or you can cut a thin piece of hard plastic in a V shape and superglue it flat on the hook. Allow it to dry before tying.

CHAN'S ICE CREAM CONE MIDGE

(Brian Chan, Canada)

Hook: Daiichi Alec Jackson Chironomid Hook CTH
Bead: White metal
Thread: Black 6/0 Danville
Body: Black 6/0 Super Floss thread to match pupal color. Adding clear fingernail polish makes the body glossy.
Rib: Red Ultra Wire (ultrasmall)
Thorax: Black thread

Notes: Diptera play a significant role in S/R trout feeding behavior. Learned behavior from getting hooked on larger, more common patterns will force the fish to feed on minutiae. These fish require exact imitation and size; the difference between a size 24 and 28 midge is huge. Midge pupae are the most sought after because they emerge slowly and float in the meniscus for long periods while trout gulp them in vast quantities. Still waters have larger chironomids than rivers do.

Caddis

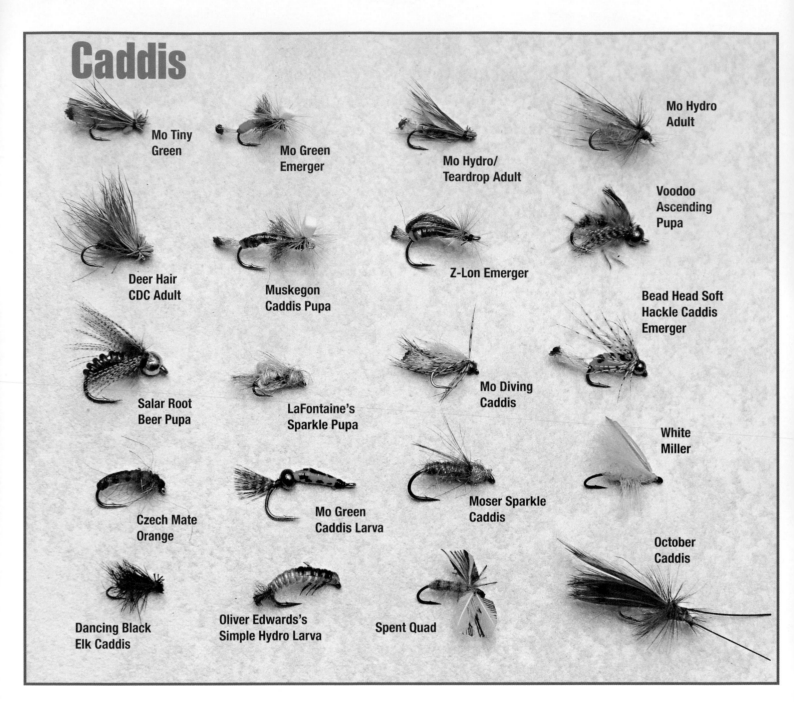

Mo Tiny Green

Mo Green Emerger

Mo Hydro/ Teardrop Adult

Mo Hydro Adult

Deer Hair CDC Adult

Muskegon Caddis Pupa

Z-Lon Emerger

Voodoo Ascending Pupa

Salar Root Beer Pupa

LaFontaine's Sparkle Pupa

Mo Diving Caddis

Bead Head Soft Hackle Caddis Emerger

Czech Mate Orange

Mo Green Caddis Larva

Moser Sparkle Caddis

White Miller

Dancing Black Elk Caddis

Oliver Edwards's Simple Hydro Larva

Spent Quad

October Caddis

BIG SPRING MOUSE

(Author)

MUSKEGON CADDIS PUPA

(Author)

Hook: Daiichi 1640; wrap light lead wire on hook for weight

Thread: Tan 6/0 UNI

Oval shell: Cut the clear hard plastic that comes wrapped around store-bought items on a cardboard back into an oval with three jagged, V-shaped grooves on each side. Superglue it flat on wrapped layers of lead wire.

Body: Dub red fox hair on thread and make an oval body using the jagged grooves

Eyes/Tailbone: Black Sharpie

Antennae: Lemon wood duck

Notes: This pattern is from my first *Fly Fisherman* magazine article, a 1980s piece on big limestone trout. This is a "honey bug" pattern that mimics clumps of hatchery fecal matter, which are a slimy tan color and are loaded with the chironomid larvae large trout key on. Its shape looks like a large sow bug. It's a ghastly looking thing, but this fly serves two purposes for me: S/R Big Spring trout take it when nothing else will work, and it often wakes up P/D fish that are totally satiated but would not pass up a clump of midge larvae.

Hook: Daiichi D1130

Thread: Brown 6/0 UNI

Tailing shuck: Bronze Metz Z-Lon, burnt to a teardrop

Body: Golden yellow latex rubber glove cut into tiny strips or Cascade latex sheets marked with brown Sharpie

Side wings: Dark dun Metz Z-Lon, cut short

Post: Rainy's white foam (2 mm) cut into tiny strips

Parachute: Light dun hackle

Notes: A Carl Richards–inspired Michigan pattern, I tied this version for trout on tailwaters that were targeting pupae suspended in the film despite the presence of egg-laying adults. Its segmented body, extremely important with caddis, is suspended below the surface and easily visible to trout; the foam makes it easier for the angler to see. Caddis pupae gyrate, float, and pulse as they drift in the current and each S/R caddis-feeding trout seems to have its own preference. Switch your presentations with each and allow the pupa to hang on the surface after the drift. Pump the fly to imitate a struggling emerger. This will often trigger a violent take!

Midge

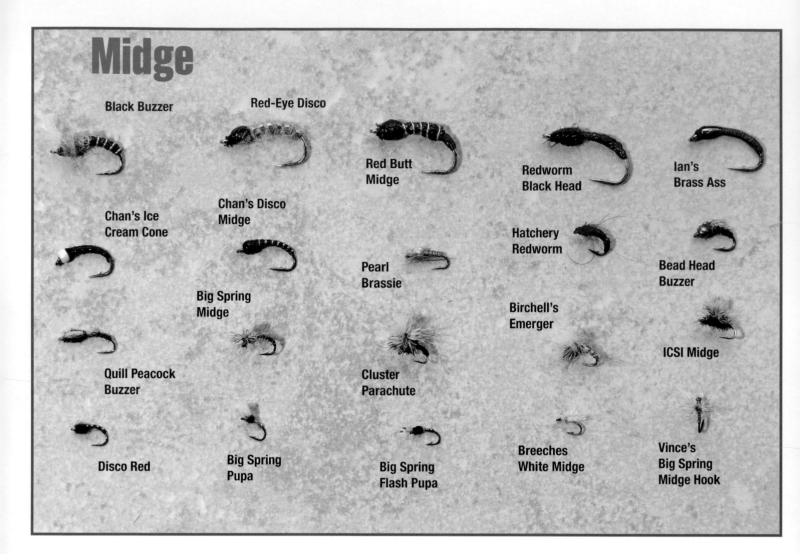

Black Buzzer

Red-Eye Disco

Red Butt Midge

Redworm Black Head

Ian's Brass Ass

Chan's Ice Cream Cone

Chan's Disco Midge

Hatchery Redworm

Bead Head Buzzer

Big Spring Midge

Pearl Brassie

Birchell's Emerger

ICSI Midge

Quill Peacock Buzzer

Cluster Parachute

Disco Red

Big Spring Pupa

Big Spring Flash Pupa

Breeches White Midge

Vince's Big Spring Midge Hook

Stonefly

Oliver Edwards's
Yellow Sally

Morrish
Golden Stone

Traditional
Golden Stone

Oliver Edwards's
Black Stone

CDC Early
Black Stone

Brooks's
Giant Stone

Kaufmann's
Stone

Roman Moser
Traun River Stone

Senyo's
Wiggle Stone

Traditional
Brown Stone

Mayflies

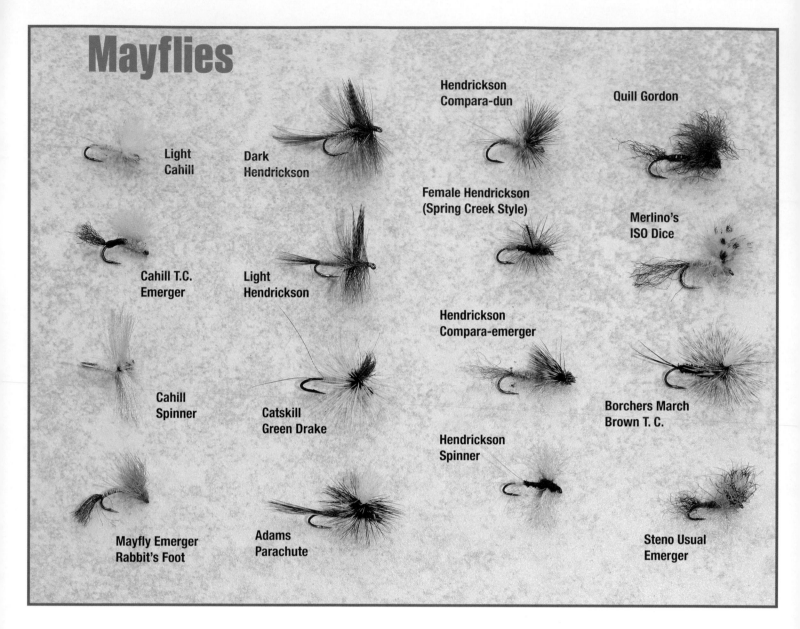

Light Cahill

Dark Hendrickson

Hendrickson Compara-dun

Quill Gordon

Female Hendrickson (Spring Creek Style)

Cahill T.C. Emerger

Light Hendrickson

Merlino's ISO Dice

Cahill Spinner

Catskill Green Drake

Hendrickson Compara-emerger

Borchers March Brown T. C.

Hendrickson Spinner

Mayfly Emerger Rabbit's Foot

Adams Parachute

Steno Usual Emerger

Nymphs/Soft Hackles

Selectivity
Pheasant Tail

Sawyer
Pheasant Tail

Copper
Pheasant Tail

Soft Hackle
Pheasant Tail

Hare's Ear

Sulphur
Soft Hackle

Steno Bead
Head

Sulphur
Pheasant Tail

Sulphur Bead
Soft Hackle

Hendrickson
Nymph

Cadillac Nymph

Mayfly Wiggle
Gray Fox

Isonychia
Nymph

Gray Drake
Soft Hackle

Otter Sucker
Spawn Trout
Smack

Steno
Hare's Ear

Matt's Marabou
Hex Wiggle

Moser's
Emerger

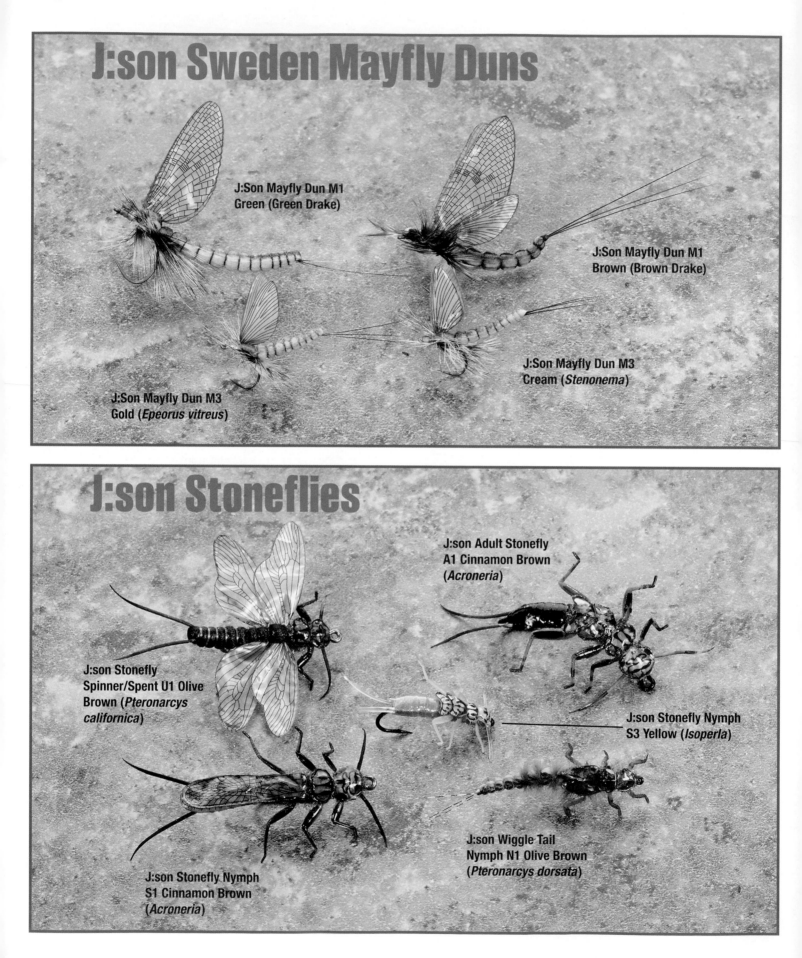

J:son Sweden Mayfly Duns

J:Son Mayfly Dun M1
Green (Green Drake)

J:Son Mayfly Dun M1
Brown (Brown Drake)

J:Son Mayfly Dun M3
Cream (*Stenonema*)

J:Son Mayfly Dun M3
Gold (*Epeorus vitreus*)

J:son Stoneflies

J:son Adult Stonefly
A1 Cinnamon Brown
(*Acroneria*)

J:son Stonefly
Spinner/Spent U1 Olive
Brown (*Pteronarcys
californica*)

J:son Stonefly Nymph
S3 Yellow (*Isoperla*)

J:son Wiggle Tail
Nymph N1 Olive Brown
(*Pteronarcys dorsata*)

J:son Stonefly Nymph
S1 Cinnamon Brown
(*Acroneria*)

The Aggressive/Active Trout

A/A trout are exciting to fish for. Watching a brook trout in a fast-flowing mountain freestone stream take every Quill Gordon mayfly adult that floats by is exhilarating. Putting your favorite stiff-hackled dry fly in front of the fish will most likely catch it. Likewise, watching huge selective brown and rainbow trout on a taskmaster spring creek get stupid when fat, juicy cicadas and hoppers are being blown around into the water on a windy August afternoon will get your adrenaline flowing. In this case, a good imitation will yield a fish that is rarely caught. In a pure and perfect wild world free from angling pressure or rapidly changing and often deteriorating ecosystem conditions, A/A behavior can still be the dominant phase for trout. This is possible in wilderness locales like Kamchatka and elsewhere. But most of us don't have the luxury to frequently fish in such primordial places.

Au Sable Michigan browns hammer large articulated streamers. It is common when you see a fish attacking your streamer to pull the fly out of the fish's mouth or set poorly with the rod rather than strip-setting. Let the fish take the fly before striking. If refusals continue, pause or speed up your stripping. RICH FELBER

The A/A phase is a pure and simple search-and-destroy predator drive that all animals and humans possess at one time or another. The trout is no exception. But this phase only exists when all signals are affirmative for highly aggressive, confident, and consistently active feeding to an abundant and desired food form. A big mayfly hatch like the Green Drake or *Hexagenia* will unleash the beast in an S/R trout that has been sipping tiny size 20 Blue-Winged Olives for weeks. A lower river estuary teeming with schools of emerald shiners will cause orca-like hunting behavior in browns fresh from a sea or lake.

For trout to operate in the A/A phase, it is critical that certain components come together. The abundance, timing, ease of capture, and caloric value of a particular food source or prey, such as a heavy mayfly hatch or a school of baitfish, is paramount. In addition, the security of its microhabitat is key for the trout to ambush and pounce on its vulnerable prey with kill-artist perfection. Undercut banks, bridges, dams and mills, overhanging woody debris, and large boulders and pools offer staging points for the trout to ambush its prey. By combining the food and habitat components with ideal conditions, seasonal behavior, and the specific trout's unique innate instincts, you will find A/A behavior at its ultimate levels.

But as reckless and vicious as the A/A phase may seem at times, a trout can also be quite deceiving and coy in its A/A feeding. Trout, like all predators, use deception as a vehicle to pounce on their prey. Just as a tiger can lie in ambush, a large brown trout hiding under an undercut bank can swiftly attack a helpless sculpin that has drifted down the stream channel into the trout's target zone. Even when it exhibits such aggressiveness, the trout retains calculation, accuracy, and precision. He is a kill artist.

Aside from feeding, which is the trout's number-one daily task, the A/A phase is important for establishing hierarchical dominance in the competition for habitat and sexual spawning supremacy, which fulfills the trout's three main primary drives of food, shelter, and successful reproduction.

Cost-Benefit Principle

A/A behavior often comes with risks that can turn deadly for a predator trout. The cost-benefit metabolic analysis is central to a fish's existence. This is the fish's internal calculator and template used to manage its feeding, sustain its life, and ensure future generations are procreated. The trout must measure an action's metabolic cost against the benefit it reaps, and vice versa, when it comes to energy exerted for predation, concealment, and spawning success. Waterways—be they rivers, streams, brooks, lakes, seas, or oceans—are like giant fluctuating global stock

Anglers often underestimate how big a streamer a trout will take. Here the A/A trout's "gotta have it" mentality overtook its more realistic cost-benefit metabolic rule and caught this gorgeous little wild Letort brown. When hunting big trout, throw really big streamers—even up to 10 inches and bigger! MATT SUPINSKI

markets. Because trout and other salmonids must adapt to certain behaviors and take risks, they constantly must define and redefine security and comfort based on their own metabolic needs and budgets. But it is always predator risk that is foremost on the minds and behavior of all wild creatures subjected to the chaos of the natural world. How trout and salmonids adapt and function to specific river systems is a balancing act. In the stock market, do you stay with stocks and bonds that have consistent and secure but small returns or do you gamble on high-yield mutual and hedge funds? Some waterways allow salmonids to dabble in both risky and conservative feeding and security behaviors.

The amount of nourishment in large prey such as hoppers, cicadas, mice, and large mayflies justifies the cost of expending large amounts of energy to take it, and so the trout becomes totally focused on the kill. Often trout will gorge themselves to death. Leviathan browns have been found with exploded stomachs and bellies caused by overindulgence.

The story of the "fat bastard" brown trout comes to mind. It was February on Michigan's Muskegon River. Snow was melting fast as a result of a warming dip in the jet stream. Rain was falling hard, causing water to rise and spill over the reservoir. A quick and unexpected reservoir "turnover" (a coldwater/warmwater inversion) happened faster than normal. Panfish like bluegill and perch don't like that quick temperature change. Some died from it and washed over the dam spillway, or were cut up in the hydroelectric turbines.

While guiding, I watched two bait fishermen netting the water, which is illegal. As I got near their boat, I saw this huge, 28- to 30-inch brown floating belly-up down the river—but still wiggling its body. The other guy pulled the big fish into the boat, and much to our amazement the fish had a huge bluegill stuck in its throat, with the tail of the fish sticking out. "That son of a gun couldn't get that thing down the pipe," I said. "I think it's choking." The two bait anglers slowly pinched the spiny back fin of the bluegill down and eased it out of the fish's mouth—a fish tracheotomy! They put the brown trout back in the river and revived it a bit even though it seemed dead. The fish came to life, shook its head, and swam away. The brown's insatiable lust for food almost caused its own death. Greed thus becomes the predator. As in humans, the drive to compulsively overeat plagues trout and all animal species. It's what ensures maximum caloric intake when the opportunity strikes.

Wild trout quickly and innately learn the most efficient way to feed without expending too much caloric output and thus tend to be more S/R in their behavior. But when the trout act in the A/A mode they risk a strong chance of violating what is right for their own long-term survival. On the flip side, the binge feeding aids in surviving the rigors of harsh P/D conditions when feeding can't take place due to environmental and procreation metabolic stress.

Mr. Big

The true A/A trophy-trout hunter most often is a streamer or large nymph fisherman who learns to stalk leviathan trout like a big game hunter. I personally became afflicted with the fanatical pursuit of large trophy trout with streamers in the 1980s when I was working as a hotelier in Washington DC. The spring creeks of Pennsylvania's Cumberland Valley were a quick one-hour, fifteen-minute drive from my Georgetown door. Here legends like Ed Shenk and Joe Humphreys perfected spring creek sculpin fishing, and I soon became a disciple. At the local fly shop, the occasional rumor of a humongous trout haunted my dreams.

My pursuit of "Mr. Big," a brown close to 24 to 26 inches who cruised around Fox's Meadow at certain times, took place back in the 1980s. I must have walked this stretch of the Letort a thousand times. I would sit at Charlie Fox's benches, listening to the trucks rolling down Interstate 81 and waiting for something to happen. I remembered the days when all the heavy-hitter Letort regulars held high court here. Most of them have since passed away; others gave up hope on this tiny little jewel after the 1981 pesticide spill that killed many of this section's wild trout. But there were still some huge monsters to be had, and I relished the fact that hardly anybody was pursuing them. Back in those days, I was just a Washington yuppie and outsider "wannabe" to the Cumberland limestone regulars. I would keep my distance and would just sit and listen to the ramblings of the stoics on "how it should be done, son!"

In the spring creek hunting game, you start by first establishing the beast's home. Undercut banks, woody debris, tree stumps, old bridges, railroad trestles, and culverts are good places to start. Many spring creeks still have old mill dams that have been breached, resulting in a deep pool below them. Most large spring creek trout are dark because they shun light as much

Mike Schmidt lives for A/A trout. "My go-to presentation is a variation of a jerk strip that I call the 'Pump and Pause,'" Schmidt says. "I make an across-stream cast followed by an up- or downstream mend to help control depth and speed. Once depth is achieved I use a few short and sharp strips followed by a pause, then repeat in various changing intervals. The strip quickly accelerates the fly and may entice a predatory chase, while the pauses allow the fly materials to breathe as the fly comes to a stop and falls a bit in the water column, imitating injured and fleeing prey." MIKE SCHMIDT

as possible and spend most of their time in concealment. When they cruise about a spring creek vegetation channel, you can't miss them. Once you spot one, you must then return again and again to determine its behavioral pattern. Each fish will have a unique personality and peculiarities. This is when the chase (and the fun) begins.

Though I often waited for a hatch to begin or sight-nymphed Sawyer Pheasant Tails, small scuds, and sow bugs for modest-sized but finicky wild browns, I mostly waited for Mr. Big. I first noticed him after a small Blue-Winged Olive hatch in February. It was a rainy day, and I was pleased to land a 12-inch brown on the surface, all brightly colored with red spots and a mocha-tinted orange belly. To catch a fish like this on the new Letort after the pesticide spill was a major accomplishment. Just as I was releasing the fish, Mr. Big showed up. He cruised downstream, sending smaller 8- to 10-inch trout scurrying. I was crouched on my knees in awe and admiration. It was about four o'clock in the afternoon when he came downstream, hovered over a bed of stream vegetation, poked his nose into some weeds, and took a bite. It then turned

upstream and took something off the surface, along with one hapless Olive floating by. The fish rooted around the channels for a good distance, probably about ten yards. Every once in a while it would yawn and stretch its large white mouth, with a kype like an Atlantic salmon. As it swam past me, it was totally oblivious to my presence and soon vanished.

For months I probed and stuck my nose in every possible undercut bank, logjam, woody tree stump, and bridge abutment. Mr. Big was nowhere to be found. One day I left the rod in the car and went hunting without it. If you are a trophy hunter, the worst thing to have in your hand is a fly rod. It will only distract you. I did take along a wading staff as I went to look for Mr. Big's home den. My poking around turned up some nice Letort brown trout, but no Mr. Big. But there was one more stump and undercut bank that was yet to be explored. It was a big old oak tree stump with roots in the undercut bank that were collecting tons of surface debris in a backwater eddy. I stood up on the rotting roots overhanging the water and one leg crashed through the roots and down into the creek. I thought I had broken my ankle. Just then, Mr. Big came flying out of that stump and circled around three times in the main channel. As I moved away, he went right back to his home. It was time to plot the attack.

First I had to decide on prey, and I chose an over-size sculpin pattern. This section of the Letort had a

Sculpins, darters, and gobies all have the same V-shaped body profiles and twice the amount of meat as baitfish of equal sizes. They are highly relished by *Salmo trutta* wherever they are found. They like dark undercut banks and weed beds, and spring creeks provide the ideal habitat. They also are slow moving and bottom darting. In the Great Lakes, the sculpins and gobies are relished by the 20- to 40-pound brown trout, which attack more slowly than salmon. MATT SUPINSKI

good sculpin population, along with some darters, V-shaped creatures that rest on the bottom and scurry from one place to the next. I visited this section of Letort for several months, and having made some positive sightings, I decided Mr. Big was notorious for early morning and evening forages out into the mainstream channel. During the warmer months of summer, he probably hunted all night—gorging on everything from field mice to sculpins to large cicadas and grasshoppers. One late April morning, after months of stalking, I found him by accident upstream near the Bonny Brook Bridge waterwheel. He must've come up there in December to spawn by the gravel gradient near the quarry, and decided to keep going upstream. I threw my 5-inch-long black Shenk's Sculpin below the waterwheel, and there he was. I had a small split shot above the sculpin's head. I cast it downstream, let it rest, and then lazily pulsed and pumped the streamer toward the bank. Mr. Big crushed it! I waited for him to get his whole mouth around it, and then set the hook. My old Battenkill CFO reel screamed as the fish tore upstream toward the bridge. I ran along the banks holding on for dear life. My 2X tippet tore against the limestone bridge until I turned the fish into my net. The case of Mr. Big was finally closed.

I saw him again later that fall. He had an interesting mark under his right eye, probably from some battle with another fisherman or with an alpha dominant brown trout. He swam by me again in his usual arrogant, oblivious way, but this time, he must've recognized me, because he swam away a lot quicker.

THE FIGHT

When fighting leviathan trout, don't panic! Let's say you hook your 20-inch dream fish. It is now a psychological battle where a cool, calm mentality must prevail if you want to land the fish. That is tough to do when you are excited. Remember, some of these bigger fish are not used to being hooked, and some might have never been hooked at all. They are just as surprised as you are. They will most often head toward security, typically after several head shakes and boils.

My experience has taught me that if you apply too much pressure at the start of the fight, you will probably lose the fish. Maintain a steady but light pressure and allow the fish to tell you what it will do. Firm but slightly light horizontal rod pressure is often the best. A large trout can only go so far under a logjam or an

undercut bank before it must turn sideways or back out. On spring creeks, the trout will sometimes bolt through weed channels; that's okay so long as you keep your rod high as to not collect any vegetation debris. If you built your leader butt section heavier, it will handle the weed buildup. If the trout burrows into weed channels, as they often do, once again it can only go so far. When I have waders on, I often walk into the spring creek to net the fish while it has its head buried in the vegetation. Sometimes that is the only way to get them, and it also prevents them from suffocating.

But if the fish is headed for a huge piece of cover that will surely break you off, such as a downed tree or a bridge abutment, I use what I call the opossum technique. In this tactic, you let the line and rod go completely limp. This often stops the fish from battling and fighting and it will take up a sedentary position in the main channel, often in a stunned fashion, possibly not realizing it remains hooked. I have played this game many times and emerged the victor. A large trout resting after a fight usually has a lactic buildup in its bloodstream and is quite tired. If it decides to do a second battle, the fight is usually a lot less eventful and the trout will succumb easily.

On larger water, you should let the fish rip you into the backing when it is first hooked—it has a straight runway to do so. Once the fish is in a somewhat controllable situation and the blistering runs are less frequent, applying pressure to either side with a low rod profile, thus allowing the long, light rod tip to wear down the fish, will eventually make it succumb. Don't hurry. Fish in cold water have plenty of energy. The biggest concern to the angler is vegetation buildup on the leader, which can be discarded during battle by carefully and gently shaking the rod left to right and gently banging the cork handle with the palm of your hand. Getting the fish as close to shore as possible also helps you net it. Steer the fish away from any weedy underwater obstacles by placing the hand that is not holding the rod on the butt section of the rod for leverage. Use large, soft catch-and-release nets that have a deep bag and a long handle. The new extendable-handle, deep-mesh Measure Nets are ideal for wading anglers on tailwaters and spring creeks.

The Dark Side

The A/A state in reclusive big brown trout is a result of extreme dominance and assuredness born amid the

Mill dams are synonymous with spring creeks around the world. They were used for gristmills and tanneries and also diverted water for irrigation by the farmers. On the Big Spring in Pennsylvania, the famous state-record brown was caught by Don Martin in 1947 by the old mill. Here in England's Hampshire chalkstreams, they are known to be home to large brown trout. KEN TAKATA

seclusion and comfort of dark microhabitats. The trout attacks with confidence and precision. Leviathan trout are rarely caught to become selective; they often choose impossible-to-reach lies or choose conditions that give them comfort, like the darkness of night.

Vince Marinaro, told me about the large browns that never get touched in England. These monster beasts of the deep and dark were revealed to me when I fished the wild trout waters of England's River Itchen near Abbots Worthy Mill. The ghost of G. E. M. Skues still haunts these hallowed waters in the Hampshire country. The chalkstream spring creek runs through beautiful pastoral farms, manicured lawns and gardens, and courtly country mansions and estates, and it has the most amazingly clear and gentle spring creek waters a soul could ever lay eyes on. Its wild browns have a spectacular orange hue and red spotting, and they can be seen nymphing all day, occasionally rising when the Blue-Winged Olives begin to hatch. Clad in Wellington boots and proper English attire, I pursued the Itchen's noble brown trout back in the 1980s with my angling cohort Ashok. In the proper English fashion, we used tried-and-true Frank Sawyer pheasant

tails, buzzers, and scuds. I had with me my Pezon et Michel bamboo nymphing rod and Orvis CFO reel. I felt quite elite.

Abbots Worthy Mill, at the top end of the Piscatorial Society's beat, caught my interest. The mainstream Itchen trout were almost Letortlike in their stubbornness to take a fly. Only a stealthy approach would work. There was a deep, dark pool under the waterwheel at the old mill that had the smell of hog brown trout. "Anybody ever fish under there?" I asked the gillie, who was munching on his afternoon lunch of smoked salmon and cucumber sandwiches, washed down with dark English ale. In a rough English accent he commented, "There are two big bastard brown trout that live under it—a male and female, the river's brood stock. But you won't catch them! They only leave during spawning season to find spawning gravel, and then it's back home under that bloody waterwheel!" he said in disgust. "Dermot Wilson, who used to own the beat, said that he once saw one of those browns eat a duckling in the mill pond."

On the chalkstreams, the preferred presentation was upstream nymphing and dry flies. The dark side of me carried a hidden Pandora's box of streamers including Shenk's Sculpins in case the gillie wasn't looking. Streamers were considered lures in England and were much frowned upon. After using a pheasant tail to fool some nice handsome browns in the 12- to 14-inch range, our gillie felt comfortable with us and asked if we would mind if he ran to the market to pick up some meat for his family dinner. "We don't mind at all. Take your time, we'll be fine!" we told him with Cheshire-cat grins. "I'll be back around dusk," our gillie remarked. Like giddy little schoolboys, we ran for the mill. "I got that sculpin box," I told Ashok. "No harm, just a few throws. I'm dying to see what that big monster looks like. If it's there I can catch it!" I spoke with the attitude of a cheeky, confident young man.

As it got darker, I attached the black sculpin to 2X. My hands were shaking, as I knew I was about to commit a moral crime, at least from the British standpoint. The problem was the pool of the mill was right below the waterwheel. My only approach was to throw the sculpin at the descending waterwheel steps, give it slack, and let the undercurrent of the wheel pull the sculpin back out to the undertow of the pool. After several practice attempts I got the cast down and honed my new "waterwheel cast." (Eat your heart out, Lefty!) My fifth attempt at tossing the sculpin into the boiling undertow brought out the huge brown trout. The big brown followed the fly and slowly engulfed it. It sounded like a dog trashing the pool! I tamed the fish quite quickly due to the lack of space it had to fight, and Ashok put the telegraphing net underneath it. My hands were still shaking from excitement and the fear that the gillie would soon return and catch us and that, along with the low light, blurred the image of this 25-inch toad in the Kodachrome shot. After we got back to the gillie shed, he finally returned and asked us, "Catch a hatch this evening, lads?" "Nahhh!" we retorted. "Nothing happened."

General small-stream and spring-creek hunting tactics for A/A trout entails fishing with short, stout 7-foot rods if you prefer to cast. If you like to use the "dapping" method, an 11-foot, 5-weight or the new 12-foot, 3-weight switch rod is perfect. Throw large sculpins and "roadkill" articulated streamers up to ten inches long. Huge foam terrestrials should be slapped hard on the water to trigger the A/A response. It's also important to lower your profile on the water and consider sun and shadow issues. Fish small spring creeks on cloudy, windy, rainy days for success; forget it on sunny bluebird days. Fish short, stout leaders

When hunting large A/A trout—which are meat-eating machines—stripping big streamers and imparting lifelike movement to the fly, or concentrating on heavy hatches of big bugs, is the ultimate way to go. With today's incredible selection of lifelike materials, articulation, and prismatic eyes, streamers look so realistic and irresistible that no trout can refuse them. JOHN MILLER

with 8- to 10-pound test to horse your fish away from obstacles. If the trout boils on or chases your fly, but doesn't commit, stop and let the fish return to its concealment lie and come back later when the light is lower. Don't beat it to death with casts; this will only make it go in into the P/D mode fast.

Tailwater A/A Behavior

Certain streamer-fishing events are common on tailwaters: bait fish being chopped up in the hydro turbines of the reservoir, the introduction of smaller, recently stocked rainbow trout, scurrying sculpins and darters, or alewives being washed over the spillway like on the Catskill tailwaters. If you can use a drift boat to fish these rivers at the high flows, streamer-stripping rainbow trout, alewife, and shad patterns is your best bet for catching these big trout. Throw streamers along the shoreline where baitfish are pushed by the high currents. This will push these smaller fish next to the shoreline where minimal currents exist, and it's also where the leviathan browns lie in ambush. Gizzard shad and alewives that have been released from the stagnant waters of the reservoir are slow-water impoundment creatures, and are not used to strong current flows. They find comfort next to shorelines.

Many tailwaters, like the White in Arkansas, receive massive amounts of yearling rainbow trout. The big browns target the hatchery trucks just as the great blue herons do. Here the A/A baitfish hunting behavioral mode will remain intact until the fish becomes satiated. Then P/D behavior resulting from digestion overload will take hold, making the trout feed less frequently or not at all.

Some of the tailwaters in the Southeast, like the Clinch and Holston, have a unique humid, subtropical climate of hot summers and mild winters. This constantly affects the temperature inversions in the reservoirs, creating baitfish kills that ultimately come through the reservoir turbines. This is a food factory for the larger trophy browns and rainbows. Given this great, consistent food source, some of the bigger fish remain in the A/A state all the time.

Here the largest alpha predator fish in the river systems have no natural enemies other than anglers. They move up and down rocky flats, pools, and gravel bars and aggressively hunt small to medium-size baitfish and trout. These fish are not waiting for the river

to bring them bugs as tailwater trout in the S/R mode do, but instead they are actively looking for the one big meal.

Montana's Kelly Galloup and Michigan's Bob Linsenman advocated fishing big streamers with the "strip-jerk" method in their epic work *Modern Streamers for Trophy Trout*. This revolutionized the method of presenting "big uglies" to river beasts on freestoners. These patterns emulate sculpins, dace, shiners, smaller trout, crayfish, and just about anything else that looks like food. "Mousing," or fishing mice patterns, is also a popular nighttime fishing technique for freestoners and tailwaters all over the globe, particularly in New Zealand and Michigan. Mousing is a common practice on the Pere Marquette River, where guides like Mike Batcke and Tommy Lynch fish through the night for amazingly huge brown trout.

When fishing streamers, expect a good amount of long follows and refusals up to your drift boat. A particular fish may chase your streamer on several occasions. At this point, stop and rest your fish like you would an Atlantic salmon. Then repeat the process.

Night fishing on the White and other tailwaters with mice and large cannibalistic trout streamers can bring world-record leviathan browns to the net. Here Tommy Lynch, a famed Michigan guide, hoists a massive "donkey" caught in the night A/A mode prowling for prey. ALEX LAFKAS

Shawn Murphy with a tailwater brown. High water flows are ideal when streamer-stripping for A/A. trout. Some water discoloration is best. MATT SUPINSKI

Blizzard hatches occur on insect-rich tailwaters like the Delaware system of New York and Pennsylvania and the Bighorn and Missouri Rivers in Montana. These are the top tailwaters for consistency in aquatic invertebrate life, environmental stability, and wild trout. A drift boat is the best way to cover a dozen miles in a day. JOHN MILLER

It's amazing how the second or third time around the fish will get aggressive enough to hammer the streamer out of frustration. Most importantly, let the fish take the streamer and don't pull out the fly too early! Another extremely effective technique is the classic "wet-fly swing" where you are not stripping much at all. It allows you to cover lots of water.

Fishing Big Bugs

Many dry-fly fishing addicts have visions of big trout slashing at the first large mayfly hatch of the year in a frenzied fashion. I know I do! Even though the trout are often aggressively chasing these insects, timing, satiation, time of day, fly patterns, and the trout's feeding rhythm all come into play.

The timing of a hatch can make the difference between angling success and failure. Say you are dealing with a big hatch of Gray, Brown, or Green Drakes. When the bugs first emerge, their arrival is not so well understood by the trout; you can have hundreds of large drakes everywhere with no surface

feeding occurring. But give these trout a day of such a heavy emergence, and the fish will be feeding aggressively on them. One often-neglected facet to remember is that there are usually good biological drifts or shoreline emergences of nymphs (like some *Isonychias* and stoneflies), which distract trout from surface feeding.

You always want to time your angling for the second or third night of the hatch when the trout is in its most A/A mode. This is when the new mega-feast has proven irresistible to the fish. As the hatch phase peaks, the fish still feed in A/A fashion, but some fish that have been caught or have more cautious S/R manners will start to become finicky. The trout will often target crippled duns, stillborn nymphs, and smaller spinners as the quirks of S/R behavior kick in. Sometimes a streamer, a mouse pattern, or a large Royal Wulff goes against the hatch-matching grain and fools a fussy and stubborn trout. But the fish will turn back to a careless A/A hatch feeding state as the hatch wanes and the bugs become fewer. This is when the leviathan trout is most vulnerable.

Hopper Madness

If you don't have the time to see the beautiful spring creeks of Montana's stunning Absaroka Range, Virginia's Shenandoah Valley can give you the same experience. Vast farmland pastures, tall mountains, and wide-open, big sky country create a panorama like no other. There are several spring creeks in this region, but none produce big selective brown trout like Mossy Creek near Bridgewater, Virginia. Here pastures, gentle rolling hills, eighteenth-century limestone churches, and Amish buggies contribute to the magnificent pastoral ambience. The Mossy's brown trout are stocked into the fertile, vegetation-rich waters as tiny fingerlings. There is also good natural reproduction in the creek's headwaters. As the small fingerlings reach the 10-inch range, they become brightly colored and as wild in personality as any other fish. Due to the heavy angling pressure and extremely rich aquatic food sources the trout's S/R meter is always in place—except when large terrestrials fill the meadows and the A/A behavior comes out. But what starts out as reckless feeding behavior can quickly turn to finicky feeding.

Shenandoah summers can be hot and humid, ideal for pasture grasshoppers to go wild. My first consistent encounter with big browns feeding on hoppers was here on Mossy Creek. To watch a big brown come up to a grasshopper imitation or natural and follow it beneath the surface hanging vertically, and then turn downstream and pursue only to go back to its original feeding lie, and then in a last-minute panic, swim back downstream to inhale it, was simply an amazing visual experience. These riseforms become Marinaro's epitome of the ultra-complex riseform, and I've only noticed them on spring creek waters that have long pool and run windows. These ultra-complex riseforms don't happen often on many fisheries, only occurring when a highly valuable, slab-of-meat food source like large grasshoppers or cicadas are around.

Fishing hoppers on the Mossy is a high art form. Some big bruiser browns will only take patterns when they are smacked on the bank and then forced to plop and fall on the water tight to the bank. Others required the fly to swim sideways, imparting twitches to it. Other fish like total dead drifts. Others like constant twitching and long pauses. Regardless, a firm "plop" presentation is required to get trout's attention and trigger the "search and destroy" response.

Success here is narrowed down on most occasions to the fly imitation's body color, form, and the space between legs and appendages. I kid you not, this

There is nothing like the drop, plop, skitter, and squirming of a helpless large terrestrial insect—like a hopper or cicada that mistakenly flew or was blown into a spring creek—to trigger the A/A hunter instinct in a leviathan predator trout looking for a quick and easy, delectable meal. But the A/A drive is not without subtle discretion. Even in the "kill artist" mode, the predator trout carefully examines acute particulars like behavior, body and appendage color tones, segmentation, and silhouette to discern the imitation from the natural, especially on heavily fished, flies-only, catch-and-release spring creeks, which are often the norm and fished by skilled anglers with their precise imitations. The dozens of grasshopper species in your spring creek pastures and the 8,000 varieties globally put the trout's selectivity meter in high overdrive even when they are in the A/A state. MATT SUPINSKI

The next time you fish grasshoppers for selective trout, carry a small field net and find out which species are in the meadows and on the trout's table—they can vary from month to month. BRIAN TROW/MOSSY CREEK OUTFITTERS

seems to be a critical factor. The Mossy's particular grasshoppers have divergent colors: yellowish-cream, olive yellow, deep green-yellow, and more. As the trout season moves into the fall, smaller, immature hoppers are preferred to the large imitations—probably because everyone is fishing large adults.

Hopper fishing can bring you the trophy trout of a lifetime during daylight hours. Focus your angling on hot windy days because hoppers love the heat. If you have farmers plowing or haying the fields in late summer, those conditions are perfect. One trick I learned to induce large brown trout activity (and is legal) is chumming up the hopper hatch. I usually walk a good distance downstream close to the banks and scare hoppers into jumping into the creek. A fair number will do so and thus sound the feeding bell to a large trout in waiting. Once you reach the downstream end of your walk, have a late breakfast or lunch and some cold drinks and take a good long break before you head back upstream. You will be amazed how

the trout's fine-tuned hunting behavior has been unleashed. You should also follow herds of cows and sheep, which stir up a ton of hoppers.

If you have refusals, change sizes and colors. Vary the presentations I described above. Never go smaller than 4X tippet or you will be sorry! Long 10- to 12-foot, 3- to 5-weight rods allow you to dap close to tall grassy banks and undercut banks in knee-creeping situations. These areas are the ones to target because they are where hoppers are most likely to fall, leap, or be blown into the creeks. The undercut banks are big brown trout condos!

The small dimple risers are often confused with smaller fish, but the bigger fish have learned to feed with a highly developed and precise efficiency. Thus they often displace little water. Often the less-adept and smaller fish feed with a splashy youthful enthusiasm. Regardless, do not judge a fish by its riseform. I've had many 20-inch-plus trophy trout feed like small chubs. It was shocking to see their efficiency. ■

Despite the low light levels, brown trout are able to discern natural prey from the imitation. Having the right pattern and making a correct presentation is often the difference between netting a few 20-inch-plus browns and getting skunked. JOHN MILLER

On the long, flat pools and eddies, trout will be seen rising everywhere during a significant hatch. Violent rises usually indicate quick-emerging insects like caddis, or swimming mayfly nymphs like *Isonychia*, *Hexagenia*, *Potamanthus*, and *Stenonema*. Steady back-and-tail bulging rises to emergers in stillborn nymphs, along with crippled adults, can be the most difficult to decipher since this type of feeding also indicates a trout is sipping spinners. The bigger the circle formed by an air bubble after a rise, usually the bigger the fish. Concentrate on one good fish at a time. If you jump from fish to fish, you will fail and spook all the fish in the pool. Concentrate on the closest fish to you and save the ones farther out for later.

When you have a popular venue, like night fishing for big browns during the famous *Hexagenia* mayfly hatch, the trout can go from S/R or even P/D mode to a frenzied A/A phase in a heartbeat. Knowing how to identify riseforms of the various emergence stages is paramount for success. In Michigan, the largest burrowing mayfly is *Hexagenia limbata*. These cyclops-like beasts hatch at dark in June and July. For the nocturnal photophobic brown trout, it's a feast like no other!

The hatch goes on all night, but the spinner flights at dusk will stir the most A/A behavior. On the wooded, spring-fed waters of the Pere Marquette, Au Sable, Manistee, and hundreds of other streams, you plan your night around a series of logjams and pools that harbor the night-stalking beasts. With the help of RIO Products' glow-in-the-dark lines, infrared glasses, and short 6-foot leaders with 10-pound test, you launch fly patterns as big as your palm. You fish by sound and feel, listening for gulping grabs and feeling the tugs of line between your fingers.

Hex fishing is not for the fainthearted. As a human predator, you fish by sound and feel, and the challenges of nighttime depth perception make this a highly specialized game. Your prey, the trout, must judge the legitimacy of your presentation and fly imitation, making Hex fishing a standoff with both sides having a fifty-fifty chance of winning.

All dry-fly night fishing to hatches must be calculated. Stake out your night pools and make notes on distances and locations of obstructions where a trout might break you off. Once situated on your Hex beat or pool for the night, you wait for the swarming, buzzing sounds of the Hex spinners. As you hear the surface-feeding trout, which sound like dogs slurping their water bowls, you will start to perceive the distance, which darkness normally does not allow. Practice your short casts tight to the logjam feeding lies in daylight hours before the hatch—some anglers even mark their lines with glow-in-the-dark tape, or markers to denote the right amount of line to have out. When you hear the gulp of your leviathan beast close to where you think you put your fly—or where it has drifted—lift the rod in hope of a hookup. Or wait for the gentle tug of the line on your fingers, with a slightly slack loop, allowing the fish to take and engulf the fly and turn. This is similar to the fly-swinging hook set for Atlantic salmon and steelhead. If this all comes together like you planned, the fish of a lifetime can be caught.

In the Hex hatch and other large mayfly hatches like the Gray, Brown and Green Drakes, A/A trout feeding takes place at the spinnerfall stage because the fish have relative ease in capturing the insects. Garbage feeding and targeting clusters will occur. Large fish will maximize the energy they exerted moving to the surface by capturing multiple insects. Spinners love to collect in the counterclockwise slackwater eddys. The trout almost always faces downstream at the curve of the current where it spins back upstream. Approach the fish coming downstream at a low profile. Make sure you're puddle-casting the fly high and stopping it at 12 o'clock, allowing the tippet to puddle up and slowly uncoil to reduce drag; using the longest and lightest tippet you can get away with is important. Make sure the tippet and fly land in the backward-swirling current. Watch how your fly moves

with the current and make adjustments. It's important to not add any movement whatsoever to your fly because this will spook the fish. Repeat again and again until you achieve success. As the spinner supply wanes, the odds of a hookup increase, so stick it out for the long haul, even late into the midnight hours.

Microhabitat and Night Feeding

Wherever you go in the world, find a bridge over a trout, steelhead, or salmon river, and you will find big fish! On Virginia's Mossy Creek, a tiny trestle always harbored a beast of a trout. On Maryland's Beaver Creek, a gentle little limestoner, an iron and stone bridge always had one or two good browns living under it. I caught my first steelhead during a blinding lake-effect snowstorm on New York's Cattaraugus Creek under the New York State Thruway bridge when I was twelve years old. I was looking for cover from the storm when the big fish slammed my fly.

The gentle rolling hills and farm country of New York's southern tier is where my passion for trout took root. My dad and I would leave our home in Niagara Falls at three o'clock in the morning to go to our favorite trout stream. It was a full-day affair that often turned into a weekend camping trip. Driving through the slopes and valleys, with their cattle farms and orchards, reminded me of my youth in the European foothills of Poland. Our favorite streams were the East Koy and Wiscoy, two gentle, spring-fed freestone streams that harbored wild brown trout that relished mayfly hatches. These little streams had diversified mayfly hatches, and they also had large black and

As long as I've trout fished, whether it be at a covered bridge on New York's Willowemoc or under the Whirlpool Bridge of the mighty Niagara, bridges have always brought me leviathan fish. Bridges come in different sizes and shapes. Here on New York's Wiscoy Creek, they are simple concrete structures carrying farm roads. If you want to catch a big trout, always consider bridges. LUCAS CARROLL

Bridges are leviathan trout magnets for all the reasons I describe, but they also make casting and presentation a nightmare. An on-your-knees approach is often necessary, along with a sidearm cast. I have found the single-handed Snap-T Spey cast to be the most effective. Point your rod at the water's surface to generate the cast's low-profile clockwise wrist snap horizontally. JAY NICHOLS

golden stoneflies. It was here that I learned of the power of night fishing.

The Albro Bridge was my workshop. It was nothing but a dirt road in the middle of a cow pasture, but the old concrete bridge spanned a deep pool on Wiscoy Creek. Fishing to the finicky wild trout by this bridge taught me how to do a sidearm or slingshot fly cast. It also taught me that bridge pools often harbored more big browns in greater numbers than I originally perceived. Despite brown trout being territorial, they learn to cohabitate together peacefully when given such perfect shelter.

Bridges, like Albro, create their own habitats. Their concrete walls or iron trestles provide excellent surfaces for stoneflies to crawl up on and hatch, they often have undercut banks where the water had worked against the foundation that large trout love, and the concrete and iron structure attract mayflies that have just hatched in the dark and will molt from adult to spinner. They would stay in the cool, moist shade of the bridge, especially on warm summer days. The rafters of the bridge housed tiny field mice, which occasionally fell into the water and created another huge meal for the carnivorous browns. There are also

small snakes around bridges. For a large brown trout, bridges are the ultimate hunting ground.

Night fishing the giant black stonefly hatch in summer also showed me how P/D trout set their clocks to become A/A nocturnal feeders. When I worked second shift in a small factory while in college, I usually quit around 10 o'clock in the evening. I would get in my old Buick and drive to the Albro Bridge, which took me about an hour and a half. I wouldn't start fishing until midnight. Then I would break out size 2-4 Brooks and Kaufmann stonefly patterns. What looked like a bridge pool devoid of trout by day turned into a monster den at night. Multiple 18- to 22-inch brown trout nights happened when the magical stonefly hatch was occurring. Fishing with heavy tippet, I would hook the fish from the top of the bridge, and run along the side to the low ground to land them and photograph them.

Not only do bridges provide cover, but there are other facets that make them prime habitat for lunkers. State fish agencies, which are often short on manpower, love to pull up their trucks to bridges and just dump fish in the river. The newly stocked trout are a delight for a large, lurking, carnivorous brown trout and can take it from the P/D to the A/A phase in an instant.

Eventually the stocked survivors will find refuge in the pools and cover, thus also becoming big brown trout. During mating season, trout will imprint to the gravel where they were hatched or to the place they were stocked. Thus some trout are just going home to their natal roots, which for many is the bridge from which they were released and spent their first few weeks.

Night-Stalking Tips

Ever since the late great Pennsylvania author and fly fisherman Jim Bashline wrote *Night Fishing for Trout* and *The Fly Fishing Bible* in the 1970s, night fishing for large trout has been an extremely productive technique that a few die-hard trophy hunters have pursued with passion and cultlike obsession. I was glued to both those books as a teen growing up and fishing the Allegheny foothills of western New York. There the night game and its tactics were the subjects of small talk in barbershops and bait shops, but the night-stalking gurus were tight-lipped about how to do it right. Night fishing is a powerful method when P/D trout of summer shut down completely during the heat of the day. Water temperatures can get uncomfortably warm as the trout wait for the cool nights when the ecosystem's critters come alive. Camping by a stream in summer gives you a sense of how the night is alive with activity.

1. HABITAT/BIG BROWN TROUT WATERS

The legacy of night fishing began on the Pennsylvania–New York border streams and rivers of the Allegheny mountains, where large freestone trout came alive at night and went on the hunt for anything that moved. These were primarily brown trout waters, and A/A browns are notorious nocturnal feeders. These freestone rivers can have marginal trout temperatures in the summer, along with heavy canoe and kayak traffic that puts trout into a P/D mode all day. Some of the smaller creeks are excellent nighttime waters. Combine these waters with nice woody debris, big tree downfalls, undercut banks, and small deep pools in the deep woods, and the setting is perfect. Michigan's Pere Marquette and Au Sable Rivers, Pennsylvania's Potter County streams, and the Ausable of New York are ideal waters for big flies and big browns.

Tailwaters are usually cold and have trout feeding all day. But when they are running low (no coldwater generation) and with warmer temperatures, the big pools and runs on the easily navigated tailwaters can get some big nighttime brown trout action.

2. SCOUTING IT OUT

Stories of big night fish are always told at fly shops. Getting in on the gossip and skinny is a good place to start. Go visit the rivers by day and look for wooded or rocky structures with pools. Make sure you have good, easily navigated paths and perhaps even carry some reflective orange tape with you to mark trees in case you get lost. Using the navigation features on your smart phone is a good idea; make sure you use it by day to see how it directs you. Also check for posted property signs. The last thing you need is a state trooper waiting for you at your vehicle when you return. Bridges are powerful big-trout magnets at night.

3. DRESS REHEARSAL

Once you target these perfect night pools, go there and practice your casts and presentations during the day. Look for backcast obstacles like trees. Learn how to toss an underhand bridge cast or figure out how to cast tight to the logjams where the fish hang out. Measure how much line and leader you will need by marking the correct lengths with fluorescent Sharpies or thin tape. If you wade, make sure your entrance to the water doesn't have sharp dropoffs. Mark the spots where you will stand while casting and note what the water is like downstream, along with obstructions like mid-stream boulders or stumps that the trout must be turned away from during a fight.

4. TACKLE

Battling big trout that need to be tamed quickly calls for short, stiff 9-foot, 5- through 7-weight rods with short leaders and heavy tippets. Night fish aren't as leader-shy as they are during the day, so 6- to 10-pound, 1X or 2X tippets are the norm. A good drag on a large arbor is important; there will be no palming as you use two hands on the rod handle and butt to steer your fish. Make sure your knots are ultrasecure and your hook points are sharpened. RIO's glow-in-the-dark lines are perfect on really dark moonless nights. But they spook fish during a full moon. Make sure your lines are weight-forward in order to cast big flies.

Leave the small fly patterns at home. Big browns have been known to eat mice, snakes, and even small ducks at night. If it moves and it can fit in their mouths, they will eat it. Baitfish, small trout, crayfish, big mayflies, stoneflies, and the above-mentioned critters are all part of the mix. Hellgrammites, dobsonflies, big moths, and hoppers and cicadas are game.

The Big Hole is perhaps Montana's most beautiful river, and it holds trophy trout. When waters are low, careful presentation is required. GREG THOMAS

5. PRESENTATION

On big freestoners and tailwaters the down-and-across big wet-fly approach imitates a host of emerging and swimming big flies, plus it appeals to the search-and-destroy instinct of A/A night-feeding trout. Streamer-stripping large roadkill patterns and mice calls for throwing the patterns next to the structure and stripping to create waking and noise against the surface. You can't be loud enough here because trout use their sensory vibration detection to night feed. During big mayfly hatches, the complex mix of emerger, adult, and spinner all enter the same S/R conundrum so drag-free floats and perhaps a twitch here and there are needed to imitate the natural. The fussy nature of trout doesn't disappear at night. Waking a big Morrish surface stone or a Wulff is perfect when there is no hatch.

6. DETECTING STRIKES

When fishing a hatch, both the sound of a slurping fish and the gentle tug on the line in your fingers signal the take. Lift the rod and set the hook if the slurping or gulping sound is near where you think your fly is. On the wet-fly swing the fish hooks itself; just a gentle tightening of the line does the trick. Streamer fishing

can be tricky, as the fish often miss the fly since you are moving it fast and under little light. If you bump a fish and it doesn't take, cast again and again. It's likely the fish hit the fly, tail rabbit, or marabou and wasn't pricked. Even a pricked fish at night will return to the fly again since it is so A/A in nature. Cloudy overcast nights are best. No wind is preferred since riffles and wakes spook even nighttime fish and make it difficult to detect fish takes by sound and feel.

7. FIGHTING NIGHT FISH

Once hooked on your trophy, take control and steer it from the cover and debris that you scouted out during the day and that the trout will seek immediately. There is no time for gentle play here. Your careful selection of tackle and knots must be trusted. Use a long extension net to land the trout. The worst thing is for the fish to come off next to shore as you dally around to net it.

8. NIGHT SAFETY

Carry your cell phone in a sealed container. Have a wading staff in case you fall into a quicksand sinkhole. The new powerful small halogen flashlights are a must, along with a headlamp. If you can afford infrared glasses, great. Wade only in waters that were scouted out during the day. If drift boating, make the trip several times by day to know the obstacles and obstructions. Realize that the boat's oars and your paddling send sound waves, as does the dropping of the anchor. Be aware of your sound footprint. Don't shine the light on your pool since it can put cautious browns down for the night.

Flipping the Switch

My most consistent success with getting trout out of the P/D state revolves around a series of techniques that I have developed over many years that I call flipping the bipolar switch. Often it is just a matter of slowing down and resting the pool and/or fish, showing the fish something new, exciting, and invigorating in fly or presentation, or returning to the stream at a time when the fish is more likely to be a taker, like at dawn or dusk or a cool summer morning. Waiting for the warmest part of the day in cold winter and spring conditions or a huge cold front storm in the heat of summer can see the P/D switch reversed.

Once you target a listless P/D fish, try sight-nymphing minutiae with light fluorocarbon tippets. The persistent "right on the nose" presentation of a size 20 midge larva or scud can get a quick snap-at-it reaction by the trout, which won't budge an inch to take a fly like it does when normal feeding occurs. Try a big dry fly that goes against the grain of the hatches that are normally present. A large streamer that consistently torments a stationary P/D trout sometimes arouses the dormancy for a quick strike on a down-and-across strip. Most often the fish will target the streamer as it swings away from it downstream.

Watch the Weather

Sometimes a break in the weather pattern can flip the switch. One time back in the 1980s on the Big Hole River, I had two days in August to float with an outfitter called, appropriately, Wise Outfitters. "Fishing has been really tough," the outfitter said when I called. "No one has been catching anything with the real bad drought we have been having. Hell, we even stop fishing for a long time. You still want to go?" "I'm booked, I'm here, and I'm going!" I said with some enthusiasm.

A big cold front with pounding rain finally relieved the P/D phase of the trout, as relief came in both cooler

When large trout assume the P/D mode during the day, anglers typically wait for evening for a hatch or to throw streamers. We are often duped into thinking that trout are lethargic and don't seek food on a bright sunny day—a big misconception. This massive Delaware brown was stalked in skinny water by selectivity guide and expert John Miller as it was scavenging for wiggling Iso nymphs that preferred the warmer, shallow waters on a river that runs extremely cold (40 to 50 degrees) even on a blistering July afternoon. MATT SUPINSKI

water and a massive stonefly hatch, and a rising off-color water that gave the pent-up browns A/A hunting security. The big selective browns lost their minds and went on the hunt to compensate for all the weeks they lived in the P/D phase. The final tally was seventeen brown trout landed in the 16- to 25-inch range. As a Brit would say, "That is just not cricket, is it?"

The San Juan Shuffle

An abundance of food can flip the switch. The San Juan Worm is world famous. It's a wormlike fly with a red chenille body that resembles the aquatic worms that live in the silt bottom of the San Juan River. The fly was developed by Paul Pacheco in the 1960s. The trout fancy them, especially when worms are abundant, but rarely are they a big component of the river's biodrift since they dig into the mud of the river bottom. So how do you generate an abundance of the silt-burrowing worm? You dig, kick, and shuffle them up! Enter the San Juan Shuffle, the fly fisherman's contribution to the world of chumming. This tactic is against the law and you will be cited if a conservation officer sees you doing it. Even extremely fussy, size 28

Montana's other jewel, the Madison River, is known for its trophy browns and rainbows that love taking big streamers and large stoneflies. GREG THOMAS

midge larva-eating trout love to take the San Juan Worm regardless of how satiated and P/D they are.

A more natural "chum line" can occur during a heavy hatch. A sudden biological drift of nymphs or larvae, coinciding with a fast spring warm up or a cold snap and storm in summer can quickly spur massive feeding. A sudden temperature inversion in a lake or dam impoundment can cause a massive release of freshwater shrimp and *Daphnia* on a tailwater. The same inversion can kill and stun baitfish, which fuels the switch in trout behavior. A sudden flash flood can scour the river bottom, especially when mayfly and caddis nymphs are mature, and send them downriver in massive quantities rather than their typical gradual emergence.

I recall the good old days on the "ditch section" of Pennsylvania's Big Spring. The trout here were ultra-selective, as I consistently allude to, but became extremely P/D when satiated. The old primetime polluter—the hatchery—was churning out nutrient loads like a Purina food factory. The feces of hundreds of millions of trout were channeled through the affluent conduit pipe like demi-glace. The decaying clumps of fecal matter held tons of chironomid midges and sow

bugs. These morsels were referred to as "cream pancakes." Thus enter the Pennsylvania Honey Bug, a pattern every Pennsylvania trout fisherman is aware of. Often the sullen and dour fish would take my version of the Honey Bug, my Big Spring Mouse, regardless of how well-fed they were. Below the private trout hatchery on Nelson's Spring Creek in Montana they loved it just as much. Many a good old boy from Pennsylvania, fishing heavy 3X tippet, would catch these large P/D browns and rainbows with this pattern when everyone was flogging the trout with 8X and size 28 midges with no success.

Another bipolar selectivity oddity is a big Olive Bugger, fished dead-drifted to schools of nymphing and bulging San Juan fish. "Light Olive Buggers? No way!" you are thinking. But many of the San Juan's large rainbows and browns have learned to eat pieces of algae and vegetation, which are chock full of Blue-Winged Olive nymphs and midge larvae. Why take one fly when you could take one hundred? Not all fish have figured this one out, but the ones that have are real pigs. I have had the same luck on Western spring creeks where the trout have learned this high-calorie food form.

Favorite A/A Trout Flies

3-D PLUSH SCULPIN

(Roman Moser, Austria)

Thread: Tan 55-decitex Power Silk or GSP
Front hook: #4 Dohitomi Saltwater or short shank #2 Aberdeen
Tail hook: #4-6 VMC Octopus (or similar)
Connector: Gray Hareline Senyo's Intruder Trailer hook wire
Fins: Peach Poly Fiber
Body/Head: Sheep wool, polyamid, or polypropylene fibers cut with Exacto knife or razor; splay out material with metal comb; use black marker for banding
Tail: Any color Poly Fiber (tapered) and some Micro Pearl Flashabou fibers
Weight: Gold Hareline Faceted Slotted Tungsten Bead (5.5 mm)
Belly: Peach or pale pink Glo-Bug Yarn
Eyes: Agate Clear Cure Adhesive eyes (5/16), or Ice Fish-Skull Living Eyes; superglue and light epoxy finish

Notes: This Roman Moser creation is without a doubt the most lifelike in shape, silhouette, and color combination of any sculpin pattern. Sculpins, due to their bottom-dwelling, scurry-and-hide behavior, love boulders, undercut banks, and vegetation cover. This fly is deadly on alpine freestoners and limestone spring creeks where clear water allows trout to inspect the flies carefully. Letort brown trout love this pattern. On Fox's Meadow, where the trout of the Letort are easily spooked, I had a 20-inch brown chase the pattern from one bank to the next for about ten feet. It jumped from one weed channel to the other as I furiously stripped the fly back toward me.

COHEN'S DOUBLE-D RAINBOW TROUT

(Pat Cohen, New York)

Back hook: Mustad 2/0 34007
Tail: Four green or white schlappen feathers, white bucktail, lime-green and red Flashabou, Pearl Krystal Flash
Connector: White Senyo's Intruder Wire with eight red and white glass beads
Front hook: #2/0 Mustad 34007
Top wings: Pink and green bucktail with pearl Krystal Flash
Side/Cheek: Grizzly hackle feathers with mallard cheek
Underwing: Pink and green bucktail with red or pearl holographic Flashabou
Eyes: 1/2-inch Clear Cure Eyes
Head: Clear Cure Goo hydro

Notes: Use this pattern on rivers that are heavily stocked with fingerling and yearling rainbow trout, especially the big tailwaters of the White, Cumberland, and Muskegon. Large A/A browns have a nose for newly stocked and dumb rainbows and follow the hatchery trucks like bait fisherman and herons, quickly taking advantage of naïve, newly stocked fish trying to figure out their new and unfamiliar home. It is also a great pattern for sea- and lake-run browns all over the world since these A/A carnivores never lose their taste for fish flesh and often get harassed and annoyed by young river trout.

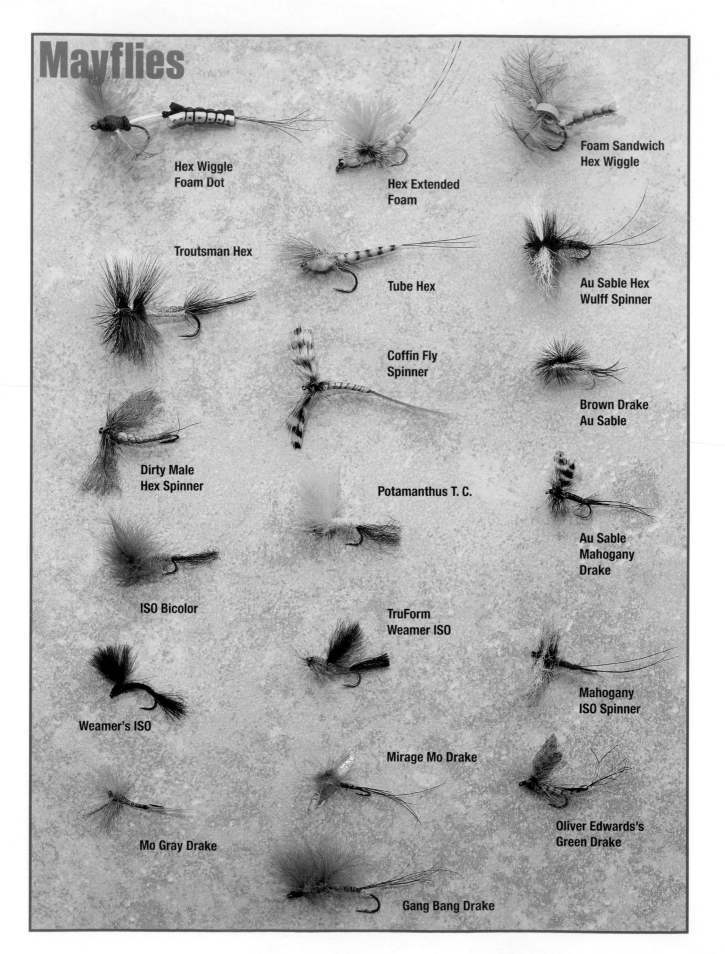

Mayflies

Hex Wiggle
Foam Dot

Hex Extended
Foam

Foam Sandwich
Hex Wiggle

Troutsman Hex

Tube Hex

Au Sable Hex
Wulff Spinner

Coffin Fly
Spinner

Brown Drake
Au Sable

Dirty Male
Hex Spinner

Potamanthus T. C.

Au Sable
Mahogany
Drake

ISO Bicolor

TruForm
Weamer ISO

Weamer's ISO

Mahogany
ISO Spinner

Mirage Mo Drake

Mo Gray Drake

Oliver Edwards's
Green Drake

Gang Bang Drake

COHEN'S DEER HAIR MOUSE

(Pat Cohen, New York)

Hook: 3/0 Mustad 34007
Tail: Rabbit strip; 50-pound mono loop
Bottom body: White deer hair spun
Top body: Natural deer belly hair spun and trimmed
Whiskers: Pheasant tail
Ears: Tan Rainy's foam (2 mm), cut in circle and folded
Eyes: Red with black pupil Clear Cure Monster Eyes (15 mm)
Underbelly: Clear Cure Goo (thin); cover belly for slick finish

Notes: This is a killer pattern for low-light trout around the world. The mouse often is just the right size for a big meal for an A/A predator.

SENYO'S TRUTTANATOR SCULPIN

(Greg Senyo, Lake Erie)

Trailer hook: Daiichi 2557
Thread: Tan 3/0 UNI
Connector: Olive Senyo's Intruder Wire
Body on back hook: Pearl Hareline Ice Dub
Zonker body: Green rabbit strip barred black
Top hook: Green Senyo's Articulated Intruder

Main body: Bottom is orange Hareline Ice Dub trimmed flat; head is pearl Ice Dub and brown Ice Dub sculpin head barred with a black marker
Legs: Lime/black Hareline Crazy Legs
Eyes: Ice Fish-Skull Living Eyes

Notes: This streamer is deadly for A/A lake- and sea-run brown trout, as well as for resident trout who relish deep water and river sculpins and who always seem to have a huge appetite. Since the sea- and lake-run browns seem to have even slower attack speeds than a steelhead, the sculpins swim at just the right speed.

MORRISH HOPPER

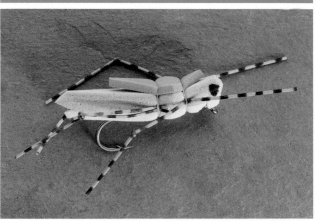

(Ken Morrish, Oregon)

Hook: Dai-Riki 730
Thread: Tan 140-denier UTC Ultra Thread
Foam: Yellow Rainy's foam bottom (2 mm, 4 mm, 6 mm), tan or green foam hopper body, orange foam top post indicator (cut with double-edge razor blades)
Legs: Gray/black Montana Fly or Hareline Grizzly Barred hopper legs
Eyes: Black marker

Notes: Hopper fishing can be a frenzied affair on big, wide-open rivers like the Yellowstone or the Snake. On those waters rainbows and cutthroat can throw discretion to the wind. But for ultrafussy spring creek trout, details are critical even when the fish are on the A/A hunt. Morrish's Hopper is one of the most effective and realistic hoppers I've used and can be tailored to match the various colors of Orthoptera by varying the foam and the synthetic legs. Present it with a plop, a gentle twitch, or a drag-free float depending on what the trout prefer. It is effective later in the season when trout become more critical.

Freestone Dry/Prospecting

Mr. Rapidan Parachute

Mr. Rapidan Traditional

Adams Deer Hair

Dark Wulff

Usual

Ausable Bivisible

Haystack

Ausable Wulff

Au Sable MI Madame X

Au Sable MI Green Madame X

Au Sable MI Black Caddis

Ausable Caddis

Mahogany Borchers

Au Sable MI Haystack

Béliveau's Gaspé Wulff

Au Sable MI Patriot

EP SHAD/ALEWIFE

(Pat Cohen, New York)

Thread: White 95-denier Lagartun X-Strong
Back hook: #4 Mustad 34007
Tail: 50-pound mono with EP Fibers wire connection

Front hook: #2 Mustad 34007
Body: Black, white, gray, yellow, or blue EP Fibers
Cheek: Pink Magic Marker with black dot
Eyes: Fish-Skull Living Eyes or Clear Cure Eyes

Notes: This is a lethal pattern when alewives or shad are spilling over reservoir dams on the Delaware or being chomped through turbines on the White. The pattern's articulation provides movement and vibration, especially when used with a Petitjean Magic Head to give the strip, jerk, and pause added attraction to baitfish-hunting trout. It works on sea- and lake-run trout, landlocked Atlantics, and fresh-run steelhead.

Even though A/A trout feed ravenously on baitfish they are still discriminating and pick up prey features such as a dot by the gill plates, the eye, and other discernible details. The more realistic the pattern the more effective it is, especially in clear waters of the Great Lakes and some tailwaters.

HEXAGENIA EXTENDED PARACHUTE

(Author)

Hook:	Daiichi D1280-2X
Thread:	Beige 95-denier Lagartun X-Strong
Tail:	Moose mane
Bottom body:	Yellow deer hair
Top body:	Olive deer hair
Rib:	Olive 95-denier Lagartun
Post:	White calf tail
Parachute:	Brown grizzly or badger hackle

Notes: With its origins on the fabled Au Sable River of Michigan, which has one of the largest and most storied *Hexagenia* hatches in the world, the deer-hair Hex has become the standard since Richards and Swisher perfected its design in *Selective Trout*. An extended body on larger mayflies gives the adult body a natural looking curve. Deer hair is buoyant and creates a durable pattern that floats well and catches many fish without falling apart (nobody likes to change flies in the total darkness). The rib is important: keep threads on top of each other to form distinct banding. Use 1X mono for the extension tied off the back of the hook. Take the yellow deer hair in a half-pencil-sized clump and tie in at the top of the hook by the eye base hairs first. Fold them backward and pinch at hook gape as you rib backward the thread to form the banding.

MORRISH'S FLUTTERING STONEFLY

(Ken Morrish, Oregon)

Hook:	Daiichi D1280
Thread:	Red 3/0 UNI
Body:	Brown and tan foam (2mm)
Rib:	Red 3/0 UNI
Legs:	Brown or black Hareline Flutter round rubber, knot-tied at joints
Back wing:	J:son stonefly wings (large)
Indicator wing:	Orange Hi-VIZ
Wing case and head:	Brown and tan foam (2mm)

Notes: This pattern's foam shape mimics the natural's, and it is deadly for stoneflies (East and West), cicadas, and hoppers. It signals big food. If you are looking for one fly pattern to get trout out of the P/D funk, this could do it!

Night Uglies and Mice

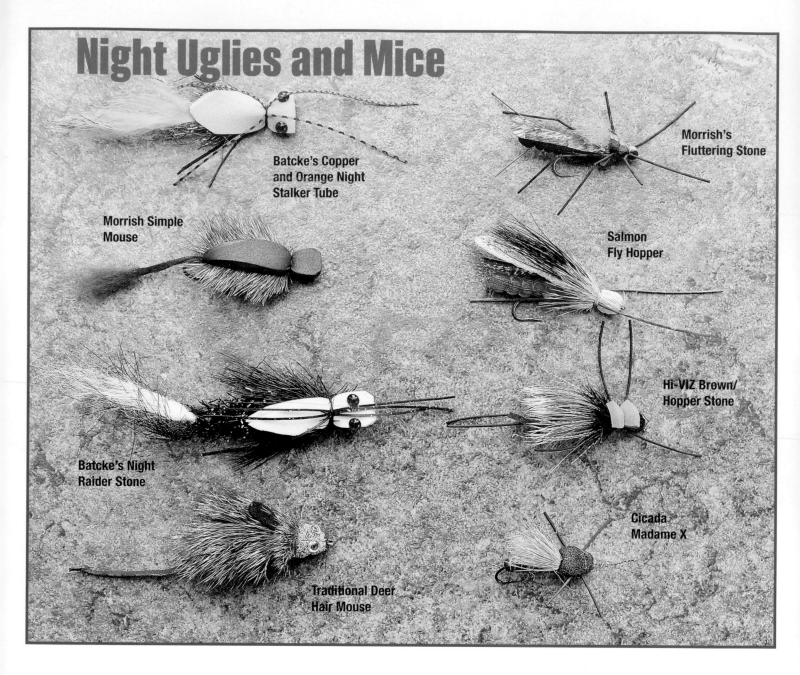

Batcke's Copper and Orange Night Stalker Tube

Morrish's Fluttering Stone

Morrish Simple Mouse

Salmon Fly Hopper

Batcke's Night Raider Stone

Hi-VIZ Brown/ Hopper Stone

Traditional Deer Hair Mouse

Cicada Madame X

Trout Streamers/Sculpins

Sculpin
Hammer

Mike's
Mufasa

Senyo's
Truttanator

Mike's Red
Rocket

Scott's Green
Butt Monkey

Morrish
Sculpin

Moser's
3-D Plush
Sculpin

Mike's
Butter
Churn

Terrestrials

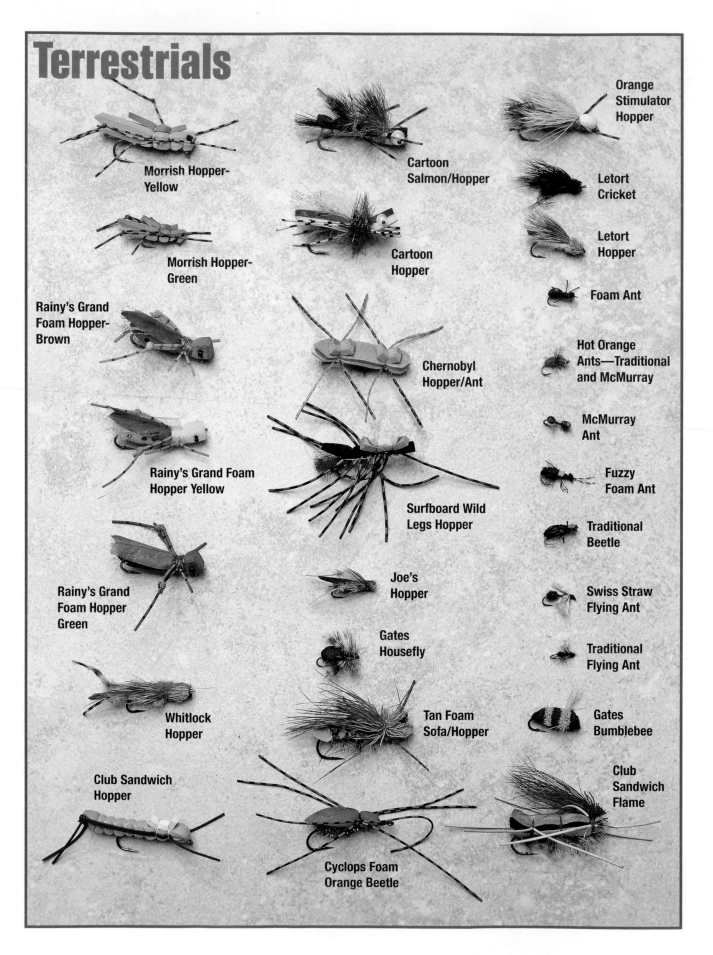

Morrish Hopper-Yellow

Morrish Hopper-Green

Rainy's Grand Foam Hopper-Brown

Rainy's Grand Foam Hopper Yellow

Rainy's Grand Foam Hopper Green

Whitlock Hopper

Club Sandwich Hopper

Cartoon Salmon/Hopper

Cartoon Hopper

Chernobyl Hopper/Ant

Surfboard Wild Legs Hopper

Joe's Hopper

Gates Housefly

Tan Foam Sofa/Hopper

Cyclops Foam Orange Beetle

Orange Stimulator Hopper

Letort Cricket

Letort Hopper

Foam Ant

Hot Orange Ants—Traditional and McMurray

McMurray Ant

Fuzzy Foam Ant

Traditional Beetle

Swiss Straw Flying Ant

Traditional Flying Ant

Gates Bumblebee

Club Sandwich Flame

Steelhead

I am convinced that the steelhead, like all the rest, are at times motivated by agitation, anger, territorial protection, curiosity, sex, hunger, instinctual imprinting. Or fear. It could be a blending of those so subtle and intertwined it will never be completely unraveled. It is indeed the mystery grab.

Lani Waller, *Wild Steelhead and Atlantic Salmon Magazine*

I've been fly fishing for steelhead since the age of six. I've been drawn to these fish in a spiritual way. The majestic steelhead rainbow trout represents the three selectivity phases in overdrive. If one fish had the ability to be totally concentrated and focused on the A/A mode, it would be the steelhead. That they can be coaxed to take a fly several times in the same day has also given them a "dumb" label by those who don't understand the fish. Their extreme aggressive behavior leads them to strike the fly a majority of the time. But those diehard aficionados that

The art of steelhead fly fishing lies in the transcendental realm of waiting for a grab. It becomes the ultimate test of mental discipline—a thousand casts to a fish that does not need to feed in the river on a daily basis. JEFF BRIGHT

Steelhead Selectivity

A/A
Fresh fish new to the river

Alpha males that are jousting for dominance

Rivers on the spate, rising and slightly off-color

Target your fishing around full moon cycles

S/R
Fish have been in the river for a while; settled in and more cautious

Feed on nymphs, larvae, and eggs

Use small patterns, fished slowly

Most active during the sweet time from 2 p.m. to dark

P/D
No feeding or dominant behavior (when trout are biting in steelhead lies you know this phase is occurring)

Unstable weather and barometric pressure; extreme weather conditions

Result of extreme angling pressure and susceptibility to catch-and-release for prolonged periods of time ■

know steelhead—both West Coast and Great Lakes—know these fish can turn S/R and P/D in a heartbeat. They can also remain in those states for a long time, leaving you skunked on a fishless day. Hence the nickname "fish of a thousand casts." Or sometimes the first cast! These qualities often make steelhead difficult to decipher, but this puzzle, this uncertainty, is part of the mind game known as steelheading.

No fish other than a steelhead can leap from A/A to S/R to P/D states in the blink of an eye. The dual personalities of the steelhead are to blame. The mature, giant chrome warrior of the big oceans and lakes is combined with the precious childlike curiosity of small river rainbows to create a fish that can be at times stubborn and impossible, other times playful, and sometimes easy to catch.

A/A States

Fresh-run fish from the ocean or lake—on the Dean River in British Columbia, for example, or on New York's Salmon River off of Lake Ontario—are exclusively in the A/A state as a result of the predator hunting drive needed in the big open water. Such fish have the mindset to eat everything in their path. Vertebrate, invertebrate—if it moves and it's smaller than the steelhead, the fish eats it. Once in the natal river system, where their youthful encounters with insects and other prey forms bring back memories of hunting in the

The steelhead/Atlantic salmon game is a battle of wills, patience, cunning, maneuverability, chances, risks, new calculations, and often unpredictable moments—often brilliantly fused together to create success or utter catastrophe. But with each passing year success becomes more steady and predictable. ANDREW BENNET

Michigan rivers produce six million wild Chinook salmon by natural reproduction. By mid-February, the fry hatch and the aggressive, dominant steelhead males and females are driven crazy by the constant intrusion. At this time they crush sac fry patterns.
MATT SUPINSKI

rivers, the steelhead recognizes prey forms that it has not focused on for years while it was out in the big seas.

Ocean and lake steelhead have a higher diversity of food forms to prey on compared to their cousins the Pacific salmon, which are actually quite particular about what they eat. The latter usually target a select group of pelagic baitfish and crustaceans that are to their liking and are easy to capture through the salmon's pack hunting methods. Steelhead, having slower attack speeds (7 to 12 mph, versus a salmon's quick and agile 35 mph), must be more opportunistic in their predator behavior in order to capitalize in a consistent manner. The A/A behavior regularly comes out throughout a steelhead's river occupation, primarily during stable water flows and barometric pressure readings.

The most prized river spots—the primary, or alpha, lies—are held in high esteem by steelhead and anglers from year to year and generation to generation. These spots attract large alpha A/A fish because of their perfect hydrological and habitat makeup: they are inside or outside bends with jagged boulders and rocks for current deflection and adjacent deep pools and runs with perfect seam water, which has fast- and slower-water holding capabilities. These lies prompt the fish to be curious and aggressive, with each facet playing off the other. In a river world of competitive dominance, the steelhead that occupies these prime lies is destined to be an A/A ravenous beast whether it likes it or not. It must take the throne and guard it, warding off any other subordinate fish who want the spot.

The prime pool guts, buckets, and sweet spots of a run or the moderately deep pool or pocket water, preferably next to obstruction cover like woody debris, bridge abutments, dams, and deep water, are usually primary winter steelhead holding spots. On smaller rivers these spots can be two to four feet deep; on big rivers, six to twelve feet deep. The insides and outsides of river bends are home to these jagged river-bottom rock contours, which act as current deflection for the trout's additional comfort. When looking for these prime holding lies, keep in mind that the slower-swimming steelhead's preference is for a moderate water speed—not too slow, not too fast.

A/A behavior shifts during seasons and to different lies. Secondary lies are secondary choices or moving water. This is usually water with gradient elevation coupled with boulder-strewn or pocket or bucket water, where some concerted effort by the steelhead is required to hold there. They are highly utilized as migration staging areas and are only deemed secondary because the comfort-loving steelhead generally prefers more subtle flows. During the summer and fall runs, when water temperatures can be on the warm side, these areas are infused with oxygen. They also contain much of the insect and sculpin life of the river. Together with tailouts, they comprise the gravel spawning areas of salmon and brown trout in the fall and steelhead in late winter and spring. These are primary hunting lies for A/A steelhead—particularly in Great Lakes fish—which will conduct the bulk of their salmon egg binge-eating frenzy here, but will always have escape plans to a pool below.

When steelhead spawn and are sight-nymphed with egg or nymph fly patterns—again a Great Lakes tradition—they switch from extremely A/A behavior to the complete opposite P/D behavior. Here their preoccupation with spawning can keep their mouths zipped tight, or just the opposite. Males will begin attacking each other near gravel areas around mid-February, particularly in the Great Lakes on rivers that have the tremendous salmon fry hatching that steelhead devour.

Steelhead will go to tertiary lies for refuge from extreme angling pressure, water conditions like floods, and predators. The steelhead will either be S/R or P/D here. Many times we just wade past these spots heading to the primary locations. They are usually in shallow or obstruction-filled water next to the primary lies, sometimes several bends up- or downstream. These can take the form of shallow, rocky sections than most anglers wade through to get to the primary pool.

All primary, secondary, and tertiary lies require jagged rock and gravel bottoms with good foam bubble line flows. These foam lines funnel the current and oxygen, and also create creases and seams of comfort and resting lies along the demarcation areas of current and slack water, which all migratory salmonids use for comfort and metabolic preservation. Steelhead, with their more lazy stream-life disposition, love to glide between these two areas.

A/A behavior is highly prized for the "big bite," but it doesn't last as long as we anglers would like it to. Those multiple-fish days are few and far between—

and I'm so happy about that. It gives us more respect for the fish and allows us to hone our skills and craft to a higher level, which gives us a higher degree of satisfaction when a steelhead is caught. If steelhead were in the A/A mode all the time, they would lose the appeal and challenge the sport brings. In my opinion, it is the anticipation of the "pull," the searching and reading of the water, and the endless skunked days spent trying to understand the mind of a nomadic warrior steelhead that give us extreme pleasure once we capture a magnificent trophy fish by doping out all the tactics—both mental and fly presentation—necessary for success.

Selective/Reflective States

In the S/R state, a steelhead goes from a big piscivore hunter to a gentle observer of its new river world and its regime. It now acts much like a trout; but unlike a trout, which has to go about the day foraging for substance, a steelhead doesn't have to feed—it seems to do so on a whim, a mysterious impulse. In the S/R mode, steelhead are like felines playing with their food.

Once a steelhead is in a holding lie, the biological drift of insects, sculpins, and baitfish piques the fish's S/R inquisitive interest. Prime times of the day do the same. It can be dawn, dusk, or the middle of the warm afternoon on a cold January day, when the waters warm a degree or two and send the biological drift into a springlike state of arousal. Midge larvae, stonefly nymphs, and crustaceans scurry about, basking in the two-degree increase.

S/R steelhead can occupy all holding lies. When the steelhead is most secure, it feels dominant in its hierarchical standing among the other fish of the pool. Or perhaps it has been hooked before, which is when the S/R mode manifests itself best. This is where steelheading becomes closer to trout fishing, a thinking man's game that I love.

Passive/Dormant States

As much as we know steelhead to be aggressive and selective, they can become P/D in extremely cold water or oxygen-depleted hot water. This also occurs if they are startled, if they are saltwater steelhead adjusting to freshwater, or after long, severe migrations, which deplete metabolic energy. But the steelhead's cocky, gregarious, and cavalier personality

A release on the Dean in British Columbia. Time, curiosity, irritation, and persistent fly presentation eventually break down the fish for an A/A attack or bite. Most steelheaders and guides can neither handle the mind game nor have the necessary patience to hunt selective steelhead. They jump around the rivers in their jet and drift boats like whirling dervishes. ANDREW BENNETT

doesn't like the P/D stage for too long. Knowing when your attempts at P/D fish are futile saves you much aggravation. Go tie flies, take a nap, or read a fly-fishing book. Resume fishing at dusk or at first light, or wait for conditions to improve.

The Codes of Hunting and Migration

Oncorhynchus mykiss, the modern-day steelhead, evolved around two million years ago in the rivers and streams around the Gulf of California. Thought to be descendants of the various red-band rainbow trout species, the pure ancient steelhead lived in roughly one hundred small creeks and rivers from the Santa Maria River to Malibu Creek. At one time the runs were in the tens of thousands. Today, they are on the endangered species list in their area of origin; all Southern California steelhead have unique strains and are identified as ecological significant units (ESU). In some creeks, only a dozen fish return each year to spawn and carry on the remaining bloodline. The steelhead spread into the Klamath and McCloud River

systems and eventually to the Columbia River valley thirty thousand to fifty thousand years ago, and they soon spread up the West Coast to British Columbia and all around the Pacific Rim to Russia's Kamchatka Peninsula. At the species' peak, all major river systems and isolated coastal basins held tremendous numbers of steelhead. Today that is not the case. Runs of wild steelhead have peaks and valleys, with the trend toward the latter.

The urge to run rivers and spawn from the big oceans, seas, or the Great Lakes makes anadromous (salt- to freshwater) and potamodromous (freshwater to freshwater) salmonids' lifelong journey for procreation a never-ending quest. Millions of years of intricate timing and navigation have made steelhead and salmon evolutionary successes. Their finely tuned biological clocks help them arrive at spawning grounds hundreds of miles upstream at the same time, allowing them to spawn and carry on their unique genetic code.

Natal imprinting to river food forms teaches the young salmonids predatory behavior, hierarchy-based feeding and pecking orders, and the importance of fleeing from danger. One need only watch a small

Careful commercial fisheries management, catch-and-release protection of wild steelhead strains, and the closure of key rivers to fishing has been vital to protecting wild steelhead on vast river systems like the Skeena in British Columbia, shown here. The Wild Steelhead Coalition has been a powerful force in the fight to save this magnificent beast. JEFF BRIGHT

school of steelhead fry along the river shoreline feeding on midges and plankton before you'll notice this hierarchical behavioral code developing. The S/R feeding starts here: learning to identify a midge larva versus a piece of weed, for example. Since a wild steelhead will spend up to two to three years in a river system, it will develop all the skills of hunting and selection of an 18-inch resident rainbow trout. Its success here feeding on mayflies, stoneflies, caddis, midges, and other aquatic and terrestrial invertebrates and vertebrates will dictate its aggression or passivity as it hits the wide-open waters of the big seas. Once a steelhead is in its large ocean or Great Lakes environment, hunting prey becomes a combination of learned and innate behavioral factors developed in its earlier river life. These traits will make the fish either an A/A alpha predator or an inferior subordinate that will have little chance of continuing to procreate at a high level and contribute to the gene pool.

As a general rule, the river attributes that allow for a healthy trout stream will provide great conditions for migrating steelhead and salmon. Stable river ecosystems and flows generally yield the healthiest wild steelhead populations. Aquatic vertebrate and invertebrate populations are diverse, thus allowing for

healthy natal imprinting to food forms and the early development of predator skills and familiarity with all three selectivity phases. The greater the predator skills developed by a juvenile steelhead, the more aggressive and selective the fish will be as an adult.

Dystrophic rivers—ones that have lumbered forests, with heavy deciduous and coniferous tree cover along with peat and marl bogs—have a deep tannic tea satin, which is welcomed by the fish populations because it creates a cloaking security blanket and heightens sensitivity to alarm and predation. Here the fish are less wary and can be approached much easier by the fly fisher. Dystrophic rivers also run slightly acidic, favoring the large, shredding insect life like stoneflies—food items highly sought after by parr and adults. These freestone rivers can be excellent habitat. Oligotrophic, volcanic, or calcareous rivers in high alpine environments, such as those found in river systems from British Columbia to Oregon and northern California, have clear water and fish with enhanced selectivity. In the Great Lakes region, Michigan's Platte River is a crystal-clear spring creek with highly wary and selective trout and steelhead. When enough fertility elements kick in—sometimes as a result of hydroelectric dam impoundments, where

these backwaters become infused with plankton and various other nutrients—they can fuel and enhance the insect life below the impoundment dams, thus allowing mayflies, caddis, and stoneflies to proliferate. Here oligotrophic waters of various rock substrata become more fertile and alkaline, especially if they have subterranean calcium carbonate deposits.

Severe "hydroelectric peaking operations," or steep valleys funneling runoff water and forcing fast river flows can scour the benthic environment of aquatic insects and other food forms. They also scour and eliminate silt and clear up much of the spawning gravel necessary for the steelhead. Wild steelhead success is directly related to the abundance of cold, oxygenated gravel nursery waters on the fishes' natal rivers. On Michigan's Muskegon, hydro operations once scoured the river, leaving it infused with steelhead spawning gravel over nearly 95 percent of its length. This created a magnificent fishery.

The Importance of Light (Phototropism)

For steelhead cruising their home hunting grounds of the Pacific Ocean or the Great Lakes, light is everything. Low light allows steelhead a cloaking device to hunt in three ways: pelagic, benthic, and coastal. Due to the slower attack speeds of steelhead, they take

Fly Fisherman magazine editor Ross Purnell with a British Columbia chrome. The gradient will dictate a river's stability or volatility and its propensity for spates and run-off. Washington's Skagit and Sauk Rivers and British Columbia's Dean have a clear bluish color, resulting from diverse oligotrophic infusion from volcanic rocks like black shale, basalt, and limestone, demanding precise presentations when waters are low and fish are wary. STEVE MORROW

what food they can whenever they can. In pelagic baitfish hunting, most of the prey's food, such as plankton, is in the upper water strata. Here the steelhead corral schools of menhaden, alewives, smelt, anchovies, shiners, chubs, and other sardines. At

Steelheading at dawn on the Muskegon River. Steelhead selectivity is heavily tied to phototropism, just as it is with brown trout. Successful steelhead fishing is sometimes impossible in bright sunny conditions, the same as it is for selective and wary brown trout. JOHN MILLER

The intricate circuitry of the neuroendocrine and sensory system allows the fish's lateral line to detect the earth's electromagnetic field for use in cross-ocean migration, making the migrating steelhead and salmon supercomplex organisms. MATT SUPINSKI

Left: If steelhead seem impossible to catch in any given pool or run in the afternoon, try them again at first or last light. You'll be amazed at how aggressive they are at these times and how they'll smash your swinging fly. The scar on this steelhead's side was caused by a lamprey. MATT SUPINSKI

slightly deeper levels, the steelhead target squid, elvers, crabs, sea urchins, jellyfish, large shrimp, and other light-sensitive creatures. When hunting they are opportunistic and feast on sticklebacks, sculpins, gobies, perch, other salmonids and a great host of shallow, warmwater prey. The frequency and efficiency of their big-water hunting shapes their A/A behavior on the return to their natal rivers.

The length of daylight (and moonlight) triggers the steelheads' finely tuned biological clocks, letting them know when it is time for upstream spawning migration. Each trout and salmon has its own photoperiod. Brown trout, Atlantic salmon, and Pacific salmon gen-

erally spawn during the diminishing daylight of fall and winter. Steelhead spawn as daylight increases in late winter; the exception to this is the fall-spawning rainbows found in the Great Lakes tributaries and South American rivers. The incredible neuroendocrine pineal gland is the steelhead and salmon's top-of-the-head dermis window, which allows the fish to be constantly measuring light. With the help of the enzyme HIOMT, the gland regulates the melatonin in the blood that basks all the internal organs. The pineal gland is linked to the optic, olfactory, and lateral sensory lines to perform a biologically specific series of functions that will aid in the fish's migration, river life, spawning, and return to the large seas for future growth and spawning migrations. The melatonin, or lack thereof, speeds up migration or slows it down. On full moons, which are powerful migration igniters, the 24-hour length of light slows melatonin production, thus producing a round-the-clock migration. Always time your steelhead and salmon trips to coincide with full moon cycles.

The optic nerve triggers sexually A/A behaviors by causing a change in the morphology of a steelhead. It is the source of the kyped jaw and the bright red bands and cheeks, and gives the other rainbow trout steelhead an optic signal as the egg and sperm production increases in their bellies. The olfactory mechanism has an incredible capacity to pick up the scent of water in the river to one part per eight million. This gives a steelhead the ability to find its natal river of origin from thousands of miles away at sea and hone into within dozens of feet from where it was born or released as a smolt. Lateral lines can detect the slightest increase of water flow. Thus a small rain or slight increase in river flow will trigger upstream migrations, especially in smaller creeks and rivers close to estuaries, from California to the Great Lakes.

Successful steelhead fishing is sometimes impossible in bright sunny conditions, except when the fish are extremely A/A and near spawning, when there is a tremendous insect hatch, or when the winter sun warms up the water temperatures and slightly perks the fish's metabolism. It can take only a several-degree change in water temperature to do this, particularly in winter. Going from 34-degree water to 36-degree water is a major milestone in the metabolic world of salmonids. The increase in temperatures will encourage insects, sculpins, scuds, and baitfish to scurry around and increase the steelhead's propensity to feed. But, in general, give me a cloudy, rainy, snowy, nasty day.

Besides providing the security and comfort needed for predation, the first light of dawn and the last light of dusk correlate with the fish's nightly migration, which culminates with the fish finding slow-speed current runs and deeper pools for rest and cover. Steelhead and salmon migrate on diminishing light periods. So at dusk, the steelhead that was in its holding lie all day gets antsy and becomes more curious, making for a powerful A/A bite as the fish prepares for upstream migration. As it migrates through the night, melatonin builds up (except during full moons), which will slow the fish down until it finds a holding lie or pool at dawn. A pool void of fish one day can be teeming with steelhead the next.

Low light levels are the signal for a steelhead to begin feeding. Consider the vertical migration of ocean shrimp and Great Lakes *Mysis* shrimp, both highly favored food items of the steelhead. The shrimp migrate to the surface and benthic environments following their prey, zooplankton, based on light levels. The biological time clocks of hunting steelhead, passed down through innate genetic behavior, have been programmed to be on full alert during these low-light periods. The same scenario exists for pelagic baitfish. Both prey and predator are active at night and when their paths cross, it creates A/A predator responses.

Water Temperature

Water temperature is one of the most important variables in speeding up or slowing down a salmonid's metabolism. Steelhead and Atlantic salmon prefer water that is 42 to 58 degrees. However, winter and summer steelhead display incredible variations. Winter steelhead, which run from August through June depending on where in the Western Hemisphere they are found, can exhibit A/A and S/R responses to your fly at water temperatures as low as 32 to 34 degrees. Summer steelhead can tolerate water in the low 70-degree range and can be aggressive if water temperatures range from the mid to upper 60s.

Steelhead will migrate the lowest level of drought-stricken rivers and creeks if water temperatures are perfect. In the fall or spring, water temps are in the ideal 45- to 55-degree migration range. If ocean or lake temperatures align with river temperatures, the scenario will be ideal for upstream migration. Here the shoreline and offshore thermoclines of the ocean or the Great Lakes are in the 45- to 55-degree range and align perfectly with the temperatures in the river-mouth estuaries. This ideal scenario will send steelhead and salmon up the river systems in good numbers because they do not need to make any metabolic adjustments to water temperature.

In the fall of 2010 Lake Michigan tributaries were running extremely low. Everyone including myself thought the run would be poor. River-mouth estuaries had shallow gravel bars that made upstream migrations difficult. But despite the low water flows, large steelhead slithered up the rivers in skinny water and made the 35-mile trek up the Muskegon River. Much to our pleasant surprise, the fishing was exceptionally good. Even though higher water flows and a spate would have helped, ideal temperatures took precedence over flows since the river and lake temperatures aligned perfectly between 48 and 52 degrees.

In 1999 I saw the same thing happen on the Lake Erie tributaries along the "Steelhead Alley," which was running at a trickle. And yet good numbers of steelhead ascended the rivers because of the ideal "magic carpet ride" water temperature range. Here huge schools of steelhead packed the few pools that had enough water depth. When water temps are too cold or too warm, steelhead will become P/D. The metabolic survival mode kicks in when temperatures drop below 32 degrees or exceed 75 degrees; this applies to both winter and summer steelhead. Winterstrain steelhead had evolved to tolerate the lower temperatures in the 30s, while summer strains tolerate the opposite extremes of the lower 70s.

Steelhead Guide Secrets

I spend close to three hundred days a year on the water with these fish. For years, steelhead guiding gave me schizophrenic days filled with elation, defeat, predictions gone wrong, and thoughts of "I thought so," or "the barometer is going up and down like a seesaw." Of course, there are also the "you should've been here yesterday" days. Here are some of the most important lessons I have learned that have helped me catch fish for myself and clients.

BELIEVE

You must believe in your flies, your approach and presentation, your timing, your tackle, your tippet strength and choice of fly lines, and your wardrobe. Neurotic hopping around from pool to pool will lead you to nothing but failure and kill your chances for success, except for the fortunate timing when you stumble on a fresh-run batch of A/A fish. That is a nice but rare bonus in today's heavily fished river systems.

STUDY AND KNOW YOUR RIVER ONE SECTION AT A TIME

The study of steelhead rivers is the study of a lifetime. They are changing worlds of holding lies, structure, newly migrating personalities, and shifting ecosystems. Time spent observing and watching the water will allow you to know the river's secrets. If you're

Dissect each section of the river and observe each section closely. Pretend you have no boat and can wade only a small section of river. Think like a migrating steelhead or salmon would and have confidence in your fly choice. HAKAN STENLUND

confident that steelhead are in the river and you know your holding lies well, you will catch trophy fish eventually. Most steelheaders learn only certain sections of the river and are usually clueless about other sections that may produce fish. You must not be a creature of habit unless you are constantly rewarded from consistent spots. Try to change this. Every other trip, explore new water and try to think like a steelhead by figuring out new holding lies that may have never produced for you in the past.

SLOW DOWN AND REPEAT

By carefully fishing each pool thoroughly and consistently, and varying your approach and time of approach, you will start to catch S/R steelhead more consistently, including more trophy fish, than ever

A Michigan winter buck that crushed a Hang Time Leech at dusk. The "mystery grab" that Lani Waller talked about can be calculated and conjured up by the angler who reads conditions and is in the right place at the right time. MATT SUPINSKI

before. Age and temperance force you to slow down (at least in my case they have). By doing so, you tend to catch more difficult fish.

Here is where I increase my success from year to year. Everybody has been taught that they will have immediate gratification if they hire the right guide, use the right fly, and have the latest high-tech fly rod and reel. This is not so. You're not going to get immediate gratification from a steelhead that has all the time in the world to not take your fly.

Pick two or three runs, pools, or beats each day and give them 110 percent concentration and presentations in different venues. When you are certain fish are there, because you see them or have seen them before, stick with these spots. Never leave fish to find fish. Take hours to fish them thoroughly if they are consistently producing primary alpha lies. These spots remain constants unless there are significant ecosystem changes from floods and droughts, logging, fallen woody debris, or bank erosion, which can cause silting and a hydrological current change. Cover the entire run with each length of your cast and work it down once, twice, and then again at the prime big-

bite hours of dusk and dawn. Some anglers will look at you like you're an idiot when wading or anchoring your boat in the same spot and working the same pool. Don't worry—they have no clue.

The good steelheader stays consistent, will change flies and presentations, and has an open mind, but stays focused on the primary productive water. I can't tell you how often I come into a new run or pool in rotation, after several boats have thrown spawn, hardware, or even flies. Those anglers left hastily and looked disgusted for not hooking anything. I never worry about pressure. I can always come in last and catch fish. This is the confidence I'm talking about. That's steelheading in a clairvoyant way—you must see and envision success.

If I arrive and my favorite pool is occupied by other anglers or boats, I will come back later and rest the pool. Most steelhead anglers only scratch the tip of the iceberg when covering a run or pool because of their impatience and need for a quick hookup. Always remember that being in the water of a beautiful steelhead river, whether it be Cleveland's Rocky River or British Columbia's gorgeous Babine River, your soul and spirit need to be one with your surroundings and the fish. The bite will come.

A GAME OF "PUSH COMES TO SHOVE"

"There can't be steelhead holding in that pool. I fished it all morning!" That's what I usually hear when I drift or jet-sled into one of my favorite pools as a wading angler or other boater is leaving. This is music to my ears! Whether consciously or by innate genetic design, steelhead love playing mind games with their fly-angler pursuers. The cautious yet cocky disposition of S/R steelhead is notorious in clear-water holding positions no matter where they are found, thus challenging your commitment and resolve.

But if you stick with it long enough, rest the pools and runs, and show the fish something different in fly pattern silhouette, design, and sparseness over and over again, inevitably they will make a mistake. They will attack, even if only for a brief moment. They will get their aggressive dander up with each passing swing or drift of the fly, just like in trout fishing where Marinaro talked of the "game of nods."

THE QUIET TIME OF DAY

The magic bite often comes from nowhere, when all is still, calm, and there is no noise or clatter from boats and wading anglers. I will often pull my boat or wade into a pool and do nothing for an hour. I'll have lunch, smoke a cigar, and calm down. When I see eagles, which are normally wary of man's intrusion, flying about my rivers I know success is soon to be had. Steelhead will acclimate to your surrounding and become more aggressive when they feel safe from predators. This feeling of safety is the single-most important situation necessary for success with steelhead, which are more wary than given credit for. This often occurs later in the day when the cars and boats have all left in frustrated disgust after not catching anything. The dusk bite is a powerful period. In the fall and winter it's when the afternoon football games come on, meaning you're more likely to have the water to yourself.

SHOVING AND BULLYING

When I was a soccer player (a center fullback), I loved to do this to my opponents, even at the cost of a yellow or red card. It was intimidating. One thing steelhead have in common with athletes is that they hate to be shoved around! Their serenity and reflection revolves around comfort on their terms in their chosen holding lies. When you methodically work a run or pool from top to tailout, you will eventually push fish down to the trough, bucket, or spot below their lowest possible holding threshold in the primary lie system. It is here, maybe after an hour or so of "pushing them down," that the explosive take or mystery grab will occur. Plug fishermen fishing from drift boats do it all the time. By a series of calculated drops of the anchor, or by wading down the pool in calculated steps and casting distances, you, or someone, will hit the magic button to grab. You do it enough times, the odds will be in your favor.

Scott Howell, the master steelhead guide of the North Umpqua in Oregon, and star of the *Skagit Master 2* DVD series, sums up a steelhead's ego and personality by comparing the fish to Alaskan bears. "If you stand still, chances are they will leave you alone," Howell says. "If you run out and panic, chances are they will attack you! Thus you need to provoke their A/A predator instinct." Here is the fine line between A/A and S/R steelhead behavior. Some of you might think I'm speaking out of both sides of my mouth since I said earlier that the quieter, dusk moments when all is calm bring out the bite, which is true. But on the flip side, a steelhead, like any aggressive animal, doesn't like shoving or bullying. It will cause them to inevitably react and snap back and strike the fly. You just have to try both approaches. Each fish and strain has its own personality based on their evolutionary survival strategy that they developed within their unique ecosystem.

"DRIVE-BYS" AND CLUMSY WADING

I guide on a heavily trafficked Great Lakes steelhead river that can be full of idiots driving jet boats and ripping through your pools, or anglers recklessly wading. Most of these boaters have no idea what they're doing, and the same is true of wading steelhead anglers. There is no need to break your nerves and get your blood pressure up. This sometimes clueless, rude display of non-sporting courtesy is no longer frowned on by me, even when a steelhead angler trashes through my pool like a clumsy rhino. Now I actually welcome it! Sound bizarre? Here's why: when steelhead are in the S/R or P/D mode, an unwelcome intrusion often creates a mystery bite. This continues to amaze me, but the more I see it happen the more I understand the behavioral process of the fish.

When I was a more insecure steelheader, I used to say, "Ah crap, those guys beat me to the pool. They are going to catch all the fish." Not anymore. I always welcome a drift boat pulling plugs such as Hot N Tots. In clear-water S/R steelhead conditions, the plugs will push the fish around, annoy them significantly, and actually do the fly fisher a big favor. Yes, they occasionally pick up a fish, mostly in high-water conditions. But you should always work these pools thoroughly after hardware anglers have molested the steelhead and created an artificially induced A/A antagonistic state in our chrome warriors.

It became clear one November day when I was swinging flies in a great run with Spey casting aficionado clients Phil and George. We had just gotten a "drive-by waking" from a jet boat driver going 50 mph, almost knocking us out of our boat. "That son-of-a-bitch!" Phil said, flashing his Italian temper. "Don't worry," I told him. "Stay focused on the next several swings." Phil looked at me with a crazy glance, thinking I was nuts. Sure enough, on the second cast a steelhead slammed his Hang-Time Leech and went cartwheeling into his backing. Phil couldn't believe it. We fished that spot with more than one hundred casts with no luck until we got the rude drive-by. Phil was baffled, but I've seen this situation play out too many times.

My theory is that the comfortable fish was rudely moved from its primary holding lie into another position, and thus its first response was aggressive and reactive with frustration. This is like trying to get a dog off a comfortable sofa position; it will growl and snap even at its owner. The steelhead, seeing Phil's leech, unleashed the aggressive response of a disturbed fish. The fish most likely did not understand that the commotion and disturbance was caused by the boat. The only thing it had to react to was the fly. So it took out its frustration on the fly. Its aggression is manifested through its mouth, both from feeding and territorial dominance perspectives.

CHANGE FLIES? NOT REALLY!

Every river has its flies that consistently catch steelhead. They vary from one river to the next. They embody the makeup of the river's biological drift and water color and appeal to the steelhead's vision. So you refine your patterns, three or four of them, for continuous success, and stick to them, right? Sort of, but not really.

There is no question that showing the fish something different can be the key, and I strongly urge everyone to experiment. As a guide I have my favorites—all

A/A behavior occurs in deep, dark runs even when pools are waked by boats and stirred up by plug-pullers. As long as no predator is seen or viewed, only perceived through the commotion, aggressive behavior can happen. MATT SUPINSKI

guides do. When a new client shows me his boxes of flies and says, "What about these?" I always respond with, "Sure, let's give it a try!" Not because I'm trying to be a nice guy (most guides try to be) but because the novelty of new patterns sometimes rattles the fish. If you believe strongly that fish are holding in your run, change your favorite fly to something totally different for a short time, but constantly go back your favorite.

This can go on for several changes or for hours, but eventually the fish will be provoked and antagonized enough to take the original fly you chose. I've seen this happen too many times. Fishing a two-fly rig where legal will give you good insight into your fish's selectivity preference and mindset at that season or time of day. In the fall of 2012 the water flows were low, the steelhead run was poor, and the fish were few and far between. Also, the unsportsmanlike practice of chumming—throwing real salmon eggs into the river to coax the steelhead to eat—was made legal again in Michigan after a five-year ban. In these situations, the steelhead become fixated on the "chow line" of eggs tossed by the angler and focus on nothing else at times.

Since I mainly swing flies with two-handers, and it is legal to fish two flies on our rivers, I would rig a large, flashy leech or intruder on top and a dropper Otter Egg about a foot below. This was my attempt to pique the two selectivity profiles of the steelhead. The flash was taken by the fresher-run fish that were not yet tainted by the eggs. The egg was taken by the steelhead that was already exposed to the caviar. It also

A steelhead hopper/dropper rig is deadly for autumn swinging and large, indecisive, S/R winter males. MATT SUPINSKI

defined steelhead personality by gender: 90 percent of the males took the flash, and 70 percent of the females took the egg. Thus it seemed clear to me that males were more aggressive and the females more opportunistic and S/R.

PRESENTATION SPEED AND ANGLES

To S/R steelhead—stubborn ones—change is somewhat essential. Varying your presentation in whatever way possible is often the key to success. As long as it makes sense, approaching a run or pool from a different direction, side of the river, or angle of the swing and drift has produced many hookups that otherwise wouldn't have happened. Guides and anglers are creatures of habit—just look at the footprints along the pools. Speeding up or slowing down your drift or swing by nymphing, swinging, or waking dries is another technique to try after you've exhausted all the possibilities. But you should always return to your primary presentation of choice after you have experimented—persistence and a proven tactic are omnipotent! It is important to start your casts short

and as close to you as possible. Eventually work your presentations outward and downriver in order to not spook fish, which are often laying right under your waders or boat.

"TEASING THE CROC"

This technique has proven itself time and time again for steelhead and Atlantic salmon. In essence, it is provoking the fish to strike. It is simple: assuming you know where your steelhead are holding, but you have not received responses to your presentation, start by giving the fish only quick and minimal glimpses of your offering just as it enters the fish's underwater window.

Pulling the fly out broadside just as it is starting to enter the strike zone may make no sense, but for extremely selective steelhead it is often the ticket to success. As we saw in our studies of refraction and reflection, the fish's window of vision has its limits. Objects outside the window of distortion have double imaging. If you repeatedly present your fly upstream of the window, and cut off its drift or swing several feet upstream of the fish, the fish might catch several glimpses of your fly in a distorted fashion. This might be enough to rouse its curiosity from an S/R state to a more A/A state once it sees the complete fly and drift.

A note here about tippets and knots, because you want to go as light as possible without losing fish to breakoffs. I like a Double Duncan/UNI. By doubling up the line through the eye of the hook you double the breaking strength. But to secure this knot properly you must use saliva on your knot, and once the knot is secure, you must rotate the tag end of your knot three-quarters of a turn to secure it and tighten it. Most people complain about fluorocarbon knot strength, but this is a result of not following the proper tying steps. Though not always possible, try to match your line with water types. I typically use green, blue, and clear lines.

HANG TIME AND SETTING UP

I'm a firm believer in resting pools. Often a selective steelhead will get so accustomed to an angler's drifts, swings, and presentations that it will develop a staccato rhythm of continuously turning away and avoiding your junk. Bright-colored fly lines, sloppy presentation, sound, and vibration all play key roles in the fish avoiding your fly. The longer you rest the water, the better off you'll be. You allow the fish to revert to its desired lies and not have to carry on the P/D avoidance behavior. Their comfort lies in bathing in the ideal flow of their holding lie, just like you sitting in your recliner, flipping through the channels on your remote until you find something you like.

Another problem is aborting your drifts or swings too early. Allowing "hang time" on your flies is extremely important, especially in late fall and winter when a steelhead's metabolism is lower. S/R steelhead like lots of time to look at your flies. A/A fish hit as soon as provoked, often hitting in a broadside fashion during mid-swing or drift. This is not the case with more S/R fish.

I once had a client with extreme Parkinson's disease. Another client had extreme alcohol problems. Both wiggled and shook their arms a great deal at the end of the drift. They caught fish consistently, believe it or not, and this told me something about hang time drift at the end of your swing. Adding a few pumps, pauses, twitches, and strips when you drift or swing your fly as it completely straightens out, and doing it for up to a minute or two in good flowing water, can turn an indecisive fish into a grabber. I know it

"Teasing the croc" brings volatile strikes. Remember, unorthodox presentations can often be the key to catching pressured fish. MATT SUPINSKI

sounds absurd, and even I was a skeptic until I witnessed it time and time again. We also tend to work our swings and drifts way too quickly, especially for winter steelhead. The drift and swing need to slow down to less than the speed of the current.

DON'T TRUST SNAGS

Deep nymphing or fly swinging with heavy T-14/20 sink-tip sections includes the occasional snag. This is the inevitable result of dredging in cold winter water, especially on cold Great Lakes rivers. I can't tell you how many times a client gave me the rod to pull out a snag, only for me to say, "That's no snag, it's moving. It's a fish!" The steelhead in the S/R state has complete peripheral vision of the surface, both sideways and top to bottom. If something moves off the bottom and starts to drift away, it could resemble dislodged salmon eggs, nymphs, scuds, crayfish, or a sculpin scurrying about; the fish will attack this movement.

Many times, the slow attack speed of the steelhead will cause it to follow your offerings, only for the fly to vanish in a snag or underwater obstruction, and then mysteriously pop up again as you dislodged it. So treat every snag as a possible fish, or hold on tight once dislodged. Sounds crazy, but it's a fact.

Another reason for this behavior is the new prey ecosystem in the Great Lakes. Steelhead chow down big-time on round gobies and deepwater sculpins. These creatures rest on the bottom and scurry about to another lie, hopscotching along the bottom. The steelhead's predator searching behavior is firmly ingrained, and when it sees this, it attacks.

Steelhead Dichotomies

WEST COAST VS. GREAT LAKES STEELHEAD
The chief difference between the two steelhead strains is the West Coast steelhead's biological transition from salt water to fresh water, which requires salinity regulation by the steelhead's renal and circulatory systems as the fish enters the freshwater environment. This transition has a pronounced effect on a steelhead's willingness or ability to ingest food. Potamodromous (freshwater to freshwater) Great Lakes fish don't have this biological complication, and thus they retain the urge and ability to feed much longer in the river system than their West Coast cousins.

Ocean-run steelhead tend to be more aggressive perhaps because of the larger variety and size of ocean food they prey on. After feeding on large prawns, squid, eels, and pelagic baitfish in the ocean, the fish's search-and-destroy drive is geared toward the larger prey. This makes the larger flies like Intruders, leeches, and prawns effective for West Coast steelhead. Both Great Lakes and West Coast fish take large flies, but, in my opinion, the ocean fish tend to prefer them on a more consistent basis throughout the year.

The ultimate selectivity deciders are fertility and natal imprinting to river food forms. Here the S/R curiosity will be stronger in the Great Lakes fish, almost like resident rainbow trout. This is due to the higher fertility and variety of food forms in the steelhead's lake and river estuary systems, which have a great interchange in biodiversity. Saltwater and freshwater steelhead both have the same primary behavioral characteristics: sexual reproduction, aggression, a hierarchy of territorial dominance, the metabolic cost-benefit analysis of river lies during migration,

and imprinting and feeding to natal food forms. It is this last phase—feeding—that has a longer and more profound impact. It constantly tugs at a Great Lakes steelhead's psyche, as compared to an A/A ocean hunter steelhead, whose taking drive continually manifests itself in aggressive responses.

WILD VS. HATCHERY
It goes without saying that wild steelhead and salmon are genetically and behaviorally superior to hatchery fish. What took nature millions of years to produce doesn't just turn up in a hatchery raceway overnight—but its genetics can. The slow and consistent infusion of genetic diversity over time in the feral state makes for a strong, unique, evolutionary significant steelhead strain. Thanks to intricate analysis of West Coast rivers made possible through the endangered and threatened species programs, biologists now know the importance of fragile wild steelhead fisheries. To maintain those fisheries today, hatchery programs have become a necessity. If carefully done, they have a great ability to create amazing fisheries.

Michigan is one example of a state doing it the right way. The state's wild Little Manistee strain has

Fly master Greg Senyo with a rare 20-pound Steelhead Alley Lake Erie steelhead, most likely Michigan strain. As long as they learn how to hunt prey rather quickly upon their release, stocked fish of wild genetics have the potential to become as savvy as their wild counterparts. However, some never do! It is the two years of natal imprinting and dodging predators that gives the truly wild fish a survival advantage, and also makes them more selective in their daily mindset. GREG SENYO

evolved for more than 140 years on the crystal-clear, insect-rich, spring creek-influenced waters of the river that bears its name. The rate of wild reproduction and survival to adulthood for these California transplants is high. The state catches steelhead in a trapping weir, where male and female adults are stripped of their sperm and eggs, respectively. Their offspring are raised in a state-of-the-art, spring-fed facility. They are checked for disease, fed extremely well, and tucked into bed (not really) by careful hatchery personnel. When stocked in steelhead rivers as smolts, they are in all essence wild steelhead that have been raised in a concrete prep school environment, versus the rough and not-so-caring real world that the born-in-the-gravel steelhead must endure. They also have a higher survival rate due to their stocking at a larger size.

Wild fish have innate learned behaviors and stimuli recognition to diverse food forms that can't be replicated, making them more selective and versatile than hatchery fish in their overall prey foraging. When bacterial kidney disease (BKD) wiped out millions of hatchery salmonids in Lake Michigan back in the late 1980s, the alewife population—the chief prey of choice and 90 percent of the salmonids' diet—plummeted to an all-time low. This caused the hatchery salmonids to go on an endless search for a vanishing prey and made them expend more energy than they were able to consume. This put a massive physical strain on the fish and led to autoimmune deficiencies which allowed the BKD—sort of like the AIDS virus—to consume the fish, causing the salmon to starve and succumb to the disease. Even though there was plenty of other pelagic prey in the lake, the hatchery fish did not have the versatile hunting skills of the wild salmon and steelhead, species that learned predator strategies since birth in the wild, allowing them to quickly exploit new food items and adjust to the changing ecosystem. The vast array of food forms in their natal, wild rivers further enhanced their creativity in obtaining prey.

SWINGING VS. NYMPHING

The West Coast steelhead aficionado uses two-handed rods and the greased-line techniques of A. H. E. Wood. The presentation includes swinging flies downstream and broadside with a series of line folds or mends. This was the proper way to fish when West Coast steelhead angling started, and it was extremely effective. With the warmer Pacific coastal rivers and their summer and winter strains of steelhead, the A/A

Steelhead can become extremely selective to the shape, color, translucency, and opaqueness of eggs as the steelheader "matched the egg hatch." Great Lakes and West Coast fusion steelheading allows the angler to explore all fly methods with a "kitchen sink" box full of everything. MATT SUPINSKI

behavior of salt steelhead could be solicited in a consistent manner using this technique. The West Coast rivers have significant river gradients and longer riffles, rapids, and pocket boulder waters, which set up primary taking lies much better than low-gradient rivers. This makes a swung fly effective in generating an A/A response from the steelhead.

Nymphing for steelhead was mostly unheard of on West Coast rivers except for a handful of California watersheds that held resident rainbows in addition to saltwater chrome. On the Eel, Klamath, Trinity, McCloud, and Sacramento River systems, the overlapping

Heavily rooted in the English and Scottish Atlantic salmon school of Spey rods and Spey- and Dee-style flies, which made their way to the early West Coast school of steelheading in the 1900s, the new nymphing technique of the Great Lakes soon became highly scorned as unethical. Today two-handed Spey-fishing fuses with nymphing to give the Great Lakes steelheader options. MATT SUPINSKI

rainbow populations of various sea and resident strains allowed nymphers to catch steelhead in conjunction with resident non-migratory mykiss rainbows. As the steelhead spread to the Great Lakes, so did the nymphing technique. Prior to the Pacific salmon boom, Great Lakes anglers fished for "large rainbows," their term for steelhead. The freshwater steelhead are exposed to a greater biological drift of insects and inhabit relatively low-gradient rivers, causing a higher rate of selectivity. Because of this, "trout-style" presentations suited the Great Lakes fishery.

The different techniques—swinging and nymphing—used in different parts of the country were practical solutions to differences in the fisheries. Purism had nothing to do with it. That conundrum came about after anglers haggled over whose steelhead were the "real deal." What polarized these two schools was the invention of the Glo-Bug in Anderson, California. Steelheaders had known for more than a century that their quarry were compulsive salmon egg eaters. The genetic code of every steelhead includes a strong prey stimulus for eggs and small round objects.

Having migrated on the heels of the massive Pacific salmon runs for millions of years, rainbow trout and steelhead are insatiable when it comes to salmonid eggs. Steelhead rivers all over North America are loaded with bait anglers fishing egg sacs, skein, and plastic clusters. It is a downright lethal method and its impact on steelhead is never ending. Hundreds of thousands of steelhead are killed every year by anglers using this technique. The Glo-Bug eventually turned into one hundred different egg pattern variations, and so steelhead nymphing became a game of fishing a nymph and egg—or just egging.

Today, nymphing with an egg and a nymph is a Great Lakes tradition just as much as swinging flies is a West Coast tradition. They are both proven methods and have their purposes for selective steelhead. Today you'll find just as many fly-swinging steelheaders in the Great Lakes you do on the West Coast, while many West Coast purists are changing to light-tippet nymphing when low-water conditions cause the steelhead to become fussy and selective. They are both valid techniques with unique applications for success.

Catch-and-Release vs. Harvest

Everything about catch-and-release steelheading makes perfect sense. Amid global climate change, salmonids will suffer and become fewer and farther between. Just as the great ice ages and warmups of the last seventy million years have dictated the northward or southward expansion of trout, salmon, and steelhead populations, global climate change may do the same. Catch-and-release steelheading is already serious stuff and is actually mandated on West Coast rivers with shrinking runs of wild fish. The massive runs of the Great Lakes still get butchered. But they are getting less massive each year due to myriad ecological and man-made causes, including invasive exotic predators, foolish and gluttonous harvest by unappreciative anglers, and destruction of spawning habitat through siltation caused by overdevelopment.

Catch-and-release fishing is selectivity's incubator. When these fish get caught and are released, their learned and innate behavioral instincts start molding future behaviors, thus making them more S/R and a greater sporting challenge. They also have a greater propensity to contribute to the gene pool when they return to the ocean or lake bigger and more aggressive and selective. The progeny will carry innate genetic attributes that will contribute to greater diversity in the fishery. When catch-and-release creates larger

The opaque beauty of a steelhead tail as a fish is being released is a cherished moment of sporting conquest. Steelhead can survive the hardships of nature and its extremes, but not the blatant stupidity of man when he kills them indiscriminately. We need only reflect on the collapse of the great West Coast steelhead fisheries over the past century to understand what can happen. MATT SUPINSKI

runs and stable river populations (and this is documented), you have stronger territorial and hierarchical competition between salmonids, thus creating better takers and players to the fly—the ideal steelhead-fishing situation.

Killing steelhead and Atlantic salmon makes no sense if you are a serious sporting angler. When you kill a steelhead or salmon, you cull the A/A behavior that brought the fish to take your fly in the first place—a fish that needs not feed on anything when it is in the river system! By negating this mysterious instinct by killing the fish, you, in all respects, are putting yourself out of business.

By killing fish you are preventing any potential progeny from carrying learned S/R or innate A/A behavioral responses to your fly. The steelhead and salmon feed primarily in the oceans and lakes; in the rivers they play with their food. Needless to say, we need more players—wild ones are preferred, but any and all will do. Every fish must be cherished.

Summer-strain vs. Winter-strain Steelhead

To this day, summer- and winter-strain steelhead still confuse even the most ardent steelheader. Their personalities and selectivity preferences, while similar, have variations. Summer steelhead evolve mainly on massive river systems like the Columbia in Oregon and Washington and the Skeena River in British Columbia. These are long, steep-gradient rivers with their heavily oxygenated flows that traverse mountain ranges and cold boulder-strewn rapids. The evolution of the summer strain was necessitated by the long upriver migration times. The steelhead were forced to navigate hundreds of miles of steep gorges and waterfalls. They needed a jump start on their migration runs to be in order to be at the right place at the right time so they could contribute to the gene pool.

Unfortunately, after westward expansion and industrialization occurred, logging, dam building, and roads destroyed good portions of these vast superhighways. Summer steelhead need the canopy of forest-lined rivers to keep them cool in the summer. The more remote and protected areas like Oregon's Umpqua, Washington's Cascades and Olympic Peninsula, and the vast wilderness of British Columbia (particularly the Dean River system) still have excellent summer steelhead runs. The shorter, easier-to-navigate coastal rivers that had quick access to

Winter and summer steelhead rarely spawn together in the wild, though this does occur. The spatial separation of their migrations and river locations, along with the uniqueness of each ecosystem, have kept them separate. Summer Skamania Washington-strain steelhead in Lake Michigan's St. Joseph River spend three years in the ocean or lake before first returning to the river. MATT SUPINSKI

spawning grounds in the oceans were dominated by winter strains, which usually ascend rivers around September and spawn in the late winter and spring. Summer-run steelhead begin migrating as early as March and continue through October and spawn into late winter. With the two strains sharing watersheds and entering the river nearly every month of the year, genetic selection has given the steelhead a strong life spatial separation and genetic diversity.

Summer steelhead selectivity is much like that of Atlantic salmon. They usually migrate en masse when spate river conditions caused by a cold front allow comfortable upstream migration. With summer water temperatures ranging from 50 to 64 degrees, the initial migration phase of summer steelhead sees the fish acting as bulls in a china shop, displaying strong A/A behavioral qualities. They have highly charged metabolisms and take aggressive lies in the cold, fast, oxygenated pocket water and runs, acting much like aggressive rainbow trout. Once their bodies stabilize to the river conditions, they are forced to conserve energy and become more S/R in their behavior.

Effective techniques for landing summer steelhead include swinging heavy Spey flies on floating lines (the Bill McMillan, dry-line steelhead style, which uses the greased line approach) and skittering waking dry flies and large stoneflies on the surface. These techniques turn the fish into incredible leaping beasts with their noses looking up. The jumping and cartwheeling leaps are a product of the warmer waters, which are close to their ideal preferred range. As the fall approaches, the fish will exhibit extreme P/D behavior and become almost impossible to catch at times. Prolonged heat and drought will drive them to this state more quickly.

Winter-strain fish have a tendency to be heavier and larger in girth because they spend less time in the rivers and more time feeding in the ocean or Great Lakes. They migrate in smaller schools and are more bottom oriented, conserving energy in low water temperatures. A/A behavior on their initial upstream river migrations is very prominent, and they strike the fly willingly with reckless abandon, similar to summer runs. But if they winter over in the river systems, as the Great Lakes fish do, they display S/R behavior on a consistent basis. The personality and selective demeanor of winter fish is akin to that of a big wise old brown trout. Solitary behavioral preferences and territorial dominance are traits of winter strains; this makes them fussy steelhead one moment and aggressive "orcas" the next. When winter fish are in the S/R or P/D phases, the aggressive behavior will only be unleashed for short bursts at dusk or dawn or during the warmest parts of the day on a cold January afternoon. It is an extremely short-lived, yet powerful bite.

The gender difference in steelhead selectivity, which we noted earlier with the flash and egg dropper system, also reveals itself in winter-strain S/R behavior. On the Muskegon River, strike indicator nymphing for brown and resident rainbow trout in winter is effective. When using tiny scuds, sow bugs, and midge larvae on 6X tippet with 4- and 5-weight rods, you often hook winter steelhead by chance. Imagine a 12-pound steelhead taking a size 18 scud or midge pattern, and then exploding downstream! In 99 percent of such cases, it is a female steelhead. Their S/R curiosity is much higher than males who are busy guarding lies and asserting territorial dominance. The females seem to retain the eating strike response much longer and view their environment as a resident trout would.

Migration Behavior: The Path of Least Resistance

Migration shapes steelhead and Atlantic salmon behavior similarly, since the fish have almost identical migration lifestyles and both freely switch between

Here the Babine in British Columbia is in ideal flows—a steelheader's dream! Higher water can bring fresh fish, but you must adjust your tactics. Fish the periphery of the primary lie pools, especially the long, flat, boulder-strewn tailouts. Fish large, dark flies.
JOHN FLAHERTY

the three selectivity phases. Ideal migration conditions occur when a river is in spate, or when flows have increased from rain or snowmelt runoff. The pulse of an increased flow triggers the fish's sensory lateral line. But the waters can often become swollen and off-color from serious flooding.

However, we can't always plan our destination trips for ideal water conditions. So what do you do when water conditions are not ideal? Go fishing, of course. You'll be surprised at what may transpire. Catching steelhead when conditions are right is probable, but it takes a real hotshot to catch fish when they are not! With this "the tough get going" mentality, I began to fish waters that were on the rise, at stable highs, or slowly coming down. You know that rising waters bring fresh runs of salmonids, so the good news is that fresh, A/A fish are moving through the system. They are the prime targets for a steelheader, but with less than perfect conditions, they are tough to locate. I'd much rather face this scenario than try to catch dour, lockjawed, P/D salmon and steelhead in low, warm water. When waters rise,

salmonids choose the path of least hydrodynamic resistance. They edge along the demarcation lines of creases and seams, areas where currents meet slack, or sometimes backwater eddy areas. These areas are near shore and many anglers wade way out past them. Look for current-obstructing boulders, shale shelves, woody debris, and bridge abutments that shield the moving fish. Waterfalls, braided river channels, tributaries entering the main river, and dams are great areas in which to target bunched-up migrating steelhead and salmon. Their A/A personalities may be in overdrive with the frustration of congested pods of fish and the indecision of trying to figure out "which way to go." Spend a good amount of time studying the river's hydrodynamic flow to pinpoint these bottlenecks. Steelhead and Atlantic salmon will enter these areas either alone or in schools. Cover each of these areas thoroughly and slowly with every presentation. Deep-water bottom presentations are best because the fish hang out at the bottom where there is the least amount of current and they can take advantage of rock deflection.

Migrating steelhead or salmon will be hell bent on remaining in the slots of the pool's tailout, often behind a boulder, which they worked so hard to reach in the heavy currents. Here the fish finds comfort and a rest from the brutal challenges of migrating against heavy flows. Find these spots and your rod will become bent with "fish on!" ARNI BALDURSSON/LAX-Á

During spate conditions, you do not want to use the traditional hotspots in pools as points of reference. Fish the periphery of these primary lies; focus on the long, flat tailouts, particularly those that are boulder strewn. Heavy 550- to 600-grain Skagit lines allow you to throw heavier and longer T-14/20 sink tips or use bottom-drift nymphing techniques (aka swinging and chucking, Great Lakes–style). Both methods are ideal. You want to fish a big and gaudy fly that generates lots of movement from materials like rabbit strips, schlappen, or marabou. As for color, in heavily stained water, black and purple are sure bets, as are hot pink or red. Even when the rivers are running high, some can still be crystal clear. In this situation the colors of choice are chartreuse, gold, yellow, and light blue, all with ample amounts of Lateral Scale Flashabou.

A perfect example of finding A/A fish where most anglers don't look happened to me on British Columbia's Thompson River. I stood with my guide on the famous Graveyard Pool, watching swollen water crash through after several days of torrential rain. There was another Spey caster in our group who decided to make the best of a bad situation and work on perfecting his double-Spey and snap-t casts. Wading out knee-deep in an area that would normally be dry gravel, he proceeded to work on the anchoring of the line with a long sink-tip section and a big black string leech, a pattern made famous by British Columbia guide and steelhead master Bob Hull. Because he was still learning he was having a tough time lifting the sinking tip and big fly off the water in his mouse and d-loop. He created a lot of back dropping, rolling, and curling of the rod tip and line in the same area. The fly never seemed to leave the water, with the Spey line in a "perpetual mouse," and was pushed around a lot with 40 feet or so of line just dragging behind the near-shore boulders close to the tailout. To the amazement of everyone, a 20-pound chrome steelhead slammed the leech right behind him and went airborne.

The next day, the same spot produced three more fish at different times of the day. It was obvious that these A/A fish were moving through the lip, resting at the tailout slots. They had enough time to crush an annoying big black leech that was sloppily getting in their path. This goes to show that sometimes the slow, dragging hang time on the drifts allows the fly to stay in the strike zone longer and can result in a fish when you least expect it.

Low Light and Prime Light

Steelhead and salmon migrate through the river systems from dusk through the night, eventually settling in comfortable pools by dawn. At these times, you can have the best fishing for them. For example, once I was guiding some clients for steelhead on my home waters of Michigan's Muskegon River. It was a long, tough day with lots of boats and wading angler traffic; needless to say, the bite was slow. My favorite pools had been hammered to death throughout the day by both fly and bait-tossing anglers. We decided to wait for the last light advantage and return before dusk. Since I knew there were fish in the pool, we started at the top and worked our way down, methodically using many different fly patterns and techniques. My clients that day, the Murphys, are skilled and have the patience of Job. They knew we'd have to intricately work each lie, slot, seam, and gut. After an hour and a half, with my boat doing numerous anchor drops down to the tail end of the run, we were fishless and ready to pack it in for the day. Just as we reeled in the last rod at twilight, a steelhead boiled in a tail slap on the surface. Almost immediately, another boiling fish responded by smashing its tail about twenty feet from

the first one. Both fish were ten feet below where our last drifts and presentations occurred, and in the spot where most guides quit fishing the pool. It seems that the anglers and guides had pushed the fish as far back into the tailout as they could comfortably tolerate.

My client instantly started his drift, swinging ten feet lower than he had left off on his last cast. Wham! Fish on! A 14-pound, double-red-banded buck slammed the Bunny Bugger leech and all hell broke loose. As the fish struck the fly and broke the water, two other fish simultaneously boiled and porpoised on the surface. Was this a sign of territorial marking behavior by the fish, or were they extremely agitated because they had been pushed out of the primary parts of the run by the all-day river traffic? One thing is for certain, this scenario is dependable and repeated, whether you are on a steelhead river in the Great Lakes or Oregon or chasing Atlantics in Russia or Québec. Bring on the night bite!

BAROMETRIC PRESSURE

In my book *Steelhead Dreams*, I tackled the issue of barometric pressure using data I've collected and the rationale I've developed over my years of guiding. I compared fishing results to each day's barometric pressure. Some correlations were made, but there were many obvious gaps, quirks, and contradictions that made me reevaluate the whole issue.

One certainty is that all steelhead and Atlantic salmon have finely tuned air bladders. These life-

A rapidly falling barometer is the death knell for winter steelhead that have been in the river system for several months. All my angling data verifies this, and now that I have the luxury of just looking at my smart phone, I can see the bite turning off with methodical accuracy. When the ice starts to build up on the guides and a cold damp wind kicks up, like here on British Columbia's Babine, things get tough.
PIERCE CLEGG

support systems allow them to dive 200 to 400 feet in oceans and Great Lakes in search of food. Some leading salmonid biologists say the fish consume aquatic invertebrates that live at the deepest benthic levels of the ocean. A fluctuating barometric pressure condenses and expands the waters of rivers and seas, particularly in surface, near-shore, and shallow river environments.

I now have a highly accurate iPhone weather app, and my eyes are opened on a daily basis. I have learned that the impact of barometric pressure on salmonids is highly variable by species, time of year, and migration stage. Yes, a slightly consistent high pressure (30.10 for example) can be conducive to a good, steady all-day bite. But so can a steady low pressure. The key is rapid fluctuations that cause fish to go from A/A to P/D, thus making them migrate and move as their genetic innate programming has dictated for millions of years.

Those deep-sea fish that have comfortably adapted to their new river homes and stabilized their air bladders do not respond well to rapid fluctuations in barometric pressure. Good signals that the barometer is falling—other than the obvious signs and the weather conditions—are fish gulping the surface for air, fish located in shallow river lies, and other despondent P/D behaviors. On the flip side, a rapidly falling barometer and inclement weather are ideal for producing a fresh run of A/A fish, especially early migrating summer steelhead and Atlantic salmon in the fall, summer, and late spring. A strong cold front produces the necessary heavy rains and dark, inclement-weather conditions that cause ocean- or lake-migrating fish to take the big step of leaving their comfortable big-water hunting grounds and travel up the rivers. Prior to this initial run, the rivers are often low and the fish need a good spate to give them a migration signal. The morning after a cold front, a previously fishless river could be full, flowing, and heavy with fresh steelhead and salmon—the ideal A/A beasts that are ready to smash your fly!

Presentations for Selective Steelhead

No matter where you encounter steelhead, almost everybody can catch the fish that are fresh in from the ocean or Great Lakes. A skunking only occurs if something is fundamentally wrong with the angler's rigging, or if he or she is fishing in a place that is completely devoid of holding water. I love it when kids fishing gummy bears, marshmallows, or peel-and-eat shrimp–all topped off with a night crawler—catch bold A/A summer steelhead on Zebco Snoopy spinning rods. But once these fish acclimate and settle into the S/R mode, our tactics must change and be refined. Steelhead presentation revolves around three main styles: swinging, nymphing, and dry-fly. Each has its own unique characteristics that require modifications based on the fish's selectivity phase and seasonal demands.

On the complete opposite spectrum from the fresh-run A/A steelhead, you have the S/R deep-winter Great Lakes steelhead. These fish are exposed to near total freeze-up situations, causing cautious and conservative S/R or P/D behaviors. The cost-benefit metabolism challenges of the steelhead's winter river environment, tremendous pressure from two-thirds of North America's population, and incredibly diverse and fertile ecosystems force the angler to adopt the thinking-man's approach to the these unpredictable and selective fish.

On my home waters in Michigan, winter steelhead stay in primary lies and holding pools typically four to ten feet deep. I find steelhead don't care to venture any deeper; often the deepest pools won't hold fish. There is tremendous daily diversity in the biological drift. On any given day, midges, scuds, small drifting stoneflies, and burrowing mayflies like *Hexagenia* are seeking out new homes, as are caddis larvae. Sculpins, darters, and shiners also move in the afternoon as the sun warms the water. Given the fact that most Michigan steelhead rivers contain excellent populations of wild brown, brook, and rainbow trout, there is heavy competition for position.

The winter steelhead's bite is short when the fish are in the S/R mode. In ideal water temperatures between 38 and 40 degrees, winter-strain steelhead can go on the bite at any given moment. P/D behavior usually occurs when low-pressure systems and frigid subarctic nights cause severe drops in water temperatures. Most of the fish have been in the river system since fall and have acclimated well. They've already gone through the A/A stage of feeding on salmon eggs and chasing swung flies, lures, and spawn dunker bags. They are now as cunning as a 25-inch spring creek rainbow on Idaho's Silver Creek. But they are still steelhead with behavioral tendencies toward big-water pelagic baitfish hunting mode. These contrasting personality traits tug at the fish daily. This is where the fun begins.

A prime winter steelhead from the Muskegon. Michigan's rivers are wild steelhead factories with incredibly diverse food forms and habitat-rich ecosystems. The state's low-lying forests and sandy soils trap every ounce of moisture, just like the chalkstreams of England's Hampshire country. Spring creeks and seeps abound throughout the Lake Michigan shoreline of western Michigan. MATT SUPINSKI

Below: The steelhead's careless penchant for eggs of any type, be they orange, pink, or chartreuse, is firmly implanted in the fish's DNA. But this behavior subsides through the winter, making the fish more introspective of its natural world and the food in it. MATT SUPINSKI

As the daylight photoperiod lengthens in early February, the neuroendocrine hormones trigger territorially dominant movement, especially among the more dominant double-red-banded buck males. These fish, along with larger females, have taken up the prime pools, guts, and holding lies and do everything they can to hold and dominate them. They must dodge the motors and anchors of drift boats and jet boats, numerous wading anglers, and every fly, bait, and lure that comes at them.

Since steelhead have egg-eating encoded in their DNA, I see this big turn in their preference every year around Valentine's Day, when the fish are no longer fond of egg patterns and instead completely focus on sculpins, Hex nymphs, leeches, Bunny Buggers, Chinook salmon fry, and stoneflies. If they share a river environment with other resident trout, the alpha steelhead's A/A personality will cause it to react to the competitive nature of the mix.

With the increasing clarity of most Great Lakes rivers, steelhead can be extremely wary and obvious to all predator advances. During deep-winter ice-up, murky runoff waters are nonexistent. One particular 18-pound double-red-banded steelhead, caught on a

cold February day in 2012, comes to mind. It happened on the ultrafertile and heavily fished clear waters of my home Muskegon River. This large Western-style river has riffles and pools ranging from several inches to twenty feet deep. Its winter fish hold in pool guts averaging six to ten feet deep. They shun light, but at the same time they use it to warm up their metabolisms in the shallows, when river temperatures are 33 degrees. These fish love balmy water temps from 36 to 38 degrees if they can get them.

My client was Dr. Matt Zaccheo. Despite it being the dead of winter, there was heavy angling pressure from guide boats and other anglers that needed a "cabin fever" getaway, along with it being a holiday weekend. The Muskegon's Sycamore Run pool has always held large fish, being of ideal depth and having a jagged rock and gravel bottom along an outside river bend. We had gotten a nice 12-pound male steelhead there earlier in the morning, which made my client happy. But Dr. Matt wanted a trophy and would spend three days with me in search of one.

"I have never got one close to twenty, like you guys over here in this part of the Great Lakes have," Matt said. He went to medical school in Erie, Pennsylvania,

The beauty and stillness of an early winter on the hallowed Babine of British Columbia. PIERCE CLEGG

and was used to fishing the Steelhead Alley, which typically produces much smaller fish. My intuition told us to hang out and wait for the dusk bite, which is the most explosive time in winter steelheading. With the sunset light diminishing later as daylight is getting ever so longer, coupled with dusk being the time of the warmest water temperatures, there is a small window that triggers the A/A bite—the timing can be as short as a few minutes. At this time of year it's all about hormones and sex, and natal imprinting to food, as the big boy and girl steelhead jockey for dominance. "We're going to hit the Sycamore Run pool at 5:30," I told Dr. Matt. "We have consistently picked up large brown trout in that pool, but not lately. They either moved out or there is a 'new sheriff in town' in those waters. It could be a real big buck steelhead keeping the smaller inferior browns off the bite!" We worked the pool hard for at least thirty minutes. Our fingers were getting frostbitten. There was no porpoise behavior like we had seen on previous nights. As it was becoming more difficult to see as night was approaching, all the other guide boats and anglers left the river.

We went through the motions of our last casts into the dusk. It was looking hopeless, leading me to believe that my intuition had led us down the wrong path.

With just enough light to see, I put a small sculpin pattern on Dr. Matt's line. "You sure you don't want to try a pink Otter Egg?" Matt asked. "Nope, if there is a huge male—the leviathan trophy that you're looking for—it has seen every egg pattern from here to the Salmon River in New York," I assuredly told him. "We are probably barking up the wrong tree since it is getting dark, so make two more casts and we are out of here."

In what may have been the next cast, Matt's switch rod went crazy as the pool boiled with a huge fish. I took my prescription sunglasses off and I couldn't see a damn thing. "This thing is a pig, whatever is," Matt said. "It busted water twice with its tail." On a wing and a prayer, fifteen minutes into the total blackout of night, I slipped the net under a massive beast. It was a beautiful sight to see: an 18-pound, kype-jawed male of perfection. It had two pronounced red bands. "How the hell did that fish see that tiny sculpin in ten feet of water at total darkness?" Matt asked.

In my opinion, this large alpha male fish waited until the comfort of darkness to make its move—way after all the other guide boats and anglers were headed to the bar or the dinner table. It waited until everything was safe and totally quiet. The light conditions were so dark that the small bottom-dwelling sculpins found it safe to come out and forage. The fish waited for the safe darkness to throw its weight around like a big-time boxer, and it pushed other competitive steelhead and large brown trout out of its way as it went in for the kill. It had viewed close to one hundred casts by us over the previous forty minutes, not to mention hundreds of casts by other guides and anglers throughout the day. It had also seen hovering birds of prey like eagles and ospreys, which were already building their nests. Like a thief in the night, this male had waited and lusted for the right time to make its move. We were lucky to be there in that moment it did!

Was it incredible eyesight that allowed this winter male to see a tiny sculpin in ten feet of water in a fifty-yard-long pool? Or was it the vibration of the marabou-barred rabbit strip pulsing along the bottom that triggered detection? Or could it have been the transparent tippet was no longer visible in the dusk? I believe it was a combination of all of the above. Fishing sparse and minute egg patterns, sculpins, nymphs, shrimp, and newly hatched Chinook fry minnows is the ticket for the winter bite. The winter biological drift is microscopic: tiny scuds, midges, and immature aquatic insects that have a ways to go before they mature and hatch.

Swing Chucking

Swinging flies Skagit-style in icy-cold water is not the most productive technique. You can hook a fish or two on occasion by deep dredging, but this is long labor when water temperatures hover near freezing. Large 600-grain Skagit heads with heavy T-14/20 sink-tip sections, bumped on the bottom and skipped, can turn on a fish here and there. Chasing flies is just not in the cards for selective steelhead bent on energy conservation in the dead of winter. Here the switch rod comes in handy for "swing chucking."

In my valiant attempt to combine swinging and nymphing, I've come up with a deadly system whose rewards far outweigh any other presentation technique for Great Lakes steelhead on ultraclear waters of the late fall, winter, and early spring.

Swing chucking, or swing drifting, involves light, two-handed switch rods (11-foot, 7- or 8-weight rods) that are casted like two-handed rods. As with all Spey casting, the elbows never leave the sides of the body—an effortless technique that can be used for days on end. It is so simple that many fly fishers want to complicate it and put too much power and muscle into the presentation. For stealth purposes, I use Rio's AquaLux intermediate and floating lines, which were created for fly presentation on crystal-clear lakes. They come in weight-forward 3- to 9-weight versions. For smaller steelhead streams with shallower depths, you can use the floating lines to match the rod in weight. For penetrating deep pools on big heavy Great Lakes rivers, use intermediate sinking lines brought down two to three line-weight sizes from your rod's designated weight. By using a 4- or 5-weight intermediate sink on an

Dr. Matt Zaccheo and his dusk monster. Winter steelheading is all about stealth, fly choice, and timing. It's a game of nerves and patience most anglers can't handle.
MATT SUPINSKI

A massive "swing-chucked" February male on my Muskegon. A switch rod and clear intermediate line made the presentation that fooled this S/R monster. MATT SUPINSKI

11-foot, 7-weight rod, which is the desired system for depth presentation, you are controlling line speed and mending qualities. You can't do that with "chuck-and-duck" running lines.

The weight needed to get the flies down comes in several varieties. First you can tie in Fish-Skull Sculpin Helmet heads; the new weighted version for streamers, leeches, and small baitfish can get your fly down in shallow to mid-depth runs and pools. A short section of T-14 sinking line can be used with the head as long as the sink tip has a long leader to the fly to ensure stealth presentation. One of the chief obstacles in extra-clear winter water is the ability of S/R steelhead to pick up the colored fly line with their impeccable vision. This does not matter in the fall, spring, and early winter when the water temperatures are higher in the 40s and 50s and the A/A fish is targeted on your leech, tube, or fly. Finally, I use a few tungsten split shots attached to a monofilament tag off a two-way swivel. These are allowed to "slip sink," which will put your fly or flies down to whatever depth you need. They can be used anywhere from the Niagara Gorge to deep Michigan tailwaters.

The technique begins with a water load, similar to a Spey cast or Scandinavian underhand cast. With the two-handed, pull-push done tightly and gently, over either the left or the right shoulder, the weighted system can effortlessly punch out hundred-foot casts. By making one or two mends and allowing your presentation to get near the bottom, you set your rod tip in the eight o'clock–four o'clock position, at a 15- to 20-degree angle slightly upstream of where your clear line enters the water. This is the difference between standard "chuck and duck," and "swing chucking." The former promotes a square line presentation or drags the flies downstream with the rod leading the line.

With this slight 15- to 20-degree angle you are constantly presenting your flies swinging across and broadside in the standard presentation for steelhead swung flies and Atlantic salmon flies. This is similar to the greased-line method. With the heavier, weight-forward AquaLux intermediate clear lines, you can maneuver the line just like any other fly line, Skagit or long belly, but on a more delicate scale. It is a combination of deep bottom nymphing and fly swinging, allowing for two flies (where legal) and an egg–leech or nymph–Spey combination.

By steadying the extended two-hand fighting butt to your chest, you allow for steadiness in drift and swing, whereas a freehand grip tends to wobble all over. By varying the height of the rod tip—lower for quicker swinging presentation, higher to slow the presentation down against the current and in cold water—you have total command of what your flies are doing just by moving your "push" hand up or down.

Why is this technique so deadly for selective deep winter steelhead? First, stealth is everything. Selective steelhead take up holding lies in slots from one bank to another. Often we overcast many lies with bright-colored green or peach Skagit lines, spooking holding steelhead. This does not occur in off-color, blue-green rivers like West Coast waters with a good winter spate or chalky waters like New York's Cattaraugus Creek.

Next is penetration. Steelhead, especially fussy ones, like to play with their prey. Yes, a perfect dead-drift egg or nymph pattern under a strike indicator or

Steelhead rivers have pocket water and shale shelf dropoffs like these on Lake Erie's Steelhead Alley. These formations create an undertow and can spin the natural prey in counterclockwise or zigzag motions. Fish can be ultra S/R here in clear waters, demanding tiny nymphs. BRETT MCCRAE

center-pin will take fish. But most selective fish like a steadily swinging, broadside, down-and-across presentation. They often pick up the fly when the drift stops, or when the fly is on the hang time directly below your wading position or where your boat was anchored. This drift triggers the innate predator curiosity and gives the fish long inspection times during which it chases the fly sideways and sometimes even downstream. Natural prey does not always float helplessly with the current like many of us are led to believe. Mayflies, stoneflies, caddis nymphs and larvae, small sculpins, and salmon sac fry all have some kind of movement.

If you are using an indicator, use a white or clear one; those colors best imitate the bubble line flotsam of the river. Wade as little as possible or slowly. Work every swing or drift one rod length at that time, constantly feeling the gentle bumping of the bottom to make sure you are in the strike zone (long leaders and flies will be swinging in the zone one foot above bottom). Wait for two or three good head shakes by a steelhead once it takes your fly before you set the hook. Usually the fish hook themselves, just like on a swinging fly. In winter steelheading, don't set the hook too early and pull the fly out of the fish's mouth before it can take it. Wait a bit, and then hold on tight! The strikes are severe even in the dead of winter.

Two-Handed Swinging: The Skagit Revolution

The United Kingdom tradition of swinging flies on Spey rods for Atlantic salmon is a beautiful thing. In rivers with mild and moderate temperatures, the innate curiosity of the Atlantic salmon and its ability to target swung down-and-across flies near the surface has made this technique a centuries-old tradition. In the early twentieth century, the temperate conditions of the Pacific West Coast steelhead rivers allowed this technique to become highly appropriate and effective for those waters. Spey casting was perceived as technical, expensive, and totally foreign to many, but the West Coast steelhead angler embraced it.

Winter-strain fish, which are bottom oriented, have slower attack speeds and can be more downright stubborn thanks to river conditions and the fishes' innate personalities. Long, double-taper Spey lines didn't give enough advantage in these conditions and were impractical with the demands of winter fishing. Skagit lines, which had shorter bellies, were perfect for the job.

These heavy-grain heads, which looked like cut Hula-Hoops, would lift the heavy sinking heads that traditional lines couldn't. By measuring sink tips in inches per second or grains per feet (T-8/11/14/20, for example), these systems allow you to dredge deep steelhead lies with large leeches and intruders. Since Great Lakes steelheading is predominately a late-fall, winter, and early spring affair, nymphing and egging was the desired technique. Known as "chuck and duck," the technique employed lead and running lines to keep the flies down in the guts and runs of deep winter lies. But now, with the Skagit system, the new Spey technique made the two-handed method practical and easy to cast with either traditional Spey methods or an overhead style.

With the Skagit method comes flies that breathe motion without movement. From the early Atlantic salmon "breathing" flies like the General Practitioner came Skagit innovations like Gallagher's prawns, Kinney's Speys, and John Farrar and George Cook's marabou/Flashabou concoctions. The modern school of "curling, snaking, and breathing" leechy long flies came from Bob Hull's string leech invention that he used on the Dean River in British Columbia. Rabbit strips and shoemaker's string were replaced with background and extended trailer hooks in innovations like Ed Ward's Intruder. The hallowed Skagit waters developed a system for deadly deep swinging methods. Contemporaries like Dec Hogan, the author of *Passion for Steelhead*, have provided much insight into the taking and holding lies of deep-water steelhead.

When swinging flies for steelhead in the three main selectivity phases, the angler will notice varied responses from the fish. In the early migration, fresh-run A/A state, the fish is by no means a connoisseur and will crush just about any gaudy colored fly at all stages of the swing. Once past the early fresh-run A/A aggressive state, steelhead in the S/R mode develop curiosity and reflection, which can pique briefly and cause the fish to take the fly. The later the season rolls into winter, the more S/R or P/D the fish will get.

FOCUS ON THE WATER

When we are armed with a new two-handed rod of our dreams and use the Skagit head and sink tip combo, we often feel like Thor, ready to conquer the river. That's all fine if you just plan on practicing your casting, but when steelhead fishing, you must focus on the job at hand, which is trying to locate taking lies and catch steelhead. Time and time again, on both the West Coast and the Great Lakes, I have watched anglers get in the water and start launching casts, over and over, with no intention of actually fishing. Nothing puts down selective fish more quickly than a big fluorescent green, 600-grain Skagit head coming through their lies.

You should start targeting holding lies and fish short to your bank, working down the pool, before you come back up and start again. Each time your cast should go farther out. On a pool or run, a targeted primary holding lie can be worked for hours. It's amazing how little attention we give the entire piece of water, only to poke our lines in certain spots and leave. Dissect each piece of water carefully and

acutely. Treat it like its own unique sector, especially if it has diversified character such as pool or pocket water, boulder buckets, river bends, or tailouts, coupled with obstruction and woody debris. This water demands more than just a few casts and swings. Carefully time your way down the pool and use measured intervals—you never know where you will find a taker. Analyze all seams before casting; these hidden buckets are especially important areas when fish are spooked from lots of pressure.

MENDING

A fly swings when the line is sweeping down and across and under tension. Mending can get a sinking

Clients who cannot master the Spey casts can be instructed in a single overhead cast with the Skagit line, putting them well on their way to West Coast swinging. The thrill and exhilaration of hooking a large A/A steelhead on the swing can now be enjoyed by all steelheaders. MATT SUPINSKI

Left: When steelhead are in a funky and pressured S/R state, there are no rules to your presentation. Thinking outside the box and fishing tertiary water and lies— the water that most other anglers pass—on heavily pressured weekends is the key, like it was here for Shawn Murphy. MATT SUPINSKI

head down quicker or straighten out your line for the swing, but the fly plays the most vital role in attracting the strike. Proper fly speed broadside that is with, or slower than, the current, combined with motion without movement of the fly and its profile in the water, is the desired goal of all swingers. But to an ultraselective, picky steelhead this may not be the answer.

Most fly swingers are creatures of habit. They use the same flies, and often rightly so—they consistently produce fish. But for tough fish, it is worth trying unconventional presentations. I like to use such presentations in each piece of water I fish after I have tried standard swings and had no luck.

As bizarre as it may seem, I have had steelhead strike just as I made the initial mend, sometimes with reverse mends downstream to speed up the fly and all kinds of mistakes in between. I have had brutally windy days with the wind coming upriver and blow-

ing my Skagit line upstream like a flag, and fish slamming the fly as it was carried by the line in an awkward upstream fashion, not at all with the traditional broadside tension. Remember, an S/R steelhead wants something it can't have or it wants to play with its prey. Test it and be curious!

HANG TIME ANTICS

It's extremely important to let your fly pulse and flutter at the end of your swing. Most Spey casters like to cast and cast, but one of the most common mistakes I see is anglers rushing to the next cast without finishing off the swing with long hang times as the fly line is extended at the end of the cast. New materials and fly designs move and breathe better than anything before. They allow the fly to hold motionless but still swim like natural prey. In any presentation, a steelhead will often chase the fly before it abandons the pursuit. But if you let the fly hang in the current

April Vokey (pictured), a noted Dean River and saltwater guide, says: "Swinging for steelhead is a stalking and an exploration that human beings were born to do . . . what a satisfying feeling it is to know that we can still live parts of our lives knowing that we are doing something so incredibly right, something we were made for. I spend a lot of time 'slow swinging' my fly through fishy seams. I make it a common practice to walk (while swinging) my streamer slowly through a pool, all the while allowing it to efficiently cover a river's lie and tempt a fish that may need that slight extra persuasion." STEVE MORROW

Below: One of April Vokey's gorgeous Intruders for the Dean River. When water conditions are low and clear, like on the Dean in summer, the Sugar Pop rides high in the water column as the natural fibers of arctic fox tail and ostrich herl breathe in the current. APRIL VOKEY

downstream of you, that same fish can turn on again and become a grabber.

The way you set yourself up in the upstream position for the swing is also significant. This helps you cover the down-and-across prime broadside approach through the guts and pockets of the primary taking lies. Your fly often ends its swing on the seams and creases demarking the current and slack water. Moving fish, resting fish, and plain "bored to tears" fish slide into these secondary lies, which are not normally targeted by your perfect primary swing presentation. This is mainly a result of practicality, since the slack water demarcation lines do not provide enough flow to get the proper current speed for your fly swing. But that doesn't mean they don't hold fish on a far more regular basis than you think, particularly fussy, pressured steelhead. Here your fly lands in the "bucket" a great percent of the time without you really being aware of it. Surprise hookups here often baffle the steelhead as much as the steelheader, who has been targeting the main run and slots. I have had steelhead strike a fly as long as several minutes into the hang time. Adding rod pumps, lifts, tugs, and twitches increases the chances for hang-time strikes. But beware. Striking too hard when completely startled on a hang-time grab, or having a strike while stripping in line, can cause a breakoff.

BUMPITY-BUMP

"I just felt a bump," the client says. Or it's, "I felt two bumps and nothing." If you swing flies you will definitely experience what I'm talking about. Are you feeling strange things? Is it the bottom? Or are you bumping into a fish? Is the fish striking the fly but missing it? This happens more than you think with S/R fish. But maybe the fish is telling you something about its personality that you never thought of. It's a combination of the "cat playing with a mouse" behavior that steelhead love.

I never fully understood how or what was occurring with these USO (unidentified striking object) sightings. Sometimes it is a river trout or parr playing with a 5-inch-long leech; sometimes you strike the back of a sucker.

It wasn't until one fall day that I had my epiphany on a famous pool on my home river. The water was running low and clear, yet held good numbers of steelhead. For several days these USO sightings and "things that go bump" plagued me and my clients, and we were baffled as to why we were not hooking up.

Scott Howell, noted dean of the North Umpqua and a Skagit master, sums up deep-water presentations best: "When times get tough, the tough are going down. If a fish is reluctant to move vertically in the water column under colder conditions, the closer I take my fly to the fish, the more likely it is to respond." SCOTT HOWELL

Using long string leeches with the hook penetrating the rabbit strip tail at the end, or tube flies with which short strikes are not possible, we still missed strikes. I eventually went to a hill overlooking the pool, where I could see what was going on. Watching a client swinging flies with my partner, I could decipher a half dozen holding steelhead in the lies he was penetrating. The fish occasionally would move to the left or right, avoiding each approaching fly. Since it was a sunny day, they were mostly P/D and were basically ignoring or oblivious to the fly anglers' approach. "Switch flies," I shouted to him. After two or three swings by the client toward the holding lie a steelhead came to the fly, bumped it twice, followed it downstream, and then turned upstream on the fly's hang time and smashed it! It was soon cartwheeling in the air downstream. Later, at cocktail hour, the client described what he felt about that particular take. "It bumped once . . . bumped again . . . nothing. Three seconds later, slam! Fish on!" It was amazing

British Columbia's Dean is a hallowed dry-fly river for majestic, surface-oriented fish—and a stonefly utopia. ANDREW BENNETT

for me to watch this whole procedure and combine it with a perfect verbal explanation by the angler.

The same quirky behavior happens when streamer fishing for trout on the chase. This behavior is particularly common in males starting to sow their territorial oats. It is interesting to note that a good amount of them attack large, undulating swinging flies, which turn on the A/A "kill artist" behavioral mode from the fish's time in the big ocean or the Great Lakes. The "bumping" behavior, which is often done with the fish's snout or cheek, simulates pelagic baitfish hunting, which is what the male steelhead will be doing in a few months. It also simulates fending off other males for spawning dominance with their kyped jaws and teeth.

The Dry Fly and the Summer Steelhead

God could not have created a more perfect river for *Mykiss* than the Dean in British Columbia. The immense bluish-green eutrophic waters cascade through boulder-strewn canyons, pools, and tailouts. The region's snowcapped Kitimat Mountains are surrounded by dense valleys of conifers and alders in the canyon section. Closer to the tidal saltwater area, large broad-shouldered A/A steelhead are hot in pursuit of a swung fly in their newfound river environments. The Dean's large boulder and flat-rock waters offer steelhead opportunities to bask in perfect taking lies that provide current deflection comfort. This can stimulate the S/R fish's introspective taking mindset. They love to eat dry flies here!

On the Dean, there is something strongly instinctual that causes steelhead to become so surface oriented. Like all eutrophic alpine rivers with pristine forests and an ideal mix of alkalinity and acidity, the Dean harbors massive populations of *Pteronarcys* stoneflies. Stoneflies of all sizes and colors (golden, black, brown) shed their shucks on the rocky boulders along the banks as they crawl up to hatch. The steelhead relished them when the fish were young juvenile river residents prior to going to the ocean, and so do their returning parents and siblings.

In order for steelhead to be surface oriented, there has to be heavy populations of crawling and shredding insects, which pique the natal parr imprinting to food forms. Another must is ideal water temperature. Perfect water temps are in the 50-degree range, with highly oxygenated flows and boulder or flat-rock waters that provide ideal holding and taking lies

In his fabulous book *Steelhead Fly Fishing*, Trey Combs talks about his experience fishing the Dean River at the Anchor and Rabbit pools and runs. He set up camp with noted West Coast steelhead guide John Farrar and the great fly tier and steelheader Jimmy Hunnicutt.

Combs writes: "When we reached the Dean, I immediately noticed thousands of nymphal skins left on rocks by emerging Pteronarcys stoneflies. This was the end of the hatch, but the next day I watched a parr chase an enormous wing adult down the river. My amusement changed to astonishment when it finally took the stonefly down."

The availability of stoneflies and caddis—aquatic insects that make strong fluttering and agitated surface movements—is vital to having steelhead respond to the dry-fly stimuli. To imitate the stoneflies and giant October caddis, Farrar came up with his "Sputterkicker" deer-hair dry-fly pattern, which soon took a selective 18-pound Dean River fish.

Scott Howell, today's New Age West Coast steelhead master and star of the *Skagit Master 2* DVD series, wakes dry flies like bass bugs. He pops and sprays water and fishes his swung flies fast and broadside to illicit A/A behavior from the fish on his home waters even when they are passive. Here is Scott's philosophy:

To me, fishing the dry fly on the North Umpqua is the pinnacle of the sport. If I have one day left, place me on the North Umpqua and let me chase a dry fly across one of her greasy tailouts. It's not just the visual rush of the actual take that makes dry-fly fishing so exciting. It is the extra element of actually getting to watch your fly as it swims through the pool that makes your heart beat just a little faster. I tend to fish my dries by incorporating a little popping action as the fly skates around. Not so much a "pop" created by stripping the line as in bass fishing, but more of disturbance created by twitching the rod tip into a tight line as the fly swings around. Aside from just being a fun

way to fish, over time I have found that there are many instances where this added action really makes a difference.

Dry-fly steelhead will take either skating or waking patterns or dries on a dead drift. In my experience it really depends on what type of holding or taking lies the fish are in. On the slower-moving tailouts with large flat rocks and boulders to cushion the river's current, you'll get a ton of looks and maybe a take on a dead drift of your fly. The faster pocket water will hold more A/A fish, since they must really move fast in order to inspect the fly. The slower current of a tailout's lip water allows more S/R refusals than takes. Paramount to all of this is allowing the fish time to take the fly and turn down with the dry fly in its mouth—too often we set the hook way too early. It is my opinion that a lot of refusals are actually takes, we just pulled the trigger too early!

Bill McMillan shares his dry-fly experiences on British Columbia's Vancouver Island in his brilliant book *Dry Line Steelhead*. Of one experience, he writes: "Over the next three days, summer run steelhead from 2 to 10 pounds came readily to the surface showing marked preference for a naturally drifted dry fly. Only a few were hooked with the surface fly on the drag (commonly preferred by steelhead); even fewer were hooked using traditional wet patterns and methods."

This account of dead-drift dries is rather unusual. But it happens in rivers with caddis and stonefly populations that have summer steelhead in good numbers that have not been fished heavily. That's the key word—pressured. Steelhead are not ardent takers of dry flies in these waters.

Another icon of dry-fly steelheading was Mike Maxwell. His Telkwa stonefly deer hair pattern perfectly imitates the *Acroneuria* brownish stonefly, which his Bulkley and Kispiox fish adored. He used a down-and-across Spey cast in which he mended and fed line, bringing the fly under waking tension. Then a second mend and feed takes place, making the fly more erratic and under tension; here it can be pumped and pushed. The hang time is stripped back in various exaggerated pulses. With this method you can affect the dry fly's speeds and actions. Lani Waller's approach is similar, but he imparted a more upstream approach and cast when he combined the dead-drifting and waking presentations in one. This is deadly since an S/R steelhead, like a brown trout on a

Indiana first imported Washington's Washougal River summer-strain fish back in the early 1970s. Now these monster "three-salt" steelhead can run as big as 26 pounds. They are extremely A/A when fresh on a new migration to the river and their leaping abilities are unparalleled in the salmonid world. They are steelhead on steroids! Double-digit catch days of fresh chrome are possible here in August on Indiana's Trail Creek, a spring-fed limestoner. MATT SUPINSKI

spring creek, will follow the dry in a complex rise-form, only to take it as the fly sweeps and wakes away. For really exciting action to A/A fresh-run fish, cast directly downstream across a fast tailout, with lines straightening out in violent upstream stripping pauses and pulses. A/A steelhead will go crazy for this approach.

The Skamania summer-strain steelhead of Michigan and Indiana's St. Joseph River and New York's Salmon River can provide dry-fly action if you are willing to put your time in. They will chase just about anything that moves, making them perfect takers of large leech patterns or dry flies.

But water temperatures in the low-gradient rivers where the fish are stocked heavily (close to a million fish are released yearly into the "Skamania Alley" from Indiana's Lake Michigan shoreline to the St. Joseph River) can get brutally high during hot summers, thus causing dour P/D behavior. Locating spring creeks in the tributary system, along with faster-gradient riffles and pocket water, is the key. The St. Joe River valley has a good amount of limestone aquifers. The upper fly-fishing-only zone on New York's Salmon River has faster, oxygenated boulder and canyon water ideal for swinging muddlers, leeches, and dries to fish fresh in from the lake almost overnight.

As freshwater-to-freshwater migrators, steelhead seem highly preoccupied with natural foods like frogs, water beetles, cicadas, and grasshoppers. They are surface oriented in shallow environments, and we can bring them to the surface by using fluorescent strike indicators while nymphing—the fish take the indica-

tor. One pattern that works well for St. Joseph fish was created by steelheader Bob Bemmer. His Excavator is a spider-style Bivisible in a green and black coloration. It can be fished dry or allowed to sink wet and it accounts for hundreds of fish each year.

Lake Erie's Steelhead Alley, with its early returning steelhead of late summer and early fall, also has fish that are known to be extremely surface oriented, again depending on the proper conditions. Karl Weixlmann, noted Lake Erie tributary guide and author, explains his method for surface-oriented fish:

I've learned that dry-fly and dry-fly dropper presentations solve the problem of fishing over extremely spooky and skittish steelhead. It's an unobtrusive presentation and works especially well when steelhead suspend in the water column. My first presentation to low-water steelhead will be a down-and-across waking dry that creates a nice V wake on the water's surface. The V wake of a dry fly can really turn on a steelhead that has never seen this presentation on a Great Lakes tributary. You should target those individual fish whose behavior tells you they are susceptible to being caught, the ones that move for the fly or follow it. These fish will often take a second or third presentation. If no fish in the pool show interest in the waking dry, I'll then fish them up and across with a dead drift.

If you want numbers, stick to swinging or nymphing egg patterns; that is a given. But when conditions are perfect—the key words Karl uses here are "low and clear waters"—and pools are filled with freshly migrated A/A fish that become stuck due to the low-water conditions, you can use a dry fly with some success.

The wild steelhead rivers of Michigan in the late winter and spring have incredible early black stonefly hatches of *Taeniopteryx* and *Allocapnia*. There are days in late March and April where my home waters of the Muskegon and Pere Marquette turn dark dun with the flotilla of egg-laying females. It looks like thousands of large gray ashes are falling from the sky! The resident browns and rainbows, already fat and plump on steelhead eggs during the spawning, will go crazy for this egg-laying phenomenon. The large spawning areas contain smaller, 2- to 4-pound non-alpha dominant jack male steelhead who usually back away from the larger aggressive alpha bucks for fear of losing their lives. These fish have been caught on skittering CDC adult stonefly dry-fly patterns.

Dry flies really give us insight into an S/R steelhead and how its instincts can be tricked into taking surface insects. Keep in mind that in the big lake environments, there are "scum lines" twenty miles out where cold- and warmwater demarcation lines hold tons of food like shrimp, water beetles, and terrestrials. The amount of surface feeding done by steelhead out in the big open waters is open to speculation. It could be substantial. If it is, we may be all too often ignoring the dry-fly approach.

Great Lakes steelhead can also be caught in the surf if conditions are ideal. From the Steelhead Alley of Lake Erie to New York State's Tug Hill Plateau along the Lake Ontario shoreline, steelhead can feed aggressively on the large amounts of baitfish—emerald shiners, alewives, deep-water sculpins, gobies, bloater chubs, sticklebacks, rainbow smelt—and this affinity for baitfish stays with the fish once it enters the rivers. The hunting behavior is particularly noticeable along the steep-gradient, rocky shoreline river estuaries of the Niagara Escarpment, where shale caverns and canyons of small streams allow for short migration distances from the big lake to river holding pools. Often the lake's pelagic baitfish will inhabit the lower river systems. Here, swinging and stripping small Ice Dub minnow patterns makes for exciting, troutlike streamer fishing. Magog and Grey Ghost smelt patterns, Emerald shiner tube flies, and any saltwater-style patterns that have holographic eyes or breathing material to create movement can bring

CDC stonefly dry flies. This pure hatch-matching steelhead fishing is possible in the spring. MATT SUPINSKI

about exhilarating strikes and action. I have seen steelhead bust through ice along estuary shoreline pools when hunting emerald shiners and smelt.

The Dynamics of Change

Global climate change is on a rampage. Predictable weather no longer exists. Winters can be warm or brutally cold—same with summers. Lately, it seems we're constantly reeling from the last ice storm, ravaging windstorms, or some other record-setting weather event. These factors wreak havoc on and destabilize river systems, water temperatures, and flows. The steelhead and salmon must adjust quickly to these seasonal fluctuations. We see more quick and abrupt changes in the selectivity behavioral phases—the fish go from A/A to P/D in a much quicker manner as a result of frontal system weather extremes that cause fluctuating barometric pressure and temperature regimes and hydrological chaos. With the heat, drought, and flood effects on rivers, migration timing is dramatically affected. The swings are often quick and severe.

Couple the weather with biological ecosystem disruptions like the exotic zebra and quagga mussels invading the Great Lakes (just to name one example) and you have complex negative environmental impacts. The clarity of the Great Lakes and its rivers has been extreme. The plankton nutrient load has been depleted as a result of the filter feeding of the mussels. This has disrupted pelagic baitfish and has made the steelhead extremely wary. They switch

When the fresh ocean- or lake-run steelhead enters a river on a quick spate of water, it will usually harbor the A/A attack mode and crush a swinging fly. But several days later, a drought and heat wave can push the fish back to a P/D state. There is no regularity or predictability in our new meteorological equation. MATT SUPINSKI

quickly from A/A to S/R, both in the lake and river environments, more so now than in the past.

Add hundreds of thousands of new steelhead anglers each year on waters already saturated to the limit with angling pressure, and you create hyperselectivity—a tense steelhead looking over its shoulder at all times as it migrates up the river.

Barometric pressure affects steelhead and all migrating salmonids. Evolutionarily speaking, dropping barometric pressure affects the fish's air bladder system, giving it a sign to head upriver. Migration movements may increase in anticipation of higher water flows and spate-driven hydrodynamics. Steelhead moving fast upstream are usually P/D and have migrating, not taking, on the mind. Stable barometric readings usually mean holding, stationary, taking steelhead. With the new weather patterns caused by global climate change, the barometric pressure seems to be in a constant state of flux—or a permanent state

of stagnation—thus putting steelhead off the bite for longer intervals. Fluctuations are also causing delays in return migration. Long, stable weather patterns are now giving way to short windows of run opportunities. The summer steelhead are forced to stay out of the rivers during extremely hot summers and early hot falls, and migration will be quick and accelerated in late fall and winter, causing extreme A/A behavior to occur simultaneously. Winter-run steelhead in the Great Lakes are being genetically selected to run later in the spring than the customary fall returns. More time in the big lakes feeding on pelagic baitfish, and less cold-water freezeup and metabolic stress, will genetically favor the late-returning spawners, which have ideal water temperatures and the season's last gravel redd digging opportunity; this allows them to circumvent the spawning efforts of their late-winter or early-spring counterparts. Survival of the fittest often coincides with timing and global climate changes.

Favorite Steelhead Flies

STEELHEAD SOFT HACKLE

(Author)

Thread:	Black 6/0 UNI
Tail/Body:	Hareline Gadwall feathers; take whole feather and lay it over the hook
Body segments:	Black thread
Thorax:	Fluorescent Shell Pink Hareline Ice Dub
Hackle:	Hungarian partridge soft hackle

Note: Soft hackles are deadly for stream trout, which is what S/R steelhead will eventually become. The early Great Lakes steelhead fishermen were troutsmen who used wet flies on the swing. This pattern is equally deadly on the Pere Marquette River in Michigan and the Bois Brule River in Wisconsin.

COHEN'S PELAGIC GENERAL

(Pat Cohen, New York)

Hook:	Daiichi 2546
Tail:	Grizzly hackle
Body:	White bucktail with grizzly feathers; sprigs of yellow, blue, and pink bucktail
Flash:	Hareline Mirage Lateral Scale (large and regular) in regular, chartreuse, and red in moderation
Topping:	Sparse blue, pink, and pearl Hareline Ice Dub shimmer fringe with peacock herl strands
Eyes:	Clear Cure Eyes or Fish-Skull Living Eyes (6 mm)
Head:	Clear Cure Goo (thin)

Notes: The Carrie Stevens-developed Grey Ghost was one of the best baitfish patterns for imitating smelt on Maine's Rangeley Lakes. Pat Cohen turns it up a notch with this hot pattern. It is a deadly pattern that mimics all fresh- and saltwater baitfish. It can be used in the river or surf for trout, seatrout, steelhead, or landlocked Atlantic salmon; each species keys in on different features like the subtle color hues, eyes, and iridescence indicative of a pelagic baitfish. The pattern also has a good swimming movement. For Great Lakes and Baltic Sea surf fishermen, especially those targeting the shoals, offshore bars, and shelves where the baitfish accumulate (such as Lake Ontario's Niagara Bar), this fly is a killer for all salmonids feasting on alewives, smelt, herring, capelin, and anything sardine.

Steelhead Egg/Nymph

Krystal Meth Egg

Dr. Tom

Krystal Blue Parr

Senyo's Black Skam Electric Stone Purple

Steelhead Hare's Ear

Clown Egg

Senyo's Teardrop Orange

Matt's Steelhead Soft Hackle

Senyo's Teardrop Blue

Emerald Erie Shiner

Senyo's Black Skam Stone Blue

Smith's Nympho

Cerise Comet

Matt's Mykiss Shrimp

Matt's Chinook Fry

Chicago Leech

Pom Pom Girl

Iceman Creepy

Baconator Mysis

Ripple Crush Niagara Gold

Otter Sucker Nuke Gummie— Pink Ice

Summer-Run Stone Blue

Iceabou Nuke

Otter Sucker Nuke Gummie— Niagara

Bear's Head Banger Hex

Summer Stone Purple

Senyo's Polish- Woven Balloon Stone

Bemmer's Skamania Excavator

Polish-Woven Green Caddis

Ripple Crush Fruity

Otter Wiggle Egg

Disco Stone

Maggot

Nagy's Niagara

Merlino's Sculpin Hex

Lime Weenie

Scrambled Egg

Ice Man Sac Fry

Matt's Latex Wiggle Hex

Senyo's Flashback Wiggle Stone

Czech-Style Caddis

Oppossum Caddis

SENYO'S SLIM SHADY INTRUDER—FROSTY

(Greg Senyo, Lake Erie)

Shank: Black Flymen Senyo Steelhead and Salmon Articulated Shank (25 mm)
Thread: Black 6/0 UNI
Eyes: Silver Hareline bead chain (medium)
Wire: Blue Senyo Intruder Wire or 30-pound Berkley Fireline
Hot spot: Chartreuse Hareline Estaz
Hackle: UV silver Hareline Polar Chenille
Back wing 1: Natural Hareline Lady Amherst center tail feather
Back wing 2: Pearl or silver Flashabou
Body: Silver Hareline Diamond Braid
Hot spot: Chartreuse Hareline Estaz
Hackle: UV Silver Hareline Polar Chenille
Wing 1: Natural Hareline Lady Amherst center tail feather
Wing 2: Pearl or silver Flashabou
Collar: Natural guinea
Eyes: Jungle cock (optional)

Notes: You can't have enough flash when fresh-run A/A steelhead are in search-and-destroy mode, especially on off-color, chalky spate rivers like Steelhead Alley of the Great Lakes or the rivers of British Columbia and Washington State. Great Lakes fly-tying master Greg Senyo has incorporated all the elements of the Intruder fly with myriad synthetic flash and MWM (motion without movement) materials. The combination drives fresh-run A/A steelhead crazy; until their recent river migration these fish were hunting pelagic baitfish in the big lake, and their hunt mechanisms are still fully intact.

BABINE ELECTRIC CANDY CANE

(Author)

Hook: Daiichi Alec Jackson Heavy Spey 2061
Thread: Black 3/0 UNI
Tail: Black rabbit strip
Body: Alternating bands of black chenille with black schlappen and Hareline's Edge Bright over holographic tinsel
Head/Collar: Red-dyed guinea feather, jungle cock

Notes: This is a deadly steelhead pattern for West Coast and Great Lakes alpha dominant fish. When the two-handed rod is pumped and tight-mended by holding the rod in a horizontal position and pushing forward and backward, it snakes and curls fly in a way that gets noticed. Black and red tones are aggression-stimulating colors to steelhead, particularly large males. I designed this pattern on the Babine in the 1980s and was inspired by the Hull String Leech. I was glad to hear that my good client John Flaherty, who fishes the Babine often, continues to punish large A/A steelhead with this pattern. It even gets them out of the P/D funk when necessary. It is also very effective for fall Great Lakes steelhead and was responsible for my first 20-pound Michigan steelhead.

Senyo A-1 and Slim Shady Intruders

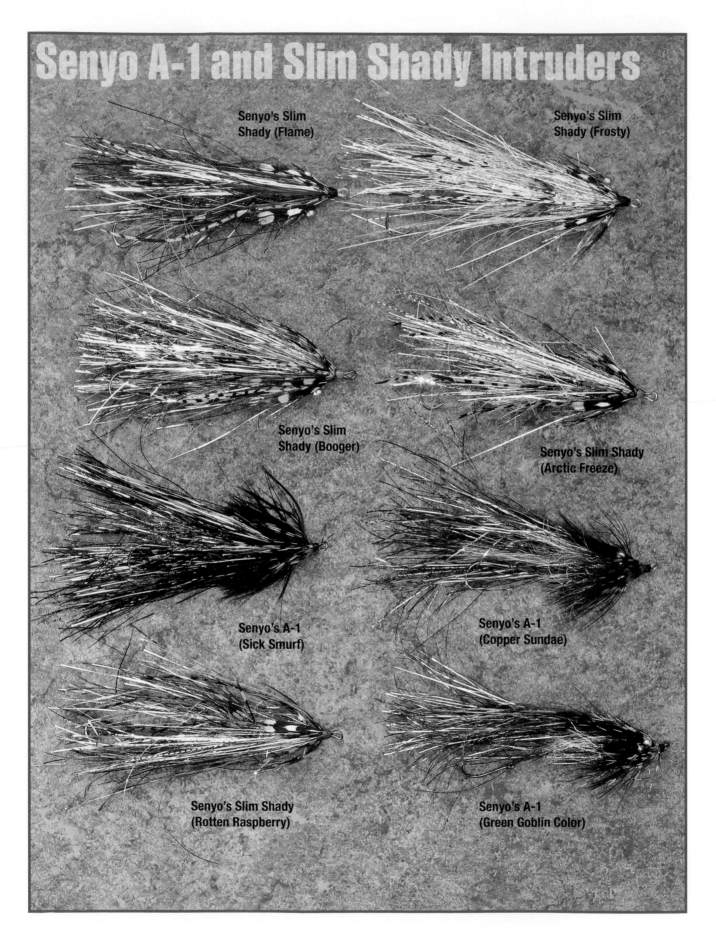

Senyo's Slim Shady (Flame)

Senyo's Slim Shady (Frosty)

Senyo's Slim Shady (Booger)

Senyo's Slim Shady (Arctic Freeze)

Senyo's A-1 (Sick Smurf)

Senyo's A-1 (Copper Sundae)

Senyo's Slim Shady (Rotten Raspberry)

Senyo's A-1 (Green Goblin Color)

MATT'S MYKISS SHRIMP

(Author)

Hook: Daiichi X120
Thread: Hot pink UNI-Stretch
Tail: Pearl Krystal Flash with strands of chartreuse, candy cane, and cerise Glo-Bug yarn
Body: Otter's Soft Milking Egg (sucker spawn, tangerine regular, and kiwi opaque glow)
Shell back: Glo-Bug Yarn and Krystal Flash

Notes: I call this "mykiss" after the Latin word for steelhead. The larger freshwater *Mysis* shrimp exist in the Great Lakes and are a highly favored food source for steelhead. The addition of the Otter Sucker spawn body and color combinations fuse the crustacean motif with the steelhead's love of eggs, giving the fly a dual purpose. This pattern can be tied small for low flows or large if water is high and offcolor.

MERLINO'S SCULPIN HEX

(Rich Merlino, Michigan)

Hook: Gamakatsu B10S
Thread: Tan 6/0 UNI
Tail: Tan and brown barred rabbit strip or Australian opossum
Body/Thorax: Tan Ice Dub

Wing/Collar: India hen neck
Back: Gold pheasant tail strands and pearlescent flat tinsel coated with epoxy
Eyes: Black Hareline mono eyes
Cone: Clear Cure Goo

Notes: Rich Merlino of Orvis Detroit came up with this pattern. When I first tested it for winter and spring steelhead it triggered deep-holding S/R and P/D steelhead to absolutely crush the fly. By far one of the most deadly Great Lakes steelhead patterns, it has a dual imitation of the abundant *Hexagenia* mayfly and sculpins, both prime food targets for the fish. Most anglers don't realize the vast amount of deepwater sculpins Great Lakes fish consume.

ICE MAN SAC FRY

(Author)

Hook: Daiichi X120
Body: Tangerine Otter Soft Milking Egg (6 mm) glued to hook
Wing: Hareline Senyo's Laser Dub, tying in layers bottom up Laser Dub silver minnow belly, hot pink, orange and topping of mottled mini marabou sand or tan.
Eyes: Black Hareline Oval 3-D Pupil

Notes: This is an effective pattern when chinook salmon and steelhead sac fry have hatched in the spring. Territorially dominant A/A steelhead, both prior to and during spawning, target any fish that intrudes into their areas of dominance. (Tiny fry often invade the spawning redds in search of kicked-up minutiae.) When wet, the Laser Dub's translucence is irresistible to trout and steelhead. The strikes to this pattern are violent. It also works well for large brown trout.

Leeches and Tubes

Red Cyclops
Intruder Tube

Humphreys' Olive
Templedog Tube

Hang Time
Leech

Humphreys' Black and
Purple Templedog

Copper Olive
Sculpin Hammer

Blue Ray
Tube

Flamethrower
Leech

Grapefruit
Sculpin Bugger

Ripple Crush
Bugger Leech

Evil
Flamethrower
Leech

Skamania
Leech

Senyo's Steelie
Parr Tube

HANG TIME LEECH

(Phil Pantano, Connecticut)

Trailer hook:	Daiichi 2557
Thread:	Black 6/0 UNI
Braid connector:	Black Senyo's Intruder Wire trailer hook
Body hook:	Black Senyo's Fish-Skull articulated shank
Body:	Black rabbit strip, then cross-cut black rabbit around hook shank
Flash:	Wapsi Lateral Mirage Scale in orange, gold, and fluorescent yellow with copper Flashabou
Collar:	Hot pink and orange Senyo's Laser Dub
Head:	Gold barbell eyes and orange Hareline Senyo's Laser Dub

Notes: Fresh-run A/A and cautious autumn S/R steelhead are usually found in low, clear water and are wary of the ever-present aggressive nature of spawning king salmon. They tend to hang in the long pool tailout areas and inspect the fly for good distances. The gold barbell head allows you to dip and curl it on the hang time at the end of the swing, which is where 80 percent of the strikes occur with this pattern.

HOWELL'S SKA-OPPER

(Scott Howell, Oregon)

Hook:	Daiichi D2110 Bomber
Thread:	Tan 6/0 UNI
Tail:	Orange Krystal Flash with orange arctic fox
Body:	Orange Senyo's Laser Dub with orange rubber legs
Back:	Brown foam (4 mm)
Collar:	Orange dyed guinea
Head:	Deer hair trimmed in ball with natural tip wings
Head flap:	U-shaped piece of black foam

Notes: On rivers like Oregon's North Umpqua, the A/A steelhead are heavily surface oriented and can be provoked to take a down-and-across, stripped and waked surface fly. It's amazing to see how A/A fresh-run fish that have pooled up react to the surface waking and commotion. On rivers that have large stonefly populations, the foam Ska-oppers are deadly in restoring natal feeding and reflective behavior in fresh-run and holding steelhead.

Howell and Senyo Intruders

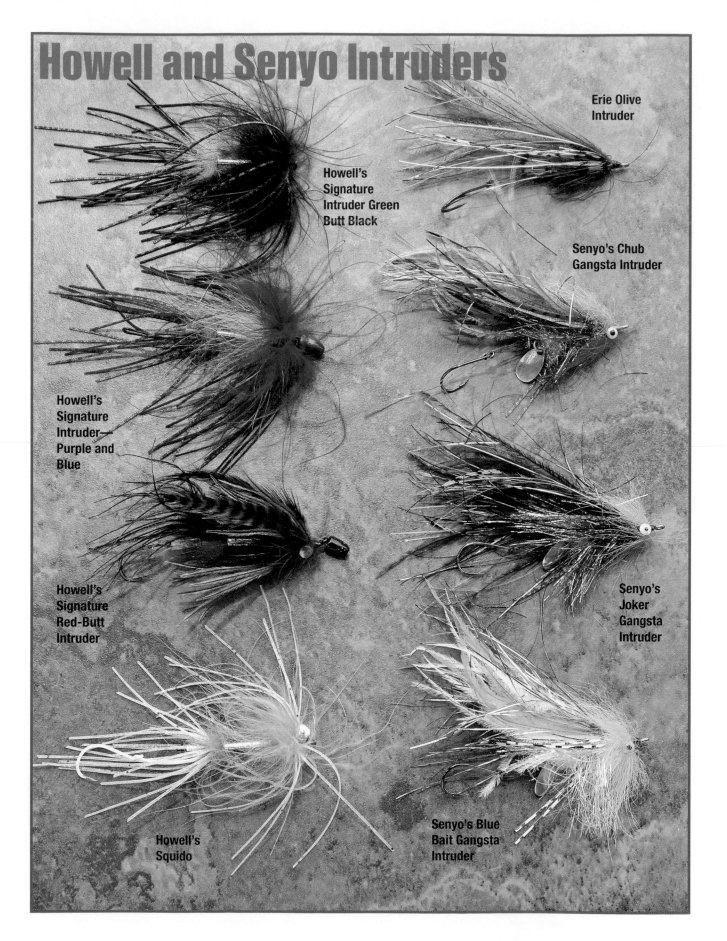

Howell's Signature Intruder Green Butt Black

Erie Olive Intruder

Senyo's Chub Gangsta Intruder

Howell's Signature Intruder—Purple and Blue

Howell's Signature Red-Butt Intruder

Senyo's Joker Gangsta Intruder

Howell's Squido

Senyo's Blue Bait Gangsta Intruder

Tubes and Minnows

Senyo's Pink Sculpin Tube

Senyo Sculpin Thugmeister

Orange and Blue Templedog Tube

Egg Leech Shaggy Gray

Red and Black Templedog Tube

Autumn Gold Templedog

Black Collie Orange

Senyo Orange Club Sculpin Tube

Nuke Pearl Amherst

Doddi Orange Tube

Marabou Parr

Torch Pelagic

Egg Invader and Space Invader

Black Egg Raider

Green Butt
Blue Intruder

Pearl Squid
Egg Invader

Opaque Ghost
Egg Invader

Emerald
Ghost

Thugmeister
Egg Invader

Senyo's Space
Invader Fish Food

Blue Opal
Invader

Senyo's Crawfish
Space Invader

Atlantic Salmon

And so it becomes the angler's job to dope out the right fly and technique to appeal to one of the predatory stimuli, whether it be as rudimentary as sheer opportunism or as tricky as excitation—even perhaps having to stretch the point to try to convince a fish, if only for one critical instant, that it's hungry when it isn't. No mean feat. This is why fly fishing for Atlantic salmon has to be among the most intriguing sports on Earth.

Art Lee, *Atlantic Salmon Journal*

The Atlantic salmon is perhaps the most majestic creature that has ever swum. Man's initial infatuation with the fish is detailed in a series of amazing cave paintings in Lascaux and Les Eyzies, along the Vézère River, a tributary of the France's Dordogne River. A beautiful floor painting of the Atlantic salmon made by some Cro-Magnon fisherman embodies the admiration

Fresh migrators are ultimately in search of deep pools below the gravel areas and sections of river where they were born. But they also stop at temporary obstacles and barriers to migration like waterfalls, which cause indecision, frustration, and also curiosity—all perfect A/A fly-taking traits. ARNI BALDURSSON/LAX-Á

Atlantic Salmon Behavior

A/A PHASE

Fresh-run spring and fall; rising spate waters
Most aggressive salmon at tailouts of the pool and
at the head of the pack in pools
Post spawn kelts need to feed
Freud's Id stage

S/R PHASE

Fish have settled in to holding and incubator pools
Focus on smaller flies, imitating naturals
Preoccupied with the surface and presentations
there
Essential to rest fish between refusals
Freud's Ego stage

P/D PHASE

Prevalent in pooled-up Atlantic salmon in late
summer
Physiological metamorphosis of salmon during the
pre-spawn phase
Renal system is taxed
Freud's Superego stage ■

the one they called "salmo"—it was godlike worship. The meat was so highly prized that returning Roman legions brought pelts of smoked salmon and it traded equally with gold in open-air markets.

The passion for the "king of all fish," as the Atlantic salmon is known, reigns supreme wherever the fish are found. Fresh out of the sea on their river migration, chrome-silver and dripping sea lice, Atlantic salmon will smash a Lady Amherst or Green Highlander fly with the vengeance of a shark or an orca. Once habituated to the river environment and their selected holding pool, their curiosity will baffle even the most ardent brown trout observer. If steelhead like to play with their prey like a cat, Atlantic salmon will play with your mind and break your spirit. Later in their pre-spawning phase, when they become dour, they can become downright impossible to catch.

Untold numbers of books have been written on the Atlantic salmon and the species' glamorous sporting qualities. The sight of an Atlantic salmon swimming in a crystal-clear pool is enough to send chills of excitement down your spine. When fishing for Atlantics, anglers will inevitably experience frustration and lack of success. Yet we keep coming back for that magical take that washes all the frustration away in a flash. This often happens when you least expect it and you have essentially given up on casting. Then the fish takes your fly when it should not have. They can turn

and worship these fish were accorded. The fish's full body profile and kype are portrayed in remarkable detail on the floor of one particular cave known as L'abri du Poisson.

There is evidence along these rivers that early man modified pools and channelized tributaries to capture the massive Atlantic salmon that once saturated the rivers of these enchanted mountains and forests. Today the region's waters harbor wild brown trout, grayling, and seatrout, and the area is included in Europe's massive restocking program to reestablish the mighty *saumon de l'Atlantique*. Today only the Brittany district maintains small migration runs of Atlantic salmon.

When the Roman legions conquered this massive area, then known as Gallia Aquitania, they called the salmon *salar*, or leapers, for their ability to jump high waterfalls while on upstream migration. The earliest writings by Pliny, in the era of Caesar Tiberius, said the people of Gaul had no greater love for a fish than for

Atlantic salmon master Arni Baldursson of LAX-Á Iceland shows off a dime-bright A/A Kola Russian salmon still dripping sea lice. Atlantic salmon are the "king of all fish." They have been worshipped by cavemen, Roman legions, and aristocracy all over the world. No other fish equals their paradoxical nature. LAX-Á

France's rich and beautiful Dordogne River valley boasted massive Atlantic salmon runs centuries ago. BEN HEINE

Right: The cave drawing at Abri Du Poisson show that *Salmo salar* has been worshipped for a long time. PHILIPPE JUGIE/CMN

off and on in a heartbeat, and take the fly on their terms. The numbers-game anglers are better off to stick with stripers or Jackson Hole cutthroat trout.

One important clue to understanding these enigmatic fish is to look at their lineage. In *Ecology of Atlantic Salmon and Brown Trout*, Bror and Nina Jonsson examined how Atlantic salmon (*Salmo salar*) and brown trout (*Salmo trutta*) evolved from a common ancestor approximately seventy to fifty million years ago. Their work suggests that brown trout initially inhabited the cold, nutrient-rich waters of Europe and the North Atlantic, with Atlantic salmon evolving later after having access to the ocean and seas. The fact that the species can mate together and have offspring further strengthens their genetic bond. Given that Atlantic salmon and brown trout are so extremely closely united, can it be that our techniques for presenting a fly to them may overlap?

It is a fusion of factors—the ocean predator instincts of the fresh-run migrators and natal imprinting to river food forms—that gives the fish a strong,

aggressive urge to take the fly. Lee Wulff sums up the fresh-from-the-sea-mentality well in his book *Atlantic Salmon*: "Coming back from the sea, where the feeding reflexes have been maintained, to rest again in the turbid flows of sweet fresh water, it must be a remembrance of many things. When an insect comes wandering by, there can only reasonably be a deep basic instinct to make a pass at it. It should be remembered that the period of parr feeding in most cases is longer than the sea-feeding portion of the salmon's life. Its effect must be a strong one."

Trying to back up theories often based on intense, passionate observation and speculation, and to combine folklore and angler observations with actual scientific evidence is quite difficult. However, there are many qualities and behaviors of Atlantics worth examining for clues to how we might fool them with a fly.

First, Atlantic salmon, like brown trout, are extremely surface-oriented. The reasons for this behavior can only be speculated, but I think it has to do with the habitat in which they grow up. Young Atlantic

Leaping salmon on the Sardine Box pool on the Gaspé's Grande Riviere. *Salar* means "leaper" in Latin, a term coined by the Roman legions who watched the salmon jump massive waterfalls. They do the same when hooked, producing in the angler an amazing adrenaline rush like no other! GORDIE PECHUER

salmon parr can spend up to three years in the river systems before smolting to the ocean or sea. Here they look like and feed with a focus on aquatic insects like stream brown trout. From the time they are born in the river and become small parr, their pectoral fins, which are larger than a stream trout's, are a vital part of their physiology. These powerful propellers will eventually allow them to jump incredibly high waterfalls and obstacles unimaginable by Pacific salmonids, but as parr these fins allow them to take up positions in faster, shallower runs, away from the larger, deeper pools dominated by fish that would eat them.

An interview with Bror Jonsson of the Norwegian Institute of Fisheries confirmed this: "The large pectoral fins make it easier for Atlantic salmon than brown trout to be pressed against the bottom substratum in strong water current," Jonsson said. "By that, the less aggressive Atlantic salmon parr have a suitable feeding habitat out in the strong current not exploited by brown trout."

This faster water is where most of the aquatic insects emerge. Hatching and darting nymphs and lar-

vae are propelled upward in these shallow environments, where they can be trapped in the turbulent surface and become easy prey for the juvenile salmon. Their surface vision is good in shallow environments due to the amount of light infused into these skinny-water habitats. This looking up for food and surface curiosity will become an important behavior for the rest of the Atlantic's life. Keep in mind also that both brown trout and Atlantics are photophobic; they prefer low-light conditions when in the A/A and S/R states. In low-light situations the surface environment is easily discernible, as opposed to a bright sunny day where glare and the direct, powerful sun make surface feeding and items of prey or curiosity difficult to detect.

Another surface orientation behavior takes place in the big-water hunting grounds of the adult. Atlantics are pelagic (upper-water) baitfish hunters. They are in a constant search for schools of herring, capelin, smelt, and all sardines. These schools are visible in the dark ocean and sea environments, as the dark clusters of the baitfish schools are backlit by the light filtered through the surface waters. If the salmon

Atlantic salmon colonized the rivers that ran into the Baltic Sea and Atlantic Ocean, allowing their unique qualities to be documented from North America to Europe. Here Thomas Woelfle Spey casts on the Ranga River of Iceland, an Atlantic salmon mecca. THOMAS WOELFLE

Right: An Atlantic salmon that took a Royal Coachman Wulff. The color red has always been a powerful stimulant for salmon and trout, a trait first noted in the "red fly" documentation of the Roman Claudius Aelinus in Macedonia around 400 AD. Lee Wulff in *The Atlantic Salmon* writes: "The appetites of these returning, mature salmon are curbed to great degree but not so completely that they, on rare occasion, will take a fly." MATT SUPINSKI

cruised the surface while looking down into the dark abyss, these schools of prey would not be detected as well. Attacking from the bottom, camouflaged by their steel-gray and blue heads and torsos that the prey cannot detect, has proven to be a successful hunting style. Once the salmon corral the baitfish they smash their bodies upward into the schools, stunning the fish and eating them. So from the early youth through adulthood, surface orientation is a constant need for the Atlantics. Keep in mind that when the parr are in shallow-water river environments they are extremely vulnerable to birds of prey like ospreys, hawks, kingfishers and the like. Keeping one keen eye upward at all times is paramount to survival.

Atlantic salmon have acute vision and see color and movement well. Bror Jonsson confirmed this: "Atlantic salmon and brown trout have impeccable vision," Jonsson said. "Brown trout are known to be photophobic, preferring dim light—Atlantics probably less so in my experience." Atlantics will take flies in brighter, clearer conditions than will steelhead and browns. The eager disposition of Atlantic "takers"

The vast array of salmon flies that young parr imprint to causes photographer and Gaspé game warden Jean Guy Béliveau to examine his fly box carefully for just the right "dope." JEAN GUY BÉLIVEAU

Right: Always have a positive attitude when on a Atlantic salmon river. If the water is low, or it is hot and sunny and not at all "taking conditions," try tiny doubles and tubes down to size 16 for P/D fish. The Atlantic's vision is that good. ARNI BALDURSSON/LAX-Á

makes them highly sought after in June and July from the Canadian Maritimes to Russia.

My first truly eye-opening experience with the incredible perception of Atlantic salmon happened years ago on Québec's Grand Cascapedia River. During my first visit in 2001, the famous Charlie Valley rock pool had been the hot pool for success the previous year and I couldn't fish the beat due to its high demand. When I eventually got to fish it in 2004, it was fishing poorly and nobody had caught salmon out of it the entire season. There had been a drastic flood the year prior that had realigned the river's substratum, thus changing the hydrodynamics for a holding salmon pool. The pool was not holding fish, plain and simple. All the guides knew it.

My good friend, lodge owner David Bishop, always gave me the "short straw" river beats. I was a guide and so I was at the bottom of the food chain for the owner, who saved the good pools for the less talented, older, and wealthier clientele. Each morning he would hold a lottery and have every guest line up to get their designated beat for the day. When David told me I was going to Charlie Valley, I really didn't care because I knew it was fishing terrible. I just wanted to see it and take some pictures of it. A fish would be a bonus. I lit up a cigar in the morning and hopped in a vehicle with my two less-than-enthusiastic guides. They knew I was screwed, and so they anticipated a fairly easy day of drinking coffee and smoking cigarettes as they sat and talked in French about everything but fishing. The moment they got there, the guys were talking about having lunch—that is not a good sign!

As I made ready my rod and tied on my own fly, they told me, "Knock yourself out. It has been pretty tough here lately with the water low, eh!" I was not going to let their downer attitude mess up my day.

My favorite fly on this river has always been the Undertaker. Starting with the large size 6 double, I began my swinging and stepped down the faster water above the rock pool with no luck. There was not a fish showing, and I could see no fish in the low water. As I approached the steep 12-foot drop-off into the massive pool near a rock the size of the house, I decided to go really small—a size 12 Double Undertaker. I swung it at a good speed right below the surface because in warmer waters the A/A metabolism of the fish would be quick and fast. Now the guides really thought I was crazy. "You might want to put a short-sink tip on. That pool is deep plus it is hot and sunny. Fish will be holding as deep as possible," shouted my guide. "Nah!" I told him. "I will stick with what I have." They looked at me with that French-Canadian "whatever" look.

On the second cast, as the fly swung near the surface of the deep drop-off, the taking fish exploded on the surface—I almost soiled myself! Twenty minutes of intense battle yielded a magnificent chrome-colored 28-pound female Atlantic that was straight from the salt. The vision capability of that fish, its being able to see a micro fly by Atlantic salmon standards from the bottom of the deep, dark, tannic-stained pool, absolutely astounded me. Moral of story: stay positive and experiment or rely on old standards. The Undertaker has never led me astray.

Vision acuteness is a function of light variation and how much a salmonid experiences light's variances and extremes. In the ocean, Atlantics can dive down to depths of a couple hundred feet to hunt benthic crustaceans and squid and other food forms when pelagic fish like herring and capelin are scarce. All benthic food forms in places where light doesn't exist possess a chemical property known as bioluminescence. Atlantic salmon like to hunt in the upper surface waters where eutrophic nutrients are highest and pelagic baitfish, small sea urchins, crabs, and jellyfish are abundant. For the salmon to go down to extreme depths to hunt, they must make amazing adjustments in their vision capabilities, which are

The strong, vibrant colors of a Willie Gunn tube fly trigger territorially aggressive behavior within alpha males, such as this large-kyped Atlantic salmon in Iceland, just prior to spawning—what I call A/A behavior. Here is when a salmon's color preference goes from blue/green to red.
HAKAN STENLUND

Art Lee writes in *Atlantic Salmon Journal*: "Unless you simply choose to play 'chuck-and-chance-it,' which is about as exciting as watching someone make a telephone call, you must be well enough informed, cagey enough, to know how to read the fish's genetic mind." ARNI BALDURSSON/LAX-Á

used in tandem with their sensory vibration perception. A 12-foot-deep river pool is really not that deep when compared to 300-foot ocean depths. So when waters are low, the sun is out, and salmon are P/D dour, or when your gillie says "salmon are not supposed to be there," think smaller and darker in your fly patterns. The proverbial, "bright day, bright fly" never seemed to work for me!

At smolting, the visual pigments in Atlantic salmon's eyes change. While the young in fresh waters are most sensitive to colors in the red spectrum, salmon at sea are most sensitive to colors in the blue spectrum (Hoar, 1988). The cones of the retina are responsible for the color vision and physiologists such as Allison et al. (2006) and Raine et al. (2013) have described how the thyroid hormone is necessary to induce ultraviolet sensitive cone loss in juvenile salmonid retinas, altering the vision of the fish when they move from fresh to salt water, and how the cells are regenerated when the adults return to rivers.

The colors red and orange may also be important for other reasons. My experience is that prior to spawning, a salmon's sexual aggression is piqued by red or orange flies. I asked Bror Jonsson whether this was a result of river life vision or if these colors aggravate spawning fish, and his response was interesting:

You know Atlantic salmon spawning status starts with colors: dominants exhibit red and light colors (typical dominant male colors) whereas subordinates exhibit dark colors and often a dark band that goes through the eyes and along the flanks of the body (typical color of females and male parr). However, large subordinate males also exhibit dark colors in the river, particularly towards the end of their spawning period. Males showing subordinate colors are less often attacked. Males with dark sides and back are "wallflowers" on the spawning ground and not esteemed by dominant males. Thus, by showing the right color, a male can sneak sperm with greater success. I have even observed dominant males quivering and squirting milt towards subordinate males displaying female colors, indicating that this camouflage is efficient.

Stages of Migration

Just saying that the hyperselectivity of these fish is rampant and unpredictable doesn't stop the head scratching we do every time we fish for them. We need some basis for establishing fundamentals that carry over from river to river and continent to continent. This will give us a selectivity framework that holds true most of the time. The exceptions, however, are still all too numerous. I like to think of the three stages of selectivity as correlating to Freud's stages of the id, the ego, and the superego. In my never-ending attempt to bring human qualities to fish, I know this may be going a little too far, but it helps me understand and explain a fish that has no rhyme or reason as to when it takes the fly.

The id or A/A state is one of reckless abandonment, or the pleasure principle. It is the basic predator drive of the hunting animal. It knows no judgment or value or any consequences for its actions. A fresh-run salmon can be labeled as such when in its A/A search-and-destroy phase. The ego or S/R state is the reality principle, the one that seeks to organize the world around the animal. This phase includes planning, metabolic cost-benefit analysis, attempts at organizing and controlling the environment, and the realization that impetuous actions may have consequences, often negative ones. The salmon does not need to feed or take the fly for nourishment; it does so because the inquisitive devil inside makes him do it. The pool of holding salmon fits this mold perfectly, as it is almost continuously in the S/R state of mind.

The final stage, superego, or P/D, is a state where the fish strives to aspire to a higher moral plane of being and evolutionary survival. Unlike humans, it is not religion or the law that brings it to this higher sense, but instead it's the fish's natural evolutionary imperative to spawn and propagate the species in order to ensure the life cycle survival strategy remains in place for millions of years to come. Hapless mistakes like taking the fly or chasing small brook trout around because they are invading space will cost the fish precious metabolic reserves, possibly killing it and negating its genetic infusion into the next generations. P/D stages occur during the pre-spawning of Atlantic salmon, starting in late September and continuing through November in most of North America. However, when provoked, aggressive, territorial, and dominant behaviors can occur.

Fresh-Run A/A Stage

Atlantic salmon will start to migrate from ocean hunting grounds near Greenland and the Faroe Islands up to a year before they ascend their natal rivers of origin. Little straying from one river to the next occurs thanks to the Atlantic salmon's finely tuned imprinting to natal rivers. The migration usually starts under darkness and with a firm river spate of snowmelt or rain runoff. The alpha predator is still in full attack mode.

Some will say that moving fish are totally preoccupied with the task at hand, that it is only holding fish that will take the fly. I have found that both stages produce results. Since most of the moving occurs in darkness or under full moons, or under "white light" in the near-arctic regions of places like Iceland, Norway, and Russia, we normally never fish to Atlantics that are on full migration; even in the above mentioned countries, white-light fishing is discouraged.

Inclement weather produces moving behavior in pools, including a lot of porpoising, splashing, and jumping. This is especially true for salmon in low, drought-stricken waters. This, combined with falling barometric pressure, is usually enough of a spark to get salmon to be A/A again and strike the fly.

A fat Swedish Mörrum River salmon fresh in from the Baltic. Some of the largest salmon of the season are caught when they are A/A and straight out of the ocean. These fish are packed full of pounds gained from eating capelin and herring in the big seas. As they harbor over in rivers, they rely on stored body fat for energy. ANDERS SORENSON

Classic Atlantic salmon holding lies are similar to steelhead lies, with the exception that the Atlantics can hold in stronger, faster flows. River islands, tributary confluences, strong gradient rapids, pocket water, large boulders, high waterfalls and dams, and rigid bottoms and river channels all produce temporary holding lies and indecision. Usually it takes dominant males and females leading a school of migrating fish to show the proper way through an uncertain path.

After spawning, the salmon's urge to take a fly is significant. This fairly short period of the river-run stage makes Atlantic salmon fishing look fairly easy and is a blessing for anglers who endure hundreds or thousands of hours of futility. Presenting your fly to A/A salmon is a fairly simple affair. Start casting near shore and increase your line length and swings with each cast; a standard down-and-across fly swing works. The strike occurs either as the fly is swung broadside or as the fly starts to turn upstream at the conclusion of its swing. I have even had A/A fish hit the fly as soon as it hit the water! In this state, the salmon is the least concerned about the speed or perfection of your presentation.

Strikes tend to come violently and takes are solid. The tension of the swung fly in the current of the river will cause the salmon to hook itself. High-leaping aerial displays and violent runs show the anger of the fish, which has probably never felt a hook in its mouth before. Heavier tippets and larger flies are more common here due to the salmon's lack of caution and the higher water flows, which are often discolored from snowmelt and spate runoff. Most Atlantic anglers use Maxima's Ultragreen leaders and tippet in clear oligotrophic waters and Maxima Chameleon in stained tannic waters. The lines are stiff, have great knot strength and abrasion resistance, and hold a fly's profile well, especially when tied with a turle knot.

Perhaps the most important aspect of fishing for fresh-run salmon is fly selection. Scientific studies have shown that fish fresh from the sea, dripping sea lice and tapeworms, show a particular preference for the blue/green light spectrum. This is most likely a function of the fish's life spent at sea, but not necessarily. This would explain why flies such as Green Highlanders, Blue Charms, and Sunray Shadows always produce well at this time of year.

But let's also look at the naturalistic side of this equation. Lee Wulff's amazingly lethal Surface Stone Fly is a parachute fly with many variations. The green version has a bright green body, which consistently produces salmon all year, particularly in June. The Green Stonefly emerges in good numbers starting in June on the northeastern Appalachian rivers extending to the tip of the Gaspé. Does this natural emergence coincide with the blue/green vision spectrum of the Atlantics at this time, or does the natural itself do the job of stimulating the take? To play devil's advocate, are the bluish-green waters of Québec's Grande Riviere and St. Jean part of the vision and fly-preference equation? This theory has led to green fly creations like the Pompier, Butterfly, Green Machine, and others. Only salmon can tell us the exact answer, but I tend to believe that it is a combination of all these things.

Patterns like the Magog Smelt, the white and dark Wulff Muddlers, and the Alley's Shrimp often resemble the baitfish and crustaceans that Atlantics encounter in the estuaries prior to river migration. If you ask anyone in the Canadian Maritimes what his or her go-to fly is, their answer will always be a muddler. This fly's silhouette resembles the sculpin, baitfish, gobies, and sticklebacks that Atlantics can encounter as they approach the brackish estuaries where these pelagic fish love to hang out in the springtime. Warmer river waters heat up the colder estuaries, attracting baitfish schools.

The Ponoi River, on Russia's Kola Peninsula, offers a rare exception to the norm of selective and P/D salmon and offers some insights into aggressive salmon behavior. When the river was first fished by the wealthy American and European anglers (I got to fish it back in the early 1980s because my uncle was a Polish diplomat in Moscow), the first Western rods to wet a line here were astonished by how willingly the Atlantics came to the fly on a consistent basis, resulting in double-digit hookups. This was most unusual when compared to the waters of the Canadian Maritime provinces, the United Kingdom, and Scandinavia. In 2003, the salmon catch rate at one camp of 20 people was 1,812 fish. That is astonishing!

A series of ecological factors go into creating such an amazing fishery. The unusually mild winter climate and short summers provide perfect water temperatures (52 degrees) for *Salmo salar*. The river's fast, oxygenated, somewhat stained waters have ideal holding lies. The river is close to the sea, which not only helps in smolt survival but also increases your chances of encountering fresh-run fish.

And there are enormous numbers of fish. Each year the Ponoi receives two migration runs: immature grilse fish in the spring, and heavy, multi-sea mature males and females in late summer, which spawn the following fall. Thus you have tremendous numbers of two spawning year class groups in the river system at the same time. As a result of this overcrowding, there is a lot of territorially dominant behavior among the various year classes.

The tremendous gravel and cobblestone river bottoms, which are free of silt, contribute to high reproductive success. Closeness to the sea results in high smolting success rates, which in turn create a high percentage of returning adults. The Ponoi's immense Diptera and stonefly life, a result of the acidic waters, provides food for the young salmon in a region where rivers are normally sterile.

Once the smolts and post-spawn adults return to the Barents Sea, the tremendous phytoplankton blooms produce incredible schools of pelagic baitfish such as herring and capelin, which are the primary food sources for the salmon. Since all large piscivorous predator fish of the Barents Sea feed on these capelin, the survival rate of young salmon at sea here is high, since the salmon are not specifically targeted as yet another baitfish. Even orca whale migrations are tied to the Norwegian spawning cycle of herring, not the migration of the Atlantic salmon as they are in other parts of the ocean.

The Ponoi's unique environment gives us some interesting looks into the world of A/A Atlantic salmon behavior. Though the salmon will take just about every traditional and modern style of Atlantic salmon fly found, it has a strong penchant for a Willie Gunn tube fly, designed by Scottish gillie Willie Gunn for the deep, rich, tea-stained rivers of Scotland. The orange, black, and yellow color scheme is easy to see in these conditions, which are similar to the Ponoi's. The fly has a tremendous ability to nudge the A/A response in the highly territorial dominant salmon jockeying for holding slots, as well as in salmon that are in sexually aggressive spawning states.

Finally, since the late-summer runs of larger salmon on the Ponoi don't spawn till the following fall, they have a long river life. Once a salmon is in this river niche, its visionary rods and cones switch from the blue/green spectrum to the red/yellow spectrum.

An example of A/A behavior in fresh-run fish on the Ponoi manifests itself on other salmon rivers. A good deal of bumping and nosing goes on when swinging flies to fresh or congested Atlantics in primary taking lies. I think this bumping and nosing, fol-

In Kola rivers, there is one king—*semga* (Russian for salmon)! The healthy brown trout populations take second billing. The Ponoi, like its sister rivers the Litza and the Karlovka, originates from lakes, swamps, and peat and marl bogs as they collect snowmelt throughout the summer. It is a wide-open river plain with constant boulders and gravel runs, providing perfect holding and taking lies for its abundant salmon.
ARNI BALDURSSON/LAX-Á

lowed by a chase—typical Atlantic behavior—comes from how Atlantics attack the pelagic baitfish schools. Usually they will circle the pack of capelin baitfish or herring, and will slam into them in an attempt to stun and confuse the tight school of fish, picking up the injured prey. I asked Bror Jonsson about this and he told me, "In my experience, most of the behavioral traits develop when the fish are young and they use similar behavioral patterns later in life—but ocean-learned hunting behavior is important.

This appears to be the reason why farmed salmon compete so poorly on the spawning ground. They use competitive displays that had previously proven successful among equals in hatchery tanks, but are useless when meeting wild species in the river. They don't fit into nature's grand scheme of things.

The Ponoi and other rivers in the Kola are unique because their salmon spend most of their time in the A/A state. This is rare for *Salmo salar*. Everyone must treat themselves during their lifetime and fish these rivers. It will totally transform the way you think of this fish. ARNI BALDURSSON/LAX-Á

The Ponoi is one of those few big rivers where salmon chase and roll on waking dry flies. Waking and stripping dries here produces a higher rate of acceptance than on the Gaspé, for instance. There a dead-drifting fly is more effective for the more P/D and S/R fish pent up in pools. This is mostly due to the faster, boulder-strewn holding slots of the Russian rivers, where movement and agitation by the prey stirs strong A/A behavioral responses. Everything about the Ponoi is unique, including the fact that the salmon spend a majority of their time in the most desirable aggressive state.

Selective/Reflective Mode

Except for the landlocked Atlantic salmon of short river systems close to the ocean and lakes, most fish start up the rivers as early as April for spawning in the fall and early winter. Given this long river incubation period, the "settling in" allows the fish to ponder and become S/R in their nature—they have a lot of time on their hands to think about stuff! Given their already high level of curiosity, this circumstance makes them take the fly often enough to be a prized game fish. Late-running fish are still takers, but they tend to get on with spawning activity more abruptly since time is of the essence.

Once an Atlantic's initial bull-in-a-china-shop, fresh-run phase slows down, or perhaps after the fish has already been hooked and released, it finds a holding pool to its liking. Then it becomes S/R. Freud said ego behaviors take hold when a person sees that actions produce consequences; so it goes for the holding salmon, who is now conserving energy for spawning. The fish must move, think, and act wisely. Since it is now in the world of the biological drift of the river ecosystem, and no longer the hunter of baitfish, or the hunted by killer whales or commercial fishing fleets, it now sees life differently and more cautiously. Here natal imprinting to food forms, reminiscent of river life behaviors as a parr, begins to rekindle the curiosity of these prodigal sons and daughters returned home and grows increasingly important for a S/R fish. Yet at the same time, its evolutionary strategy causes a tightly clamped jaw. This is the yin and yang struggle of Atlantic salmon in the river.

Once the salmon chooses its holding pool—usually the deepest water with much room for escapement, often near spawning grounds—it will stratify at all depths, depending on hierarchy, comfortable flow, and water temperatures. It will also pick holding pools next to fast, deep, well-oxygenated runs with boulders and jagged rock. It will slip into these areas when summer temperatures soar and oxygen becomes necessary for survival. On Norway's famous Gaula River, the salmon love the deep pools, yet they lie close to shore in fast, boulder-strewn rapids, which are often tea-stained from peat and marl forest bogs. Thomas Woelfle, master German trout and salmon fly fisher and photographer, is amazed by the ability of salmon to go from S/R to A/A behavior in a heartbeat as they occupy the near-shore niches. "Norway to many means big rivers, lots of space and long casts with two-handed rods and shooting heads," Woelfle said. "Well, not always. During high-water periods lots of fish move up near shore, so it's better not to wade too deep into the river. The salmon shouldn't see the fly too soon—the later the better. It should surprise him and trigger its strike behavior and the bite."

Woelfle describes my "wants something it can't have" theory I talked about earlier. You always want to surprise the Atlantic and change the status quo of its somewhat boring river life. Sometimes changes of light or a situation in the river system, like the arrival of ocean salmon in the pool of established resident fish, makes all the salmon more aggressive. You will

Arni Baldursson lands a huge Norwegian salmon from a well-built boat. The big waters of Norway's Alta River are ideal for giant Atlantic salmon. Though not easy to fish and turbulent, world records are meant to be broken here. ARNI BALDURSSON/LAX-Á

often see fish chasing each other and jockeying for position. This is a good time to present the fly.

In this phase, the salmon can take your fly at any given time. It has total mobility and metabolic stability, so you might be caught off guard when its taking urge happens. Concentration on each cast and presentation is more critical here. Having a game plan and sticking to it—along with its variations—or not being afraid to make unorthodox changes must be done methodically for success. This is what separates the great Atlantic salmon anglers from the average Joes. The greats consistently catch fish because of their adaptability and willingness to try something against the grain. Here is a list of important strategies.

DON'T BE A CREATURE OF HABIT

Every day, all spring, summer, and fall on Atlantic salmon rivers throughout in the world, a guide's SUV pulls up to the beat for the day. Doors and truck tailgates are slammed shut at the same time each day. Anglers walk to the water like clockwork on the same path, make the same fly selection with the same cast, and fish it the same way. They catch nothing, then

have lunch. Maybe there is a hookup or a refusal. They come back to the lodge for drinks and dinner, then repeat the same thing next day.

Instead, try approaching the pool or beat you are assigned to from a different side or direction. Try a different fly than recommended—this will drive your gillie crazy, but the good ones know variety is the spice of life. Try different presentations from different angles. Remember gillies and guides work seven days a week from June through September. To survive this grueling work schedule, their whole existence must be regimented in order to avoid burnout. So their fly choice is usually the one that caught the last fish, same with presentation. Everything about an Atlantic salmon guide's survival strategy, just like that of the fish, has to be calculated and rigorously stuck to if they want to guide every day.

There is not much room for the "what if" mentality when a guide is going on weeks of sleep deprivation. This is where the spark and enthusiasm of the client dreaming weeks ahead and tying new flies in anticipation of the trip adds to the whole relationship. I often say, after a client has showed me his new flies,

Atlantic salmon, like those of the Mörrum River in Sweden, love the down-and-across swinging fly and two-handed Spey fishing has become a must for serious Atlantic salmon chasers throughout the world. Although true Spey casts take time to master, a simple overhead can be learned by all fly fishers in a matter of minutes and accomplishes the same goal. HENRIK LARSSON

that something really cool or great can be found in their novel approach. I mumble, "Why didn't I think of that?"

No fly is a sacred cow. As I mentioned above, every lodge, gillie, and river has its hallowed tried-and-true flies that are consistent producers of fish for one reason or another. As a guide, I have my own. But to an Atlantic, whose whims change by the minute, presenting a series of flies in all sizes and color combinations makes sense. Traditionalist patterns, new-age rubber-legged creatures, tube flies, and natural baitfish patterns all have merit. Traditional fly-swinging, riffle-hitching, pumping and stripping, and dead drifting all have their place. Sound confusing? It is. That is why this Atlantic salmon phase is so much fun.

TAKE TIMEOUTS

Take timeouts between fly changes. Sit and study the salmon. Look around you at the beauty; Atlantics live in natural wonderlands. By looking around, you might see the angle of the sunlight, a mayfly mating swarm well above your head, or an impending storm coming

over the mountains, which will change barometric pressure and possibly stir up the bite. Yes, you probably paid a fortune for your trip and your cost-benefit calculations directly reflect how much you paid. You can always tell the "newbies" in the salmon camp— their amount of casting correlates directly to the dollars they spent. By slowing down, you give the fish a chance to behave normally and not have to adjust to your changing flies or your quirky casting intrusions. You also allow your mind to think like a predator.

Sit and reflect upon your fly boxes and ask yourself, "What worked for me in the past and what would I eat if I were a salmon? This fly worked in a similar situation I encountered years ago." Take a nap. I always bring a flask of scotch or bottle of beer, along with the fly-tying vise and some materials in my backpack to every beat I go to. Good cigars also. The joy one should experience just by being on a hallowed river of *Salmo salar* should be a bonus unto itself. Go poke around the woods for some mushrooms to bring back to the lodge chef. Sharpen your hooks. Test your knots. Pick up some rare stones (the Gaspé is full of the most beautiful exotic stones you have ever seen). Flogging the water for a return on your investment only puts salmon into a disdainful P/D attitude. So take a break. Oftentimes the first few casts back in the water can produce an explosive strike. Your patience earned you this!

Atlantic salmon will give you chases, bumps, long looks, slow follows, refusals, and downright disdainful "yawns" as their big white kyped mouths open for oxygen while they fin in the pools. When the salmon shows interest in your fly, your gillie will always tell you to wait before the next cast is executed.

If you have a quasi-acceptance, try this. First change your fly. Your guide might flip out since the common practice is to wait and show the fish the same fly. For me, a take occurred more often than not on the casts after flies were changed. You can also drop down or go to a smaller fly size. Show a fly pattern that has similar color combinations but might have more movement. Change tippet diameter. Tie a loose Duncan rather than a sturdy and rigid Turle knot in order to change the fly's profile and how it sits in the water. When in doubt, put a riffle hitch on it!

SALMON WANT WHAT THEY CANNOT HAVE

Once a fish shows intent or gives pursuit but ultimately refuses, a good salmon angler will stop casting and rest the fish. Guides insist upon this. This is to allow the fish to go back to its holding or taking lie and brood over the refusal that just occurred. Atlantic salmon, like steelhead, want something they can't have. Like a lovesick puppy, it must reflect on what it could have had if it had only committed to the fly. In essence, you are giving the fish a chance to think about it what it could have had. This is the stimulating thing to do.

The next cast can bring a take, another refusal, or a total scorning. If it's the latter, then it is time to switch flies and continue the process. This may go on for hours when approaching a 30-pound trophy! By the fish continuously reacting to your offering, you and your guide have established a taker. When my client, and I as guide, caught the IGFA world-record landlocked Atlantic salmon on Torch Lake in Michigan by sight-nymphing, we switched flies seventeen times before the fish finally took. Each time the trophy fish came to the fly with its mouth open before it refused at the last second and went back to its lie, reflecting on what wasn't right or lacked appeal.

THE POWER OF THE UP-AND-ACROSS PRESENTATION

My good friend Bill Greiner of Malbaie Lodge in the Gaspé taught me some pretty unorthodox presentations for selective or passive Atlantic salmon. When salmon were pooled up in waters with little flow, which is common on the Gaspé rivers in late summer or early fall, Bill employed a streamer stripping/bass popping technique that was absolutely deadly. His rubber-legged concoctions imitated a brindle bug in all sizes and colors, including Labatt's blue, orange, black, and red. With the grizzly hackle and the pulsating black, yellow, and white barred rubber legs, the

The array of Atlantic salmon flies is an incredible artistic display of the passion of fly tying. You can never have enough patterns, and you are constantly looking for that special fly that will turn the salmon's fancy in your favor. MATT SUPINSKI

Eric Clapton with a leaping Iceland Atlantic. Besides his world-renowned guitar prowess, he is a master fly fisher who loves spring creeks and salmon. ARNI BALDURSSON/LAX-Á

flies would wake the water like giant cyclops trying to make it from one bank to the next.

To present this fly, you position yourself downstream from the pod of pooled-up fish and cast your fly to the top of the pool's riffles. Then start stripping it back toward you as fast as you can, waking water—or with the fly slightly sunk—so it pushes water past the school of fish. This drives the salmon absolutely crazy! But it is hard work. When the salmon comes to the fly, it often chases it for long hard inspections. The fish mostly refuse them, but when they take, watch out for the explosion!

I turned over two dozen salmon in one afternoon on the Miramichi in New Brunswick by stripping a large size 4 double-hook orange Francis. I hooked at least six grilse and adult fish that "were not supposed to be takers" due to low, clear water. It is now a mainstay presentation used throughout the Canadian Maritimes and has spread to Iceland, Norway, and Russia. Try it and you'll be amazed by its explosive qualities. But make sure your stripping arm is in good shape. Work out at the gym before you go on your salmon trip—trust me.

Nowhere is the surface-oriented S/R Atlantic salmon personality more prominently displayed than on the Big Laxa River of Iceland. This is a land of fire, ice, and stark beauty like nowhere else on earth. Basalt lava eruptions thousands of years ago created fertile lakes like the Myvatn, the source of the Laxa's flows. The Laxa is a giant spring creek where precipitation percolates through the bedrock, just like it does in the chalkstream downs and low-lying limestone spring creeks. It spills warm and cold spring water into the lake. Much like Yosemite, volcanic activity is constant here, either in the full-blown or planning stages. With the massive amount of dissolved minerals and plant growth, the waters are extremely fertile and eutrophic.

The Diptera midge life of the lake and river is mind boggling, as is the amount of small crustaceans like scuds and water fleas, which feed the river's resident brown trout and duck populations. They are also food for the small Atlantic parr. Trophy brown trout inhabit the entire system. But the largest Atlantic salmon of Iceland ascend this river and are as selective as those in spring creeks. The Myvatn Valley of the Laxa is so

The Big Laxa emanates from Lake Myvatn through channels loaded with vegetation and algae. Buttercups, lavender wood cranesbills, mixed fir trees, and lush tundra grasses blanket a deep emerald-green valley that is in stark contrast to the snow-covered volcanic peaks. Sheep graze in the lush pastoral meadows as flocks of tufted ducks and goldeneyes abound. It is a pristine primordial utopia protected by Iceland's conservation agency. ARNI BALDURSSON/LAX-Á

intense with black fly *Simulium* that black insect clouds will arrive and disperse with the wind; the brown trout will feed on these midge clusters and grow to enormous sizes. But what makes the Laxa's Atlantics unique is the smooth-flowing, stillwater character of the river, combined with the impeccable clarity and weedy channels of a chalkstream. The modern Atlantic salmon dean Art Lee rated the Laxa I Adaldal as one of the most selective Atlantic salmon rivers on earth. He writes in the *Atlantic Salmon Journal*:

> Heading my list in a class all by itself, is Iceland's Laxa I Adaldal to which I made 34 trips and into which I would like to have my ashes spread in a statement of both affection and gratitude. The specific challenge with which we're dealing is getting multiple-risers to finally take. By the way, Big Laxa, as she is widely addressed as a sign of respect, is the ultimate laboratory, casting up to 14, 15, 16 times in numerous different fly patterns before takes on

the 16th, 17th or 18th, is not unusual on this, the world's largest spring creek, and accounts in some measure, anyway for why the typical catch per rod/week isn't as high as on those rivers where they typically bite or don't. It takes considerable time, after all, to mess with finicky fish, and there are only so many hours in an angling day.

Arni Baldursson is an Icelander who has probably caught more Atlantic salmon than any other angler on the planet. As the owner of LAX-Á Worldwide Destinations, he has the chance to fish for Atlantic salmon from Scotland to Russia. His suggestion for fishing "the Big Laxa" is to go tiny and on the surface:

> The Laxa is a tricky river with clever fish. I use long leaders, all floating lines, normally smaller tube flies. long wings, greenish colors, riffling hitch, nothing big and clumsy, delicate fishing where you do not rush through one pool to

hurry up to get to another pool, here you take your time . . . change flies. Change speeds of the flies, present them at different angles and from different sides of the river . . . you are fishing over fish and you have to earn their interest, it is not high volume fishing, it is fewer but bigger and clever fish that love to come up to the surface to take your fly if you present it right.

As with searching dry-fly patterns for trout, the hitch fly can also show you which fish out of a pod of salmon in a pool is most likely to have a taking instinct and mentality. One common practice is to target the fish at the tail of the pool, which are usually non-alpha-sized males that vie for alpha dominance. The author is shown here with a large "hitched-up" York River Gaspé male, caught right at dark on a size 12 Blue Charm. B. GREINER

In *Riffling Hitch*, author Art Lee detailed his love for and study of this motion technique, which wreaks havoc on the minds of S/R salmon—especially on the Laxa.

The hitch is also useful strategically, both to spot salmon and to bring reticent risers to strike the fly. A quick hitch over that lie where "you just know there's a fish" after having failed to stir any action by the usual means, often gets results. A hitch can also work as, "something out of left field" to show to salmon that have looked at patterns conventionally but have stubbornly refused to latch hold. Or as a teaser to reintroduce to a fish that have risen several times to your offerings, then seemingly called it quits. Or as a trick to tweak the salmon you really hope to hook on the next presentation.

The riffle hitch was invented by Art Perry and pioneered by Lee Wulff on Portland Creek in Newfoundland. Wulff made the technique extremely deadly in rivers that also produce dry-fly fish. When fished in water with enough speed to wake and wiggle the hitched fly and change its speed and direction, this technique raises more fussy—and at times dour—salmon than any other, especially on clear Icelandic rivers and the Gaspé. Riffle-hitched micro tube flies (size 16-18 plastic tube trebles) like the popular Blue Charm, Laxa Blue, Monroe's Killer, and Sunray Shadow, will take selective Atlantics when nothing else will.

My experiences with the hitch are the same. Just the right amount of river speed—not too fast, not too slow—is paramount for the hitch to work effectively. River depths must also be ideal, preferably nothing deeper than eight to ten feet. The clearer the water the better, but dark tannic rivers still produce fish to the hitch.

What I found with the hitch, as did Art Lee, was its amazing ability to take fish in conditions when it shouldn't work, such as cold, stained, heavy-flowing rivers in spring spate, when sink heads and large 2/0 Green Highlanders dredged deep is the standard technique. I believe the wiggling and twitching movement constantly piques the natal parr instinct of the young salmon in the riffles and fast pocket water where aquatic insects must swim to escape fast flows.

Dry Flies

As with the hitch, we have dry-fly presentations that work extremely well for Atlantics. Some anglers fish dries exclusively. Bombers, Wulffs, and greased-up Muddlers will all take salmon on the surface. Dead-drifting is popular on the Gaspé rivers since waking flies rarely catch fish there. Russia's fast, tannic rivers favor the waking method. The jury will never be concluded on the effectiveness of dry-fly fishing for Atlantic salmon, but here are my observations.

Though I know I will stir a lot of controversy here, I use the dry as much as or more often than the wet fly for Atlantics due to the salmon's extreme surface orientation. S/R Atlantics tend to have long inspection times and will regularly rise to dead-drifted dry flies. I find salmon in lower pools and in still tailouts to be the best risers to the dead drift. The fish tend to ascend slowly like a surface submarine, taking on the form of the compound rise, and usually refuse the fly. This can go on for more than a dozen times to one fly in the same fish. It is unnerving to say the least, or if you're twisted like me, absolutely fascinating!

Waking or riffle-hitching dry flies at a quicker speed tends to work best in broken, fast, boulder or slot water in pools and runs. A/A salmon fresh from the salt are the best takers for this method, since their hunting instincts are still in full effect. Heavy competition for space and territorial dominance also evokes more chasing behavior.

Similar to Lani Waller's Dean River steelhead techniques, a combination of wake, dead-drift, wake, can be accomplished in one presentation and produce explosive results with Atlantics. This will either excite the salmon or send them scurrying into passive dormancy.

Refusals and the Take

When you experience a nice rise and refusal to your dry, that is a start. To many Atlantic connoisseurs this is cause for joy and elation. Atlantics, when they commit to the fly in the S/R state, will make a full-blown commitment and take it. There is a ton of foreplay—refusals, bumps, tail-whacking—that goes on. These

The Grand Cascapedia River in Québec. Dead-drifting or waking a dry just before dusk is a powerful tool for catching S/R Atlantics. Low light brings out the curiosity in the pooled-up fish. MATT SUPINSKI

The Doddi Orange

One particular summer, the Gaspé was gripped by a 90-degree heat wave. River temps soared and bright, hot, cloudless days were the norm. My guide Gordie and I concentrated on the Grande Riviere and Pabos systems, two cold, spring-fed rivers where the salmon were the least stressed and affected by the ghastly and unwelcome heat. Even here, the morning and afternoon bite was nonexistent. Fish did not get active in the holding pools until an hour before dusk, when the hot sun sank below the treeline of the Chic-Choc Mountains, typically around six o'clock in the evening. Our daily routine was to have a late brunch of crab and herring on a French baguette with Canadian beer at the Le Pechuer restaurant along the beach in the resort town of Perce. We would then make sure we would be at the Sardine Box beat—a crystal-clear, limestone rock pool carved deep by glaciers—on the

Grande at six as the sun started setting, and from then until dark we got serious for the big 10- to 30-pound salmon.

As I stepped into the water along the edge of the calcareous rock formations that plunged into the 15-foot-deep pool, I noticed an orange item floating downstream. It looked like the Icelandic Doddi Orange fly I was about to cast. "Gordie, is there anyone fishing the sector upstream from us that could have dropped a Doddi Orange fly out of his or her box and into the water by accident?" I asked. "Doubt it. We are the only ones on this river today!" Gordie shot back. Just then, the orange "whatever" started to swim to the rocky limestone shelf. "Gordie, get it!" I screamed. Gordie ran over and grabbed it. A 6-inch-long orange juvenile spotted eastern newt was in his hand—the cutest little bugger I've ever seen. I told Gordie to

Dry-fly salmon fishing plays an important part of presentation on vodka-clear waters that have good aquatic insect life like stoneflies that juvenile parr imprint to. MATT SUPINSKI

empty his Thermos, put cool river water in it, and keep the newt for dinner conversation at the lodge. As I started casting, another juvenile newt swam across the pool, and this time two 20-pound-plus Atlantics came from eight feet down to take a swipe at the little cutie, only to quickly turn off in disdain. Here the fish were reflecting on their surroundings and tried to assimilate their normal hunting behaviors even if they didn't have to since they were there to spawn. But reflective behavior and curiosity killed the cat. My reflective angler's mind went to work; in Polish there is a saying: *glowka pracuje*—the mind is always working even when not obvious.

Bill Greiner, the lodge owner, said the Doddi Orange was an Icelandic fly that *Salmo salar* fly-fishing guru Art Lee brought to the Matapedia and other Gaspé rivers. It's the go-to fly once a salmon's thoughts turn to spawning aggression and territorial dominance. "This is the fly for this time of year," Bill said, as he held up a bright size 6 Doddi Orange tied on a double salmon fly hook. "The males are particularly interested in it."

Could the fly be challenging the reactive color impulse of these Atlantics from their aggressive spawning mode, or was it an S/R response to the orange newt? I immediately began to do a little research. Newts, both the North American and Icelandic species, like dense wet forests with lakes, ponds, and alkaline limestone rivers. So the Grand Pabos and alkaline-rich Big Laxa (Mr. Lee's favorite) fit the description. Newts also give off a poisonous chemical reaction from their skin when predated upon. Could that be the reason behind the Atlantic's quick change, stop, and retreat response to these lovely orange wiggling delectables? Can this be a case of natal imprinting to juvenile food forms in the Atlantic salmon, or the result of a strike response to vibrant red/orange colors fueled by sexually dominant responsive behavior? We may never know.

Here is one absolute fact that I know, as gillie Gordie will attest to. As I stepped up to the plate in the Sardine Box beat at 6:45, the light was low and dim. Dark gray-backed silver shadows of salmon were ominously on the prowl as the low light fostered more comfortable conditions. All day long they reflected on their pool surroundings, watching newts, small parr feeding, insects hatching—a river full of life they perhaps were detached from due to their drive to procreate. Eventually their urge to strike like the big-ocean

A guide gets ready on this crystal gem, the Bonaventure River in Québec. The brisk morning yields fog, cool air, and the hope of Atlantic salmon biting again after weeks of relentless heat and drought. Global climate change is altering the timing of Atlantic salmon runs, river flows, and temperatures, and makes planning fishing trip destinations more difficult. One year rivers are at drought levels, and the next they flood. MATT SUPINSKI

hunter they are takes over. After two down-and-across swings, with hanging slack-line mends similar to an old-fashioned A. H. E. Wood greased-line method, a 31-pound, kype-jawed male engulfed my Doddi Orange with white and black rubber-legged tentacles. ■

are good behaviors that are usually preludes to the take.

When an Atlantic salmon shows interest, the seasoned dry-fly addict will usually rest the fish. This allows the fish to go back to its taking position and brood over what it just did, causing it to want the fly the next time it sees it. After a short minute or two wait, the re-presented dry will produce another refusal, a take, or no response whatsoever.

If refusals occur, change fly color and size. Something might just not be right with the fly in the Atlantic's mind. Sometimes imparting several twitches of the fly as it enters the salmon's field of vision does the trick.

For ultraselective salmon, I found changing the fly after the first refusal, rather than sticking with the original, usually seals the deal. We often bore the salmon to tears with repeated presentations of a tried-and-true pattern, and eventually the fish loses all interest in the imitation. Many dry-fly anglers have experienced repeated refusal rises to multiple flies. Sometimes resting the fish for a longer period, or going to a tiny swung tube or small triple in size 14-16 (yes, even for salmon!) on a riffle hitch does the trick.

As for the take, allow plenty of time for the salmon to come up, put its mouth over the fly, and turn down; then you strike. "God save the queen," is what is customarily said in your mind when the fish takes the fly, in order to allow for the pause. Unlike trout, who spit quickly, Atlantics hold on longer to the fly. Once they commit, they commit!

I can't tell you how often a gillie will break your concentration by saying, "It's coming, it's coming, oh my god! It's huge!" This only causes the client to pull out the fly as soon as he or she sees the wide white mouth come over the top. I know this because I've done it many times. Good guides say nothing but "Strike!" It takes several rises of the salmon to the dry fly for you to get the hang of it. So tell your gillie to shut up if they haven't already figured it out!

Passive/Dormant

Unfortunately, this is perhaps the most familiar state a fly fisher finds in Atlantic salmon unless you are on the Kola in Russia. Summers on Atlantic salmon rivers can be cruel to both the fish and the fishermen. Warm, low, clear water and stifling temperatures with no rain mean radical approaches must enter the picture.

Nowhere is this more perfectly depicted then in Québec's Gaspé. Its magnificent Chic-Choc mountains, the northernmost tip of the Appalachian range, drops down to the Bay de Chaleur with magnificent wild Atlantic salmon rivers sprinkled through its valleys. Here, cut by glacial movements fifty million years ago, are some of the most pristine and clear rivers a person will ever lay eyes on.

Each river is unique and special. The Bonaventure has waters of impeccable emerald transparency where you can see down into a pool twenty feet deep and swear you are only in two feet of water. The Grande Riviere and Pabos River's calcium carbonate rock create unparalleled spring creek clarity. The larger Cascapedia and Matapedia, along with the York and Dartmouth, emanate from peat marl bogs and lakes, which have a heavy conifer and hardwood forest influence. (Logging is quite prominent here.) Their salmon grow to massive sizes of up to 70 pounds and are multi-sea fish that impart strong genetic selectivity codes to ensure survival. When the taking is on, it's on. But when it is not, the fishing is really demoralizing. Looking into pool after pool loaded with hundreds of Atlantic salmon is overwhelming, especially if not one of those salmon is willing to take your fly!

Fishing Roadkill

It was an early September day on the Grand Cascapedia. Air temperatures were soaring into the upper 90s and the rivers were getting warm. The pools were loaded with 15- to 40-pound Atlantic salmon. You could stand above the Salmon Run pool and watch these giants yawn, occasionally quiver, or jockey for territorial dominance. Yet changing flies and trying new patterns led to daily frustration. Weeks went by without a hookup in camp. Even when cold spells arrived and cooled things down, *Salmo salar*'s attitude was impenetrable.

In the days of old, Scottish salmon gillies would stone a pool to get dour salmon to become agitated enough to bite. Many salmon seem to desire something they can't have, or in this case, something they have never imagined in their wildest fish dreams.

Targeting the sexually aggressive nature of these fish is obviously the way to go. What could aggravate a serene pool of Atlantics as it goes through the daily stages of boredom, watching the same Lady Amherst or Blue Charm fly patterns come by them on an amazingly regular schedule? Then something as big as a 6-inch-long sculpin, a leechy-looking thing, or a big ugly, nasty fly terrorizes the serenity of the Atlantic's regal disposition. This is a grand awakening similar to the gillies of Scotland stoning the pool. Difference is you're doing it with large and gaudy fly patterns—roadkill.

Does it work all the time? No. But when it does, it's lethal! Roadkill, a term coined by the late Gaspé guide Lee Fortan and inspired by Atlantic salmon addict Steve Stallard and myself, enticed 40-pound Atlantics when nothing was working. Was it a fluke, the product of circumstance, or a consequence of the fly's presentation? All we know was that it worked and it was deadly.

This method for stubborn P/D Atlantics is actually quite simple. Vary your fly choice between traditional and roadkill patterns, and your presentation between conventional and non-established methods. Start by asking your gillie and other anglers on the river and at the lodge what has been the hot pattern of the year so far, and tie variations on that theme in different sizes and with uncommon materials. Make the flies look like something a truck ran over! Use motion-without-movement materials like marabou, rabbit strips, schlappen, rubber legs, arctic fox, and foam. Ask your guide to look at your fly box. It's amazing how West Coast steelhead patterns and Great Lakes fly patterns will pique your guide's interest and willingness to experiment.

When fishing roadkill, vary your fly speed constantly from slow to fast and then to erratic stripping and twitching. If the fish moves to your fly, show it a variation of the pattern in either a larger or smaller size, or go to something totally different. My client Bill Mattea caught a trophy Atlantic salmon on the Petite Cascapedia that moved to a gaudy purple Great Lakes egg-sucking leech.

When the traditional down-and-across swing doesn't excite the fish, try the down-and-straight-up presentation. Position yourself at the top of the run or pool, directly in the center, and cast completely to the tailout of the pool. Then rapidly and repeatedly strip the fly high above the fish. Occasionally stop the pattern cold, allowing it to dead-drift. Then once again strip it rapidly upstream. If the fish shows interest yet does not commit to a down-and-across presentation, present your fly with a rapid lift and rise to the surface, just upstream from the fish's holding lie. The key is to constantly speed up, slow down, and lift your fly to the surface, thus confusing the fish. Your provoca-

Quentin, a Mic-Mac Indian guide on the Cascapedia, holds the author's male Atlantic salmon that clobbered a "roadkill." P/D dour Atlantic salmon need a huge stimulus fly to wake them from their funk and stimulate the A/A response that is present on their first arrival to the river and in the ocean hunting grounds. MATT SUPINSKI

tion will lead to either a massive, boiling strike or scare the hell out of the whole pool. It's that simple.

What's the bottom line? When traditional tactics and flies are working, honor them and find joy in them. When they are not, have fun breaking away from tradition. When you unhook your roadkill pattern from a massive Atlantic's kype after it has inhaled your fly, you'll treasure the astonished look from both the salmon and the gillie. Those moments are priceless!

Timing

Make sure you take the water temperature—the ideal range is 45 to 60 degrees. Do not fish for Atlantics if the water is warmer than 70 degrees—you will only kill them. But if waters remain cold even when bright sun and low water is making the fish P/D, they can be caught. This late-year stage of the river lifestyle includes the pre-spawning A/A mode of both the male and the female. Females will begin "mock fanning."

Scotland's Rivers Tay, Dee, and Spey are synonymous with Atlantic salmon, scotch drinking, and Spey casting. It's funny how the scotch bottle becomes empty at the lodge no matter what—when people are hooking fish and are happy, or when they are not catching anything and in a miserable state. The "dram of whiskey" is part of the salmon-fishing tradition. ARNI BALDURSSON/LAX-Á

You will see this as they quiver in the mid-depths of the pool, practicing their tail wagging to dig gravel, even though they are weeks or months away from needing to do so. Males start to chase other males now that they are at their highest weight. The males carry heavy milt and the females have egg sacs stored firmly in their bellies, producing massive weight in the females and large kyped jaws in the males. If you hook these fish at this time of year, they will tear you up beyond comprehension! They are angry and destructive in this pre-spawning state. If your timing comes along when they turn from passive to aggressive—what seems like an overnight shift—you can have some of the best fly fishing for Atlantic salmon you'll ever experience. It usually comes on the first cold spell of fall, prior to the season's closing.

FORGET THE CHEF'S SCHEDULE

It was the summer from hell in the Gaspé. August temperatures soared into the upper 90s. The sun and heat were relentless in what is supposed to be a cool, damp Canadian Maritime province. Nobody was happy. All the guests at the lodge were complaining about the heat and the fishless days.

My wonderful guide Gordie asked what time he should pick me up after breakfast. "Let's shoot for noon!" I said. Gordie was shocked, but adjusted quickly to his new schedule, which let him sleep in for a change and do some chores in the morning.

I knew the drill all too well. The sun would stir the pooled-up salmon as it rose over the Atlantic Coast around four o'clock in the morning. The fish in the pool would move around for about an hour, line up in pool pecking order, bump each other a little bit, and then settle into a long, dour P/D sleep for the rest of the day. It happened with uncanny regularity and regiment.

When Gordie picked me up I said, "Let's go grab a lobster sandwich at Le Peschuer." We drank a cold pitcher of Labatt ale and watched the cute French-Canadian girls walk by. "Great idea, Matt!" Gordie said, loving his new guide schedule.

For several days, we were assigned to the Sardine Box beat of the Grande Riviere. It's an absolutely beautiful, blue, crystal-clear, transparent set of pools holding some large salmon that are extremely selective and sometimes almost impossible to catch. "Let's make sure we are at the Sardine Box about 5 p.m., is that good with you?" I asked Gordie. "Sounds great Matt!" Gordie was loving life. He was amazed that he was getting paid to have fun—he was like a kid in a toy shop.

We arrived at the gazebo hut for cocktail hour at 5 p.m., overlooking the pool that had about four hundred Atlantic salmon in it. They all seemed motionless, holding several feet below the surface in one pool that had to be 20 feet deep. They were comatose, totally P/D. That was fine for me since I knew things would change shortly. I kicked back as I poured a scotch and lit up a Cuban, rigging up with my ugly Labatt Blue grizzly rubber-legged concoction. "As soon as the sun goes over that peak of the Chic-Choc Mountains, those fish will start stirring around," I said to Gordie. "Trust me. They hate that blazing sun, understand Pat?" (Every Irish person in the Gaspé calls another Irishman Pat or Patty.) "Yes sir," he replied. "Makes sense to me!" At the top of the Sardine Box was a narrow fast-water chute, well-oxygenated and emanating out of an underground spring. The fish are drawn to this area especially when it gets hot and the sun goes down. They are too big (some are approaching the 30- to 40-pound range) to sit in that shallow water during the day because of their paranoia.

Once I moved into position, I made a well-calculated up-and-across downstream fast-stripping presentation right below the surface. As the fly pushed water, my fourth cast yielded an explosion on the surface as the fish absolutely hammered the fly. Gordie was screaming in disbelief. After about a thirty-minute battle for fifty yards up and downstream, the still-dumbfounded Gordie tailed the fish. We snapped pictures of the beautiful 32-pound, kype-jawed male as it swam off into the darkness.

I showed up back at the lodge well after dinner. The chef was not happy with me and had left my tinfoil-covered plate next to the microwave. The other rods at the lodge went skunked. They had fished all day and looked dejected and extremely sunburnt. After seeing the pictures of my catch, the next day everybody slept in, opting to go to the beach resort, have a lobster sandwich, and go to their designated river beats for the day with a whole new attitude. That evening everyone came back to the lodge late, salmon on the camera, and the chef was not thrilled.

Austin Clark releases a wild Atlantic salmon. Catch-and-release angling and a sporting thought process born out of respect for the god-given resource will hopefully determine intelligent management decisions. This can bring about a whole dogma and process that allows us and the natural world to parley for what is the fundamental beauty of fly fishing: the selection process that embodies every motive, thought, and interaction between the angler and fish, and that can forever bring us joy and sporting closure. MATT SUPINSKI

Timing is everything for P/D salmon. Whether you have to get up and get on the river well before breakfast, or stay well after dark, the chef can leave you your dinner in the microwave. Besides, you didn't come to eat. Make sure your camera batteries are charged and your flash is working—you'll need it!

Flipping the Switch

As with trout and steelhead, sometimes natural or manmade events can occur that switch fish from P/D to A/A. One of those events can be an insect hatch. Though Atlantic salmon don't partake of the daily insect hatches like stream trout do, they are exposed to them and sometimes they can't help but to instinctively react to them in a way that benefits the angler. A massive infusion of food, be it a great hatch or one artificially chummed up by man (see San Juan Shuffle, page 113) can often cause a drastic change in the fish's behavior and its selectivity phase. In the White House pool, the appearance of the natural Ephron hatch woke the fish up.

It was another late-August dog day on the Gaspé's York River. Low water and extremely warm temperatures made pods of pooled-up Atlantic salmon extremely dour and totally uninterested in the fly fishers' offerings, no matter what time of day one fished. The White House and Keg pools had to have 1,000-plus Atlantics in them ranging from 10 to 50 pounds.

Each evening the dinner and cocktail discussion among the guests was bleak—no hookups no matter what and where you fished. Having access to more than six world-class rivers, it was clear that the salmon bite and behavior was dormant. Everyone awaited a big cold front with precipitation to break the stalemate. Excellent underwater photographer and fly fisher Jean-Guy Béliveau, who is also a river keeper and game warden with the local Zone of Ecological Control (ZEC), gave me some interesting information as I talked to him streamside. Jean-Guy is world famous for scuba diving into the world of salmon to obtain his excellent photography. He had been filming on the York's premier pool and beat, the White House pool, and he noticed how the large salmon became quite agitated just before dusk. They went from a purely listless state to showing reactive behavior. Jean-Guy saw the emergence of large wiggling mayfly nymphs. It was the *Ephoron leukon* (White Fly) hatch, which occurs at that time of year. To the fly fisher, curious Atlantic behavior is a good sign that can mean a hookup or at least a good strong look and inspec-

Atlantic salmon on Québec's Dartmouth River school up by a spring seep under the shade of a tree during an extreme drought and heat wave. MATT SUPINSKI

Gillie Austin Clark and angler Shawn Murphy with a 38-pound, kype-jawed male Atlantic from the White House pool. Since the White Fly hatch was on the water, I tied up a handful of size 12 Double White Muddlers to imitate the emerging nymphs. Greasing the fly and riffle-hitching it landed this beautiful Atlantic. JOHN MURPHY

tion, a welcome change from the sulking salmon. Since I was familiar with the *Ephoron* from my days on Pennsylvania's Yellow Breeches and my Michigan trout streams, it was time to take this observation to the next level.

The White House pool comes with a high premium and is not always available (it is booked years in advance), but you can go there and walk the bluff stairs and watch the chosen few anglers fish with the guides. I got there several hours before dark and stared down into a pool filled with behemoth Atlantics in the 30- to 50-pound range. They were holding in the gentle flow of the pool and constantly maintaining their hierarchical pecking order. Occasionally you would see a white kype-jawed mouth open and seemingly yawn out of total boredom; in reality, this large inhalation of oxygenated water is a means of stretching the salmons' ever-growing kypes.

Two anglers per beat and two guides is the standard setup here. One angler presented fly after fly—dries, traditional salmon wets, riffle hitches, and ugly rubber concoctions—generating not an ounce of interest from the several hundred fish crammed in the pool. Just before dark, as the anglers were sadly packing up to get to the lodge for the last dinner bell seating, I saw my first white mayfly come off the water, followed by another. At the tail end of the pool a gregarious young male made a quick swiping swirl near the surface. This seemed to agitate the entire pooled-up pod. As more flies and darkness approached, the pool's salmon went from listlessness to a reactive frenzy, with fish chasing each other and boiling the surface. Was it dusk and the approaching night delivering the stimu-

lus for the sudden salmon frolic? Or was it the reflective and reactive behavior triggered by the White Fly emergence? This is the conundrum of selectivity.

The next morning at the lodge I received the good news that my two travel colleagues and clients, the Murphys, had won the privilege to fish White House that day. I was busy at my fly-tying vise that morning, drinking my coffee and trying to put away thoughts of the previous night's dialogue over cocktails, which lasted well past the midnight hour as everyone tried to solve all the world's problems. I pulled out a box of Daiichi double salmon hooks in sizes 12 and 14, small by Atlantic salmon standards, and tied tiny, short white muddler minnows. I put them on a china plate lined with green ferns and presented them to Shawn Murphy as a good luck token while she ate breakfast. "Try these please, especially when all else fails," I told her.

The day started with a cold front finally coming to the Gaspé, bringing cool temperatures and threatening storms. John Murphy, fishing with respected and extremely knowledgeable guide Austin Clark, caught a nice kype-jawed, colored-up male on a Blue Charm right at the start. Austin then went to work on getting Shawn out of the weeklong skunking. As threatening thunderstorms moved in, Shawn was getting nervous, this being her last day on the water before their departure. Austin and Shawn moved into the run that holds some monstrous males that are known to be more aggressive. "Matt told me to put this tiny white muddler on, grease it up with floatant and a riffle [Portland] hitch, and work it from the top to the bottom of the run," Shawn told Austin. As the dark sky boded ominously, Shawn noticed white mayflies emerging

A rainbow after a storm usually means your luck will soon change. From the Baltic states to Iceland, Scotland to the Canadian Maritime provinces, the rainbow will always bode well for salmon anglers looking for that little sign and bit of magic that will make the fish bite. Climatologically, rainbows usually mean a cool front just came through and turned fish on, but according to Icelandic folklore, if you are under a rainbow your wishes will come true. For anglers, that means catching the salmon of their dreams. MATT SUPINSKI

from the water. As is the case with all aquatic invertebrate insect hatches—mayflies, caddis, stoneflies—the whites are sensitive to barometric pressure changes and diminishing light levels. Since the White Fly is an evening emerger, a sudden change of light conditions has been known to fool them into an emergence.

After working the run to its tailout, one of Shawn's last casts produced a jolting strike. She let the line and hook set itself, as is properly done on the riffle hitch, and a gigantic kype-jawed male broke the surface and began to leap all the way down the pool. Shawn has seasoned big-fish fighting skills honed by hours of steelheading, and a magnificent 38-pound male was tailed by Austin forty minutes later. Yes, it is an interesting story riddled with what-ifs and many agnostic speculations and theories. But subduing a smart, large Atlantic with a fly that was not the orthodox pattern for that time of year was the sweet end that justified the unusual means.

Landlocked Atlantics

As a result of their freshwater-to-freshwater nature, landlocked salmon are a fusion between true seagoing salmon and lake-run brown trout. Though they are *Salmo salar*, not having to undergo the salinity balance when entering fresh water gives them a greater disposition to take the fly and eat food. Their migrations up the river systems usually occur in the late fall just prior to spawning, similar to a brown trout. This allows the fish to maximize its feeding and predating opportunities.

Landlocked Atlantic salmon exist in the Scandinavian countries, particularly the deep reservoirs of Sweden, where they were landlocked either in the past couple hundred years through dam-building, or millions of years ago through geological isolation. In North America, they are found on a slew of lakes and river systems in Québec and Maine; Lake Champlain, Lake George, and the Finger Lakes of New York; and the Great Lakes themselves. Lake Ontario once had an indigenous Atlantic salmon population that was extirpated by rampant destruction by the European settlers and pollution caused by the Industrial Revolution. Today, thanks to the efforts of New York's Department of Environmental Conservation and the Ontario Ministry of Fisheries, the lake's Atlantic salmon populations are coming back. Documented natural reproduction is taking place on New York's Salmon River and Ontario's Credit River. In the Rangeley Lakes system of Maine, the landlocked salmon average about 3 to 5 pounds. They feed like brown trout in that they target aquatic insect hatches and rainbow smelt.

The dual nature of landlocked salmon makes them a pleasure for fly fishers to target. Many of the salmon's lakes are dominated by aquatic invasive species like zebra mussels, and the impeccable water clarity demands presentations be incredibly detailed and accurate. Imitating the various baitfish populations through exact fly duplication is important. Their ability to ascertain all aspects and complexities of an insect hatch is equal to that of their cousin the brown trout. On one inland lake system in Michigan, the landlocked stocked salmon were known to take midges off the surface in the fall near the shoreline. In the St. Marys River of Lake Huron, they aggressively

feed to small caddis pupae all day—8- to 20-pound Atlantics feeding like brown trout in the middle of summer! That is the unique aspect of these fish.

On the rivers in which the Atlantics run early, like New York's Salmon River and the St. Marys, they will target large classic Atlantic salmon flies, rainbow smelt patterns, and yellow, black, and white muddlers on the swing in an A/A fashion. This is an absolute joy to experience in May and June. In the fast, cool, oxygenated rapids and canyon water of these two systems, the salmon will also target bombers and other dry flies on the surface.

With Atlantic landlocked salmon, you have it all: the "king of the sea" and a selective brown trout all packed to one fish! Some would say the Atlantic salmon is the poster child of selectivity.

Dr. John Murphy with a 27-pound landlocked salmon caught on Torch Lake, Michigan. This water is also home to the IGFA world-record fish the author and his client caught. Landlocks can grow to enormous size since they don't travel thousands of miles like ocean fish do. They usually concentrate on pelagic baitfish schools and *Mysis* shrimp near shore. MATT SUPINSKI

Right: Landlocked male kype jaws are amazing structures. Males use them to maintain spawning dominance as they fight with their rivals. Like elk, deer, and moose—all species that rely on their antlers in duels—the male with the biggest kype is often the winner in the mating game. LAURIE SUPINSKI

Favorite Atlantic Flies

ROB'S WILLIE GUNN TEMPLEDOG

(Rob White, Scotland)

Hook:	Daiichi 7131 double
Tube:	Clear Eumer/Pro Tube plastic (large)
Connector:	Orange silicone tube
Thread:	Fluorescent red 95-denier Lagartun X-Strong
Tag/Tail:	Neon fluorescent orange UNI floss with Mylar through it.
Rear body/Rib:	Gold Ultra holographic tinsel with oval gold UNI French tinsel (large)
Front body:	Black Veniard's Tri Lobal Hackle Medium Crystal mix; hot orange cock hackle palmered back the body and ribbed with gold tinsel
Wing:	Orange arctic fox; yellow arctic fox; yellow goat; black arctic fox with some strands of Krinkle Mirror Flash on top
Hackle:	Hot orange cock
Cheeks:	Jungle cock
Head:	Clear Cure Goo Thin

Notes: The Willie Gunn is the most universally effective Atlantic salmon fly because its color combination piques the A/A response of Atlantic salmon, lake- and sea-run trout, and even steelhead. This fly is the go-to pattern on fresh-run Atlantics in the tea-stained tannic waters of early spring and summer in Norway, Sweden, Russia, and the United Kingdom, and in the Canadian Maritime rivers like the Grand Cascapedia, Margaree, and Miramichi. It also can be a strong bipolar switch fly that puts P/D fish back into the taking mode because the red/orange spectrum stimulates the optic sexual spawning aggressive strike response. Scientific studies have proven that the red/orange spectrum stimulates fish that have been in the river systems for some time and that have a tendency to go dour and P/D, whereas the blue/green spectrum is favored by fresh-run fish from the ocean or sea. This fly can be fished at all sizes and tubes.

DODDI ORANGE

(Tube: Paul Marriner, Canada; Traditional: Author)

TUBE

Tube:	Orange Eumer/Pro Tube plastic (medium)
Thread:	Black 95-denier Lagartun X-Strong
Throat:	Yellow arctic fox
Overwing:	Black bucktail Krystal Flash

TRADITIONAL

Thread:	Yellow 6/0 UNI
Hook:	Daiichi Salmon D7131 double
Tag:	Holographic silver Lagartun Mini Flat Braid
Tail:	Orange bucktail with pearl Krystal Flash
Body:	Hot orange UNI-Stretch
Throat:	Yellow soft hackle
Overwing:	Orange bucktail
Cheek:	Jungle cock

Notes: The Doddi Orange is an Icelandic fly introduced to North America by Art Lee. It works well on Atlantics as fall nears. The salmon's spawning aggression is piqued by the bright orange. The color also imitates the orange newt, which loves rocky limestone caverns along oligotrophic waters like those in Québec. I believe orange piques the A/A behavior in spawning salmonids since genetic optic attraction to the color of roe is a constant theme in migratory salmonids. Orange is also associated with various sea crustaceans and squid.

Icelandic/Scandinavian/Russian

Ranga Tube

Francis Black Micro

Munroe Killer Longtail

Green Highlander Micro Treble

Black and Blue Riffle

Francis Red

Icelandic Rat

Francis Black

Black Sheep

Micro Sunray Shadow

Green Butt Longtail

Black Sheep Micro

Silver Stoat Longtail

Green Brahan Long Tail

Black and Blue Longtail

Crossfield Micro

Green Butt Micro Treble

Green Highlander Conehead Tube

Black and Blue Micro Riffle

Stoat Low Water

Arni's Favorite— Underwing Brown

Collie Dog Riffle

Green Brahan Micro Cone

Vidar Red Francis

Salmon/Steelhead Dries and Subsurface Wets

Bomber
Green

Labatt Blue
Bomber

White Wulff
Bomber

Orange Crush
Bomber

Creamsicle
Moose Turd

Béliveau's Green
Wulff Stone

Wulff Original
Green Stone

Gaspé Green
Stone

Green Butt
Stone

Orange
Autumn
Stone

Francis Green

Royal
Coachman
Wulff

Hot Orange
Francis

Sunray
Shadow

Blue Charm
Riffle Hitch

Undertaker

Hairy Mary

York White
Muddler

Foam
Spudder
Tan

October
Caddis

Waller
Waker Gray

Waller Waker
Orange

Babine Turd

Babine
Sputter Kicker

BÉLIVEAU'S GASPÉ GREEN STONE

(Inspired by Lee Wulff, tied by Jean-Guy Béliveau, Québec)

Hook: Daiichi 2052
Thread: Black 6/0 UNI
Body: Fluorescent chartreuse Hareline Pearl Diamond Braid
Wings: Flashabou Mirage sheet (opal crinkle), black bucktail
Post: Black bucktail
Hackle: Tan/ginger rooster

Notes: The green Gaspé stonefly is abundant throughout the upper northeastern United States and the Canadian Maritimes. It has a significant role on the ultraclear blue-green waters of the Gaspé, where it is the top Atlantic salmon pattern after the Blue Charm. Jean-Guy's pattern is a takeoff on the original Lee Wulff design and incorporates the new synthetic materials available. Its green color is highly favored by fresh-run A/A Atlantics, which tend to devote much of their optic attention to the blue/green color spectrum.

BOMBARDIER

(Author)

Hook: Daiichi 2110
Thread: Black 95-denier Lagartun X-Strong
Tail: White calf tail

Tag: Green deer hair spun; you can also use orange and red deer hair tags.
Body: Natural deer hair spun and palmered brown hackle
Wings: White calf tail, ginger hackle

Notes: This bomber is extremely effective in low, clear pools when fishing for P/D salmon, which are cautious of bright colors. It can be fished and tied in all sizes and it's worth it for the angler to change sizes if refusals occur. The darker colors work well on rivers with good caddis and stonefly populations. It can be fished dead-drifted or slightly twitched. I find the darker bombers work better dead-drifted, but be prepared for many refusals along with the rises.

MALBAIE RUBBER LEGS

(Author)

Hook: Daiichi 2110
Tail: Squirrel
Body: Electric blue (left) or orange Hareline variegated chenille
Rib: Flat oval silver Veniard tinsel, grizzly palmer
Rubber legs: Both flies use white/black mottled Hareline grizzly natural—or you may experiment.

Notes: Bill Greiner, former owner of Malbaie Lodge in the Gaspé, introduced me to the effectiveness of these patterns when Atlantic salmon are dour and P/D. These uglies are streamer-stripped at a rapid pace in a trout/bass-fishing style that goes totally against the grain of traditional wet-fly swinging, but is highly effective nonetheless. Cast these patterns up and across and strip down as fast as you can on the surface or under it, and be prepared for jaw-dropping follows and refusals. When your fish commits and takes the fly, allow it to put its mouth totally around and engulf the fly before setting the hook—don't set the hook too early as you would in trout fishing.

Roadkill and Traditional Atlantic Flies

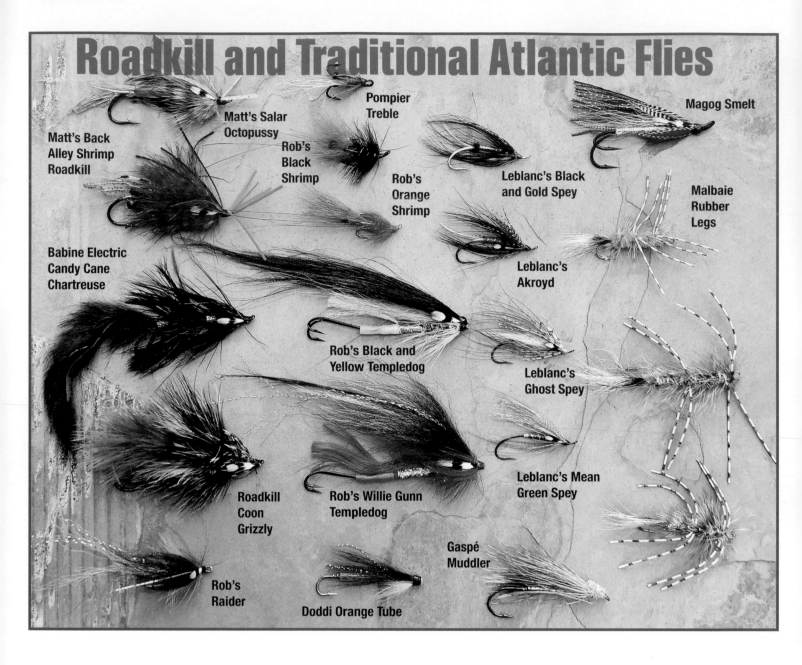

Matt's Back Alley Shrimp Roadkill

Matt's Salar Octopussy

Rob's Black Shrimp

Pompier Treble

Rob's Orange Shrimp

Leblanc's Black and Gold Spey

Magog Smelt

Malbaie Rubber Legs

Babine Electric Candy Cane Chartreuse

Leblanc's Akroyd

Rob's Black and Yellow Templedog

Leblanc's Ghost Spey

Roadkill Coon Grizzly

Rob's Willie Gunn Templedog

Leblanc's Mean Green Spey

Rob's Raider

Doddi Orange Tube

Gaspé Muddler

HOT ORANGE FRANCIS

(Author)

Hook:	Daiichi 7131
Thread:	Fluorescent hot orange UNI-Stretch
Tail:	Two hackle form ginger and grizzly rooster hackle stems stripped and cut in triangular shapes for the claws; pheasant tail
Body:	Wrap hot orange UNI-Stretch in cylindrical shape for shrimp body
Eyes:	Black Hareline mono
Rib:	Round silver Veniard tinsel (medium) with ginger rooster hackle

Notes: This Icelandic fly is deadly on crystal-clear Gaspé rivers or tea-stained tannic waters in Norway, Sweden, and Russia where salmon pool. On the Grand Pabos in Québec, the fish in a nasty P/D phase for weeks, I switched my approach point to the other side of the pool on the opposite bank. I had close to two dozen follows to the rod tip when stripping this fly in one pool, something that my gillie said "was not supposed to happen." I eventually hooked a 34-pounder.

BLUE CHARM RIFFLE HITCH

(Author)

Hook:	Daiichi 2441
Thread:	Black 6/0 UNI
Tag:	Black Lagartun Mini Flatbraid, silver oval mini braid, yellow Lagartun floss

Tail:	Golden pheasant
Upper body:	Black Lagartun Mini Flatbraid, silver oval Lagartun embossed tinsel
Throat:	Blue dyed webby goose feather
Wing:	Gadwall feathers
Underwing:	Golden pheasant
Cheek:	Jungle cock

Notes: The Blue Charm is the universal go-to fly for Atlantic salmon guides and anglers around the world. This slimmer version is meant to be used riffle-hitched (leave plenty of room at the front of the hook) and is deadly on S/R salmon in clear, blue flat waters like Iceland's Laxa and Canada's Gaspé. The hitch is effective in triggering a surface response, especially on rivers with large populations of aquatic insects. The hook is never set when a fish takes the hitch; instead, gently tighten the line, allowing a hand loop of the line to slip through the fingers, and tug the rod horizontally.

CASCAPEDIA ROADKILL COON

(Author)

Hook:	Daiichi 2151
Thread:	Black 3/0 UNI
Body:	Alternating bands of black and white marabou to create barred look; palmered
Whiskers:	Aqua Glow Hareline Crazy Legs (medium)
Cheek:	Jungle cock

Notes: I invented this fly one September by going totally against the grain of what *should* work. It was a hot and dry late summer when no fly pattern worked on the Cascapedia. The fish were hyper P/D and the outlook was bleak for salmon angling. We had taken every salmon fly pattern ever invented and fished them hard with no results. One evening we passed a dead raccoon on the road, and I joked to a guide, "I bet that would work on a hook!" The next day I was up to the challenge, and I tied this. Hookups came from huge P/D fish that had previously scoffed at everything. I landed a 31-pound Atlantic on it that evening. The marabou and rubber legs pulse in the water when the swing/strip method is used on a traditional down-and-across method.

Fly Plate Recipes

TROUT CRACK BWO

(Author)

Hook:	Daiichi 1160
Thread:	Olive 6/0 UNI
Tail:	Brown Metz Betts' Z-Lon
Body:	Green Hareline Dubbing to match natural
Wing:	Dun CDC

TROUT CRACK BWO EMERGER

(Author)

Hook:	Daiichi 1160
Thread:	Olive 6/0 UNI
Tail:	Brown Z-Lon
Lower body:	Dark brown Hare-Tron Dubbin
Thorax:	Apple Green Caucci-Nastasi Spectrumized Dubbing
Wings:	Dark gray CDC

BUBBLE BWO EMERGER

(Author)

Hook:	Daiichi 1160
Thread:	Olive 6/0 UNI
Tail:	Bronze Betts' Z-Lon
Body:	Olive Hareline Baetis Quill II
Head:	White Hareline micro foam air bubble, gray parachute hackle

P. T. STILLBORN BWO NYMPH

(Author)

Hook:	Daiichi 1560
Thread:	Brown 6/0 UNI
Tail/Body:	5 strands natural or dyed olive pheasant tail
Thorax:	Medium olive Caucci-Nastasi Spectrumized blend

Budding wing case: Light dun CDC

Notes: Similar to the Sulphur cripple, this is deadly on spring creeks and tailwaters when trout are ultra S/R.

REVERSED PARACHUTE BWO

(Author)

Hook:	Daiichi 1160
Thread:	Olive 8/0 UNI
Tail:	Clear Antron
Body:	Olive Hareline Baetis Quill II
Thorax:	Dark Olive Caucci-Nastasi Spectrumized Dubbing
Post:	UNI glow yarn
Hackle:	Light dun

SAN JUAN MICRO BWO STILLBORN NYMPH

(Author)

Hook:	Daiichi 1140
Thread:	Brown 8/0 UNI
Tail:	Pheasant tail
Body:	Two stripped peacock quills
Head:	Peacock herl

Notes: This tiny BWO stillborn is sparseness at its finest. It has fooled many large S/R San Juan fish that have been hammered by the more traditional patterns.

RUSTY BRONZE SPINNER

(Author)

Hook:	Daiichi 1182, slightly curved
Thread:	Rust 8/0 UNI
Body:	Rusty Wapsi Antron
Wings:	Gray Hareline Organza

COMPARA-EMERGER

(Author)

Hook:	Daiichi 1182
Thread:	Tan 8/0 UNI
Tail:	Brown Betts' Z-Lon
Body:	Pale olive Caucci-Nastasi Spectrumized blend
Head:	Coastal deer hair

Notes: This Caucci-Nastasi pattern was a major innovation in selectivity fly design.

POLISH-WOVEN BWO

(Piotr Michna)

Hook:	Daiichi 1120
Thread:	Olive 6/0 UNI
Tail:	Dark brown turkey biots
Body:	Olive and brown Polish-woven UNI-Stretch

Wing pad/legs: Pheasant tail

BEAD HEAD BWO EMERGER

(Author)

Hook:	Daiichi 1140
Bead:	Gold
Thread:	Olive 6/0 UNI
Tail:	Mallard flank
Body:	Olive natural Hareline Dubbin
Wing case:	Pheasant tail
Legs:	Mallard flank

BWO PARACHUTE VIZ

(Author)

Hook:	Daiichi 1182
Thread:	Olive 6/0 UNI
Tail:	Light dun fibers
Body:	Olive Hareline Dubbin
Post:	White (or any color of choice) Hareline Hi-VIZ yarn
Parachute:	Dark dun

SPRING CREEK BWO

(Author)

Hook:	Daiichi 1182
Thread:	Dark olive 6/0 UNI
Tail:	Olive Betts' Microfibbets
Body:	Dark olive Hareline Quill II or thread
Wing:	Inverted stripped dun hackle on one side in sailboat silhouette fashion
Hackle:	Dark dun

BWO TRADITIONAL PARACHUTE

(Author)

Hook:	Daiichi 1182
Thread:	Olive 6/0 UNI
Tail:	Dark dun
Body:	Olive natural Hareline Dubbin
Wing:	Dark blue dun turkey fibers
Hackle:	Light dun

CLUSTER BWO

(Author)

Hook:	Daiichi 1182
Thread:	Olive 6/0 UNI
Tail:	Brown Z-Lon
Body:	Olive thread
Post:	White Antron
Hackle:	Grizzly

PSEUDOCLOEON DUN

(John Miller)

Hook:	Daiichi 1110
Thread:	Olive 8/0 UNI
Tail:	Two strands brown Z-Lon
Body:	Light olive thread
Thorax:	Tuft of light olive thread
Wing:	Clear Metz Betts' Z-lon

POLISH-WOVEN LIGHT BWO

(Piotr Michna)

Hook:	Daiichi 1120
Thread:	Olive 6/0 UNI
Tail:	Black hackle fibbets
Body:	Tan and olive UNI-Stretch, woven
Wing pad/legs:	Pheasant tail

SULPHUR

INVARIA DUN

(Author)

Hook:	Daiichi 1182
Thread:	Yellow 6/0 UNI
Tail:	Yellow Metz Microfibbets
Body:	Pale yellow Caucci-Nastasi Spectrumized Dubbing blend
Wing:	Light dun CDC

MARINARO SULPHUR PARACHUTE

(Author)

Hook:	Daiichi 1182
Thread:	Yellow 6/0 UNI
Tail:	Light dun
Body:	Pale yellow Caucci-Nastasi Spectrumized Dubbing
Wing:	Dun turkey quill
Hackle:	Light dun

DOROTHEA T. C. EMERGER

(Author)

Hook:	Daiichi 1140
Thread:	Yellow 6/0 UNI
Tail:	Brown Betts' Z-Lon
Body:	Pale yellow Caucci-Nastasi Spectrumized Dubbing
Wing:	White CDC

Z-LON EMERGER

(Author)

Hook:	Daiichi 1110
Thread:	Yellow 6/0 UNI
Tail:	Pheasant tail
Body:	Pheasant tail
Emerging wings:	Dark dun Metz Betts' Z-Lon
Head:	Yellow Hareline Dubbin

CENTROPTILUM EMERGER

(Author)

Hook: Daiichi 1110
Thread: Yellow 8/0 UNI
Tail: Clear Metz Betts' Z-Lon
Body: Pale yellow Caucci-Nastasi Spectrumized Dubbing
Wings: White CDC

Notes: The tiny size 20 late summer Western PMD/Sulphur emerges on inclement weather days; they love afternoon thunderstorm emergences on spring creeks and have difficulty hatching. The fish target emergers almost exclusively in these situations.

T. C. SULPHUR

(Author)

Hook: Daiichi 1182
Thread: Yellow 6/0 UNI
Tail: Brown Betts' Z-Lon
Body: Orange/yellow Hareline Dubbin mix
Wing: Dun CDC

SULPHUR/STENO USUAL

(Author)

Hook: Daiichi 1182
Thread: Orange 6/0 UNI
Tail: White rabbit's foot
Body: Sulphur gold Spirit River Antron Dubbing
Wing: White rabbit's foot

Notes: This Fran Betters Ausable River pattern is effective during *Stenonema* hatches because the adult and spinner have a blood-orange hue.

EXTENDED-BODY SULPHUR

(Author)

Hook: Daiichi 1140
Thread: Yellow 6/0 UNI
Tail body: 2X mono tied to hook shank; yellow Microfibbets for tail and yellow Antron yarn wrapped to thorax
Wing: Coastal blond deer hair

SULPHUR PUFF EMERGER

(Author)

Hook: Daiichi 1140
Thread: Yellow 6/0 UNI
Tail: Brown Betts' Z-Lon
Body: Yellow Hareline Dubbin
Emerger ball: Gray clipped rabbit's foot in a ball

RUSTY SPINNER

(Author)

Hook: Daiichi 1182; curve the body by bending it under heat
Thread: Rusty brown 70-denier Ultra
Body: Rust mahogany Wapsi Sparkle Antron
Wing: Hareline Organza

PMD DUN

(Author)

Hook: Daiichi 1182
Thread: Yellow 6/0 UNI
Tail: Light olive Betts' Microfibbets
Body: Greenish Yellow Caucci-Nastasi Spectrumized Dubbing
Wing: White CDC

PMD/CALLIBAETIS

(Author)

Hook: Daiichi 1182
Thread: Yellow 6/0 UNI
Tail: Clear Betts' Microfibbets
Body: Pale yellow Caucci-Nastasi Spectrumized Dubbing
Wing: White Hareline Thin Wing; use marker for dot segments
Hackle: Light dun

SULPHUR PT STILLBORN

(Author)

Hook: Daiichi 1182
Thread: Brown UNI 8/0
Tail/Body: 5 strands of dark European pheasant, mahogany-dyed or natural pheasant tail
Thorax: Orange gold Spirit River Antron dubbin
Wing case: Dun CDC

SNOWSHOE EMERGER

(Author)

Hook: Daiichi 1182
Thread: Yellow 8/0 UNI
Tail: Brown Betts' Z-Lon
Body: Amber stone sparkle Hareline Dubbin
Wing: Light dun snowshoe rabbit's foot shaped to form

SULPHUR SPINNER

(Author)

Hook: Daiichi 1182; bend under heat
Thread: Yellow 6/0 UNI
Tail: Yellow Betts' Microfibbets
Body: Spirit River Sulphur Antron
Wings: Clear Hareline Organza

Notes: The bent hook is important. This is the last detail S/R trout look for as spinners shrivel at death.

SULPHUR COMPARA-DUN

(Author)

Hook: Daiichi 1182
Thread: Yellow 6/0 UNI
Body: Sulphur gold Spirit River Antron
Wing: Tan coastal deer hair
Notes: The original Caucci-Nastasi design had its roots in Fran Betters' Haystack pattern. Their books *Hatches I* and *Hatches II* are the bibles for selectivity fly design and entomology.

DORTHEA/CENTROP EMERGER

(Author)

Hook: Daiichi 1140
Thread: Brown 8/0 UNI
Tail/Back body: Brown Betts' Z-Lon wrapped forward
Thorax: Yellow Hareline Dubbin
Wing: White CDC

WOOD DUCK EMERGER

(Author)

Hook: Daiichi 1182
Thread: Brown 8/0 UNI
Tail: Lemon wood duck
Body: Pheasant tail or stripped peacock quill
Legs: Lemon wood duck
Emerger wings: White snowshoe hare or CDC
Head: Sulphur Spirit River Antron

FOAM BUBBLE EMERGER

(Author)

Hook: Daiichi 1160
Thread: Yellow 6/0 UNI
Tail: Lemon wood duck
Body: Sparkle yellow Spirit River Antron with micro gold rib
Air bubble: Tuft of yellow Rainy's closed-cell foam (2 mm)
Hackle: Ginger

SULPHUR SOFT HACKLE

(Author)

Hook: Daiichi X120
Thread: Brown 6/0 UNI
Tail/Body: 6 strands of pheasant tail
Rib: Copper Ultra Wire (medium)
Thorax: Sulphur Spirit River Antron
Hackle: Hungarian partridge soft hackle

CRUSTACEAN

LETORT CRESSBUG

(Author)

Hook: Daiichi 1130
Thread: Gray 6/0 UNI
Back: Dark pheasant tail strand
Rib: Clear monofilament 5X of choice
Body: Gray olive Hareline Dubbin Scud
Eyes: Burnt 3X Maxima Chameleon
Notes: The eyes and spine of *Mancasellus* are extremely important to a spring creek trout that has eternity to examine the natural or artificial. I found this out when the other sow bug styles did nothing until I came out with this pattern. Keep a fine sewing needle with you to pluck out fibers and trim them in an oval shape.

RAZORBACK CRESS BUG

(Author)

Hook: Daiichi 1130, lightweight lead wire wrapped on shank
Thread: Gray 6/0 UNI
Shell: Cut V-shaped grooves into the side of some thin hard plastic and superglue flat on top of lead wire
Body: Gray beaver
Markings: Black marker for tail; V-shaped tail plate
Notes: Another lethal sow bug pattern for use when spring creek trout are spooked by split shot. The weight of the fly takes it down and you control the drift by lifting and dropping the rod tip.

FALLING SPRINGS SCUD

(Mark Sturtevant, Pennsylvania)

Hook: Daiichi 1130
Thread: Brown 8/0 UNI
Tail/Back: Bronze Betts' Z-Lon/Antron
Rib: Light gray thread or 5X monofilament
Body: Blend of 50 percent olive, 50 percent gray Hareline scud dubbing

HERB'S ZEBRA SHRIMP

(Herb Wiegal, Pennsylvania)

Hook: Montana Fly Company 7045
Thread: Black 8/0 UNI
Tail: Sprig of mallard
Body: White or pearl Hareline UV Ice Dub (tier's choice) with black micro plastic beads for dark banding on *Gammarus*

Notes: Herb Wiegel, the former owner of Cold Spring Anglers in Carlisle, Pennsylvania, swore by this deadly fly for Big Spring trout. It imitated the larger *Gammarus* banded scud and it works on ultra S/R fish where *Gammarus* are found.

JAN'S SKID MARK SCUD

(Jan Nemec, Nevada)

Hook: Montana Fly Company 7009 scud hook 1130
Thread: Olive 8/0 UNI
Tail: Dark dun CDC strands
Back: Clear scud back or plastic bag
Eyes: Black marker
Body: Gray olive Hareline Dubbin scud with tuft of orange Glo-Bug yarn for hot spot

Notes: Hot spots are based on the Czech practice of adding a nice suggestive hint to nymphs and scuds. Adding the tuft of orange Glo-Bug yarn here is like fishing two flies, a micro egg and scud pattern, at the same time. This is important in places where only one fly is allowed.

BRONZE BACK MO SCUD

(Author)

Hook: Daiichi 1130
Thread: Gray 6/0 UNI
Tail: Mallard
Back: Clear scud back or plastic bag strip with one strand of bronze or amber Ultra Vinyl Rib
Body: Gray olive Hareline Dubbin scud
Rib: Silver UTC wire (small)
Eye: Black marker

Notes: The blood vein on many tannic-water scuds is apparent to an S/R trout.

LETORT CRESSTACIA

(Author)

Thread: Olive 8/0 UNI
Hook: Daiichi D1120 scud or X120 X Point
Tail/Blood vein: Rust or bronze Antron or Darlon
Eyes: 3X burnt Maxima Chameleon
Body: Mix of 40 percent gray, 40 percent light olive, and 20 percent yellow Hareline sow/scud and traditional for yellow. Pluck out into oval shape and trim.

Notes: This is a lethal spring creek fly that imitates both *Mancasellus* sow bugs and scuds. Carry a needle and pluck out the fibers. This fly doesn't look like much when it's dry, but when it's wet its translucency is impeccable.

MYSIS TRANSPARENT LANEY'S

(Joe Shafer, Colorado)

Hook: Daiichi 1140
Thread: 4M UNI mono or UTC monofoil
Body: UNI mono overlaid with pearly Flashabou; five-minute epoxy
Antennae: White Antron yarn
Head: White Antron with strands of orange hair or Antron, pulled over two black micro rubber legs; clip for eyes and coat with five-minute epoxy

Notes: This pattern is perfect for when *Mysis* is released from icy reservoir depths into tailwaters.

OLIVER EDWARDS'S DEEP-DIVING SHRIMP

(Oliver Edwards, England)

Hook: Daiichi 1130
Weight: .020 Hareline Round Lead Free Wire
Thread: Gray 6/0 UNI
Tail/Body: Fine gray Antron with barbs of brown or gray Hungarian partridge hackle
Antennae: Partridge hackles
Shell back: Scud back, flexi body, or plastic bag strip— tier's choice
Rib: 3X clear mono
Legs: Partridge

Notes: Weighted scuds and nymphs are essential in places where adding split shot is forbidden and where extremely S/R fish shy away from the plop or appearance of added weight. If you add weight on spring creek scuds, the dull tungsten black, nickel, or green split shot is suggested.

ORANGE SCUD

(Author)

Hook: Daiichi 1130
Thread: Gray 6/0 UNI
Tail: Lemon wood duck and pearl Krystal Flash
Back: Scud back or thin plastic bag strip with strand of Hareline pearl flat tinsel
Eyes: Burnt Maxima Chameleon
Body: Shrimp pink Hareline UV Ice Dub

Notes: Dead and molting scuds take on an orange hue.

MOSER'S KILLER BUG

(Inspired by Frank Sawyer; tied by Roman Moser, Austria)

Hook: 1150 Daiichi
Bead: Wapsi Slotted Silver tungsten bead head ($^3/_{32}$)
Thread: Gray 6/0 UNI
Body: Gray Antron or beaver
Rib: Silver Ultra Wire (medium)

Notes: Roman's version of Sawyer's simplistic killer bug is effective for imitating sow bugs, scuds, nymphs, and caddis larvae.

SANDS'S MYSIS TRANSPARENT

(Will Sands, Colorado)

Hook:	Daiichi 1140
Thread:	White or beige 8/0 UNI mono
Eyes:	Burnt Chameleon mono 5X
Body:	Five-minute epoxy
Antennae:	White CDC cut short, three wood duck fibers for claws, and white Z-Lon under eyes

Notes: Another great transparent pattern for use when water is being released on the Colorado tailwaters. The shrimp have neutral buoyancy and can be anywhere in the water column from the top to the bottom. Watch the fish's feeding behavior.

SWANNUNDAZE SCUD

(Author)

Hook:	Wapsi SE3
Thread:	Light olive 6/0 UNI
Shell:	Light olive or olive Swannundaze scud back, or clear or olive Ultra Vinyl Rib
Rib:	Olive thread
Body:	Light olive or yellow Hareline Scud Dubbin

OLIVE KRYSTAL SCUD

(Author)

Hook:	Wapsi SE3
Thread:	Tan 6/0 UNI
Tail:	Pearl Krystal Flash
Rib:	Silver Ultra Wire (extra small)
Shell back:	Clear scud back or plastic bag with strands of Krystal Flash
Eyes:	2X burnt Maxima mono

PEARL SCUD

(Author)

Hook:	Wapsi SE3
Thread:	Gray 6/0 UNI
Shell back:	Wapsi pearl holographic tinsel (small)
Rib:	Gray thread
Body:	Pearl Hareline UV Ice Dub

Notes: This is effective where both tan and *Mysis* scuds are found with cream midge larvae.

MYSIS DEAD WHITE

(Pat Dorsey, Colorado)

Hook:	Daiichi 1140
Thread:	White 6/0 UNI
Tail/Back:	White Antron
Body:	*Mysis* white Wapsi Sow/Scud Dubbing
Eyes:	Black micro rubber legs clipped and burnt or burnt Maxima mono

Notes: Remember that Colorado tailwater fish like those on the Frying Pan will follow the *Mysis* drift for long distances. The trout are S/R to either live or dead versions and will feed to the most abundant form. The farther downriver one fishes, the more this pattern makes the difference.

CADDIS

MO TINY GREEN

(Author)

Hook:	Daiichi 1182
Thread:	Brown 6/0 UNI
Tail shuck:	Burnt bronze Metz Betts' Z-Lon
Body:	Highlander green latex rib
Wing:	Tier's choice of J:son dark caddis wing, Hareline Clear Wing mottled with brown marker, or buggy tan Hareline Medallion Sheeting. All are cut in tent wing with coastal deer hair.

Notes: The adults usually emerge a little slower due to the colder waters and often leave a tailing teardrop shuck attached. As Carl Richards noted, this can make or break a fly pattern's success.

DEER HAIR CDC ADULT

(Author)

Hook:	Daiichi 1182
Thread:	Gray 6/0 UNI
Tail:	Dun CDC strands
Body:	Brown hare's mask
Wing:	Deer hair clipped

SALAR ROOT BEER PUPA

(Author)

Hook:	Daiichi X120
Bead:	Gold
Thread:	Rust 6/0 UNI
Underbody:	Pearl holographic Ultra tinsel (small)
Rib:	Larva Lace or root beer Ultra Vinyl Rib
Thorax:	Brown ostrich with wood duck

Notes: This large caddis pupa/emerger is deadly on Great Lakes Atlantic salmon since caddis hatches are prominent on the big lakes and in all river systems. Great Lakes Atlantics feed like opportunistic browns and caddis is number one on their list, along with *Hexagenia*.

CZECH MATE ORANGE

(Author)

Hook:	Daiichi X120
Thread:	Rusty brown 6/0 UNI
Back:	Brown Hareline UV Chewy Skin, lightly marked with orange marker
Belly:	Amber Antron yarn
Rib:	Red Ultra Wire (extra small)
Thorax:	Hare's ear with tuft of hot orange Ice Dub on the hot spot

DANCING BLACK ELK CADDIS

(Author)

Hook:	Daiichi 1182
Thread:	Black 6/0 UNI
Body:	Black Antron with black hackle
Wing:	Black elk or deer hair

MO GREEN EMERGER

(Author)

Hook:	Daiichi 1160
Thread:	Brown 6/0 UNI
Trailing shuck:	Bronze Metz Betts' Z-Lon burnt to teardrop
Body:	Highlander green latex rib
Side wings:	Dark dun Metz Betts' Z-Lon
Post:	White Hareline Micro Thin closed-cell foam
Hackle:	Light dun

Notes: Devastating on ultra S/R trout on clear tailwaters like the Missouri and Muskegon.

MUSKEGON CADDIS PUPA

(Author)

Hook:	Daiichi 1130
Thread:	Brown 6/0 UNI
Tailing shuck:	Bronze Metz Betts' Z-Lon burnt to teardrop
Body:	Golden yellow latex rubber glove cut in tiny strips or Cascade latex sheets/Bob Marriott's, with brown Sharpie marker bandings
Side wings:	Dark dun Metz Betts' Z-Lon cut short
Post:	White Rainy's foam (2 mm) cut into tiny strips
Parachute:	Light dun hackle

Notes: A Carl Richards–inspired pattern, I tied this version for extremely selective tailwater trout that were targeting pupae suspended in the film despite the presence of egg-laying adults everywhere. Its segmented body, extremely important with caddis, is suspended below the surface and easily targeted by the trout. The foam gives the angler fly visibility.

LAFONTAINE'S SPARKLE PUPA

(Gary LaFontaine, Montana)

Hook:	Daiichi 1130
Thread:	Tan 8/0 UNI
Tail:	Tan Antron
Bubble:	Top and bottom, overlapping clear Antron
Body:	Yellow Antron
Wing pads:	Black marker
Head:	Bronze/amber Antron

MO GREEN CADDIS LARVA

(Author)

Hook:	Daiichi 1150
Thread:	Black 6/0 UNI
Tail:	Gadwall feather fibers
Tag:	Black tungsten bead ($^3/_{32}$)
Body:	Highlander green latex rib, black marker segments for wing pads, Hard As Nails varnish over body

OLIVER EDWARDS'S SIMPLE HYDRO LARVA

(Oliver Edwards, England)

Hook:	Wapsi SE5
Thread:	Tan 6/0 UNI
Tail:	Dyed sprig of black ostrich
Lower main body:	Light olive Danville Acetate Floss
Back:	Olive Hareline Chewy Skin or olive Hareline scud back cut thin
Rib:	Gray UNI-Flex or iron gray Lagartun X-Strong
Legs:	Black hackles stripped to base of cape for curved effect (three on each side)
Wing pads:	Black marker

MO HYDRO/TEARDROP ADULT

(Author)

Hook:	Daiichi 1182
Thread:	Brown 6/0 UNI
Trailer:	Bronze Metz Betts' Z-Lon
Body:	Tan or yellow latex rib, brown Sharpie marker for banding
Underwing:	Tier's choice of J:son caddis wing dark, Hareline Clear Wing mottled with brown marker, or buggy tan Hareline Medallion Sheeting. All are cut in tent wing with coastal deer hair
Top:	Coastal deer hair

Z-LON EMERGER

(Author)

Hook:	Daiichi CTH Alec Jackson chironomid
Thread:	Brown 8/0 UNI
Trailer:	Bronze Betts' Z-Lon, burnt
Body:	Tan yellow latex rib, brown Sharpie marker ribs, Hard As Nails polish finish
Back:	Dark dun Metz Betts' Z-Lon
Hackle:	Dark dun

MO DIVING CADDIS

(Author)

Hook: Daiichi 1130
Bead: Black tungsten ($5/64$)
Thread: Brown 8/0 UNI 8/0
Trailer: Bronze Metz Betts' Z-Lon, burnt teardrop
Body: Green or yellow latex rib; brown Sharpie marker for segments
Collar: Hungarian partridge soft hackle
Wing: UNI Glow Antron (comes in clear white only)

Notes: Many caddis, including *Hydropsyche* and *Cheumatopsyche*, dive to lay eggs. The UNI Glow looks like bubbles under the water. Cast to rising fish and pump the fly to make it sink and twitch it until it tails out. Then pump the rod to imitate struggling surface caddis.

MOSER SPARKLE CADDIS

(Roman Moser, Austria)

Hook: Daiichi 1182
Thread: Rusty brown 6/0 UNI
Body: Rust Hareline UV Ice Dub
Rib: Copper Ultra Wire (extra small) or just rusty brown thread
Collar: Ginger hackle fibers
Head: Shrimp pink Hareline UV Ice Dub

SPENT QUAD

(Author)

Hook: Daiichi 1182
Thread: Rusty dun 8/0 UNI
Body: Amber Antron
Wings: Hungarian partridge tips; cut in four wings in V shape

Notes: Deadly as dusk approaches and the spent caddis are sipped well into the night on tailwaters like the Muskegon.

MO HYDRO ADULT

(Author)

Hook: Daiichi 1182
Thread: Rusty dun 8/0 UNI
Body: Cinnamon Hareline Dubbin
Wing: Tier's choice of J:son caddis wing dark, Hareline Clear Wing mottled with brown marker, or buggy tan Hareline Medallion Sheeting. All are cut in tent wing with coastal deer hair
Wing: Coastal deer hair

VOODOO ASCENDING PUPA

(Author)

Hook: Daiichi X120
Bead: Tungsten nickel ($3/32$)
Thread: Brown 8/0 UNI
Body: Mottled tan mini marabou palmered and layered and trimmed down to pupa shape
Underwing: Mallard
Wing: Hungarian partridge tips

Notes: Used as a dropper below an adult or pupa, this fly looks like an ascending emerger and is lethal. It takes trout in a caddis hatch when nothing else will.

BEAD HEAD SOFT HACKLE CADDIS EMERGER

(Author)

Hook: Daiichi X120
Bead: Tungsten nickel ($5/64$)
Thread: Brown 6/0 UNI
Trailer: Bronze Metz Betts' Z-Lon, burnt teardrop
Body: Green or tan/cream latex, depending on species; Sharpie marker for segments
Collar: Hungarian partridge

WHITE MILLER

(Author)

Hook: Daiichi 1182
Thread: White 8/0 UNI
Body: Cream Antron, white hackle palmered and trimmed to sides
Wings: White turkey quill

Notes: August and September bring the fast-flying and egg-laying millers to the surface at dusk. Their quick movement must be imitated by twitching, skittering, and hopping the pattern.

OCTOBER CADDIS

(Author)

Hook: Daiichi 1182
Thread: Rusty brown 6/0 UNI
Body: Amber Stone Hareline or Wapsi Antron
Wings: Brown strung saddle hackle tips; black marker for dot
Collar: Ginger hackle
Antennae: Stripped ginger quill

MIDGE

BLACK BUZZER

(Author)

Hook:	Daiichi CTH Alec Jackson Chironomid
Thread:	Black 6/0 UNI
Body:	Black Lagartun Mini Flatbraid; Hard as Nails coating
Rib:	Silver Lagartun oval tinsel (small)
Side pads:	Orange Antron
Head:	Hare's mask
Cilia:	White CDC

Notes: The buzzer is deadly anywhere from high Rocky Mountain and alpine lakes to spring creeks, where they imitate *Simulium* and larger chironomids.

CHAN'S ICE CREAM CONE

(Brian Chan, Canada)

Hook:	Daiichi CTH Alec Jackson chironomid hook. (Still waters have larger midges than spring creeks and rivers.)
Bead:	White metal
Thread:	Black 6/0 Danville
Body:	Black Super Floss 6/0 thread
Rib:	Red Ultra midge wire (extra small)
Thorax:	Black thread

Notes: Clear fingernail polish makes the body look glossy.

QUILL PEACOCK BUZZER

(Author)

Hook:	Daiichi CTH Alec Jackson chironomid hook
Thread:	Black 8/0 UNI
Body:	Peacock strip quills
Thorax:	Peacock
Wing case:	White Antron

DISCO RED

(Author)

Hook:	Daiichi 1130
Thread:	Black 8/0 UNI
Body:	Red Flashabou and Lagartun X-Strong silver tinsel micro rib
Head:	Black Antron

RED-EYE DISCO

(Author)

Hook:	Daiichi CTH Alec Jackson chironomid hook
Thread:	Black 8/0 UNI
Body:	Hare's mask
Rib:	One strand of Hareline Mirage lateral scale
Red eye:	Red Lagartun Mini Flatbraid
Wing case:	Black Hareline Dura Skin
Body lacquer:	Hard as Nails

CHAN'S DISCO MIDGE

(Brian Chan, Canada)

Hook:	Daiichi 1140
Thread:	Black 8/0 UNI
Body:	Red UNI floss
Rib:	Silver Lagartun X-Strong oval tinsel
Bead:	Black Wapsi Killer Caddis glass bead (midge)
Cilia:	White Antron

BIG SPRING MIDGE

(Author)

Hook:	1130 Daiichi
Thread:	Gray 8/0 UNI
Body:	One pheasant tail fiber
Post:	White Hareline Micro Thin Foam
Hackle:	Grizzly

BIG SPRING PUPA

(Author)

Hook:	K1A Partridge Vince Marinaro Midge Hook
Thread:	Gray 8/0 UNI
Body:	Hare's mask
Rib:	Silver Krystal Flash
Head:	Black Hareline Dubbin
Air bubble:	White Hareline Micro Thin Foam

Notes: Pennsylvania's Big Spring Creek and many other spring creeks have a predominant gray midge motif in size 26-28 that must be tied sparse. Fish a pupa under a well-greased dry fly.

RED BUTT MIDGE

(Author)

Hook:	Daiichi CTH Alec Jackson chironomid
Thread:	Black 8/0 UNI
Tag:	Red Lagartun micro flat braid
Body:	Black Lagartun micro flat braid
Rib:	Silver Lagartun X-Strong oval tinsel
Head:	Black Lagartun micro flat braid tied in ball
Body lacquer:	Hard As Nails

PEARL BRASSIE

(Author)

Hook:	Daiichi CTH Alec Jackson chironomid hook
Thread:	Gray 8/0 UNI
Body:	Copper Ultra Wire (small)
Thorax:	Hare's mask
Wing case:	Pearl Flashabou strands; Hard As Nails coating

Notes: The pearl imitates the air bubbles that midges and other larvae use to propel themselves upward.

CLUSTER PARACHUTE

(Author)

Hook:	Daiichi 1130
Thread:	Black 8/0 UNI
Tail:	White Antron
Body:	Black thread
Thorax:	Black UV Hareline peacock Ice Dub
Post:	White CDC
Hackle:	Grizzly

BIG SPRING FLASH PUPA

(Author)

Hook:	K1A Partridge Marinaro Midge Hook
Thread:	Black 8/0 UNI
Body:	Green pearl Krystal Flash
Head:	Black thread
Cilia:	Silver Flashabou Accent

REDWORM BLACK HEAD

(Author)

Hook:	Daiichi CTH Alec Jackson chironomid hook
Thread:	Black 8/0 UNI
Body:	Red Lagartun Mini Flatbraid
Rib:	Silver Lagartun X-Strong oval tinsel
Thorax:	Black peacock Hareline UV Ice Dub
Wing case:	Black or mottled black Wapsi Thin Skin

HATCHERY REDWORM

(Author)

Hook:	Daiichi 1130
Thread:	Red 8/0 UNI
Body:	Red Flashabou wrapped
Head:	Red UV Ice Dub

Notes: Most spring creeks around the world have hatcheries associated with them. These hatcheries utilize the cold subterranean ground flows, which have stable temperatures that allow for growing trout year-round. The red chironomid worm in sizes 18–24 feasts on the hatchery fecal matter and is eventually flushed into the spring creeks.

BIRCHELL'S EMERGER

(Author)

Hook:	Daiichi 1130
Thread:	Black 8/0 UNI
Tail:	Brown Betts' Z-Lon
Body:	Gray turkey biots
Rib:	Black thread
Thorax:	Peacock UV Ice Dub
Post:	White CDC
Hackle:	Grizzly

BREECHES WHITE MIDGE

(Author)

Hook:	K1A Partridge Marinaro Midge Hook
Thread:	White 8/0 UNI
Body:	White thread
Slant wing:	Clear Betts' Z-Lon
Head:	Orange Glo-Bug yarn

Notes: This is the go-to pattern (in size 28 with 8X tippet) when trout are gulping midges on the flat water of the Yellow Breeches and other spring creeks in autumn. Set the hook light and slow.

IAN'S BRASS ASS

(Author)

Hook:	Daiichi CTH Alec Jackson chironomid hook
Thread:	Black 8/0 UNI
Body:	Copper UTC (brassie)
Head:	Black thread built up into an oval
Sides:	Strand of copper Flashabou

BEAD HEAD BUZZER

(Author)

Hook:	Daiichi 1130
Bead:	Copper ($5/64$)
Body:	Black thread
Rib:	Copper Ultra Wire (small)
Thorax:	Peacock UV Ice Dub
Wing:	Pearl Flashabou

ICSI MIDGE

(Tom Baltz, Pennsylvania)

Hook:	K1A Partridge Marinaro Midge Hook
Thread:	Black 8/0 UNI
Body:	One peacock strand
Hackle:	Grizzly
Post:	Orange Glo-Bug or orange Hi-VIZ Antron

Notes: Hi-VIZ posts become important as our eyesight gets worse. They are also useful for dark-colored waters where the midge is hard to see.

VINCE'S BIG SPRING MIDGE HOOK

(Vince Marinaro)

Hook:	K1A Partridge Marinaro Midge Hook
Thread/Body:	Gray 8/0 UNI
Hackle:	Grizzly Tiny Palmer

STONEFLY

OLIVER EDWARDS'S YELLOW SALLY

(Oliver Edwards, England)

Hook:	Daiichi 1560
Thread:	Olive 8/0 UNI
Tail:	Yellow Betts' Microfibbets
Body/Thorax:	Yellow or amber Antron
Rib:	5X mono
Legs:	Lemon-dyed wood duck
Back/Wing case:	Clear Wapsi Nymph Skin or Hareline Dura Skin, colored with brown and yellow marker

MORRISH GOLDEN STONE

(Ken Morrish, Oregon)

Hook:	Daiichi 1760
Bead:	Gold ($5/64$)
Thread:	Yellow 8/0 UNI
Tail:	Amber goose biots
Body:	Copper Ultra Wire (brassie)
Back:	Thin strip of black Hareline Dura Skin or Wapsi Thin Skin
Legs:	Black Krystal Flash
Thorax:	Amber Antron
Wing case:	Folded mottled peacock wing

TRADITIONAL GOLDEN STONE

(Author)

Hook:	Daiichi 1760
Thread:	Brown 6/0 UNI
Tail:	Golden goose biots
Body:	Sulphur gold Spirit River Dubbing
Rib:	Gold UTC wire (medium)
Back:	Pheasant tail, mottled turkey, or peacock wing
Legs:	Yellow goose biots
Wing case:	Folded mottled turkey or peacock wing cut in V shapes and covered in Clear Cure Goo or epoxy
Thorax:	Yellow UNI or Antron yarn
Antennae:	Brown goose biots

OLIVER EDWARDS'S BLACK STONE

(Oliver Edwards, England)

Hook:	TMC 400 T (swimming nymph)
Thread:	Black 8/0 UNI
Tail:	Two moose mane fibers
Body:	Tier's choice of Hareline Dura Skin, Hareline Cheesy Skin, or Wapsi Thin Skin or thin strips of black electrical tape to accent segments; Hard As Nails coating to give glossy sheen
Wing case:	Double-fold body material into three segments to add thickness
Thorax:	Black Hareline Dubbin
Legs:	Black/white Partridge fibers
Antennae:	Moose mane tips

Notes: Extremely realistic when imitating the early black *Allocapnia* or *Taeniopteryx* hatch in which the nymphs wiggle and swim.

CDC EARLY BLACK STONE

(Author)

Hook:	Daiichi 1640
Thread:	Black 8/0 UNI
Body:	Black hare's mask
Wing:	Four to six light dun CDC strands
Hackle:	Grizzly

Notes: Lethal when early black caddis appear in the afternoons and lay eggs. This pattern should be twitched and dead drifted. Use Trout Hunter CDC Fly Dressing.

BROOKS'S GIANT STONE

(Author)

Hook:	Daiichi 1730
Thread:	Black 6/0 UNI
Tail:	Moose mane
Body:	Black Ultra Vinyl Rib
Rib:	Red Ultra Wire (medium)
Thorax:	Peacock herl
Legs:	Black saddle hackle
Wing case:	Black Hareline Dura Skin or Wapsi Thin Skin, folded in plates

Notes: Still the go-to stone when fishing fast boulder water from the Madison to the Alps wherever *Pteronarcys* are present. Can be weighted with lead wire to get down fast in Brooks's "potshotting" method.

KAUFMANN'S STONE

(Randall Kaufmann, Oregon)

Hook:	Daiichi 1730
Thread:	Black 6/0 UNI
Tail:	Black goose biots
Body:	Lead wire weight shaped to form with black SLF Kaufmann stonefly dubbing
Rib:	Black UTC Vinyl Rib nymph
Wing plates:	Three turkey quill segments cut into V shapes
Antennae:	Black goose biots

ROMAN MOSER TRAUN RIVER STONE

(Roman Moser, Austria)

Hook:	Daiichi 1182
Thread:	Black 8/0 UNI
Body:	Black hare's mask
Wing:	J:son stone wing (extra-small)
Hackle:	Grizzly

SENYO'S WIGGLE STONE

(Greg Senyo, Lake Erie)

Back hook:	Daiichi 1182
Thread:	Black 6/0 UNI
Tail:	Black goose biots
Body:	Black UTC Vinyl Rib oval (nymph)
Connection:	3X mono superglued to front hook
Front hook:	Daiichi X 120
Wing case:	Pearl black Hareline Flashy Back
Legs:	Black goose biots
Body:	Peacock Ice Dub

Notes: This fly wiggles and swims, imparting an amazing quality of movement. It is excellent for trout and steelhead alike in the spring.

TRADITIONAL BROWN STONE

(Author)

Hook:	Daiichi 1730
Thread:	Brown 6/0 UNI
Tail:	Brown goose biots
Body:	Brown stone SLF Kaufmann
Rib:	Brown UTC Vinyl Rib (nymph)
Thorax:	Black ostrich
Legs:	Ginger saddle hackle
Wing case:	Brown or dark pheasant tail Hareline Dura Skin, Wapsi Thin Skin, or brown turkey biot quills
Antennae:	Brown goose biots

MAYFLIES

LIGHT CAHILL

(Author)

Hook:	Daiichi 1182
Thread:	Light cahill 6/0 UNI
Tails:	White Metz Microfibbets
Body:	Light cahill Wapsi beaver dubbing
Wing:	White CDC

CAHILL T. C. EMERGER

(Author)

Hook:	Daiichi 1160
Thread:	Brown 6/0 UNI
Tail:	Brown Metz Betts' Z-Lon
Body:	Brown Metz Z-Lon
Thorax:	Light cahill Wapsi beaver
Wings:	Tan CDC

CAHILL SPINNER

(Author)

Hook:	Daiichi 1182, slightly bent to mimic natural
Thread:	Light cahill 6/0 UNI
Tail:	Clear Metz Microfibbets
Body:	Pinkish cream Caucci-Nastasi Spectrumized Dubbing
Thorax:	Tinge of black Hareline Dubbin
Wings:	Clear Organza, clipped bottom and top

MAYFLY EMERGER RABBIT'S FOOT

(Author)

Hook:	Daiichi 1160
Thread:	Tan 8/0 UNI; match to insect color
Tail:	Brown Metz Betts' Z-Lon
Body:	Ginger Hareline Quill Body
Wings:	Gray or tan snowshoe rabbit
Head/Thorax:	Mahogany brown Caucci-Nastasi Spectrumized Dubbing

Notes: This is an amazing pattern that imitates many early-season may fly hatches. It fits the bill in all situations.

DARK HENDRICKSON

(Author)

Hook:	Daiichi 1182
Thread:	Brown 8/0 UNI
Tail:	Dark dun hackle
Body:	Beaver
Wings:	Lemon wood duck
Hackle:	Light dun

LIGHT HENDRICKSON

(Author)

Hook:	Daiichi 1182
Thread:	Light cahill 6/0 UNI
Tail:	Dun hackles
Body:	Dark tan Wapsi Beaver
Wings:	Lemon wood duck
Hackle:	Ginger

CATSKILL GREEN DRAKE

(Author)

Hook:	Daiichi 1182
Thread:	Light cahill 6/0 UNI
Tails:	Moose mane
Body:	Dark tan Wapsi beaver
Wing post:	Lemon wood duck
Hackle:	White

ADAMS PARACHUTE

(Author)

Hook:	Daiichi 1182
Thread:	Gray 8/0
Tail:	Brown and grizzly hackle tips
Body:	Adams gray Wapsi beaver
Post:	White calf tail

Parachute hackle: Brown grizzly

Notes: If an angler were allowed only one dry fly to fish throughout the world, the Adams would be it. When I asked the gillie what dry to use during my first visit to the hallowed chalkstreams of England, he said "the one you feel most confident in." I chose the size 14 Adams Parachute. Two hours later I was told to report to the bar at the lodge because I was catching and releasing way too many fish by British standards and was banished from the river.

HENDRICKSON COMPARA-DUN

(Author)

Hook:	Daiichi 1182
Thread:	Tan 6/0 UNI 6/0
Tail:	Tan Metz Microfibbets
Body:	Dark brown Caucci-Nastasi Spectrumized Dubbing
Wings:	Light coastal deer hair

Notes: This pattern is still the go-to fly for adults on the Delaware when *subvaria* are on.

FEMALE HENDRICKSON (SPRING CREEK STYLE)

(Author)

Hook:	Daiichi 1182
Thread:	Gray 6/0 UNI
Tail:	Dark dun
Tag:	Gold or sulphur Spirit River Dubbing, formed into ball to mimic the egg that ready to be deposited
Body:	Natural ginger quills or ginger Hareline Quill Body
Wings:	Light dun hackle tips stripped, cut, inverted, and tied by tips
Hackle:	Brown
Head:	Gray brown Orvis Antron Dubbing

Notes: The bright-orange egg ready to be deposited by the female is pronounced on *Ephemerella subvaria*.

HENDRICKSON COMPARA-EMERGER

(Author)

Hook:	Daiichi 1182
Thread:	Gray 6/0 UNI
Tail:	Light brown Metz Betts' Z-Lon
Body:	Dark brown Caucci-Nastasi Spectrumized Dubbing
Wings:	Short coastal deer hair

HENDRICKSON SPINNER

(author)

Hook:	Daiichi 1182
Thread:	Rusty brown 6/0
Tail:	Gray Metz Microfibbets, split in V
Egg:	Yellow orange Antron
Body:	Brown goose biots
Thorax:	Rusty Wapsi Super Bright Dubbing
Wings:	Clear Hareline Organza

QUILL GORDON

(Author)

Thread:	Brown 6/0 UNI
Hook:	Daiichi 1182
Tail:	Gray hackle tips
Body:	Razor stripped and varnished peacock herl tied in perfect bands to form the rib
Wings:	Wood duck
Hackle:	Brown for Hendrickson or gray hackle for black *Leptophlebia*

Notes: The Quill Gordon was the first true selective trout fly of the Americas. It was first tied by founding father Theodore Gordon in the Catskills and it set the standard for modern dry flies apart from the British school. The body segments and wing profile imitate myriad darker mayflies in the spring. During high flows of spring the pattern is unsinkable and has a sparse silhouette.

MERLINO'S ISO DICE

(Rich Merlino, Michigan)

Hook:	Daiichi 1182
Thread:	Rusty brown 8/0 UNI
Tail:	Brown Betts' Z-Lon and two moose mane strands
Body:	Rust Wapsi sparkle Antron
Rib:	Strand of copper Flashabou
Wings:	Gray snowshoe rabbit

Notes: Effective as a searching pattern when the evening *Isonychia* hatch is yet to come.

BORCHERS

(Inspired by Ernie Borchers;
tied by Gates Au Sable Lodge, Michigan)

Hook:	Daiichi 1182
Thread:	Brown 6/0 UNI
Tail:	Moose mane
Body:	Six strands of dark European red-brown pheasant, or mahogany-dyed pheasant tail
Post:	White calf tail
Hackle:	Grizzly

Notes: This is the traditional Lead-Winged Coachman that made its debut on Michigan's hallowed Au Sable river and is the go-to pattern for large dark mayflies around the world.

MARCH BROWN T. C.

(Author)

Hook:	Daiichi 1160
Thread:	Tan cream 8/0 UNI
Tail:	Brown Betts' Z-Lon
Body:	Pinkish cream Caucci-Nastasi Spectrumized Dubbing
Wing:	Tan CDC mottled with brown marker

STENO USUAL EMERGER

(Fran Betters, New York)

Hook:	Daiichi 1182
Thread:	Tan 6/0 UNI
Tail:	Brown Hareline Darlon
Body:	Orange gold Spirit River Antron Dubbing; back half colored with brown marker
Wing:	Light tan snowshoe rabbit foot, mottled with brown marker

Notes: The wing mottling on *Stenonema* is significant. S/R trout detect wings first through the refractive angle that allows them to see around corners.

NYMPHS/SOFT HACKLES

SELECTIVITY PHEASANT TAIL

(Author)

Hook:	Daiichi 1560
Thread:	Brown 6/0 UNI
Tail/Body:	Pheasant tail
Rib:	Copper Flashabou
Wing:	Wood duck
Thorax:	UV Peacock Hareline Ice Dub
Bead:	Hareline Cyclops Brass bead ($5/64$)

Notes: Adding wood duck imitates the speckled body of Sulphurs and other *Ephemerella* and *Stenonema* nymphs.

SAWYER PHEASANT TAIL

(Frank Sawyer, England)

Hook:	Daiichi 1560
Thread/Ribbing:	Red mahogany Veniard copper wire (small)
Body:	Eight strands of red brown European pheasant (if you can find it), or mahogany dyed or regular pheasant tail
Thorax:	Copper wire wrapped to form oval; body wound in union with pheasant strands
Wing case:	Pheasant strands pulled back and tied in thorax with red wire

Notes: Frank Sawyer was the master of English chalkstream nymphing. If one had to fish one fly pattern in the world,

the Pheasant Tail Nymph would be it! It was initially intended to mimic the *Baetis* Blue-Winged Olive nymphs but it is a general pattern that imitates a host of clinging mayflies, particularly Sulphurs. Like all of Sawyer's nymphs, this is simplicity through design and it is highly effective. It has no legs since the *Baetis* is a quick swimmer and its legs are tucked in.

COPPER PHEASANT TAIL

(Author)

Hook:	Daiichi 1560
Thread:	Brown 6/0 UNI
Tail/Body/Wing case:	Pheasant tail
Rib/Thorax:	Copper Ultra Wire (small)

SOFT HACKLE PHEASANT TAIL

(Author)

Hook:	Daiichi 1560
Thread:	Brown 6/0 UNI
Body/Tail:	Pheasant tail
Rib:	Copper Ultra Wire (small)
Thorax:	Hareline Senyo's UV Ice Dub
Hackle:	Partridge soft hackle

HARE'S EAR

(Author)

Hook:	Daiichi 1560
Thread:	Brown 6/0 UNI
Tail:	Pheasant tail
Body:	Hare's ear
Rib:	Gold Ultra Wire (small)
Thorax:	Hare's mask
Wing case:	Cardinal pheasant feather

SULPHUR SOFT HACKLE

(Author)

Hook:	Daiichi X120
Thread:	Brown 6/0 UNI
Tail:	Pheasant tail
Rib:	Copper Ultra Wire (small)
Thorax:	Pale yellow Hareline Dubbin
Wing:	Partridge soft hackle

STENO BEAD HEAD

(Author)

Hook:	Daiichi 1720
Thread:	Light cahill 6/0 UNI
Tail/Wing:	Lemon wood duck
Body:	Amber Hareline Dubbin
Rib:	Copper Ultra Wire (small)
Thorax:	UV peacock Hareline Senyo's Ice Dub
Eye:	Cyclops gold bead ($^5/_{64}$)

SULPHUR PHEASANT TAIL

(Author)

Hook:	Daiichi 1270
Thread:	Brown 6/0 UNI
Tail/body/Wing case:	Pheasant tail
Thorax:	Light yellow brown Caucci-Nastasi Spectrumized Dubbing

SULPHUR BEAD SOFT HACKLE

(Author)

Hook:	Daiichi 1560
Thread:	Brown 6/0 UNI
Tail/Body:	Pheasant tail
Thorax:	UV shrimp orange Hareline Senyo's Ice Dub
Wing:	Partridge soft hackle

HENDRICKSON NYMPH

(Author)

Hook:	Black Partridge Klinkhamer 15BN nymph hook
Thread:	Tan 6/0 UNI
Tail:	Lemon wood duck
Body:	Dark red fox
Wing case:	Dark mallard wing

CADILLAC NYMPH

(Author)

Hook:	Daiichi 1560
Thread:	Black 6/0 UNI
Tail:	Black dyed pheasant tail
Back:	Copper Flashabou
Rib:	Copper Ultra Wire (small)
Thorax:	Peacock
Wing case:	Black dyed pheasant tail
Eye:	Black tungsten bead ($^3/_{32}$)

Notes: This is a popular New Zealand nymph.

MAYFLY WIGGLE GRAY FOX

(Author)

Hook:	Daiichi 1150
Thread:	Gray 70-denier Ultra
Tail:	Lemon wood duck
Extended body:	2X mono
Body:	Beaver/hare's mask mix
Legs:	Cardinal pheasant feather clipped in V
Wing case:	Dark mallard wing

ISONYCHIA NYMPH

(Author)

Hook:	Daiichi 1560
Thread:	Brown 6/0 UNI
Tail:	Gadwall feather strands
Body:	Brown Antron
Rib:	Copper Ultra Wire (small)
Back:	Copper Flashabou
Gill plates:	Root beer/copper flash Hareline Crazy Legs
Wing:	Partridge soft hackle
Head:	UV peacock Hareline Ice Dub

GRAY DRAKE SOFT HACKLE

(Author)

Hook:	Daiichi 1760
Thread:	Black 6/0 UNI
Tail:	Gadwall feather strands
Body:	Large Gadwall feather wound around hook and clipped
Rib:	Silver Ultra Wire (small)
Thorax:	Peacock Hareline UV Ice Dub
Wing:	Partridge soft hackle

Notes: Gray drake nymphs migrate to shore to emerge, so one should swim and twitch this pattern along the shoreline riffles

OTTER SUCKER SPAWN TROUT SMACK

(Author)

Hook:	Daiichi 1150
Thread:	Fluorescent red 70-denier Ultra
Egg:	Tangerine Otter Soft Milking Egg sucker spawn pierced through middle of eggs onto hook and superglued

MATT'S MARABOU HEX WIGGLE

(Author)

Back hook:	Daiichi 1270 broken off
Thread:	Yellow 6/0 UNI
Tail:	Sand or tan Hareline mini barred marabou
Body:	Marabou wound forward and clipped with brown marker spotting
Attachment:	3X mono
Front hook:	Daiichi x510
Body:	Yellow amber Antron
Rib:	Silver Ultra oval tinsel (small)
Wing case:	Latex rubber glove cut into two V-shaped gill plates and marked with brown Sharpie
Hackle:	Hen ring neck feather

MOSER'S EMERGER

(Roman Moser, Austria)

Hook:	Daiichi 1150
Thread:	White 6/0 UNI
Tail:	White CDC
Body:	Cream Antron
Side wings:	White cock hackle tips
Back wing:	White CDC
Head:	Cream Antron and white CDC wing case

STENO HARE'S EAR

(Author)

Hook:	Daiichi 1150
Thread:	Tan 6/0 UNI
Tail:	Pheasant tail
Body:	Hare's ear
Rib:	Copper Ultra Wire (small)
Wing case:	Mallard feather clipped into V shape
Collar:	Tan saddle hackle

J:SON SWEDEN MAYFLY DUNS

These incredibly innovative fly designs present the ultimate natural replication to S/R trout. The new patterned swivels tied into the leader prevent the stiff wings from spinning and twisting, which can be a problem when using stiff plastic materials.

J:SON MAYFLY DUN M1 GREEN (GREEN DRAKE)

Hook:	#10 J:son Ultimate Short Shank Dry Fly Hook
Thread:	J:son Ultimate Tying Thread (transparent, unspun 50-denier Dyneema)
Wings:	J:son Realistic Wing Material RWM M1
Extended body:	J:son Realistic Colored Foam, Mayfly Selection (Ash Grey)
Hackle:	Cree/Variant (parachute style)
Tails:	Synthetic Microfibbets
J:son Realistic Color Markers:	Colorless Blender and Warm Grey No 6

J:SON MAYFLY DUN M1 BROWN (BROWN DRAKE)

Hook:	#10 J:son Ultimate Short Shank Dry Fly Hook
Thread:	J:son Ultimate Tying Thread (transparent, unspun 50-denier Dyneema)
Wings:	J:son Realistic Wing Material RWM M1 (rear wing is M3)
Extended body:	Cinnamon Brown J:son Realistic Colored Foam, Mayfly Selection
Hackle:	Cree/Variant (parachute style)
Tails:	Synthetic Microfibbets

J:son Realistic Color Markers:	Colorless Blender and Walnut
Markings:	Black fine-point waterproof marker

J:SON MAYFLY DUN M3 GOLD (*EPEORUS VITREUS*)

Hook:	#16 J:son Ultimate Short Shank Dry Fly Hook
Thread:	J:son Ultimate Tying Thread (transparent, unspun 50-denier Dyneema)
Wings:	J:son Realistic Wing Material RWM M3
Extended body:	Saffron Gold J:son Realistic Colored Foam, Mayfly Selection
Hackle:	Cree/Variant (parachute style)
Tails:	Synthetic Microfibbets
J:son Realistic Color Markers:	Colorless Blender and Warm Grey No 4

J:SON MAYFLY DUN M3 CREAM (*STENONEMA*)

Hook:	#16 J:son Ultimate Short Shank Dry Fly Hook
Thread:	J:son Ultimate Tying Thread (transparent, unspun 50-denier Dyneema)
Wings:	J:son Realistic Wing Material RWM M3
Extended body:	Vanilla Cream J:son Realistic Colored Foam, Mayfly Selection
Hackle:	Cree/Variant (parachute style)
Tails:	Synthetic Microfibbets
J:son Realistic Color Markers:	Colorless Blender and Spanish Olive

J:SON STONEFLIES

J:SON STONEFLY SPINNER/SPENT U1 OLIVE BROWN (*PTERONARCYS CALIFORNICA*)

Hook:	#8 J:son Ultimate Dry Fly Hook
Thread:	J:son Ultimate Tying Thread (transparent, unspun 50-denier Dyneema)
Wings:	J:son Realistic Wing Material RWM U1
Head/Thorax:	J:son Realistic Wing Material RWM S2
Legs:	Olive brown J:son Realistic Nymph Legs RNL S2
Extended Body:	Cinnamon Brown J:son Realistic Colored Foam, Stonefly Selection
Dubbing:	Any brand of synthetic dubbing in olive brown or brown
Body/Thorax/Abdomen:	J:son Realistic T&A Regular Olive Brown
J:son Realistic Color Markers:	Colorless Blender & Walnut
Markings:	Black regular point waterproof marker

J:SON STONEFLY NYMPH S1 CINNAMON BROWN (*ACRONERIA*)

Hook:	#2 J:son Ultimate Nymph Hook, bent
Thread:	J:son Ultimate Tying Thread (transparent, unspun 50-denier Dyneema)
Weight:	Strips from flexible tungsten sheet
Head/Thorax:	J:son Realistic Wing Material RWM S1
Legs:	Olive Brown J:son Realistic Nymph Legs RNL S1
Back:	J:son Real Skin (Olive Brown)
Dubbing:	Any brand of synthetic dubbing in light olive brown or light brown
Body/Thorax/Abdomen:	J:son Realistic T&A Regular Olive Brown
J:son Realistic Color Markers:	Colorless Blender and Walnut
Markings:	Black regular-point waterproof marker

J:SON STONEFLY NYMPH S3 YELLOW (*ISOPERLA*)

Hook:	#8 J:son Ultimate Nymph Hook
Thread:	J:son Ultimate Tying Thread (transparent, unspun 50-denier Dyneema)
Weight:	Strips from flexible tungsten sheet
Head/Thorax:	J:son Realistic Wing Material RWM S3
Legs:	Olive Brown J:son Realistic Nymph Legs RNL S3
Back:	J:son Real Skin (Yellow)
Dubbing:	Any brand of synthetic dubbing in cream or yellow
Body:	J:son Realistic T&A Regular Yellow
J:son Realistic Color Markers:	Colorless Blender and Warm Grey No 4

J:SON ADULT STONEFLY A1 CINNAMON BROWN (*ACRONERIA*)

Hook:	#8 J:son Ultimate Dry Fly Hook
Thread:	J:son Ultimate Tying Thread (transparent, unspun 50-denier Dyneema)
Wings:	J:son Realistic Wing Material RWM A1
Head/Thorax:	J:son Realistic Wing Material RWM S2
Legs:	Olive Brown J:son Realistic Nymph Legs RNL S2
Extended Body:	Cinnamon Brown J:son Realistic Colored Foam, Stonefly Selection
Dubbing:	Any brand of synthetic dubbing in olive brown or brown
Body and back:	J:son Realistic T&A Regular Olive Brown
J:son Realistic Color Markers:	Colorless Blender and Walnut
Markings:	Black regular-point waterproof marker

J:SON WIGGLE TAIL NYMPH N1 OLIVE BROWN (*PTERONARCYS DORSATA*)

Hook:	#10 J:son Ultimate Dry Fly Hook
Thread:	J:son Ultimate Tying Thread (transparent, unspun 50-denier Dyneema)
Weight:	Strips from flexible tungsten sheet (thorax)
Head/Thorax:	J:son Realistic Wing Material RWM N1
Legs:	Olive Brown J:son Realistic Nymph Legs RNL N1
Extended body:	Cinnamon Brown J:son Realistic Colored Foam, Mayfly Selection
Dubbing:	Light Olive Brown/Light Brown synthetic dubbing in (any brand)
Gills:	Natural Brown Ostrich
Body/Thorax/Abdomen:	J:son Realistic T&A Micro Olive Brown
J:son Realistic Color Markers:	Colorless Blender and Walnut
Markings:	Black fine-point waterproof marker

MAYFLIES

HEX WIGGLE FOAM DOT

(M. Batcke, Michigan)

Thread:	Brown 6/0 UNI
Tail:	Moose mane
Back:	Power Pro white cord attachment; brown and yellow Rainy's foam (2 mm), thread ribbing, red marker dots on underbelly
Front hook:	Daiichi 1120
Thorax:	Brown and yellow Rainy's foam (2 mm)
Wings:	Light dun CDC

Notes: Trout love this great, durable pattern that floats and can be twitched at night without drowning. It also can be used during the day as a terrestrial or hopper-like pattern prior to the nighttime Hex hatch.

TROUTSMAN HEX

(Gates Au Sable Lodge)

Hook:	Daiichi 2110
Thread:	Yellow 3/0 UNI
Tail:	Moose mane
Body:	Lower: Yellow deer hair; top: natural deer hair
Rib:	Yellow thread carefully and symmetrically wound in quads, first front and then back
Wing:	White calf tail, ginger hackle

DIRTY MALE HEX SPINNER

(Author)

Hook:	Daiichi 1270
Thread:	Tan 3/0 UNI
Tail:	Moose mane
Body:	Gray Spirit River Antron; lower body is deer hair; top is quad-style ribbing with thread
Thorax:	March brown Spirit River Antron
Wings:	Gray Organza with grizzly hackle

Notes: The male *Hexagenia* is darker and smaller than the female. During some nights when there are more males, the fish key on the darker spinner.

ISO BICOLOR

(Author)

Hook:	Daiichi 1150
Thread:	Brown 6/0 UNI
Tail:	Brown Betts' Z-Lon
Body:	Mahogany brown Caucci-Nastasi Spectrumized Dubbing
Wing:	Five to six light dun CDC feathers

Notes: Tie this with a thick body and splay the wings to imitate the fluttering of a newly hatched adult on the surface.

WEAMER'S ISO

(Paul Weamer, Pennsylvania)

Hook:	Daiichi 1150
Thread:	Black 6/0 UNI
Tail:	Black moose mane
Body:	Mahogany Wapsi Beaver Dubbing
Wing:	Dark dun CDC

MO GRAY DRAKE

(Author)

Hook:	Daiichi 1270, carefully bent in middle (can be heated and bent)
Thread:	Gray 6/0 UNI
Tail:	Light dun hackle
Body:	Grizzly and light dun quills soaked in water and tied in white and gray bands; apply a light coat of Hard As Nails to prevent cracking
Thorax:	Adams gray Wapsi beaver dubbing
Wings:	Gray Organza and light dun hackle

Notes: This pattern is lethal, especially when the trout have become ultra S/R and the heavy hatch continues for up to six weeks as it does on Michigan's Muskegon and Pere Marquette.

HEX EXTENDED FOAM

(M. Batcke, Michigan)

Hook:	Daiichi 2110
Thread:	Tan 6/0 UNI
Tails:	Stripped grizzly quill
Body:	Rainy's Evazote foam or small yellow float cylinders; a 3/32-inch Tomsu mayfly body cutter is helpful
Wings:	Tan Hareline Premo turkey flats
Parachute hackle:	Grizzly
Eyes:	Black Hareline mono nymph eyes (extra small)

Notes: This is a realistic and durable pattern. The thread banding takes an accented ribbing shape that is irresistible to the trout. You can use a thin brown Sharpie to further accentuate the ribbing bands.

TUBE HEX

(Author)

Hook:	Daiichi 1170
Thread:	Yellow 6/0 UNI
Body:	Tan Spirit River Lip-Stik mayfly extended body (large), tan or yellow Hareline foam cylinders, or 3/32-inch brown Sharpie bands. A Tomsu mayfly cutter may be helpful.
Thorax:	Cream Antron
Post:	White Hi-VIZ Antron
Hackle:	Ginger

Notes: The brown banding is extremely deceiving when used with the slender, realistic body.

COFFIN FLY SPINNER

(Author)

Hook:	Daiichi 1170
Thread:	Drake green 6/0 UNI
Extended body:	2X mono attached to hook and glued
Tail:	Light dun Microfibbets
Body:	Cream Antron yarn
Rib:	Dark green thread
Thorax:	Black Hareline Dubbin
Wing:	Grizzly tips with grizzly hackle

POTAMANTHUS T. C.

(Author)

Hook:	Daiichi 1150
Thread:	Cream 6/0 UNI
Tail:	Brown Betts' Z-Lon
Body:	Yellow brown Caucci-Nastasi Spectrumized blend
Wing:	Cream CDC

Notes: A must-have pattern for the Catskill rivers in July.

TRUFORM WEAMER ISO

(Paul Weamer, Pennsylvania)

Hook:	Daiichi 1230 or Montana Fly Company's Weamer Truform dry-fly hooks
Thread:	Brown 6/0 UNI
Tail:	Brown Betts' Z-Lon
Body:	Gray/olive Wapsi Antron
Wing:	Brown CDC
Hackle:	Grizzly

MIRAGE MO DRAKE

(Author)

Hook:	Daiichi 1270
Thread:	Gray 95-denier UTC X-Strong
Tail:	Moose mane
Body:	Stripped grizzly and light dun quills soaked in water and wrapped in bands
Wings:	Hareline Mirage sheet cut with Tomsu or J:son wing cutters
Topping:	Light dun CDC

Notes: The iridescent mirage sheeting takes on the sheen of mayfly wings but will twist tippets. Use minimal 3X tippet to prevent twisting.

GANG BANG DRAKE

(Author)

Hook:	Daiichi 1270
Thread:	Black 95-denier Ultra X-Strong
Tail:	Moose mane
Egg sac:	Chartreuse Antron
Body:	Grizzly and dun stripped quills for banding
Wings:	Two separate clumps of light dun CDC to imitate two insects coupling

Notes: When large A/A feeding trout get ravenous for a mouthful, they will target the multi-coupling mayfly spinners. These can have one couple paired up or two males coupling with a female. These orgies are too heavy to fly and so they fall to the water in a big clump, where a big brown will slam the surface to take them before they unravel and fly off. It's a big "steak" to a finicky fish that has learned to grab a mouthful rather than a nibble.

FOAM SANDWICH HEX WIGGLE

(M. Batcke, Michigan)

Hook:	Daiichi 1120
Thread:	Brown 6/0 UNI
Extended body:	Rainy's foam; tan for top, yellow for bottom (2 mm)
Tail:	Moose mane
Rib:	Brown thread
Attachment:	Power Pro Cord with thin strand of yellow foam (2 mm) tied to make an extended body
Thorax:	Same foam combination as above, cut wider
Wings:	Dark dun CDC

AU SABLE HEX WULFF SPINNER

(Gates Au Sable Lodge)

Hook:	Daiichi 2110
Thread:	Black 6/0 UNI
Tail:	Three strands moose mane
Body:	Yellow Antron and deer hair
Rib:	Black thread and ginger hackle
Wings:	White calf tails and brown hackle

Notes: The calf tail makes this fly a more visible spinner at nighttime and blends into the white surface bubble flotsam line.

BROWN DRAKE AU SABLE

(Author)

Hook:	Daiichi 1120
Thread:	Light olive or dull yellow 6/0 UNI
Tail:	Pheasant tail fibers
Body:	Natural deer hair
Rib:	Thread
Post:	White calf tail
Hackle:	Brown

AU SABLE MAHOGANY DRAKE

(Gates Au Sable Lodge)

Hook:	Daiichi 1120
Thread:	Brown 6/0 UNI
Tail:	Moose mane
Body:	Red or mahogany deer hair
Rib:	Brown thread
Wings:	Grizzly hen tips
Hackle:	Grizzly cock

MAHOGANY ISO SPINNER

(Author)

Hook:	Daiichi 1270, bent in middle (can be warmed up)
Thread:	Brown 6/0 UNI
Tail:	Moose mane
Body:	Rust Wapsi sparkle Antron blend
Wings:	Clear Organza
Thorax hackle:	Grizzly cock

OLIVER EDWARDS'S GREEN DRAKE

(Inspired by Oliver Edwards; tied by author)

Hook:	Daiichi 1120
Thread:	Brown 6/0 UNI
Extended tail:	2X mono secured to hook and glued
Tail:	Moose mane
Body:	Yellow Antron yarn with green Antron yarn back
Rib:	Green UNI single-strand floss
Thorax:	Hareline Insect Green Dubbing
Wings:	Olive Hareline web wing mottled with black marker
Hackle:	Long strands of light dun cock

Notes: This realistic design is simple to tie. Use heavy tippet like 3X fluorocarbon to prevent wing-spinning the leader.

FREESTONE DRY

MR. RAPIDAN PARACHUTE

(Harry Murray, Virginia)

Hook:	Daiichi 1182
Tail:	Moose mane tied in to body to form V shape
Thread:	Tan 8/0 UNI
Body:	Fly-Rite #34
Post:	Yellow calf tail
Hackle:	Grizzly cock

MR. RAPIDAN TRADITIONAL

(Harry Murray, Virginia)

Hook:	Daiichi 1182
Thread:	Tan 8/0 UNI
Tail:	Moose mane tied into body to form V shape
Body:	Fly-Rite #34
Wings:	Yellow calf tail, split
Hackle:	Grizzly cock

Notes: This is a great pattern for searching freestone rivers in the spring when dark mayflies like the Quill Gordon, March Brown, and other quills are on the water. In these situations it's important to have a fly that floats well in water that is heavy from spring runoff.

ADAMS DEER HAIR

(Leonard Halladay, Gates Au Sable Lodge, Michigan)

Hook:	Daiichi 1182
Thread:	Light olive 6/0 UNI
Tail:	Moose mane
Body:	Natural deer hair
Wings:	Grizzly hackle tips, grizzly cock palmered

DARK WULFF

(Author)

Hook:	Daiichi 1182
Thread:	Brown 6/0 UNI
Tail:	Natural deer hair
Body:	Gray Wapsi beaver
Wings:	Light dun deer hair palmered

AUSABLE BIVISIBLE

(Fran Betters, New York)

Hook:	Mustad 7957B
Thread:	Orange 6/0 UNI
Tail:	Deer hair
Body:	Rust orange-dyed Australian opossum
Hackle rib:	Grizzly
Wing:	White calf tail

Notes: A great floater and searching fly for New York's fast, boulder-strewn, and sometimes whitewater sections.

USUAL

(Fran Betters, New York)

Hook:	Mustad 7957B
Thread:	Tan 6/0 UNI
Tail:	Blonde snowshoe rabbit foot
Body:	Tan Antron or fox
Wing:	White calf tail

Notes: Betters's imitation of the Light Cahill or Sulphur hatch has great floatability.

HAYSTACK

(Fran Betters, New York)

Hook: Mustad 7957B
Thread: Red 70-denier Ultra Thread
Tail: Moose mane
Body: Rust orange-dyed Australian opossum
Wing: Deer hair
Notes: Al Caucci's article, "The Indestructible Haystack," introduced the Caucci/Nastasi Compara-Dun, which is rooted in the Haystack. The different tails and slants of the wings are the only separation.

AUSABLE WULFF

(Fran Betters, New York)

Hook: Mustad 7957B
Thread: Orange 70-denier Ultra
Tail: Woodchuck hair tips
Body: Rust orange-dyed Australian opossum
Wings: White calf tail, brown and grizzly hackle
Notes: A great fast freestone fly for the mahogany drake *Isonychia* hatch.

AUSABLE CADDIS

(Fran Betters, New York)

Hook: Mustad 7957B
Thread: Brown 8/0 UNI
Body: Brown rust hare's mask
Flat tent caddis wing: White calf tail
Hackle: Ginger and grizzly cock

AU SABLE MI MADAME X

(Gates Au Sable Lodge, Michigan)

Hook: Daiichi 1180
Thread: Black 6/0 UNI
Tail: White calf
Body: Wapsi Sparkle Braid over Hareline Ice Dub, peacock black
Wing/Head: Tan deer hair
Collar: Brown hackle
Legs: Grizzly barred Hareline rubber legs (medium)

AU SABLE MI GREEN MADAME X

(Gates Au Sable Lodge, Michigan)

Hook: Daiichi 1180
Thread: Black 6/0 UNI
Tail: Moose mane
Body: Dark olive Wapsi Sparkle Yarn
Wing/Head: Deer hair
Hackle: Light dun hackle
Legs: Olive/black Hareline Crazy Legs

AU SABLE MI BLACK CADDIS

(Gates Au Sable Lodge, Michigan)

Hook: Daiichi 1180
Thread: Black 6/0 UNI
Body: Black hare's mask palmered with black hackle
Wing: Natural deer hair
Head: Bright yellow Antron and black hackle

MAHOGANY BORCHERS

(Gates Au Sable Lodge, Michigan)

Hook: Daiichi 1180
Thread: Black 6/0 UNI
Body: Reddish-brown deer hair
Rib: Black thread
Post: White calf tail
Hackle: Brown

AU SABLE MI HAYSTACK

(Gates Au Sable Lodge, Michigan)

Hook: Daiichi 1280
Thread: Gray 6/0 UNI
Tail: Mottled turkey strands
Body: Gray or brown Antron
Wing case/post: Gray-dyed deer hair slanted forward
Hackle: Grizzly cock
Notes: A great searching or imitative pattern for Hendrickson hatches.

BÉLIVEAU'S GASPÉ WULFF

(Jean-Guy Béliveau, Canada)

Hook: Daiichi 2117
Thread: Black 6/0 UNI
Tail: Deer hair
Tag: Chartreuse UNI-Stretch
Body: Orange-gold Spirit River Antron or pumpkin orange UNI-Stretch
Rib: Brown cock hackle palmered
Wing: White calf tail and brown cock hackle

AU SABLE MI PATRIOT

(Gates Au Sable Lodge, Michigan)

Hook: Daiichi 1170
Thread: Red 70-denier Ultra
Tail: Moose mane
Body: Red thread
Rib: Pearl tinsel and blue Krystal Flash laid over each other
Post: Calf tail
Hackle: Ginger

NIGHT UGLIES AND MICE

Night Stalker Uglies and Mice drum up leviathan trout around the world.

BATCKE'S COPPER AND ORANGE NIGHT STALKER TUBE

(Mike Batcke, Michigan)

Hook:	Daiichi 1648
Thread:	Black 95-denier Lagartun X-Strong
Tail:	Tan rabbit
Tube:	White plastic Eumer/Pro Tube (small) with copper Ultrawire (small) for ribbing
Body:	Copper Spirit River holographic wrap
Back:	Tan Rainy's foam (4 mm) cut in teardrop shape and folded at head
Legs:	Brown and orange Hareline Crazy Legs
Eyes:	Clear cure Adhesive Red Monster ($^3/_{16}$)

Notes: This is an excellent searching pattern for night-feeding browns near woody debris.

MORRISH SIMPLE MOUSE

(Ken Morrish, Oregon)

Hook:	Daiichi 2110
Thread:	Black 95-denier Lagartun X-Strong
Tail:	Stripped brown rabbit strip
Body:	Deer hair spun and clipped tight to hook on bottom and splayed outward
Top:	Brown Rainy's closed-cell foam (6 mm) cut in a teardrop cylinder shape to spec

Notes: One of the best mouse patterns anywhere on the planet!

BATCKE'S NIGHT RAIDER STONE

(Mike Batcke, Michigan)

Trailer hook:	Daiichi 2157, tied on 20-pound mono attachment
Thread:	Black 95-denier Lagartun X-Strong
Tail:	White and black arctic fox
Main hook:	Daiichi 2720 broken off and rounded by flame and curled at tag
Body:	Black Spirit River Estaz
Top:	Two layers of white Rainy's white foam (4 mm) on each side, cut into triangles and folded at base
Legs:	Black/blue Hareline Crazy Legs
Eyes:	Clear cure Adhesive Red Monster ($^3/_{16}$)

Notes: Excellent at night when the big black *Pteronarycys* stones are on the water.

TRADITIONAL DEER HAIR MOUSE

(Author)

Hook:	Daiichi 1750
Thread:	Amber 95-denier Lagartun X-Strong
Tail:	Brown leather strip
Body:	Deer hair spun, clipped tight on bottom, splayed out to form
Ears:	Brown leather cut into ear shape
Whiskers:	Black moose mane
Eyes:	Clear cure Adhesive Agate ($^1/_4$)

MORRISH'S FLUTTERING STONE

(Ken Morrish, Oregon)

Hook:	Daiichi D1280
Thread:	Red 3/0 UNI
Body:	Three foam pieces sandwiched together; left and right sides are brown (2 mm), middle is tan (2 mm)
Rib:	Red 3/0 UNI
Legs:	Brown/black Hareline Flutter round rubber legs coming out of body, knotted at joints; you can also use Hareline Loco Legs
Back wing:	J:son stonefly wings (large)
Indicator wing:	Orange Hi-VIZ
Wing case/Head:	Clip body $^3/_4$ inch down the hook; tie in remainder with wing case protruding; shape head so it is round

Notes: Deadly when giant *Pteronarcys* are emerging at night or when cicadas and even hoppers are in the mix.

SALMON FLY HOPPER

(Mike Batcke, Michigan)

Hook:	Daiichi 1270
Thread:	Brown 95-denier Lagartun X-Strong
Body:	Orange Rainy's Gorilla body foam (04) with brown marker
Rib:	Brown 95-denier Lagartun X-Strong
Wing:	Orange Krystal Flash, white Hareline Thick Wing with marker spots, black bucktail
Head:	Deer hair wrapped backward
Legs:	Black Hareline round rubber legs

Notes: This is a great combo fly that imitates the salmon fly hatch and giant stones.

HI-VIZ BROWN/HOPPER STONE

(Author)

Hook:	Daiichi 1270
Thread:	Orange Lagartun X-Strong
Tail:	Black Hareline round rubber
Lower body:	Tan Rainy's foam (2 mm)
Upper body:	Dark brown Rainy's foam (2 mm)
Rib:	Dun hackle and orange thread
Wing:	Deer hair
Head:	Black deer hair wound back
Legs:	Black Hareline rubber round
Top body:	Hi-VIZ indicator; orange Rainy's foam cut square and tied in

CICADA MADAME X

(Author)

Hook:	Daiichi 1280
Thread:	Fluorescent yellow Lagartun X-Strong
Tail:	Two strands of root beer Krystal Flash
Overbody:	Black Rainy's open-cell foam (2 mm)
Abdomen/Underbody:	Gray Antron yarn
Rib:	Yellow 95-denier Lagartun X-Strong
Wing:	White Hareline crinkle Antron and elk hair
Legs:	Brown Hareline round rubber
Antennae:	Root beer Krystal Flash
Head:	Top and bottom are Rainy's open-cell foam (2 mm) cut round

TROUT STREAMERS/SCULPINS

SCULPIN HAMMER

(Author)

Hook:	Daiichi 2340
Thread:	Black 95-denier Lagartun X-Strong
Overbody/Tail:	Medium brown Hareline black barred rabbit strip tied Matuka style
Body:	Olive sculpin Senyo's Laser Dub with copper and purple Hareline Senyo's Wacko Hackle strands
Legs:	Brown/orange flake Hareline Crazy Legs
Head:	Olive sculpin Senyo's Laser Dub
Cheeks:	Jungle cock

Notes: This is a lethal pattern for big browns and landlocked Atlantic salmon.

SENYO'S TRUTTANATOR

(Greg Senyo, Lake Erie)

Trailer hook:	Daiichi 2557
Thread:	Tan 3/0 UNI
Connector:	Olive Senyo's Intruder wire
Body on back hook:	Pearl Senyo's Ice Dub
Zonker body:	Olive variant Hareline rabbit strip black barred
Top hook:	Green Senyo's articulated Intruder
Main body:	Orange Hareline Senyo's Ice Dub bottom, trimmed flat; pearl Ice Dub and brown sculpin Ice Dub head barred with black marker
Legs:	Lime/black Hareline Crazy Legs
Eyes:	Ice Fish-Skull Living Eyes

Notes: Deadly for lake- and sea-run brown trout and resident trout who relish deepwater sculpins.

MORRISH SCULPIN

(Ken Morrish, Oregon)

Hook:	Daiichi 2220
Thread:	Black 95-denier Lagartun X-Strong
Tail/Body/Back:	Natural brown Hareline barred rabbit, Matuka style
Gill plates:	Green pheasant skin feathers
Head:	EP fibers or Hareline Extra Select Craft Fur cut to head shape with black marker for banding; epoxy hard coating
Eyes:	Clear Cure Adhesive Agate ($5/16$)

MOSER'S 3-D PLUSH SCULPIN

(Roman Moser, Austria)

Thread:	55-decitex Power Silk or GSP, Hareline Dubbin
Front hook for trout:	#4 or short shank Dohitomi Saltwater, #2 Aberdeen
Tail hook:	#4 or #6 VMC Up-eye Octopus hook
Connector:	Gray Hareline Senyo's Intruder Trailer hook wire
Fins:	Peach Poly Fiber
Body/Head:	Sheep wool, Polyamid, or Polypropylene fibers cut with Exacto knife or razor; splay out material with metal comb, use black marker for banding
Tail:	Any color tapered Poly Fiber and some Pearl Flash Fibers
Weight:	Gold Hareline Faceted Slotted Tungsten Bead (5.5 mm)
Belly:	Peach or pale pink Glo-Bug yarn fibers
Eyes:	Clear Cure Adhesive Agate eye ($5/16$) or Fish-Skull Living Eyes Ice; superglue and light epoxy finish

Notes: Without a doubt this Roman Moser creation is the most lifelike in shape, silhouette, and color combinations of any sculpin pattern for selective trout around the world. It's deadly on limestone spring creeks where the water clarity allows trout to carefully inspect the offering. Letort brown trout, perhaps the most finicky trout that swim, love this pattern and lose their guard.

MIKE'S MUFASA

(Mike Schmidt, Ohio)

Thread:	Tan 140-denier UTC
Hook 1:	#1 Gamakatsu B10S
Hook 2:	#1 Gamakatsu SP11
Tail/top:	Barred marabou
Body 1:	Tan and yellow schlappen
Body 2:	Copper Ice Dub
Legs:	Medium tan Hareline Grizzly Barred Rubber
Head 1:	Dark tan and rusty brown Senyo Laser Dub
Head 2:	Coppertone Fish-Skull (large)
Weight:	.035 lead
Eyes:	Hareline 3D Epoxy, ¼-inch Super Pearl
Epoxy:	Clear Cure Goo (thick)
Connection:	Beadalon, 19 strand .018 with three size E beads

MIKE'S RED ROCKET

(Mike Schmidt, Ohio)

Thread:	140-denier UTC
Hooks:	#1–2 Gamakatsu B10S
Tail:	Rabbit strip, barred natural
Body 1:	Yellow Schlappen, yellow
Body 2:	Yellow/olive Cactus Chenille, yellow/olive
Body 3:	Tan marabou, tan
Cheeks:	Sand Grizzly Marabou
Head:	Rusty brown and tan Senyo Laser Dub
Eyes:	Hareline Big Fish, ⅜-inch Super Pearl
Connection:	Beadalon, 19 strand .018 with three size E beads

SCOTT'S GREEN BUTT MONKEY

(Scott Smith, Canada)

Thread:	Orange 95-denier Lagartun X-Strong
Hook:	Daiichi 2340
Tail:	Chartreuse marabou
Overbody:	Orange hot schlappen or Wapsi saltwater neck hackle or orange rabbit strip Matuka style
Body:	Orange/gold Wapsi sparkle Estaz
Gill plates:	Orange schlappen tips
Head:	Orange McFly foam trimmed into oval shape

Notes: This is Scott's killer pattern for A/A coaster brook trout during spate flows.

MIKE'S BUTTER CHURN

(Mike Schmidt, Ohio)

Thread:	Tan 140-denier UTC
Back hook:	#2 Gamakatsu SP11-3L3H
Front hook:	#1/0 Gamakatsu B10S
Tail:	Tan and brown schlappen
Body:	Tan, rusty brown, and white marabou
Flash:	Copper Hareline Magnum Holographic Flashabou
Body 2:	Brown and white bucktail.
Eyes:	Clear Cure Ghost Dumbbell Eyes
Head:	Clear Cure Goo (thin then Hydro)

TERRESTRIALS

Note: A complete set of River Road Creations or Tomsu's Pronotum foam cutting tools (for body, wing, and legs) and an extended body tool from J:son are recommended for best results.

MORRISH HOPPER-YELLOW

(Ken Morrish, Oregon)

Hook:	2X Dai-Riki 730
Thread:	Tan 140-denier Ultra
Foam:	Rainy's yellow foam (2 mm, 4 mm, or 6 mm) bottom, tan or green foam hopper body, orange foam top post indicator (cut with double-edge razor blades)
Legs:	Gray/black Montana Fly or Hareline barred hopper legs
Eye:	Black marker

Notes: This is the most effective and realistic hopper I've used. It can be tailored to match the colors of *Orthoptera*.

MORRISH HOPPER-GREEN

(Ken Morrish, Oregon)

Notes: Same as yellow hopper above, only with lime green foam for the bottom and dark green barred Hareline grizzly legs for the top

RAINY'S GRAND FOAM HOPPER-BROWN

(Author)

Hook:	Daiichi 1280
Thread:	Tan 3/0 UNI
Body:	Light brown foam (4 mm) cut to shape; black Sharpie spots
Wing:	Pearl Krystal Flash and brown laminated saddle hackle, folded and ironed and Scotch taped
Thorax:	Brown Antron
Legs:	Tan Hareline micro rubber legs with black markings and tied at joints
Eyes:	Burnt mono chameleon or micro black mono barbells

RAINY'S GRAND FOAM HOPPER YELLOW

(Author)

Notes: Same as above, except with yellow foam and yellow Antron and tan Hareline rubber legs.

RAINY'S GRAND FOAM HOPPER GREEN

(Author)

Notes: Same as above, except with dark green foam, green Antron, olive saddle hackle and green Hareline rubber legs with black markings.

WHITLOCK HOPPER

(Author)

Hook:	Daiichi 1280
Thread:	Yellow 3/0 UNI
Body:	Yellow deer hair
Wing:	Turkey quill
Legs:	Wapsi TNT hopper legs
Head:	Natural deer hair pulled back and clipped
Indicator:	Orange fuzzy foam

CLUB SANDWICH HOPPER

(Author)

Hook:	Daiichi 1280
Thread:	Yellow 3/0 UNI
Body:	Tan, pink, and gray Rainy's Gorilla foam bodies
Rib:	Yellow thread
Legs:	Brown Rainy's round rubber tied at joints
Indicator:	White Rainy's foam (2 mm)

CARTOON SALMON/HOPPER

(Author)

Hook:	Daiichi 1280
Thread:	Brown 3/0 UNI
Body:	Orange and brown Rainy's Gorilla bodies foam (04)
Back/Front wing:	Brown deer hair, UV orange Hareline Ice Dub rib
Body rib:	Brown thread
Legs:	Rust Rainy's round rubber legs, black marker
Eyes:	Black/white Wapsi rattle doll eyes

CARTOON HOPPER

(Author)

Hook:	Daiichi 1270
Thread:	Yellow 3/0 UNI
Foam:	Yellow and brown Rainy's Gorilla 06
Wing:	Pearl Krystal Flash and white Antron
Thorax:	Peacock Hareline UV Ice Dub and furnace hackle
Legs:	Black/white Hareline centipede
Eyes:	Wapsi rattle doll eyes

CHERNOBYL HOPPER/ANT

(Author)

Hook:	Daiichi 1280
Thread:	Yellow 74-denier Lagartun X-Strong
Underbody:	Yellow thread and fine small palmered brown hackle
Body:	Yellow and tan Rainy's foam (2 mm) or Gorilla bodies
Front/Back indicators:	Rainy's two-tone indicator strips (2 mm)
Legs:	Bonefish tan Hareline speckled Crazy Legs

SURFBOARD WILD LEGS HOPPER

(Author)

Hook:	Daiichi 1280
Thread:	Brown 74-denier Lagartun
Tail:	Red Antron
Body:	Copper sparkle Wapsi metallic Antron
Body:	Black Rainy's (2 mm) or Gorilla body
Indicator foam:	Yellow and orange (2 mm)
Legs:	Brown Hareline centipede

JOE'S HOPPER

(Author)

Hook:	Daiichi 1280
Thread:	Yellow 74-denier Lagartun
Tail:	Red Antron
Body:	Yellow Antron yarn and brown hackle
Wing:	Turkey
Legs:	Yellow Hareline Knotted Pheasant hopper
Head:	Deer hair

GATES HOUSEFLY

(Gates Au Sable Lodge, Michigan)

Hook:	Daiichi1182
Thread:	Black 6/0 UNI
Body:	Peacock
Back:	Black Rainy's open-cell foam (2 mm)
Hackle:	Grizzly
Wings:	Grizzly saddle tips

TAN FOAM SOFA/HOPPER

(Author)

Hook:	Daiichi 1280
Thread:	Brown 3/0 UNI
Body:	Tan Rainy's open-cell foam (2 mm)
Rib:	Grizzly hackle
Wing:	Deer hair
Legs:	Copper/black Wapsi Silly Chrome

CYCLOPS FOAM ORANGE BEETLE

(Author)

Hook:	Daiichi 1270
Thread:	Black 6/0 UNI
Body:	Copper Wapsi crinkle Estaz
Back:	Orange Rainy's open-cell foam (4 mm) cut in beetle/centipede shape
Legs:	Orange/brown Hareline Grizzly Barred Rubber Legs medium

ORANGE STIMULATOR HOPPER

(Author)

Hook:	Daiichi 1280
Thread:	Orange 6/0 UNI
Body:	Rust orange Antron
Tail:	Orange deer hair
Wing/Head:	Tan deer or elk hair
Legs:	Orange Hareline Grizzly Barred Rubber Legs (medium)

LETORT CRICKET

(Ed Shenk, Pennsylvania)

Hook:	Daiichi 1280
Thread:	Black 95-denier Lagartun X-Strong
Body:	Hareline black dubbin
Wing:	Black turkey quill
Wing/Head:	Black deer hair

LETORT HOPPER

(Ed Shenk, Pennsylvania)

Hook:	Daiichi 1280
Thread:	Brown 95-denier Lagartun X-Strong
Body:	Cream yellow Antron or rabbit
Wing:	Natural turkey
Wing/Head:	Deer hair

FOAM ANT

(Author)

Thread:	Black 6/0 UNI
Hook:	Daiichi 1640
Body:	Black Hareline Dubbin with black Hareline Ultra Thin foam folded over and cut to ant shape; orange painted dot on back
Legs:	Turkey biot black quills

HOT ORANGE ANTS—TRADITIONAL AND MCMURRAY

(Author)

TRADITIONAL

Hook:	Daiichi D1182
Thread:	Orange 8/0 UNI
Back abdomen:	Hot orange Hareline Dubbin
Thorax:	Grizzly hackle
Head:	Smaller dubbed version of back

MCMURRAY ANT

(Ed Sutryn)

Hook:	Daiichi 1182
Thread:	Brown 8/0 UNI
Ant back/front:	A larger piece for back body and a smaller piece of balsa for head, cut to ant shape or ovals and joined by thin mono superglued and inserted with needle; painted red or orange with hot fluorescent tip of paint; mono tied to hook in midsection
Thorax:	Brown hackle

Notes: The go-to fly when all else fails for selective trout on tailwaters and spring creeks. It can be tied in all sizes.

FUZZY FOAM ANT

(Author)

Hook:	Daiichi 1640
Thread:	Black 6/0 UNI
Body:	Black Antron
Body:	Hareline micro thin foam or Hareline furry foam
Indicator:	Yellow Hareline micro foam spec 2 mm in thorax for visibility
Legs:	Black Krystal Flash

TRADITIONAL BEETLE

(Author)

Hook:	Daiichi 1640
Thread:	Black 6/0 UNI
Body:	Peacock herl
Back:	Brown or black deer hair
Legs:	Brown or black deer hair clipped
Indicator:	Orange Hareline micro foam dot

SWISS STRAW FLYING ANT

(Author)

Hook:	Daiichi 1640
Thread:	Brown 6/0 UNI
Back/Front body:	Two oval shapes in brown hare's mask
Wing:	Tan Swiss Straw

TRADITIONAL FLYING ANT

(Author)

Hook:	Daiichi 1640
Thread:	Brown 6/0 UNI
Body:	Brown oval-shaped thread: larger in back, small in front
Thorax:	Brown hackle
Wings:	Tiny hackle tips from light dun hackle

GATES BUMBLEBEE

(Gates Au Sable Lodge, Michigan)

Hook: Daiichi 1640
Thread: Black 95-denier Lagartun X-Strong
Body: Spun black and yellow deer hair
Wings: Spun layer of natural deer hair

CLUB SANDWICH FLAME

(Author)

Hook: Daiichi 1280
Thread: Red 6/0 UNI
Body: Grizzly hackle with orange Rainy's (2 mm), black and tan foam
Wing: Flame orange bucktail
Legs: Tan Rainy's round rubber legs

STEELHEAD EGG/NYMPH

KRYSTAL METH EGG

(Author)

Hook: Daiichi X510
Thread: Hot pink UNI-Stretch; use a healthy coating on hook shank to imitate blood vein of skein
Body: Fluorescent pink and fluorescent orange Hareline pearl braid weaved together in oval bulbs on each side

CLOWN EGG

(Author)

Hook: Daiichi X510
Thread: Hot pink UNI-Stretch
Egg: Cerise, chartreuse, orange, and flame McFly foam tied Glo-Bug style

CERISE COMET

(Author)

Hook: Daiichi X510
Thread: Hot pink UNI-Stretch
Tail: Hot pink sparkle Estaz
Egg: Cerise or flame McFly foam with strand of hot pink Estaz at top for egg eye

POM POM GIRL

(Author)

Hook: Daiichi X120
Thread: Hot pink UNI-Stretch
Trailer egg: Peach pom-pom egg or baby pink Glo-Bug attached to mono with needle and glue
Main egg: Peach pom-pom or baby pink Glo-Bug with cotton candy Glo-Bug sheath

RIPPLE CRUSH NIAGARA GOLD

(Author)

Hook: Daiichi X510
Thread: Hot pink UNI-Stretch
Tail: Pearl UV Estaz
Egg: Baby Pink McFly foam Glo-Bug with Glo-Bug Niagara gold sheath; leave hot pink UNI-Stretch exposed at bottom

ICEABOU NUKE

(Author)

Hook: Daiichi X510
Thread: Hot pink UNI-Stretch
Tail: Hareline Pink Iceabou with pearl Estaz
Egg: Cerise pink McFly foam with baby pink Glo-Bug sheath

RIPPLE CRUSH FRUITY

(Author)

Hook: Daiichi X510
Thread: Hot pink UNI-Stretch
Tail: Pearl UV Estaz
Egg: Tangerine McFly foam, cotton candy sheath

NAGY'S NIAGARA

(John Nagy, Lake Erie)

Hook: Daiichi X120
Thread: Fluorescent orange 70-denier Ultra
Egg: Use blue, chartreuse, orange, and pink Glo-Bug and strand together like a clown egg Glo-Bug
Eye: Black marker or black mono eyes

SCRAMBLED EGG

(John Nagy, Lake Erie)

Hook: Daiichi X120
Thread: Fluorescent orange 70-denier Ultra
Egg: Peach and orange weave Glo-Bug sucker-spawn yarn

DR. TOM

(Author)

Hook: Daiichi X510
Thread: Chartreuse UNI-Stretch
Body: Orange Hareline micro chenille
Wing: Chartreuse Antron
Head: Chartreuse Rainy's foam (2 mm)
Throat: Orange saddle hackle

SENYO'S TEARDROP ORANGE

(Greg Senyo, Lake Erie)

Hook:	Daiichi X120
Thread:	Yellow 6/0 UNI
Egg:	Balsa cut to teardrop and covered with orange and chartreuse hobby paint and attached and glued with mono
Sheath:	Cream Glo-Bug yarn

SENYO'S TEARDROP BLUE

(Author)

Hook:	Daiichi X120
Thread:	Yellow 6/0 UNI
Egg:	Teardrop-shaped balsa painted blue, yellow, and hot-red tip and glued to mono strand
Sheath:	Blue Glo-Bug yarn

MATT'S MYKISS SHRIMP

(Author)

Hook:	Daiichi X120
Thread:	Hot pink UNI-Stretch
Tail:	Pearl Krystal Flash with strands of Glo-Bug yarn in (left to right) chartreuse, candy cane, cerise
Body:	Otter's Soft Milking Egg sucker spawn comes in a braid; cut pieces to fit size of hook used. Spawn is in (left to right) tangerine opaque, regular tangerine, and kiwi flash. They are pierced through hook evenly through body and superglued over pink UNI-Thread on the hook to form the blood vein
Shell back:	Glo-Bug yarn and Krystal Flash shell in order above

Notes: I call this "mykiss" for the Latin term for steelhead (*Oncorhynchus mykiss*). It's an absolute killer pattern that can be tied small or large depending on flows.

OTTER SUCKER NUKE GUMMIE—PINK ICE

(Author)

Hook:	Daiichi X120
Thread:	Hot pink UNI-Stretch tied to form blood vein
Egg:	Tangerine Otter's Soft Milking Egg Sucker Spawn braid pierced in the middle, slid through hook, and superglued
Sheath:	Baby pink Glo-Bug

OTTER SUCKER NUKE GUMMIE—NIAGARA

(Author)

Notes: Tied same as above, just with Niagara gold Glo-Bug sheath.

OTTER WIGGLE EGG

(Author)

Hook:	Daiichi X120
Thread:	Hot pink UNI-Stretch
Back egg:	Tangerine Otter's Soft Milking Egg slid onto 3X mono with needle and then looped to main hook and glued; keep loose to let egg wiggle
Main egg:	Tangerine Otter's Soft Milking Egg with tangerine and pink McFly Foam egg tied Glo-Bug–style in front

ICE MAN SAC FRY

(Author)

Hook:	Daiichi X120
Body:	Tangerine Otter's Soft Milking Egg (6 mm) glued to hook
Wing:	Hareline Senyo's Laser Dub tied from wing bottom up—silver minnow belly first, hot pink second, and orange and topping of mottled mini marabou sand or tan third
Eyes:	Black Hareline 3D oval pupil

Notes: An effective pattern when chinook salmon and steelhead sac fry have hatched. The translucency of the Laser Dub when wet is irresistible to trout and steelhead.

KRYSTAL BLUE PARR

(Author)

Hook:	Daiichi X120
Thread:	Gray 70-denier Ultra
Body:	Pearl Hareline UV Ice Dub
Body:	Blue barred Hareline rabbit strip with blue and pearl Krystal Flash
Eye:	Black Hareline 3-D oval pupil

EMERALD ERIE SHINER

(Greg Senyo, Lake Erie)

Thread:	White 6/0
Tail hook:	Daiichi 1182, broken off
Tail:	UV pearl Hareline Ice Dub or triangle-shaped Enrico Puglisi anadromous brush
Lower body:	Polar white EP fibers with EP anadromous brush
Upper body:	Dark olive EP fibers
Main hook:	Daiichi X510
Bottom body:	Polar white EP fibers and EP anadromous brush
Upper body:	Dark olive EP fibers
Eye:	Clear Cure Ice

MATT'S CHINOOK FRY

(Author)

Hook: Daiichi X452
Thread: White 70-denier Ultra
Lower Body/Wing: Silver minnow belly Hareline Senyo's Laser Dub
Top body/Wing: Olive sculpin and gray Laser Dub
Sides: Grizzly hackle
Eye: Hareline 3-D oval

ICEMAN CREEPY

(Author)

Hook: Daiichi X120
Thread: Gray 70-denier Ultra
Wing 1: Hot pink Hareline Senyo's Laser Dub
Wing 2: Silver minnow belly
Wing 3: Olive sculpin dub
Legs: Hareline Hot-Tipped Crazy Legs
Eye: Hareline 3-D oval

BEAR'S HEAD BANGER HEX

(Jeff "Bear" Andrews, Michigan)

Hook: Daiichi 1560
Thread: Black 70-denier Ultra
Tail: Orange Glo-Bug yarn
Bottom body: Yellow Antron
Top body: Pheasant tail strands folded into wing cases and ribbed with copper Ultra copper wire (small)
Gills: Gray pheasant underwing filoplumes
Collar hackle: Ring-necked pheasant hen webby hackle
Eyes: Black Hareline mono

MERLINO'S SCULPIN HEX

(Rich Merlino, Michigan)

Hook: Gamakatsu B10S
Thread: Tan 6/0 UNI
Tail: Tan/brown barred rabbit strip or Australian opossum
Body/Thorax: Tan Hareline UV Ice Dub
Wing/Collar: India hen neck
Back: Gold pheasant tail strands with one layer of pearlescent flat tinsel and epoxy coating shell
Eyes: Black Hareline mono eyes
Cone: Clear Cure Goo
Notes: One of the deadliest Great Lakes steelhead patterns by far, this fly is a dual imitation of the abundant *Hexagenia* mayfly and a sculpin, both of which are prime food targets for the fish.

MATT'S LATEX WIGGLE HEX

(Author)

Hook: Daiichi 1560 with hook broken off
Thread: Gray 70-denier Ultra
Tail: Sand mottled mini marabou
Body/Rib: Yellow latex glove cut into thin strips for ribbing effect and layered as such with copper Ultra Wire ribbing (small)
Back: Pheasant tail strands
Gills: Gray pheasant skin underwing filoplumes stacked horizontally
Attachment: 3X mono glued
Front hook: Daiichi X510
Body: Latex strands cut thin to allow rigged banding
Back wing case: Latex cut into V shape; V marks colored with brown Sharpie
Collar: Hen pheasant fibers or arctic or grizzly variant neck hackle
Eyes: Black Hareline mono

SENYO'S BLACK SKAM ELECTRIC STONE PURPLE

(Greg Senyo, Lake Erie)

Hook: Daiichi 2441
Thread: Black 95-denier Lagartun X-Strong
Tail: Black marabou
Body: Black electrical tape in rib wound with folded wing cases
Thorax: Purple Hareline Senyo's Laser Dub
Legs: Plain black Hareline round legs
Eyes: Black Hareline bead chain (small)

SENYO'S BLACK SKAM STONE BLUE

(Greg Senyo, Lake Erie)

Hook: Daiichi 2441
Thread: Black 95-denier Lagartun X-Strong
Tail: Black/purple Hareline Hot-Tipped Crazy Legs
Body: Black electrical tape wrapped in layers
Wing case: Blue Steelie Hareline Ice Dub; Hareline mirage sheet wing case optional
Legs: Blue/black Hareline Hot-Tipped Crazy Legs
Eyes: Black Hareline plastic bead chain (small)

SUMMER-RUN STONE BLUE

(Greg Senyo, Lake Erie)

Hook: Daiichi 2441
Thread: Black 6/0 UNI
Tail: Black goose biots
Body: Gray SLF Dubbing
Rib: Black Ultra Vinyl Rib
Wing case: Dark mallard wing segment
Hackle collar: Blue Metz Hatchery soft hackle

SUMMER STONE PURPLE

(Greg Senyo, Lake Erie)

Hook:	Daiichi 2441
Tail:	Black goose biot
Body:	Black SLF Dubbing
Rib:	Black Ultra Vinyl Rib
Thorax:	Purple Estaz
Hackle collar:	Purple Metz Hatchery soft hackle and purple dyed guinea

SENYO'S POLISH-WOVEN BALLOON STONE

(Greg Senyo, Lake Erie)

Hook:	Daiichi 1760
Thread:	Black and gray UNI-Stretch
Tail:	Black goose biots
Lower body:	Gray air balloon strips
Upper body:	Polish weave of black and gray UNI-Stretch with V-shaped strands of pearl Krystal Flash
Thorax:	Black goose biots, upper and lower are V shaped, with purple Estaz and black Hareline Dura Skin folded for wing pads
Head:	Electric blue glass craft bead (small)

DISCO STONE

(Author)

Hook:	Daiichi 1760
Thread:	Black 95-denier Lagartun X-Strong
Tail:	Black goose biots
Body:	UV purple and Blue steelie Hareline Ice Dub
Rib:	Black Ultra Vinyl Rib
Thorax:	Purple Estaz with black soft hackle
Wing case:	Dark mallard wing
Antennae:	Black goose biots

SENYO'S FLASHBACK WIGGLE STONE

(Greg Senyo, Lake Erie)

Tail hook:	Daiichi 1260, broken off after tied
Thread:	Black 95-denier Lagartun X-Strong
Tails:	Black goose biots
Body:	Black Hareline vinyl rib
Connector:	3X mono
Main hook:	Daiichi X120
Body:	Peacock Hareline UV Ice Dub
Back wing case:	Black Hareline Flashback folded
Legs:	Black goose biots

STEELHEAD HARE'S EAR

(Author)

Hook:	Daiichi 1760
Thread:	Black 6/0 UNI
Tail:	Fox hair
Body:	Comb coarse hare's ear with dubbing brush
Wing case:	Dun mallard wing flank

MATT'S STEELHEAD SOFT HACKLE

(Author)

Hook:	Daiichi X120
Thread:	Black 3/0 UNI
Tail:	Whole gadwall feather
Body:	Whole gadwall feather wound or spun to front of hook as thread is palmered
Rib:	Black thread
Thorax:	UV Shrimp Pink Hareline Ice Dub
Hackle:	Partridge soft hackle

SMITH'S NYMPHO

(Scott Smith, Canada)

Hook:	Daiichi 1760
Thread:	Brown 6/0 UNI
Tail:	Cream hen hackle fibers
Body:	Chartreuse Hareline Ice Dub
Rib:	Gold UNI French oval tinsel (small)
Thorax:	Plucked-out orange Hareline UV Laser Dub
Wing case:	Dark mallard wing flank

CHICAGO LEECH

(Author)

Hook:	Daiichi 1760
Thread:	Black 6/0 UNI
Tail:	Black marabou, purple Flashabou
Body:	Black mohair palmered with fibers brushed out
Head:	Black tungsten bead ($^3/_{32}$) and orange Hareline Ice Dub

BACONATOR MYSIS

(Jeff Bacon, Michigan)

Hook:	Daiichi 1120
Thread:	Tan 3/0 UNI
Body:	Tan Hareline sow/scud dub
Back:	Clear Hareline scud back
Antennae:	Tan saddle hackle

BEMMER'S SKAMANIA EXCAVATOR

(Bob Bemmer, Michigan)

Hook:	Daiichi 2557
Thread:	Olive 6/0 UNI
Body:	Green Hareline variegated chenille with green grizzly saddle hackle; middle section is UV hot orange Hareline Ice Dub

POLISH-WOVEN GREEN CADDIS

(Author)

Hook:	Daiichi X120
Thread:	Black 6/0 UNI
Tail:	Black saddle hackle fibers
Body:	Chartreuse and dark green UNI-Stretch woven Polish style
Thorax:	Caddis Green Hareline Ice Dub
Head:	Gold tungsten bead ($^3/_{32}$)

MAGGOT

(Author)

Hook:	Daiichi X120
Thread:	White 6/0 UNI
Body:	UV pearl Hareline Ice Dub
Rib:	Silver UNI flat tinsel (extra small)
Collar:	Black ostrich
Head:	Gold tungsten bead ($^3/_{32}$)

LIME WEENIE

(Author)

Hook:	Daiichi X120
Thread:	Black 6/0 UNI
Body:	Chartreuse Hareline micro velvet chenille
Rib:	Gold Ultra Wire (extra small)
Head:	Peacock
Head:	Gold bead ($^5/_{64}$)

CZECH-STYLE CADDIS

(Author)

Hook:	Daiichi X120
Thread:	Orange 6/0 UNI
Body:	UV chartreuse Hareline Ice Dub
Throat:	UV peacock Hareline Ice Dub
Head:	UV orange Hareline Ice Dub

OPPOSSUM CADDIS

(Author)

Hook:	Daiichi 1760
Bead:	Copper bead $^5/_{64}$
Thread:	Brown 6/0 UNI
Body:	Green Hareline velvet chenille McKenzie caddis
Rib:	Gold Ultra Wire (extra small)
Throat:	Opossum fur

STEELHEAD—SENYO A-1-SLIM SHADY INTRUDER

The entire Greg Senyo Slim Shady A-1 series fishes well on off-color spate-driven rivers, wherever you may find them. The flies also do well on oligotrophic rivers with a natural chalky lime-green color, including many West Coast waters, the Cattaraugus in New York, the Dean in British Columbia, and many northern California rivers.

SENYO'S SLIM SHADY (FLAME)

Shank:	25 mm copper Flymen Fishing Co. Senyo's Steelhead & Salmon Shank
Thread:	Black 6/0 UNI
Eyes:	Gold bead chain (medium)
Wire:	Orange Senyo's Intruder Wire or 30-pound Berkley Fireline
Hot Spot:	Pink Estaz Hareline
Hackle:	UV gold Polar Chenille
Back wing 1:	Natural Lady Amherst center tail feather
Back wing 2:	Red/copper Flashabou
Body:	Gold Diamond Braid
Hot Spot:	Pink Estaz
Hackle:	Gold UV Polar Chenille
Wing 1:	Natural Lady Amherst center tail feather
Wing 2:	Red/copper Flashabou
Collar:	Natural guinea
Eyes:	Jungle cock (optional)

SENYO'S SLIM SHADY (BOOGER)

Shank:	25 mm green Flymen Senyo's Steelhead & Salmon Shank
Thread:	Royal blue 6/0 UNI
Eyes:	Silver medium bead chain
Wire:	Blue Senyo's Intruder Wire or 30-pound Berkley Fireline
Hot Spot:	Chartreuse Estaz
Hackle:	Silver UV Polar Chenille
Back wing 1:	Chartreuse Lady Amherst center tail feather
Back wing 2:	Blue/green Flashabou
Body:	Silver Hareline Diamond Braid
Hot Spot:	Chartreuse Estaz
Hackle:	Silver UV Hareline Polar Chenille
Wing 1:	Chartreuse Hareline Lady Amherst center tail feather
Wing 2:	Blue/green Flashabou
Collar:	Chartreuse Guinea
Eyes:	Jungle cock (optional)

SENYO'S A-1 (SICK SMURF)

Shank:	Blue Flymen Senyo's Steelhead & Salmon Shank 25 mm
Thread:	Black 6/0 UNI
Eyes:	Black or silver Medium bead chain
Wire:	Hareline Blue Senyo Intruder Wire or 30-pound Berkley Fireline
Hot Spot:	Chartreuse Estaz
Body:	UV Silver Hareline Polar Chenille
Underwing 1:	Blue Hareline Lady Amherst center tail feather
Underwing 2:	Pearl Flashabou
Overwing 1:	Purple Flashabou
Overwing 2:	Blue Flashabou
Hackle:	Black Hareline schlappen
Collar:	Blue guinea
Eyes:	Jungle cock

SENYO'S SLIM SHADY (ROTTEN RASPBERRY)

Shank:	25mm pink Flymen Senyo's Steelhead & Salmon Shank
Thread:	Red 6/0 UNI
Eyes:	Silver bead chain (medium)
Wire:	Pink Senyo's Intruder Wire or 30-pound Berkley Fireline
Hot Spot:	Pink Estaz
Hackle:	UV pink Polar Chenille
Back wing 1:	Pink Hareline Lady Amherst center tail feather
Back wing 2:	Pearl/pink Flashabou
Body:	Hareline Silver Diamond Braid
Hot Spot:	Pink Estaz
Hackle:	UV pink Polar Chenille
Wing 1:	Pink Hareline Lady Amherst center tail feather
Wing 2:	Pearl/Pink Flashabou
Collar:	Pink guinea
Eyes:	Jungle cock (optional)

SENYO'S SLIM SHADY (FROSTY)

Shank:	25 mm black Flymen Senyo's Steelhead & Salmon Shank
Thread:	Black 6/0 UNI
Eyes:	Silver bead chain (medium)
Wire:	Blue Senyo's Intruder Wire or 30-pound Berkley Fireline
Hot Spot:	Chartreuse Estaz
Hackle:	UV silver Polar Chenille
Back wing 1:	Natural Hareline Lady Amherst center tail feather
Back wing 2:	Pearl/silver Flashabou
Body:	Silver Hareline Diamond Braid
Hot Spot:	Chartreuse Estaz
Hackle:	UV silver Polar Chenille
Wing 1:	Natural Hareline Lady Amherst center tail feather
Wing 2:	Pearl/silver Flashabou
Collar:	Natural Guinea
Eyes:	Jungle cock (optional)

SENYO'S SLIM SHADY (ARCTIC FREEZE)

Shank:	25 mm blue Flymen Senyo's Steelhead & Salmon Shank
Thread:	Royal blue 6/0 UNI
Eyes:	Silver bead chain (medium)
Wire:	Blue Senyo's Intruder Wire or 30-pound Berkley Fireline
Hot Spot:	Pink Estaz
Hackle:	UV silver Polar Chenille
Back wing 1:	Blue Hareline Lady Amherst center tail feather
Back wing 2:	Blue/silver Flashabou
Body:	Silver Diamond Braid
Hot Spot:	Pink Estaz
Hackle:	UV silver Polar Chenille
Wing 1:	Blue Hareline Lady Amherst center tail feather
Wing 2:	Blue/silver Flashabou
Collar:	Blue guinea
Eyes:	Jungle cock (optional)

SENYO'S A-1 (COPPER SUNDAE)

Shank:	Copper Flymen Senyo's Steelhead & Salmon Shank (25 mm)
Thread:	Black 6/0 UNI
Eyes:	Black or gold bead chain (medium)
Wire:	Copper Senyo's Intruder Wire or 30-pound Berkley Fireline
Hot Spot:	Orange Estaz
Body:	UV Copper Polar Chenille
Underwing 1:	Orange Hareline Lady Amherst center tail feather
Underwing 2:	Bronze Flashabou
Overwing 1:	Fuchsia Flashabou
Overwing 2:	Copper Flashabou
Hackle:	Brown Hareline schlappen
Collar:	Orange Guinea
Eyes:	Jungle cock (optional)

SENYO'S A-1 (GREEN GOBLIN COLOR)

Shank:	25 mm green Flymen Senyo's Steelhead & Salmon Shank
Thread:	Black 6/0 UNI
Eyes:	Olive or gold bead chain (medium)
Wire:	Chartreuse Senyo's Intruder Wire or 30-pound Berkley Fireline
Hot Spot:	Chartreuse Estaz
Body:	UV gold Polar Chenille
Underwing 1:	Chartreuse Hareline Lady Amherst center tail feather
Underwing 2:	Copper Flashabou
Overwing 1:	Gold Flashabou
Overwing 2:	Kelly green Flashabou
Hackle:	Brown schlappen
Collar:	Chartreuse Guinea
Eyes:	Jungle cock (optional)

STEELHEAD LEECHES AND TUBES

The Leech made its steelhead debut when Bob Hull of British Columbia invented the String Leech, which used the rabbit strip's lifelike movements and was an instant killer pattern for West Coast steelhead. Around the same time, Egg-Sucking Leeches were invented in Alaska for the large steelhead-like rainbows there that fed on salmon eggs. The Tube was brought from the Atlantic salmon world and incorporated into all forms of steelhead flies—even nymphs.

RED CYCLOPS INTRUDER TUBE

(Author)

Hook:	Daiichi 2557
Thread:	Red 6/0 UNI
Tube:	Red plastic Eumer/Pro Tube (large)
Body:	Silver Ultra flat tinsel (medium) with gold Ultra oval rib (medium)
Tag wing:	Black Hareline Spey plumes
Front wing:	Black Hareline Spey plumes with red Flashabou and pearly Krystal Flash
Collar:	Red Hareline schlappen
Eyes:	Hareline Tungsten Predator eyes

Notes: Red and black is a lethal color combo for large A/A male steelhead.

HANG TIME LEECH

(Phil Pantano, Great Lakes)

Hook:	Daiichi 2557
Trailer hook:	Daiichi 2557
Thread:	Black 95-denier Lagartun X-Strong
Braid connector:	Black Senyo Intruder trailer hook wire
Body hook:	Black Fish-Skull Senyo's articulated shank
Body:	Black rabbit strip; cross-cut black rabbit around hook shank
Flash:	Copper and orange/lime Lateral Scale
Collar:	Hot pink and orange Senyo's Laser Dub
Head:	Gold barbell eyes

Notes: The gold barbell eyes and Lateral Scale flash allow the angler to pump and dip the leech on the swing's hang time. It's lethal on fresh chrome fall steelhead!

COPPER OLIVE SCULPIN HAMMER

(Author)

Hook:	Black Daiichi Alec Jackson 2059
Thread:	Black 95-denier Lagartun X-Strong
Tail/Upper body:	Dark olive barred rabbit Matuka-style
Body:	Olive Senyo's Laser Dub sculpin, copper/blue Krystal Wrap shaggy chenille
Legs:	Brown/orange flake Hareline Crazy Legs
Head:	Combination of hot pink and hot orange Hareline Laser Dub
Cheek:	Jungle cock

FLAMETHROWER LEECH

(Author)

Hook:	Daiichi 2059
Thread:	Black 95-denier Lagartun X-Strong
Tail/Upper body wing:	Black Hareline rabbit strip
Tail:	Copper Flashabou
Body:	Electric purple Spirit River UV Estaz
Head:	Hot pink and orange Senyo's Laser Dub
Collar:	Pink Hareline guinea feather
Eyes:	Silver bead chain

Notes: The Flamethrower leeches are deadly for late fall steelhead that like the movement of black rabbit with hints of orange and pink.

EVIL FLAMETHROWER LEECH

(Author)

Hook:	Daiichi 2059
Thread:	Black 95-denier Lagartun X-Strong
Wing/Tail/Back:	Black Hareline rabbit strip
Body:	Electric purple Spirit River UV Estaz
Rib:	Palmered schlappen
Head:	Hot pink Hareline Senyo Laser Dub
Eyes:	Jungle cock

SKAMANIA LEECH

(Author)

Hook:	Daiichi 2059
Thread:	Black 95-denier Lagartun X-Strong
Leech:	Black or purple
Body:	Purple Spirit River UV Estaz
Eyes:	Chartreuse Hareline Predator dumbbell

HUMPHREYS' OLIVE TEMPLEDOG TUBE

(Pete Humphreys, Michigan)

Tube:	Pink Eumer/Pro Tube silicone connector with teardrop brass tube
Hook:	Daiichi 1648 Alec Jackson Tube
Thread:	Olive 74-denier Lagartun X-Strong
Wing:	Chartreuse and olive arctic fox, holographic copper and green Flashabou
Throat:	Green rhea intruder feathers
Cheeks:	Jungle cock
Cone:	Chartreuse Eumer/Pro Tube brass monster cone

HUMPHREYS' BLACK AND PURPLE TEMPLEDOG

(Pete Humphreys, Michigan)

Hook:	Daiichi 2059
Thread:	Black 74-denier Lagartun X-Strong
Tube:	Pink Eumer/Pro Tube connector with brass copper teardrop
Wing:	Blue and purple arctic fox; green, blue, copper, purple, and gold Flashabou
Throat:	Black Hareline Spey plumes
Cheeks:	Jungle cock

BLUE RAY TUBE

(Author)

Hook:	Daiichi 2557
Tube:	Blue Eumer/Pro Tube connector and silver brass teardrop tube
Thread:	Royal blue 6/0 UNI
Wing:	Purple and blue arctic fox with pearl Flashabou
Head:	Combination of purple and blue Hareline Ice Dub
Cheeks:	Jungle cock
Cone:	Chartreuse Eumer/Pro Tube brass monster

GRAPEFRUIT SCULPIN BUGGER

(Author)

Hook:	Daiichi 1750
Thread:	Black 74-denier Lagartun X-Strong
Tail:	Hareline sand mottled marabou, copper Flashabou
Body:	Copper/black Hareline sparkle chenille
Rib:	Wapsi furnace saddle hackle
Legs:	Root beer/copper Hareline Loco Legs
Head:	Combination of chartreuse and fluorescent hot pink Hareline UV Ice Dub

RIPPLE CRUSH BUGGER LEECH

(Author)

Hook:	Daiichi 1750
Thread:	Black 74-denier Lagartun X-Strong
Tail:	Black rabbit strip, copper Mirage Flashabou
Body:	Hareline copper/black sparkle chenille
Rib:	Wapsi furnace hackle
Legs:	Root beer/copper Hareline Loco Legs
Head:	Combine in layers fluorescent hot pink, red, and orange Hareline UV Ice Dub

SENYO'S STEELIE PARR TUBE

(Greg Senyo, Lake Erie)

Hook:	Daiichi 2557
Tube:	Clear Eumer/Pro Tube (small); make black parr marks with marker
Thread:	Red 74-denier Lagartun X-Strong
Wing 1:	Pink Laser Dub
Wing 2:	Pearl Ice Dub Shimmer Fringe
Wing 3::	Green EP Silky Fiber. Make parr marks with black marker and green Flashabou
Gill plate:	Red marker
Eyes:	Hareline 3-D oval pupil with epoxy head

Notes: Lethal on rivers like the Lake Michigan tributaries where good salmon, trout, and steelhead parr exsist in amazing numbers.

STEELHEAD—HOWELL AND SENYO INTRUDERS

HOWELL'S SIGNATURE INTRUDER GREEN BUTT BLACK

(Scott Howell, Oregon)

Body hook:	Black Senyo's articulated Fish Skull
Back hook:	Daiichi 2557
Thread:	Black 74-denier Lagartun X-Strong
Tail:	Black/blue flake Hareline crazy legs
Tag:	Chartreuse SLF Dubbing
Body:	Silver Ultra flat tinsel (large)
Wing:	Black arctic fox and black marabou; black and blue Hareline Crazy Legs

HOWELL'S SIGNATURE INTRUDER—PURPLE AND BLUE

(Scott Howell, Oregon)

Body hook:	Black Senyo's Fish-Skull Articulated Intruder
Back hook:	Daiichi 2557
Tail:	Deep purple/blue flake Hareline crazy legs
Tag:	Blue SLF
Body:	Silver Ultra flat tinsel (large)
Wings:	Blue Hareline Extra Select Craft Fur, purple marabou, purple Crazy Legs, blue speckled worm weight

HOWELL'S SIGNATURE RED-BUTT INTRUDER

(Scott Howell, Oregon)

Body hook:	Senyo's Fish Skull Intruder shank black
Back hook:	Daiichi 2557
Thread:	Black 74-denier Lagartun X-Strong
Tail:	Purple Hareline Spey plumes
Tag:	Red SLF Dubbing
Body:	Silver Ultra flat tinsel (large)
Wings:	Black Hareline Extra Select Craft Fur, purple Hareline Spey plumes, two purple grizzly hackles
Head:	Silver barbell or black worm bullet weight

HOWELL'S SQUIDO

(Scott Howell, Oregon)

Hook:	Gamakatsu White Octopus 02606
Tail:	Hareline Aqua Glow Crazy Legs
Tag:	Pink SLF Dubbing
Body:	Silver Ultra flat tinsel (large)
Wing:	Pink Hareline Extra Select Craft Fur; pink marabou, Hareline Aqua Glow Crazy Legs

Notes: Ocean steelhead are imprinted to the pink and orange colors of squid and shrimp, which are vital food sources in low-water river estuaries.

ERIE OLIVE INTRUDER

(Greg Senyo, Lake Erie)

Hook:	35 mm Green Flymen Senyo's articulated shank
Thread:	Black 6/0 UNI
Tail:	Golden pheasant Hareline flank and topping
Body:	Peacock Hareline Ice Dub
Head:	Copper Hareline Ice Dub
Rib:	Green guinea saddle
Wing:	Olive Hareline Spey plumes, Hareline Lady Amherst natural, copper Mirage Flashabou
Cheeks:	Golden pheasant

Notes: This is a great low-water autumn special.

SENYO'S CHUB GANGSTA INTRUDER

(Greg Senyo, Lake Erie)

Shank:	35 mm orange Flymen Senyo's Articulated Shank
Connection:	30-pound Berkley Fireline or copper/orange Senyo Intruder Wire
Thread:	Orange 6/0 UNI
Butt:	Pheasant Tail Hareline Ice Dub, gold spinner blade
Tail:	Orange Hareline Lady Amherst tail feather and copper Mirage Flashabou
Hackle:	Hareline UV Copper Polar Chenille
Wing 1:	Orange Hareline Lady Amherst tail feather
Wing 2:	White ostrich feathers
Wing 3:	Copper Mirage Flashabou
Wing 4:	Tan ostrich feathers
Rubber legs:	Pumpkin Hareline Loco Legs
Gills:	Red Hareline Senyo's Shaggy Dub
Eyes:	Yellow Hareline Predator Eyes (small)
Head:	Eumer Mörrum arctic fox
Throat:	Orange Eumer/Pro Tube arctic fox

SENYO'S JOKER GANGSTA INTRUDER

(Greg Senyo, Lake Erie)

Shank:	Black Flymen Senyo's Articulated Shank (35mm)
Connection:	30-pound Berkley Fireline; black Senyo's Intruder wire
Thread:	Orange 6/0 UNI
Butt:	UV Pink Hareline Ice Dub, silver spinner blade optional
Tail:	Chartreuse Hareline Lady Amherst tail feather and purple Mirage Flashabou
Hackle:	Silver Hareline UV Polar Chenille
Wing 1:	Chartreuse Hareline Lady Amherst tail feather
Wing 2:	Black ostrich feathers
Wing 3:	Purple/green Flashabou
Wing 4:	Black ostrich feathers
Rubber legs:	Purple/Electric Blue Hareline Crazy Legs
Gills:	Black Senyo's Shaggy Dub
Eyes:	Yellow Hareline Predator Eyes (small)
Head:	Chartreuse Eumer arctic fox
Throat:	Pink Eumer arctic fox

Notes: Extremely effective in off-color spate waters. The spinner is optional since many consider it crossing the "fly fishing boundary."

SENYO'S BLUE BAIT GANGSTA INTRUDER

(Greg Senyo, Lake Erie)

Shank:	35 mm blue Flymen Fishing Co. Articulated Shank
Connection:	30-pound Berkley Fireline
Thread:	Orange 6/0 UNI
Butt:	Chartreuse Hareline Ice Dub
Tail:	Natural Lady Amherst tail feather and pearl Mirage Flashabou
Hackle:	Silver Hareline UV Polar Chenille
Wing 1:	Natural Hareline Lady Amherst tail feather
Wing 2:	White ostrich feathers
Wing 3:	Pearl/blue Flashabou
Wing 4:	White ostrich feathers
Rubber legs:	White/black barred rubber legs
Gills:	White Hareline Senyo's Shaggy Dub
Eyes:	Yellow Hareline Small Predator Eyes
Head:	Blue Eumer arctic fox
Throat:	Chartreuse Eumer arctic fox

STEELHEAD—TUBES AND MINNOWS

SENYO'S PINK SCULPIN TUBE

(Greg Senyo, Lake Erie)

Tube:	Pink Eumer/Pro Tube (large)
Hook:	Daiichi 2557
Thread:	Pink 6/0 UNI
Tail:	Hot pink marabou, hot pink holographic Flashabou
Body:	Hareline pink UV Ice Dub
Hackle rib:	Hareline Pink UV Krystal Hackle
Collar:	Wood duck
Head:	Blue, pink, and white Laser Dub

ORANGE AND BLUE TEMPLEDOG TUBE

(Greg Senyo, Lake Erie)

Tube:	Orange Eumer/Pro Tube hook tube with silver brass teardrop (22 x 4 mm)
Hook:	Daiichi 2557
Thread:	Royal blue 6/0 UNI
Wing:	White and orange Eumer arctic fox, blue Hareline Ice Dub, silver and red holographic Flashabou, holographic Mirage Flashabou, Hareline black Spey plume hackles
Collar:	Blue schlappen
Cheek:	Golden pheasant
Cone:	Orange Eumer monster cone

RED AND BLACK TEMPLEDOG TUBE

(Author)

Tube:	Black Eumer/Pro Tube connector with black teardrop brass (22 x 4 mm)
Thread:	Black 6/0 UNI
Hook:	Daiichi Alec Jackson 1648
Wing:	Black and red Eumer arctic fox, red and green holographic Flashabou, black Hareline Spey plumes
Collar:	Red and black schlappen
Cheek:	Golden pheasant
Cone:	Red Eumer/Pro Tube monster

BLACK COLLIE ORANGE

(Author)

Tube:	Eumer/Pro Tube plastic connector and black brass teardrop tube (22 x 4 mm)
Thread:	Black 6/0 UNI
Hook:	Hareline 1648 Alec Jackson Tube
Wing:	Orange and black Eumer arctic fox; orange, silver, and black Krystal Flash
Throat:	Orange schlappen

NUKE PEARL AMHERST

(Author)

Hook:	Daiichi 2441
Thread:	White 74-denier Lagartun
Tail:	Eumer arctic fox, natural Hareline Lady Amherst
Body:	Pearl Hareline UV Ice Dub
Rib:	White saddle hackle or white schlappen
Collar:	White arctic fox, natural Hareline Lady Amherst, Mirage Flashabou
Head:	Orange Hareline Ice Dub in egg ball, chartreuse Hareline Ice Dub veil

MARABOU PARR

(Author)

Hook:	Daiichi 2557
Thread:	Gray 95-denier Ultra
Wing 1:	Silver minnow belly Hareline Senyo's Laser Dub
Wing 2:	Pink Laser Ice Dub
Wing 3:	Mottled sand marabou
Topping:	Mirage Lateral Scale
Eyes:	Clear Cure plastic barbell

SENYO SCULPIN THUGMEISTER

(Greg Senyo, Lake Erie)

Tube:	Black plastic Eumer/Pro Tube (large)
Hook:	Daiichi 1648 Alec Jackson tube
Thread:	Black 74-denier Lagartun
Tail:	Black marabou with copper and blue Krystal Flash
Body:	Purple Hareline UV Ice Dub with purple and blue UV Krystal Hackle
Collar:	Black marabou with wood duck
Head:	Blue, purple, and black Hareline Senyo's Laser Dub

Notes: The Thugmeister is an old black, blue, and purple design from the first *Steelhead Dreams* book. We showed the pattern to a steelheader on Michigan's Rogue River, not knowing he was a "fish killer." He strung up three steelhead on "death row" each day. We were ashamed of ourselves for showing him the lethal fly!

EGG LEECH SHAGGY GRAY

(Author)

Hook:	Daiichi 2441
Thread:	Black 95-denier Lagartun
Tail:	Gray marabou
Body:	Pearl Hareline UV Ice Chenille with gray heron Spey hackle
Wing:	Mirage Flashabou with black/opal Mirage Flashabou blend
Collar:	Gray Hareline Loco Legs with gray Senyo's Shaggy Dub
Head:	Pink Hareline Crystal Chenille with Hareline Senyo's pink Shaggy Dub

AUTUMN GOLD TEMPLEDOG

(Author)

Tube:	Amber Eumer/Pro Tube connector, silver brass teardrop (22 x 4 mm)
Hook:	Daiichi 1648 Alec Jackson tube
Thread:	95-denier Lagartun X-Strong
Wing:	Burnt amber and black Hareline arctic fox, black Spey plumes, copper and gold Flashabou
Collar:	Olive and black schlappen
Cheek:	Golden pheasant

SENYO ORANGE CHUB SCULPIN TUBE

(Greg Senyo, Lake Erie)

Tube:	Green plastic Eumer/Pro Tube (large)
Hook:	Daiichi 1648 Alec Jackson tube
Thread:	Orange 74-denier Lagartun X-Strong
Tail:	Mottled chartreuse marabou, Mirage Flashabou
Body:	Chartreuse Laser Dub with orange intruder Hareline rhea feather
Collar:	Mottled chartreuse marabou, wood duck
Wing:	Pearl Mirage Flashabou
Head:	Brown, chartreuse, and orange Hareline Senyo's Laser Dub
Cone:	Orange Eumer Monster

DODDI ORANGE TUBE

(Author)

Thread:	Orange Lagartun 74 X-Strong
Hook:	Daiichi 1648 Alec Jackson
Tube:	Eumer/Pro Tube brass teardrop with grooves (17 x 3 mm); red enamel ribbed with fine brush
Wing:	Yellow Eumer arctic fox, orange arctic fox with orange Krystal Flash and Mirage Flashabou
Collar:	Orange guinea hackle
Cheek:	Jungle cock

Notes: Perfect for stained and off-color water in Iceland, Russia, Norway, and Québec.

TORCH PELAGIC

(Author)

Hook:	Daiichi X452
Thread:	Gray 95-denier Lagartun X-Strong
Wing 1:	Silver minnow belly Hareline Senyo's Laser Dub
Wing 2:	Hot pink UV Laser Dub
Wing 3:	Silver Minnow Belly Hareline Laser Dub
Topping:	Mirage and Lateral Scale Flashabou with opal/black Mirage Flashabou blend
Parr markings:	Black marker
Eyes:	Hareline oval 3-D

Notes: This is the ultimate trolling fly for springtime landlocked Atlantic salmon, Carrie Stevens style.

STEELHEAD EGG INVADER AND SPACE INVADER INTRUDERS

These modern-day steelhead intruders carry the egg-sucking motif combined with modern synthetic materials, bringing loads of movement and flash that fresh-run steelhead on the high, rising waters in the Pacific Northwest and Great Lakes love. All Senyo's egg raiders follow the same basic template. Just change colors for each fly.

SENYO'S EGG RAIDER TEMPLATE

Thread:	6/0 UNI
Hook:	#1 Mustad 3366 cut off above hook bend; Daiichi 2557 Alec Jackson Intruder trailer
Bead:	Tangerine or peach bead (8 mm)
Hook connection:	30-pound Berkley Fireline
Tail 1:	Marabou
Tail 2:	Zonker rabbit strip
Flash:	Flashabou Magnum
Hackle:	Schlappen
Body:	Hareline Senyo's Ice/Laser Dub
Wing:	Marabou
Rubber legs:	Metallic fleck Hareline Loco Legs
Head:	Senyo's Shaggy Dubbing
Eyes:	Mardi Gras Plastic Bead Chain or silver barbell

BLACK EGG RAIDER

(Greg Senyo, Lake Erie)

Hook:	Daiichi 2557 Intruder as trailer; Mustad 3366 cut off above bend and pushed down into semicircle for body hook
Thread:	Black 95-denier Lagartun X-Strong
Tail:	Black Hareline rabbit, blue and purple holographic Flashabou
Body:	Peacock Hareline Ice Dub, black schlappen rib
Collar:	Black Hareline schlappen and black Hareline Senyo's Shaggy Dub
Legs:	Black/purple hot-tipped Hareline Crazy Legs

PEARL SQUID EGG INVADER

(Greg Senyo, Lake Erie)

Hook:	Daiichi 2557 Intruder for trailer; Mustad 3366 cut off above bend and pushed down into semicircle for body hook
Thread:	Black 95-denier Lagartun X-Strong
Tail:	White Eumer/Pro Tube arctic fox, natural Hareline Lady Amherst
Body:	Pearl Hareline UV Ice Dub, white Hareline rhea intruder feather
Wing:	White Eumer arctic fox, white Hareline Spey plumes, natural Hareline Lady Amherst, Mirage Flashabou, Lateral Scale Mirage Flashabou
Eyes:	Silver dumbbell, pearl Hareline Ice Dub

EMERALD GHOST

(Greg Senyo, Lake Erie)

Hook:	Daiichi 2557 Intruder for trailer; Mustad 3366 cut off above bend and pushed down into semicircle for body
Thread:	Black 95-denier Lagartun X-Strong
Tail:	White rabbit strip, emerald green holographic Flashabou
Body:	Pearl Hareline UV Ice Dub, white Hareline rhea intruder feather
Wing:	White marabou, Mirage Flashabou
Collar:	Cream and light pink blend Hareline Senyo's Shaggy Dub
Eyes:	Emerald bead chain

THUGMEISTER EGG INVADER

(Greg Senyo, Lake Erie)

Hook:	Daiichi 2557 Intruder for trailer; Mustad 3366 cut off above bend and pushed down into semicircle for body
Thread:	Black 95-denier Lagartun X-Strong
Tail:	Light purple rabbit with purple arctic fox
Body:	Blue Steelie Hareline Ice Dub
Wing:	Combination of blue, black, and purple holographic and Mirage Flashabou with black, purple, and blue Hareline Senyo's Wacko Hackle
Collar:	Hareline Senyo's Shaggy Dub

BLUE OPAL INVADER

(Author)

Hook:	Daiichi 2557 Intruder for trailer; Mustad 3366 cut off above bend and pushed down into semicircle for body
Thread:	Black 95-denier Lagartun X-Strong
Tail:	White rabbit strip with chartreuse marker for tail tips
Body:	UV pearl Hareline Ice Dub, white Hareline rhea intruder feather
Wing:	Mirage, blue, and purple holographic Flashabou

Collar:	White Hareline Senyo's Shaggy Dub
Eye:	Blue bead chain

GREEN BUTT BLUE INTRUDER

(Greg Senyo, Lake Erie)

Hook:	Daiichi 2557 Intruder for trailer; Mustad 3366 cut off above bend and pushed down into semicircle for body
Thread:	Black 95-denier Lagartun X-Strong
Tail:	Purple and blue arctic fox, mirage Lateral Scale Flashabou
Tag:	Chartreuse Hareline Senyo's Laser Dub
Body:	UV pearl Hareline Ice Dub
Rib:	Hareline rhea intruder feather
Front wing:	Purple and blue Spey plumes, natural Hareline Lady Amherst
Eyes:	Silver dumbbell

OPAQUE GHOST EGG INVADER

(Greg Senyo, Lake Erie)

Hook:	Daiichi 2557 Intruder for trailer; Mustad 3366 cut off above bend and pushed down into semicircle for body
Thread:	Black 95-denier Lagartun X-Strong
Tail:	White rabbit strip with olive marabou
Wing/Collar:	White marabou with opaque pearl Sili Legs and gray Senyo's Shaggy Dub
Eyes:	Blue chain

SENYO'S SPACE INVADER FISH FOOD

(Greg Senyo, Lake Erie)

Hook:	#4 Owner Mosquito
Shank:	Flymen Senyo's shank (25 mm)
Thread:	70-denier Ultra Thread or 6/0 UNI-Thread
Tag:	UV pink Hareline Ice Dub
Rubber legs:	Pink/blue Hareline hot-tipped Crazy Legs
Wing 1:	Pink/blue Hareline hot-tipped Crazy Legs
Body:	Hareline Diamond Braid
Body:	Blue Steelie Hareline Ice Dub Shimmer Fringe
Wing 2:	Silver Hareline Senyo's Wacko Hackle, Blue Mirage and Natural Hareline Lady Amherst
Connection:	30-pound Berkely Fireline

SENYO'S CRAWFISH SPACE INVADER

(Greg Senyo, Lake Erie)

Hook:	#4 Owner Mosquito
Shank:	Flymen Senyo's shank (25 mm)
Thread:	70-denier Ultra Thread or 6/0 UNI-Thread
Tag:	Copper Hareline Ice Dub
Legs:	Orange/purple hot-tipped Hareline Crazy Legs
First wing:	Orange/purple hot-tipped Hareline Crazy Legs
Body:	Root beer Hareline Diamond Braid
Body:	Copper Hareline Ice Dub
Wing 2:	Copper Hareline Senyo's Wacko Hackle, Copper Mirage and Natural Amherst
Connection:	30-pound Fireline

ATLANTIC SALMON—ICELANDIC/SCANDINAVIAN/RUSSIAN FLIES

Tied by Vidar Egilsson and Arni Baldursson, Iceland
Iceland's Atlantic salmon live in sparkling clean waters that have many springs draining into them. They are in many cases large spring creeks, such as the big Laxa, where the Atlantic salmon can be the most selective on earth. The ultraclear waters allow the salmon to see minutiae, and the young parr feed on the tremendous midge and Diptera life that abounds on the rivers and streams. Micro tubes and tiny treble flies are mainstays here, as is the famous riffle hitch, which creates a wake on the water. It is amazing that a micro size 18 treble can hold 20-pound Atlantic salmon here.

RANGA TUBE

Hook:	Gamakatsu C14
Tube:	Eumer/Pro Tube clear plastic micro black silicon connector
Thread:	Black 8/0 UNI
Tail:	Black bucktail and pearl Krystal Flash
Tag:	Gold oval wire and ribbing
Body:	Lower half is silver holographic flat tinsel; upper half is peacock herl
Overwing:	Black bucktail and Krystal Flash
Collar:	Black webby Australian opossum
Cheek:	Jungle cock
Cone:	Chartreuse Eumer/Pro Tube (small)

BLACK AND BLUE RIFFLE

Hook:	Partridge O2 double Wilson
Thread:	Black 8/0 UNI
Tube:	Clear Eumer/Pro Tube (small)
Overwing:	Black calf tail and Krystal Flash
Throat:	Blue Laxa mini marabou

ICELANDIC RAT

Hook:	Gamakatsu C14
Thread:	Black 8/0 UNI
Tube:	Clear Eumer/Pro Tube (small)
Wing:	Yellow-dyed squirrel and black arctic fox

MICRO SUNRAY SHADOW

Hook:	Partridge X 3BL Needle eye treble tube
Tube:	White or clear Eumer/Pro Tube (micro)
Wing:	Krystal Flash, blue arctic fox, black arctic fox
Topping:	Blue and purple Flashabou

SILVER STOAT LONGTAIL

Hook:	Partridge O2 Double Wilson
Thread:	Black 8/0 UNI
Tail:	Pearl Krystal Flash
Body:	Silver Ultra tinsel and silver rib oval
Wing:	Black arctic fox
Throat:	Black mini marabou

CROSSFIELD MICRO

Hook:	Owner ST 36 BC silver treble
Thread:	Yellow 8/0 UNI
Wing:	Mallard
Throat:	Blue Laxa mini marabou

BLACK AND BLUE MICRO RIFFLE

Hook:	Partridge O2 Double Wilson
Tube:	White/clear Eumer/Pro Tuber (micro)
Wing:	Tied upside-down for riffle hitch; throat is black arctic fox, blue Flashabou
Collar:	Blue Laxa mini marabou

COLLIE DOG RIFFLE

Hook:	Partridge O2 Double Wilson
Thread:	Black 6/0 UNI
Tube:	Clear/white Eumer/Pro Tube (small)
Wing:	Black arctic fox and Krystal Flash

FRANCIS BLACK MICRO

Hook:	Owner ST 36 BC silver treble
Thread:	Yellow 8/0 UNI
Tail/Claws:	Stripped white and ginger quill with V-shaped claws
Thorax:	Peacock
Hackle:	Ginger

FRANCIS RED

Hook:	Owner ST 36 BC Gold Treble
Thread:	Red 70-denier UTC X-Strong
Tail/Claws:	White and ginger stripped quills
Body:	Red floss or red UNI-Stretch
Rib tag:	Ginger hackle
Rib:	Silver Lagartun micro oval

FRANCIS BLACK

Hook:	Owner ST 36 BC silver treble
Thread:	Yellow 8/0 UNI
Tail/Claws:	White and ginger stripped quills with pheasant tail
Body:	Black floss or black UNI-Stretch
Tag:	Ginger hackle
Tag:	Green UNI-Stretch or green floss
Rib:	Gold Lagartun oval tinsel (fine)
Body:	Black Lagartun Mini Flatbraid or black floss
Wing:	Arctic fox
Throat:	Black marabou mini tips

GREEN BUTT LONGTAIL

Hook:	Partridge X3BL needle eye treble
Thread:	Black 8/0 UNI
Tail:	Black arctic fox with green pearl Krystal Flash
Tag:	Silver Lagartun fine oval tinsel, hot green UNI-Neon Floss
Body:	Black Lagartun flat braid or black floss
Rib:	Silver Lagartun fine oval tinsel
Wing:	Black arctic fox
Throat:	Black marabou mini tips

GREEN BRAHAN LONG TAIL

Hook:	Partridge Salar CS14/2B double
Thread:	Black 70-denier Ultra
Tail:	Chartreuse and black bucktail
Body:	Highlander green Lagartun flat sparkle braid
Rib:	Silver Lagartun fine oval tinsel
Wing:	Black bucktail with green and pearl Flashabou

Notes: An effective Icelandic and Russian salmon fly for use in stained spate rivers. This pattern is an Arni Baldursson favorite.

GREEN HIGHLANDER CONEHEAD TUBE

Hook:	Partridge Salar CS14T/1B tube
Thread:	Orange 70-denier Lagartun
Tube:	Clear or white Eumer/Pro Tube (medium)
Body:	Gold Ultra holographic flat tinsel
Rib:	Gold UNI flat varnished tinsel (medium)
Wing:	Orange, chartreuse, and black bucktail with pearl Flashabou
Collar:	Yellow and green saddle hackle webby
Topping:	Three strands of black Holographic Flashabou
Throat:	Yellow and green mini marabou
Head/Cone:	Eumer/Pro Tube orange cone

ARNI'S FAVORITE—UNDERWING BROWN

Hook:	Partridge Salar CS14T/2 B double
Thread:	Black 70-denier Lagartun
Tube:	Clear white Eumer/Pro Tube (large); no material on tube, just head
Wing:	Red squirrel, peacock strands, and black arctic fox

GREEN BRAHAN MICRO CONE

Hook:	Partridge Double Wilson 02/16
Thread:	Black 70-denier Lagartun
Tube:	Clear Eumer/Pro Tube (micro)
Body:	Highlander green Lagartun Mini Flatbraid
Wing:	Black arctic fox with green Flashabou
Throat:	Black mini Spey plumes
Head:	Eumer/Pro Tube small silver cone

Notes: This is the perfect tube for when skinny water conditions dictate that you get down in fast, oxygenated riffles during heat-filled days.

MUNROE KILLER LONGTAIL

Hook:	Partridge Double Wilson 02
Thread:	Black 70-denier Lagartun
Tail:	Yellow and orange bucktail, pearl Krystal Flash
Tag:	Gold Ultra oval tinsel (small)
Body:	Black Lagartun flat braid
Rib:	Same as tag
Wing:	Black arctic fox, several strands of black silver spec Flashabou
Throat:	Orange mini Spey plums and blue Guinea

Notes: This Scottish favorite—also my favorite—is lethal on stained waters from Russia to Scandinavia to Canada. It follows the same color concept as the Willie Gunn.

GREEN HIGHLANDER MICRO TREBLE

Hook:	Partridge X3BL treble needle
Thread:	Lagartun red 70
Tail:	Orange, yellow, and chartreuse bucktail (used sparsely); chartreuse Krystal Flash
Tag/Rib:	Gold Lagartun oval tinsel (extra-small)
Body:	Silver Lagartun flat varnished tinsel (small)
Wing:	Black arctic fox
Throat:	Yellow and green mini Spey plume fibers

Notes: An effective spring pattern when waters are low but there are fresh salmon in the rivers.

BLACK SHEEP

Hook:	Daiichi 2421 low-water single
Thread:	Red 70-denier Lagartun
Tag:	Silver Ultra flat tinsel (small)
Body:	Black angora goat
Wing:	Yellow and black calf tail, green pearl Flashabou
Throat:	Blue Hareline Spey plume fibers
Cheek:	Jungle cock (extra-small)

Notes: A wonderful low-water pattern that can be fished riffle hitched when salmon are ultra S/R.

BLACK SHEEP MICRO

Hook:	Partridge O2 Double Wilson/16
Tag:	Silver Ultra small silver flat tinsel
Body:	Black angora goat
Wing:	Yellow and black calf tail, green pearl Flashabou
Throat:	Blue Hareline Spey plume fibers
Cheek:	Jungle cock (extra-small)

Notes: A Laxa pattern for use in summertime low-water conditions.

BLACK AND BLUE LONGTAIL

Hook:	Partridge X3SL needle eye treble silver
Thread:	Black 70-denier Lagartun
Tail:	Black bucktail with pearl Krystal Flash
Tag/Rib:	Gold Lagartun oval (extra-small)
Body:	Silver Ultra flat tinsel (small)
Wing:	Black arctic fox
Throat:	Blue Hareline Spey plumes

GREEN BUTT MICRO TREBLE

Hook:	Partridge X3BL treble black
Thread:	Black 8/0 UNI
Tail:	Black arctic fox with green pearl Krystal Flash
Tag:	Silver Lagartun oval tinsel (fine), hot green UNI-Neon Floss
Body:	Black Lagartun flat braid or black floss
Rib:	Silver Lagartun oval tinsel (fine)
Wing:	Black arctic fox
Throat:	Black marabou mini tips

STOAT LOW WATER

Hook:	Partridge single Wilson 01 low water
Thread:	Black 70-denier Lagartun
Tail:	Golden pheasant
Tag:	Silver Ultra flat tinsel (small)
Body:	Silver Ultra flat tinsel (small)
Rib:	Gold Ultra oval tinsel (small)
Underwing:	Two strands of lateral scale Flashabou dyed pearl fluorescent yellow
Wing:	Black saddle hackle
Throat:	Black Hareline Spey plumes

Notes: A perfect pattern for using the riffle-hitch technique on low clear rivers in summer when salmon are extremely P/D.

VIDAR RED FRANCIS

Hook:	R. M. Jeffries QG Double Water Gold Salmon Hooks
Thread:	Red 70-denier Lagartun
Tail:	Stripped white and ginger quills and V-shaped claw clips with left fibers
Tail:	Pheasant tail
Hackle:	Wapsi furnace ginger hackle palmered
Body:	Red UNI-Stretch or red floss
Rib:	Gold Ultra oval tinsel (extra-small)
Topping:	Red Hareline Ice Dub fibers (just a few crinkles)

ATLANTIC SALMON—STEELHEAD DRIES AND SUBSURFACE WETS

BOMBER GREEN

(Author)

Hook:	Daiichi 2110
Thread:	Black 95-denier Lagartun X-Strong
Tail:	White calf tail
Tag:	Chartreuse-dyed deer hair
Body:	Green deer hair
Hackle:	Badger
Wing:	White calf tail
Hackle:	Badger

LABATT BLUE BOMBER

(Author)

Hook:	Daiichi 2110
Thread:	Black 95-denier Lagartun X-Strong
Body:	Blue-dyed deer hair
Hackle:	Ginger
Wings:	White calf tail
Hackle:	Ginger

WHITE WULFF BOMBER

(Author)

Hook:	Daiichi 2110
Thread:	Black 95-denier Lagartun X-Strong
Tail:	White calf tail
Body:	White deer hair
Wings:	White calf tail
Hackle:	White

ORANGE CRUSH BOMBER

(Author)

Hook:	Daiichi 2110
Thread:	Black 95-denier Lagartun X-Strong
Tail:	White calf tail
Body:	Orange fluorescent deer hair
Wings:	White calf tail
Hackle:	Brown

CREAMSICLE MOOSE TURD

(Author)

Hook:	Daiichi 2110
Thread:	Black 95-denier Lagartun X-Strong
Tail:	White calf tail
Body:	Cream deer hair
Hackle:	Orange
Head:	White calf tail

BÉLIVEAU'S GREEN WULFF STONE

(Jean Guy Béliveau, Canada; based on original Wulff's Green Stone)

Hook:	Daiichi 2052
Thread:	Black 95-denier Lagartun X-Strong
Tag:	Silver Ultra flat tinsel (medium)
Body:	Chartreuse Hareline Diamond Braid
Wing:	Black bucktail
Post:	Green-tipped bobby pin (bent up) or regular bobby pin painted with a green tip
Hackle:	Grizzly

WULFF ORIGINAL GREEN STONE

(Author)

Hook:	Partridge 02 Double Wilson
Thread:	Black 95-denier Lagartun X-Strong
Tag:	Silver Ultra flat tinsel (medium)
Body:	Fluorescent green UNI-Stretch or highlander green Hareline French Silk floss
Wing:	Black bucktail or calf tail
Post:	Pin turned up with micro yellow or green plastic bead under the tag end of pin; or a green or yellow bobby pinhead
Hackle:	Grizzly

GASPÉ GREEN STONE

(Author)

Hook:	Daiichi 2421
Thread:	Black 95-denier Lagartun X-Strong
Body:	Green Antron hare mix
Wing:	Green-dyed calf tail
Post:	Green-head bobby pin or burnt 50-pound mono painted green
Hackle:	Badger

GREEN BUTT STONE

(Author)

Hook:	Daiichi 7130
Thread:	Black 95-denier Lagartun X-Strong
Tag:	Silver Ultra flat tinsel (medium) with green UNI-Stretch or chartreuse Lagartun Mini Flatbraid (tier's choice)
Body:	Black UNI-Stretch or black Lagartun Mini Flatbraid
Rib:	Silver UNI oval tinsel (small)
Wing:	Black bucktail
Post:	Bobby pinhead or burnt 50-pound mono painted to preference
Hackle:	Grizzly

ORANGE AUTUMN STONE

(Author)

Hook:	Daiichi 7130
Thread:	Black 95-denier Lagartun X-Strong
Body:	Orange UNI-Stretch or orange Lagartun Mini Flatbraid
Wing:	Rust elk hair, gold and orange Krystal Flash
Post:	Green-headed bobby pin or burnt 50-pound mono painted green
Hackle:	Grizzly

FRANCIS GREEN

(Author)

Hook:	Daiichi 1730
Thread:	Green UNI-Stretch
Tail/Claws:	Ginger and grizzly stripped quills with claws cut V-shaped at tail; clump of pheasant tail strands
Body:	Green UNI-Stretch rounded into cone-shaped shrimp formation (larger in back, slim in front)
Rib:	Ginger hackle with silver Ultra oval tinsel (small)
Eyes:	Black mono eyes

HOT ORANGE FRANCIS

(Author)

Hook:	Daiichi 7131
Thread:	Fluorescent hot orange UNI-Stretch
Tail:	Two hackle-form ginger and grizzly rooster hackle stems stripped and cut into triangle shape for claws; pheasant tail
Body:	Wrap hot orange UNI-Stretch in cylindrical shape for shrimp body
Eyes:	Black Hareline mono
Rib:	Silver Veniard round tinsel (medium) with ginger rooster hackle

Notes: This Icelandic fly is deadly on crystal-clear Gaspé rivers where salmon are pooled up. While fishing one pool on the Grand Pabos, I had close to two dozen follows to the rod tip when stripping this fly. I eventually hooked a 34-pounder.

ROYAL COACHMAN WULFF

(Author)

Hook:	Daiichi 1730
Thread:	Black 95-denier Lagartun X-Strong
Tail:	Golden pheasant
Tag:	Peacock herl
Body:	Red UNI-Stretch or red Lagartun Mini Flatbraid
Thorax:	Peacock herl
Wing:	White calf tail
Throat:	Brown saddle

SUNRAY SHADOW

(Author)

Hook:	Daiichi 1730
Thread:	Black 95-denier Lagartun X-Strong
Tag:	Silver Ultra tinsel (small)
Body:	Black or pearl Lagartun Mini Flatbraid
Wing:	Light blue and black bucktail, with strands of blue and purple mirage or holographic Flashabou
Throat:	Blue-dyed guinea

BLUE CHARM RIFFLE HITCH

(Author)

Hook:	Daiichi 2441
Thread:	Black 6/0 UNI
Tag:	Black Lagartun Mini Flatbraid, silver Mini Flatbraid, yellow Lagartun floss
Tail:	Golden pheasant
Upper body:	Black Lagartun Mini Flatbraid, silver Ultra oval embossed tinsel
Throat:	Blue-dyed webby goose feather
Wing:	Gadwall feathers
Underwing:	Golden pheasant
Cheek:	Jungle cock
	Leave plenty of room at front of hook for riffle hitch

Notes: The Blue Charm is the universal go-to fly for Atlantic salmon guides and anglers around the world. This slimmer version is meant to be used riffle-hitched, which is deadly on clear blue and flat waters like Iceland's Laxa and those on Québec's Gaspé.

UNDERTAKER

(Author)

Hook:	Daiichi 1730
Thread:	Black 74-denier Lagartun X-Strong
Tag:	Gold Ultra tinsel (small) with bands of green and red UNI-Stretch
Body:	Peacock herl
Rib:	Silver Ultra round embossed tinsel
Wing:	Black bucktail
Throat:	Black saddle
Cheek:	Jungle cock

HAIRY MARY

(Author)

Hook:	Daiichi 1730
Thread:	Black 74-denier Lagartun X-Strong
Tail:	Golden pheasant
Tag:	Silver Ultra French-embossed tinsel (medium)
Body:	Black Lagartun Mini Flatbraid
Wing:	Natural squirrel
Cheek:	Jungle cock
Throat:	Blue saddle or Metz hatchery soft hackle

YORK WHITE MUDDLER

(Author)

Hook:	Daiichi 1730
Thread:	Fluorescent orange 74-denier Lagartun
Tag:	Silver Ultra flat tinsel (small), with tiny hint of orange UNI-Stretch
Body:	Silver Lagartun Mini Flatbraid or silver Ultra flat tinsel (medium)
Wing:	White bucktail
Head:	Spun white bucktail with exposed orange Lagartun thread with a tuft of orange Senyo's Laser Dub

FOAM SPUDDER TAN

(Ken Morrish, Oregon)

Hook:	Gold Daiichi Alec Jackson steelhead irons
Tail:	Orange Krystal Flash
Thread:	Beige 74-denier Lagartun X-Strong
Body:	Orange or pearl Krystal Flash
Thorax:	Ginger deer hair trimmed into wings
Foam:	Tan (6 mm) cut to shape of sample

OCTOBER CADDIS

(Author)

Hook:	Black Daiichi Alec Jackson steelhead irons
Thread:	Black 74-denier Lagartun X-Strong
Body:	Orange SLF angora goat
Wings:	Hungarian partridge tips
Head:	Spun deer hair with legs splayed out

WALLER WAKER GRAY

(Author)

Hook:	Black Daiichi Alec Jackson steelhead irons
Thread:	Black 95-denier Lagartun X-Strong
Tail:	Moose mane
Body:	Black and natural deer hair spun in bands
Wing:	White calf tail
Throat:	Black or brown deer hair

WALLER WAKER ORANGE

(Author)

Hook:	Black Daiichi Alec Jackson steelhead irons
Thread:	Black 95-denier Lagartun X-Strong
Tail:	Moose mane
Body:	Black and orange spun center deer hair
Wings:	Natural elk hair

BABINE TURD

(Pierce Clegg, British Columbia)

Hook:	Daiichi 2557
Thread:	Black 95-denier Lagartun X-Strong
Trailer wire:	Black Hareline Senyo's Intruder Wire
Body hook:	Daiichi 2461, clipped and turned back for eye
Tag:	Hot orange Hareline UV Ice Dub
Body:	Ginger deer hair spun
Rib:	Tiny grizzly hackle
Head:	White calf tail

BABINE SPUTTER KICKER

(Pierce Clegg, British Columbia)

Hook:	Gold Daiichi Alec Jackson steelhead irons
Thread:	Black 95-denier Lagartun X-Strong
Tail/Body:	Tan bucktail
Rib:	Thread
Wing:	Tan bucktail
Head:	Bucktail clipped and wound back and lacquered in a spread turkey wing fashion; must be stiff to push water

Notes: A lethal steelhead dry when the stoneflies are hatching on the Dean and Babine Rivers in British Columbia.

ROADKILL AND TRADITIONAL ATLANTIC FLIES

These flies range from avant-garde patterns inspired by dead animals on a Québec highway for P/D pooled-up salmon, to the honored and time-tested traditional noble ties.

MATT'S SALAR OCTOPUSSY

(Author)

Hook:	Daiichi 2052 Alec Jackson Spey
Thread:	Black 95-denier Lagartun X-Strong
Lower body/Tail:	Zoom Salty Super Tube rubber soft bait in pink squid body (available from Bass Pro Shops), Mirage Flashabou
Upper body:	Barred grizzly blood marabou palmered
Collar:	Natural grizzly marabou
Legs:	Hareline Aqua Glow Crazy Legs
Cheeks:	Jungle cock

MATT'S BACK ALLEY SHRIMP ROADKILL

(Author)

Hook:	Daiichi 2052 Alec Jackson Spey
Thread:	Black 95-denier Lagartun X-Strong
Tag:	flat gold Ultra tinsel (medium)
Tail/Back body:	Zoom salty rubber soft bait brown and copper speckled—Bass Pro Shops
Upper body:	Orange Hareline Lady Amherst, orange mottled grizzly chickabou
Legs:	Orange brown Hareline tipped Sili Legs
Cheeks:	Jungle cock

BABINE ELECTRIC CANDY CANE CHARTREUSE

(Author)

Hook:	Daiichi 2052 Alec Jackson Spey
Thread:	Black 95-denier Lagartun X-Strong
Tail:	Black rabbit strip
Body:	Black chenille with black schlappen bands, with bright chartreuse edge on top of a layer of silver Ultra flat tinsel (small)
Cheek:	Jungle cock

ROADKILL COON GRIZZLY

(Author)

Hook:	Daiichi 2052 Alec Jackson Spey
Thread:	Black 95-denier Lagartun X-Strong
Tail:	Brown marabou
Body:	Brown, olive, white, and black barred grizzly marabou palmered in layers
Collar:	Black natural guinea
Cheek:	Jungle cock

ROB'S RAIDER

(Rob White, Scotland)

Hook:	#2 Silver Partridge Wilson Double
Thread:	Black 3/0 Veniard
Tail:	Hot orange and yellow bucktail mixed with 2 or 3 strands silver Krystal Flash tied fairly long as an Ally's Shrimp
Tag:	Red Hareline French Silk floss
Body:	Ultra Holographic tinsel on back half and black floss palmered with a yellow cock hackle on the front half, both covered with a ribbing of silver UNI French oval tinsel (small)
Wing:	Black bucktail tied just beyond the shank of the hook
Hackle:	Orange cock long-tied after the wing long enough to come back to the shank of the hook
Cheeks:	Jungle cock tied top and bottom (as opposed to each side)
Head:	Clear Cure Goo Thin

POMPIER TREBLE

(Author)

Hook:	R. M. Jefferies X2B Esmond Drury outpoint treble
Thread:	74-denier Lagartun X-Strong
Tail:	Yellow bucktail, golden pheasant
Body:	Black Lagartun Mini Flatbraid, silver tinsel
Throat:	Green Metz hatchery soft hackle

ROB'S BLACK SHRIMP

(Rob White, Scotland)

Hook:	R. M. Jefferies X2B Esmond Drury outpoint treble
Thread:	Black 74-denier Lagartun X-Strong
Tail:	Hot orange stripped cock hackle stocks (same as above); then hot orange arctic fox tied in shorter than the bristles or stocks; lastly, hot orange tippet tied in with the black bit, no further back than the end of the hook shank
Tag:	Red Hareline French silk floss (varnished)
Body:	Black Veniard's Cactus Chenille XF palmered with a black cock hackle back the body and covered with a silver rib.
Head:	Clear Cure Goo Thin

ROB'S ORANGE SHRIMP

(Rob White, Scotland)

Hook:	Gold R. M. Jeffries X2BG Esmond Drury treble
Thread:	Orange 74-denier Lagartun X-Strong
Tag:	Fluorescent orange UNI-Stretch
Tail:	Hot orange stripped cock hackle quills; these are to be placed at equal intervals (one on every bend in the hook) so that they are not all curled in the same direction. Short-tie in hot orange tips with the black marker banded fibers (or golden pheasant tips) no farther back than the end of the hook shank; then hot orange arctic fox tied in shorter than the bristles or quills
Tag:	Fluorescent red floss (varnished)
Body:	Hot orange Cactus Chenille with a hot orange cock hackle palmered back the body and ribbed with silver UNI French Embossed oval tinsel (small)
Head:	Clear Cure Goo Thin

ROB'S BLACK AND YELLOW TEMPLE DOG

Thread:	Black 74-denier Lagartun X-Strong
Hook:	#2 Partridge Wilson Double
Tube:	Clear Eumer/Pro Tube (large), chartreuse or yellow silicone tubing for hook placement
Tag:	Fluorescent yellow Hareline 4-Strand floss.
Tail:	Thick fluorescent yellow floss with some pearl Flashabou through it.
Rear body:	Silver Lagartun flat varnished tinsel (large)
Rib:	UNI French oval tinsel (medium)
Front body:	Black Veniard Tri Lobal hackle Medium Crystal mix with a fluorescent yellow cock hackle palmered back the body and ribbed with silver tinsel
Wing 1:	Yellow arctic fox
Wing 2:	A few strands of kingfisher blue bucktail or goat
Wing 3:	Black goat
Wing 4:	Black arctic fox with some strands of Krinkle Mirror Flash on top
Hackle:	Fluorescent yellow cock
Cheeks:	Jungle cock tied on sides

ROB'S WILLIE GUNN TEMPLEDOG

(Rob White, Scotland)

Hook:	Daiichi 7131 double
Tube:	Clear plastic Eumer/Pro Tube (large); connector is an orange silicone tube
Thread:	Red 95-denier Lagartun X-Strong
Tag:	Fluorescent hot orange Hareline French silk floss
Tail:	Neon fluorescent orange UNI floss with some Mylar through it
Rear body/Rib:	Gold Ultra holographic tinsel with gold UNI French tinsel (large)
Front body:	Black Veniard Tri Lobal hackle Medium Crystal mix with a hot orange cock hackle palmered back the body and ribbed with gold tinsel
First wing:	Orange arctic fox
Second wing:	Yellow arctic fox
Third wing:	Yellow goat
Fourth wing:	Black arctic fox with some strands on Krinkle Mirror Flash on top
Hackle:	Hot orange cock
Cheeks:	Jungle cock tied on sides
Head:	Clear Cure Goo Thin

Notes: The Willie Gunn is the most universal Atlantic salmon fly. Its color combination piques the A/A response, especially in tannic waters from Russia to Québec.

DODDI ORANGE TUBE

(Paul Marriner, Canada)

Thread:	Black 95-denier Lagartun X-Strong
Tube:	Orange Eumer/Pro Tube (small)
Hook:	Daiichi 1648 Alec Jackson tube
Wing:	Black bucktail, silver Krystal Flash
Throat:	Yellow arctic fox with two strands of pearl Flashabou

LEBLANC'S BLACK AND GOLD SPEY

(Marc LeBlanc, Canada)

Hook:	Gold Daiichi 2055 Alec Jackson Spey
Thread:	Brown 6/0 UNI
Tail:	Golden pheasant
Tag:	Black ostrich
Body/Rib:	Gold Ultra flat tinsel (small), copper Ultra Wire (small)
Upper body:	Stripped peacock quills
Collar/Wings:	Black Spey hackle
Topping:	Natural Amherst
Cheek:	Jungle cock

LEBLANC'S AKROYD

(Marc LeBlanc, Canada)

Hook:	Daiichi 2051 Alec Jackson Spey
Thread:	Black 6/0 UNI
Tail:	Golden pheasant
Tag:	Gold Ultra flat tinsel (small)
Body/Rib:	Orange and black Angora with oval gold UNI French ribbing (small) for orange, silver UNI French oval ribbing for black
Wing:	Orange and black Spey hackle, gadwall
Throat:	Black Spey hackle and gadwall
Cheek:	Jungle cock

LEBLANC'S GHOST SPEY

(Marc LeBlanc, Canada)

Hook:	Alec Jackson Spey
Thread:	White 6/0 UNI
Tag:	Silver UNI French oval tinsel (extra small)
Body/Rib:	Pearl Lagartun Mini Flatbraid, silver UNI French oval tinsel rib (extra-small)
Wing:	White arctic fox, pearl Krystal Flash, olive and black Spey hackle
Topping:	Natural Amherst
Throat:	Natural Amherst and black Spey hackle

LEBLANC'S MEAN GREEN SPEY

(Marc LeBlanc, Canada)

Hook:	Daiichi 2051 Alec Jackson Spey
Thread:	Black 6/0 UNI
Tag:	Silver UNI French oval tinsel (extra small)
Body:	Hot green UNI Neon floss or green Lagartun Mini Flatbraid
Wing:	Green Krystal Flash, chartreuse bucktail, green Spey hackle
Topping:	Green-dyed mallard
Throat:	Green Spey hackle and green mallard

GASPÉ MUDDLER

(Austin Clark, Canada)

Hook:	Daiichi 2340
Thread:	Black 3/0 UNI
Tag:	Gold UNI French oval tinsel (large)
Body/Rib:	Gold Lagartun flat tinsel (large) and gold UNI French oval tinsel (large)
Wing/Head:	Natural deer hair spun and cut

MAGOG SMELT

(Author)

Hook:	Daiichi 1730
Thread:	Black 74-denier Lagartun X-Strong
Tail:	Gadwall feather fibers
Body/Rib:	Silver Ultra flat tinsel (medium) for body, silver UNI French tinsel (medium) for rib
Wing:	White, chartreuse, and purple bucktail, pearl Krystal Flash, gadwall and peacock fibers
Throat:	Red Metz soft hackle and gadwall feather tips

MALBAIE RUBBER LEGS

(Author)

Follow Same Formula for Each

1. Orange
2. Green Goblin
3. Labatt Blue

Hook:	Daiichi 2220
Thread:	Fluorescent orange or peacock blue 70-denier Ultra
Tail:	Fox, squirrel, or calf tail
Hackle rib:	Grizzly soft hackle
Body:	Hareline orange variegated chenille, green emerald sparkle, and blue sparkle chenille
Legs:	White/black speckled Hareline centipede legs

Index

[Note: Page numbers in *italics* refer to photo/illustration captions.]

Adams Deer Hair, 118
  recipe for, 226
Adams Parachute, *94*
  recipe for, 219
Adriatic Sea, *35*
Aggressive/Active (A/A) phase
  char and, 33–34
  overview of, 9–12
  salmon and, 9, 11, 78, 141, 159, *171*, 172, *172*, 174, 177, *177*, 179–182, *182*, 189, 193–194, *193*, 196–200, 203, 252
  steelhead and, 9, 11, 123–128, *127*, 130–135, *135*, 137–139, 141–146, 148, 150, 152, *153*, 156–160, *158*, *160*, 163, 165, 167, 239
Aggressive/Active (A/A) phase, trout and, 9–12, 20–24, 32–35, 50, 54–55, 62, 73, 74, 76, 78, 87, 89, *100*, *103*
  brook, 32, *32*, 55, 230
  brown, 12, *20*, 22–24, *23*, 26, 97–99, *99*, 104, *104*, 106, 108–111, 114, 115
  flies recommended for, 115–122, 225
  lake, *34*
  overview of, 21, 97–122
  rainbow, 26–30, *27*, *28*, 33, 97, 104, 114, 142
Alewife, 11–12, 24–26, 34, 103, 118
Alley's Shrimp, 180
Alta River, *10*, *183*
Armstrong Creek, 40, 42, 43
Arni's Favorite—Underwing Brown, *201*
  recipe for, 246
Atlantic Ocean, 24–25
Atlantic salmon. *See* salmon, Atlantic
Atlantic Salmon, The (Wulff), 173, *175*
Atlantic Salmon Journal, 171, *178*, 187
Ausable Bivisible, 118
  recipe for, 226
Ausable Caddis, 118
  recipe for, 227
Au Sable Hex Wulff Spinner, *116*
  recipe for, 225
Au Sable Mahogany Drake, *116*
  recipe for, 225
Au Sable MI Black Caddis, 118
  recipe for, 227
Au Sable MI Green Madame X, 118
  recipe for, 227
Au Sable MI Haystack, 118
  recipe for, 227
Au Sable MI Madame X, 118
  recipe for, 227
Au Sable MI Patriot, 118
  recipe for, 227
Au Sable River (Michigan), 39, 108, 111, 119
Ausable River (New York), 70, 111

Ausable Wulff, 118
  recipe for, 227
Autumn Gold Templedog, *169*
  recipe for, 243
Avon, River, 8, *51*, 57

Babine Electric Candy Cane, *163*
  recipe for, 163
Babine Electric Candy Cane Chartreuse, *203*
  recipe for, 250
Babine River, 133–134, *143*, *145*, *148*, 163, 250
Babine Sputter Kicker, *202*
  recipe for, 250
Babine Turd, *202*
  recipe for, 250
Baconator Mysis, *162*
  recipe for, 236
Baldursson, Arni, *172*, *183*, 187–188, 245, 246
Baltic Sea, *13*, 23, 24, *25*, 36, 161, *175*, *179*
Barents Sea, 181
Bashline, Jim, 111
Batcke, Mike, 104
Batcke's Copper and Orange Night Stalker Tube, 120
  recipe for, 228
Batcke's Night Raider Stone, *120*
  recipe for, 228
Bay de Chaleur, 192
Bead Head Buzzer, *92*
  recipe for, 216
Bead Head BWO Emerger, *84*
  recipe for, 208
Bead Head Soft Hackle Caddis Emerger, *90*
  recipe for, 214
Bear's Head Banger Hex, *162*
  recipe for, 235
Beaver Creek, 109
Beaverkill River, 15, 66, 69–70, 78
  Cairn pool, 70
Béliveau, Jean-Guy, *176*, 196, 203
Béliveau's Gaspé Green Stone, *203*
  recipe for, 203
Béliveau's Gaspé Wulff, 118
  recipe for, 227
Béliveau's Green Wulff Stone, *202*
  recipe for, 248
Bemmer, Bob, 158
Bemmer's Skamania Excavator, *162*
  recipe for, 236
Berners, Juliana, 8
Betters, Fran, 79, 226
Beveliqua, Daniela, *58*
Big Hole River, *112*, 114
Bighorn River, 44, 45, *45*, *105*
Big Hunting Creek, 56, *56*, 57

Big Laxa River, 75, 186–188, *187*, 191, 205, 245, 249
Big Manistee River, 25
Big Spring Flash Pupa, *92*
  recipe for, 216
Big Spring Midge, *92*
  recipe for, 215
Big Spring Mouse, *91*, 114
  recipe for, 91
Big Spring Pupa, *92*
  recipe for, 215
Big Spring Run, 23, 30, *31*, 83, 91, *102*, 114, 211, 215
Birchell's Emerger, *92*
  recipe for, 216
Bishop, David, 176–177
Bivisible, 158
Black and Blue Longtail, *201*
  recipe for, 247
Black and Blue Micro Riffle, *201*
  recipe for, 245
Black and Blue Riffle, *201*
  recipe for, 245
Black Buzzer, *92*
  recipe for, 215
Black Collie Orange, *169*
  recipe for, 242
Black Egg Raider, *170*
  recipe for, 243
Black Sheep, *201*
  recipe for, 247
Black Sheep Micro, *201*
  recipe for, 247
Blue Charm, 180, 188, *188*, 192, 197, 203
Blue Charm Riffle Hitch, *202*, 205
  recipes for, 205, 249
Blue English, *13*
Blue Opal Invader, *170*
  recipe for, 244
Blue Ray Tube, *166*
  recipe for, 240
Bois Brule River, 161
Bombardier, *203*
  recipe for, 203
Bomber, 189
Bomber Green, *202*
  recipe for, 247
Bonaventure River, *191*
Borchers March Brown T. C., *94*
  recipe for, 220
Breeches White Midge, *92*
  recipe for, 216
Bridges, fishing, 109–111, *109*, *110*
Bristol Bay, 29
Bronze Back Mo Scud, *88*
  recipe for, 211
Brooks's Giant Stone, *93*
  recipe for, 217

brook trout, *11*, 21, 26, 58
    A/A phase and, 32, *32*, 55, 97, 230
    coasters, 31–33, *32*, 230
    freestone streams and, *32*, 55
    overview of, 30–33
    spring creeks and, 23, 30
    S/R phase and, 31, *31*, *32*
Brown Drake Au Sable, *116*
    recipe for, 225
brown trout, 5, *8*, 20, 21, *21*, 35, *62*, *70*, 81,
    108, *114*, 126, 130, 149, 165, 173, 174,
    186, 212, 228
    A/A phase and, 12, *20*, 22–24, *23*, 26,
    97–99, *99*, 104, *104*, 106, 108–111, 114,
    115
    catch-and-release waters and, 2–4
    freestone streams and, *11*, *54*, 55, *55*, 56,
    56, 109–110
    habituation and, 17–18
    Hucho, 23, 34–35, *54*
    lake-run, 23–26, *25*, 115, 117, 229
    marble, 23, 34–35, *54*
    overview of, 22–26
    P/D phase and, 15 17, *104*, 108, 110, 113,
    114
    sea-run, 15, 23–26, *26*, 115, 117, 229
    Seeforellen-strain, 24, *25*
    spring creeks and, 3, 11, 22, 23, *42*, *43*,
    81, 97, *100*, 102, *102*, 229
    S/R phase and, *13*, 17–18, 22, *24*, 27, 31,
    31, 52–53, 59, 66, 69–70, 82, 83, 106,
    108, *130*, 199, 229
    tailwaters and, *20*, 22, 51–53, 104, *104*,
    111
Bubble BWO Emerger, *84*
    recipe for, 207
Bulkley River, 157
bull trout, 34
Bunny Bugger, 145, 147
Butterfly (fly), 180
BWO Parachute Viz, *84*
    recipe for, 208
BWO Traditional Parachute, *84*
    recipe for, 208

Cadillac Nymph, *95*
    recipe for, 221
Cahill, 4
Cahill Spinner, *94*
    recipe for, 218
Cahill T. C. Emerger, *94*
    recipe for, 218
Cajun Latex Amber Stonefly, *89*
    recipe for, 89
Cannonsville Reservoir, 44
Cartoon Hopper, *122*
    recipe for, 231
Cartoon Salmon/Hopper, *122*
    recipe for, 231
Cascapedia Roadkill Coon, *205*
    recipe for, 205
Catch-and-release waters, 7
    salmon and, 2, 15–16, 141, *195*
    steelhead and, *128*, 141
    trout and, 2–4, 15, 21, 77, 82
Catskill Green Drake, *94*
    recipe for, 219
Cattaraugus Creek, 109, 150, 237
Caucci, Al, 68, 72, 85, 227
Caucci/Nastasi Compara-dun, 227
CDC Compara-emerger, 72
CDC Early Black Stone, *93*
    recipe for, 217

Centroptilum Emerger, *86*
    recipe for, 209
Cerise Comet, *162*
    recipe for, 233
chalkstreams. *See* spring creeks; spring
    creeks, trout and
Champlain, Lake, 198
Chan's Disco Midge, *92*
    recipe for, 215
Chan's Ice Cream Cone Midge, *89*, *92*
    recipes for, 89, 215
char, 30
    freestone streams and, 55
    overview of, 33–34
Cheesman Canyon, 47, *49*
Chernobyl Hopper/Ant, *106*, *122*
    recipe for, 231
Chicago Leech, *162*
    recipe for, 236
Chinook salmon, 24, *125*, 147, 149, 165,
    234
Christensen, Peter, 33
Cicada Madame X, *120*
    recipe for, 229
Clapton, Eric, *186*
Clark, Austin, *195*, 197, *197*, 198
Clarke, Brian, 30, 64
Clinch Reservoir, 44, 104
Clinch River, 11, 45, 48
Clown Egg, *162*
    recipe for, 233
Club Sandwich Flame, *122*
    recipe for, 233
Club Sandwich Hopper, *122*
    recipe for, 231
Cluster BWO, *84*
    recipe for, 208
Cluster Parachute, *92*
    recipe for, 216
Coffin Fly Spinner, *116*
    recipe for, 225
Cohen, Pat, 161
Cohen's Deer Hair Mouse, *117*
    recipe for, 117
Cohen's Double-D Rainbow Trout, *115*
    recipe for, 115
Cohen's Pelagic General, *161*
    recipe for, 161
Coho salmon, 24
Collie Dog Riffle, *201*
    recipe for, 245
Columbia River, 127, 141
Combs, Trey, 157
Compara-dun, 11, 76
Compara-emerger, *72*, *84*
    recipe for, 207
Complete Brown Trout, The (Heacox), 21
Cook, George, 152
Copper Olive Sculpin Hammer, *166*
    recipe for, 239
Copper Pheasant Tail, *95*
    recipe for, 220
Creamsicle Moose Turd, *202*
    recipe for, 248
Credit River, 198
Crossfield Micro, *201*
    recipe for, 245
Cumberland River, 115
cutthroat trout, 173
Cyclops Foam Orange Beetle, *122*
    recipe for, 232
Cypress River, *32*
Czech Mate Orange, *90*
    recipe for, 213

Czech-Style Caddis, *162*
    recipe for, 237

Dancing Black Elk Caddis, *90*
    recipe for, 213
Dark Hendrickson, *94*
    recipe for, 219
Dark Wulff, *118*
    recipe for, 226
Dartmouth River, 192, *196*
Dean River, 74, 124, *127*, *129*, 141, 152,
    154, 156–157, *156*, 189, 237, 250
Dee, River, *194*
Deer Hair CDC Adult, *90*
    recipe for, 212
Delaware River, 22, *45*, 46, *50*, *52*, 73, 76,
    77, 80, 85, 87, *105*, *113*, 118, 219
    East Branch, 11–12, 66, 70
    Junction pool, 70
    Stockport pool, 46–47
    West Branch, 11–12, 44–46, *70*, *81*
Dirty Male Hex Spinner, *116*
    recipe for, 224
Disco Red, *92*
    recipe for, 215
Disco Stone, *162*
    recipe for, 236
Doddi Orange Traditional, 190–191, *200*
    recipe for, 200
Doddi Orange Tube, *169*, *200*, *204*
    recipes for, 200, 243, 252
Dolly Varden, 33, 34
Dordogne River, 171, *173*
Dorothea T. C. Emerger, *86*
    recipe for, 208
Dorthea/Centrop Emerger, *86*
    recipe for, 210
Dorsey, Pat, 48
Double Undertaker, 177
Double White Muddler, *197*
Downsville Reservoir, 11
Drift boating, 43, *52*, 62, 70, 71, 80, 104,
    105, 113, *127*
Dr. Tom, *162*
    recipe for, 233
Dry Line Steelhead (McMillan), 157

East Koy Creek, 5, 79, 109–110
Edwards, Oliver, 80
Eel River, 139–140
Egg Leech Shaggy Gray, *169*
    recipe for, 242
Egg-Sucking Leech, 239
Egilsson, Vidar, 245
Emerald Erie Shiner, *162*
    recipe for, 234
Emerald Ghost, *170*
    recipe for, 244
Emergers (Richards), 66, 78
EP Shad/Alewife, *118*
    recipe for, 118
Erie, Lake, 132, *138*, *151*, 158, 159
Erie Olive Intruder, *168*
    recipe for, 241
Evil Flamethrower Leech, *166*
    recipe for, 239
Excavator, 158
Extended-Body Sulphur, *86*
    recipe for, 209

Falling Spring Run, 17–18, 40, 42, 43
Falling Springs Scud, *88*
    recipe for, 210
Farrar, John, 152

Female Hendrickson (Spring Creek Style), *94*
  recipe for, 219
Finger Lakes, 198
Fishing the Dry Fly as a Living Insect (Wright), 75
Flaherty, John, 163
Flamethrower Leech, *166*
  recipe for, 239
Fly Fisherman magazine, 91, *129*
Fly Fishing Bible, The (Bashline), 111
Fly Fishing Tailwaters (Dorsey), 48
Foam Ant, *122*
  recipe for, 232
Foam Bubble Emerger, *86*
  recipe for, 210
Foam Sandwich Hex Wiggle, *116*
  recipe for, 225
Foam Spudder Tan, *202*
  recipe for, 249
Fortan, Lee, 193
Fox, Charlie, 99
Francis (fly), 186
Francis Black, *201*
  recipe for, 246
Francis Black Micro, *201*
  recipe for, 245
Francis Green, *202*
  recipe for, 248
Francis Red, *201*
  recipe for, 245
freestone streams
  char and, 55
  grayling and, 55
  salmon and, 74
  steelhead and, 74, 128
freestone streams, trout and, 4, 10, *11*, 15, 21, 53–60, 66–67, 74, 76, 77, 89, 104, 112, 226
  brook, *32*, 55
  brown, *54*, 55, *55*, 56, *56*, 109–111
Frying Pan River, 47–48, 212
Fuzzy Foam Ant, *122*
  recipe for, 232

Gallagher's prawns, 152
Gallegos River, 24
Galloup, Kelly, 104
Gang Bang Drake, *116*
  recipe for, 225
Gaspé Green Stone, *202*
  recipe for, 248
Gaspé Muddler, *204*
  recipe for, 252
Gates Bumblebee, *122*
  recipe for, 233
Gates Housefly, *122*
  recipe for, 231
Gaula River, 182
General Practitioner, 152
George, Lake, 198
Gibinski, Wojtek, 36
Glo-Bug, 140, 234
Goddard, John, 30, 64
Gordon, Theodore, 22, 83, 219
Grand Caspedia River, *12*, *189*, 193, 200, 205
  Charlie Valley rock pool, 176–177
  Salmon Run pool, 192
Grande Riviere, 78, 180
  Sardine Box pool, *174*, 190–191, 194–195
Grand Pabos River, *17*, 191, 205, 249
Grapefruit Sculpin Bugger, *166*
  recipe for, 240

Gray Drake Soft Hackle, *95*
  recipe for, 221
Gray Drake Spinner, *85*
  recipe for, 85
Grayling, 36, *36*, 55, 87
Great Lakes, 20, 24–26, *25*, 27, 32, 34, 74, *100*, 118, 124, 126–131, 134, 137–142, *140*, 144, 146–149, 152, 153, 156, 158–161, 165, 193, 198, 212, 235, 243
See also individual lakes
Steelhead Alley, 132, *138*, 148, *151*, 158, 159, 163
Green Brahan Long Tail, *201*
  recipe for, 246
Green Brahan Micro Cone, *201*
  recipe for, 246
Green Butt Blue Intruder, *170*
  recipe for, 244
Green Butt Longtail, *201*
  recipe for, 246
Green Butt Micro Treble, *201*
  recipe for, 247
Green Butt Stone, *202*
  recipe for, 248
Green Highlander, *10*, 11, *172*, 180, 188
Green Highlander Conehead Tube, *201*
  recipe for, 246
Green Highlander Micro Treble, *201*
  recipe for, 246
Green Machine, 180
Greiner, Bill, 185–186, 191, 203
Grey Ghost, 159, 161
Griffith's Gnat, 76
Gulf of California, 127
Gulper Special, 76
Gunn, Willie, 181

Hairy Mary, *202*
  recipe for, 249
Halford, Frederic, 3, 39
Hang Time Leech, *133*, *166*, *167*
  recipes for, 167, 239
Hare's Ear, *95*
  recipe for, 221
Hatchery Redworm, *92*
  recipe for, 216
Hatches I, 72
Hatches II, 72
Haystack, 118
  recipe for, 227
Heacox, Cecil E., 21
Healy, Joe, 25
Hendrickson Compara-dun, *94*
  recipe for, 219
Hendrickson Compara-emerger, *94*
  recipe for, 219
Hendrickson Nymph, *95*
  recipe for, 221
Hendrickson Spinner, *94*
  recipe for, 219
Henry's Fork, of the Snake River, *41*, 68, 73, 77
Herb's Zebra Shrimp, *88*
  recipe for, 211
Hewitt, Edward, 22
Hexagenia Extended Parachute, *119*
  recipe for, 119
Hex Extended Foam, *116*
  recipe for, 224
Hex Wiggle Foam Dot, *116*
  recipe for, 224
Hi-VIZ Brown/Hopper Stone, *120*
  recipe for, 229
Hogan, Doc, 152

Hojnik, Luka, 35
Holston Reservoir, 44, 104
Horton Brook, 69–70
Hot Creek, *38*, 40
Hot Orange Ant (McMurray), *87*, *122*
  recipes for, 87, 232
Hot Orange Ant (Traditional), *87*, *122*
  recipes for, 87, 232
Hot Orange Francis, *202*, *205*
  recipes for, 205, 249
Howell, Scott, 134, *155*, 157
Howell's Signature Intruder Green Butt—Black, *168*
  recipe for, 240
Howell's Signature Intruder—Purple and Blue, *168*
  recipe for, 240
Howell's Signature Red-Butt Intruder, *168*
  recipe for, 240
Howell's Ska-Opper, *167*
  recipe for, 167
Howell's Squido, *168*
  recipe for, 240
Hucho trout, 23, 34–35, *54*
Hull, Bob, 144, 152, 239
Hull String Leech, 163
Humphreys, Joe, 99
Humphreys' Black and Purple Templedog, *166*
  recipe for, 239
Humphreys' Olive Templedog Tube, *166*
  recipe for, 239
Huron, Lake, 26, 199

Ian's Brass Ass, *92*
  recipe for, 216
Iceabou Nuke, *162*
  recipe for, 233
Ice Dub, 159
Icelandic Rat, *201*
  recipe for, 245
Iceman Creepy, *162*
  recipe for, 235
Ice Man Sac Fry, *162*, *165*
  recipes for, 165, 234
Icsi Midge, *92*
  recipe for, 216
Iliamna Lake, 3–4, *28*, *29*
"Indestructible Haystack, The" (Caucci), 227
In the Ring of the Rise (Marino), 19, *62*, 64
Intruder, 152, 154
Invaria Dun, *86*
  recipe for, 208
ISO Bicolor, *116*
  recipe for, 224
Isocaine Wiggle, *67*, 73
  recipe for, 67
Isonychia Nymph, *95*
  recipe for, 221
Itchen, River, 3, *3*, 102

Jagger, Jason, *62*
Jan's Skid Mark Scud, *88*
  recipe for, 211
Joe's Hopper, *122*
  recipe for, 231
Jonsson, Bror, 174, 175, 178, 181
J:son Adult Stonefly A1 Cinnamon Brown, *96*
  recipe for, 223
J:son Mayfly Dun M1 Brown, *96*
  recipe for, 222

J:son Mayfly Dun M1 Green, *96*
  recipe for, 222
J:son Mayfly Dun M3 Cream, *96*
  recipe for, 222
J:son Mayfly Dun M3 Gold, *96*
  recipe for, 222
J:son Stonefly Nymph S1 Cinammon
    Brown, *96*
  recipe for, 223
J:son Stonefly Nymph S3 Yellow, *96*
  recipe for, 223
J:son Stonefly Spinner/Spent U1 Olive
    Brown, *96*
  recipe for, 223
J:son Wiggle Tail Nymph N1 Olive Brown,
    96
  recipe for, 223

Kamchatka River, 3–4
Karlovka River, *181*
Kaufmann's Stone, *93*
  recipe for, 218
Kettle Creek, 58
Kinney's Speys, 152
Kispiox River, 157
Klamath River, 127, 139–140
Kola River, *172*, 192
Kraft, Brian, 29
Krka River, 35
Krystal Blue Parr, *162*
  recipe for, 234
Krystal Meth Egg, *162*
  recipe for, 233
Kvichak River, 29

Labatt Blue Bomber, 185, 195, *202*
  recipe for, 247
Lady Amherst, 11, *172*, 192
LaFontaine, Gary, 50, 75
LaFontaine's Sparkle Pupa, *90*
  recipe for, 213
lake-run trout, 13–14, 29, 118
  brown, 23–26, *25*, 115, 117, 229
lake trout, 34, *34*, 35
Laxa Blue, 188
Leblanc's Akroyd, *204*
  recipe for, 252
Leblanc's Black and Gold Spey, *204*
  recipe for, 252
Leblanc's Ghost Spey, *204*
  recipe for, 252
Leblanc's Mean Green Spey, *204*
  recipe for, 252
Lee, Art, 171, *178*, 187, 188, 191, 200
Letort Cress Bug, *88*
  recipe for, 210
Letort Cresstacia, *83*, *88*
  recipes for, 83, 211
Letort Cricket, *122*
  recipe for, 232
Letort Hopper, *106*, *122*
  recipe for, 232
Letort Spring Run, *8*, 18, 39, 40, 61, 64, 75,
    98–101, *99*, 229
  Fox's Meadow, 99, 115
Light Cahill, *94*
  recipe for, 218
Light Hendrickson, *94*
  recipe for, 219
limestoners. *See* spring creeks; spring
    creeks, trout and
Lime Weenie, *162*
  recipe for, 237
Linsenman, Bob, 104

Little Manistee River, 138–139
Litza River, *181*
Lynch, Tommy, *104*

Madison River, 53, *114*, 217
Maggot, *162*
  recipe for, 237
Magog fly pattern, 159
Magog Smelt, 180, *204*
  recipe for, 253
Mahogany Borchers, 118
  recipe for, 227
Mahogany ISO Spinner, *116*
  recipe for, 226
Malbaie Rubber Legs, *203*, *204*
  recipes for, 203, 253
Malibu Creek, 127
Manistee River, 24, 108
Marabou Parr, *169*
  recipe for, 242
Marble trout, 23, 34–35, *35*, *54*
March Brown, 56
March Brown T. C., recipe for, 220
Margaree River, 200
Marinaro, Vince, 17, 19, 39, 42, 56, *62*, 64,
    65, 69, 75, 77, 102, 106
Marinaro Sulphur Parachute, *86*
  recipe for, 208
Martin, Don, *102*
Matapedia River, 191, 192
Mattea, Bill, 193
Matt's Back Alley Shrimp Roadkill, *204*
  recipe for, 250
Matt's Chinook Fry, *162*
  recipe for, 235
Matt's Latex Wiggle Hex, *162*
  recipe for, 235
Matt's Marabou Hex Wiggle, *95*
  recipe for, 222
Matt's Mykiss Shrimp, *162*, *165*
  recipes for, 165, 234
Matt's Salar Octopussy, *204*
  recipe for, 250
Matt's Steelhead Soft Hackle, *162*
  recipe for, 236
Matuka, *32*
Maxwell, Mike, 157
Mayfly Emerger Rabbit's Foot, *94*
  recipe for, 218
Mayfly Wiggle Gray Fox, *95*
  recipe for, 221
McCloud River, 127, 139–140
McMillan, Bill, 142, 157
Merlino, Rick, 165
Merlino's ISO Dice, *94*
  recipe for, 220
Merlino's Sculpin Hex, *162*, *165*
  recipes for, 165, 235
Michigan, Lake, 24, 131–132, 139, *142*,
    147, 158
Micro Sunray Shadow, *201*
  recipe for, 245
Mike's Butter Churn, *121*
  recipe for, 230
Mike's Mufasa, *121*
  recipe for, 230
Mike's Red Rocket, *121*
  recipe for, 230
Miller, John, 12, 46, 51–52, *52*, 67, *70*, 77,
    80, 85, *113*
Mirage Mo Drake, *116*
  recipe for, 225
Miramichi River, 186, 200
Missouri River, 44, *45*, 50, 73, *105*, 213

Modern Streamers for Trophy Trout (Galloup
    and Linsenman), 104
Mo Diving Caddis, *90*
  recipe for, 214
Mo Gray Drake, *116*
  recipe for, 224
Mo Green Caddis Larva, *90*
  recipe for, 213
Mo Green Emerger, *90*
  recipe for, 213
Mo Hydro Adult, *90*
  recipes for, 213, 214
Monroe's Killer, 188
Morrish Golden Stone, *93*
  recipe for, 217
Morrish Hopper—Green, *122*
  recipe for, 230
Morrish Hopper—Yellow, *117*, *122*
  recipes for, 117, 230
Morrish Sculpin, *121*
Morrish Simple Mouse, *120*
  recipe for, 228
Morrish's Fluttering Stonefly, *119*, *120*
  recipes for, 119, 228
Mörrum River, 24, *179*, *184*
Moser, Roman, *11*, 53–54, 115, 211, 229
Moser Sparkle Caddis, *90*
  recipe for, 214
Moser's Emerger, *95*
  recipe for, 222
Moser's Killer Bug, *88*
  recipe for, 211
Moser's 3-D Plush Sculpin, *121*
  recipe for, 229
Mossy Creek, 40, 106–107, 109
Mo Tiny Green, *90*
  recipe for, 212
Mr. Rapidan Parachute, 118
  recipe for, 226
Mr. Rapidan Traditional, 118
  recipe for, 226
Muddler, 189
Muddler Minnow, *32*
Mueller, Walt, 29–30
Munroe Killer Longtail, 201
  recipe for, 246
Murphy, John, 197, *199*
Murphy, Shawn, *104*, *153*, 197, *197*, 198
Muskegon Caddis Pupa, *90*, *91*
  recipes for, 91, 213
Muskegon River, *20*, 45, 49, 73, 75, 99, 115,
    129–132, *130*, 142, 145, *147*, *150*, 159,
    213, 224
  Sycamore Run pool, 147–149
Mysis Dead White, *88*
  recipe for, 212
Mysis Transparent Laney's, *88*
  recipe for, 211
Myvatan, Lake, 75, 186, *187*

Nagy's Niagara, *162*
  recipe for, 233
Nastasi, Bob, 68
Navajo Dam, 44
Nelson's Spring Creek, 40, 42, 43, *68*, 114
Neversink River, 52–53, *53*, 83
Ngaruroro River, 26
Niagara River, *109*, 150, 159
Night fishing, 35, *104*, 108, 110–113
Night Fishing for Trout (Bashline), 111
Nipigon River, 32
North Umpqua River, 74, 134, 155, 157,
    167

Nuke Pearl Amherst, *169*
  recipe for, 242
Nymphs and the Trout (Sawyer), *51*

October Caddis, *90, 202*
  recipes for, 214, 250
Olive Bugger, 114
Olive Krystal Scud, *88*
  recipe for, 212
Oliver Edwards's Black Stone, *93*
  recipe for, 217
Oliver Edwards's Deep-Diving Shrimp, *88*
  recipe for, 211
Oliver Edwards's Green Drake, *116*
  recipe for, 226
Oliver Edwards's Simple Hydro Larva, *90*
  recipe for, 213
Oliver Edwards's Yellow Sally, *93*
  recipe for, 217
Ontario, Lake, 124, 159, 198
  Niagara Bar, 161
Opaque Ghost Egg Invader, *170*
  recipe for, 244
Opossum Caddis, *162*
  recipe for, 237
Orange and Blue Templedog Tube, *169*
  recipe for, 242
Orange Autumn Stone, *202*
  recipe for, 248
Orange Crush Bomber, *202*
  recipe for, 248
Orange Scud, *88*
  recipe for, 211
Orange Stimulator Hopper, *122*
  recipe for, 232
Otter Egg, *30,* 135–136, 148
Otter Sucker, 165
Otter Sucker Nuke Gummie—Niagara, *162*
  recipe for, 234
Otter Sucker Nuke Gummie—Pink Ice, *162*
  recipe for, 234
Otter Sucker Spawn Trout Smack, *95*
  recipe for, 221
Otter Wiggle Egg, *162*
  recipe for, 234
Owen River, 26

Pabos River, 190, 192
Pacheco, Juan, 113
Pacific Ocean, 24, 129
Pacific salmon. *See* salmon, Pacific
Passion for Steelhead (Hogan), 152
Passive/Dormant (P/D) phase
  overview of, 9, 15–18
  salmon and, 15–17, *16, 17,* 159, 172,
    178, 179, 182, 185, 192–198, *193,* 200,
    203, 205, 250
  steelhead and, 15–17, *16,* 124, 126–127,
    132, 134, 137, 142, 143, 146, 152, 155–
    160, *160,* 163, 165
Passive/Dormant (P/D) phase, trout and,
  20, 103, 111, *113,* 119
  brown, 15–17, 104, 108, 110, 113, 114
  overview of, 15–17, 21
Pearl Brassie, *92*
  recipe for, 215
Pearl Scud, *88*
  recipe for, 212
Pearl Squid Egg Invader, *170*
  recipe for, 244
Penn's Creek, 76
Pennsylvania Honey Bug, 114
Pepacton Reservoir, 11, 44

Pere Marquette River, *11,* 39, 104, 108, 111,
  159, 161, 224
Perry, Art, 188
Petite Cascapedia River, 193
Pheasant Tail Nymph, 42, *51,* 69–70, 103,
  220
Pine Creek, 58
Piotr's Polish-Woven Mayfly, *87*
  recipe for, 87
Platte River, 128–129
PMD/Callibaetis, *86*
  recipe for, 209
PMD Dun, *86*
  recipe for, 209
Pobst, Dick, 75
Polish-Woven BWO, *84*
  recipe for, 207
Polish-Woven Green Caddis, *162*
  recipe for, 236
Polish-Woven Light BWO, *84*
  recipe for, 208
Pompier, 180
Pompier Treble, *204*
  recipe for, 251
Pom Pom Girl, *162*
  recipe for, 233
Ponoi River, 180–182, *181, 182*
Poppelhoj, Mikkel, *5*
Portland Creek, 188
Potamanthus T. C., *116*
  recipe for, 225
Pseudocloeon Dun, *84*
  recipe for, 208
P. T. Stillborn BWO Nymph, *84*
  recipe for, 207
Purnell, Ross, *129*

Quill Gordon, 3, *83, 94*
  recipes for, 83, 219
Quill Peacock Buzzer, *92*
  recipe for, 215

rainbow trout, *114,* 127, 140
  A/A phase and, 26–30, *27, 28,* 33, 97,
    104, 114, 142
  habituation and, 17–18
  overview of, 26–30
  spring creeks and, 27, 43, 97
  S/R phase and, 17–18, 26, 27, *31,* 45, *45,*
    46, 59, 60, 82
  tailwaters and, 22, 45–47, *45,* 51–52, 104,
    115
Rainy's Grand Foam Hopper—Brown, *122*
  recipe for, 230
Rainy's Grand Foam Hopper—Green, *122*
  recipe for, 231
Rainy's Grand Foam Hopper—Yellow, *122*
  recipe for, 231
Ranga River, *175*
Ranga Tube, *201*
  recipe for, 245
Rangeley Lakes, 161, 198–199
Rangitaiki River, 26
Razorback Cress Bug, *88*
  recipe for, 210
Red and Black Templedog Tube, *169*
  recipe for, 242
Red Butt Midge, *92*
  recipe for, 215
Red Cyclops Intruder Tube, *166*
  recipe for, 239
Red-Eye Disco, *92*
  recipe for, 215

Redworm Black Head, *92*
  recipe for, 216
Reversed Parachute BWO, *84*
  recipe for, 207
Richards, Carl, 1, 5, 50, *66, 67,* 72, 75, 78,
  81, 91, 119, 212, 213
Riffling Hitch (Lee), 188
Ripple Crush Bugger Leech, *166*
  recipe for, 240
Ripple Crush Fruity, *162*
  recipe for, 233
Ripple Crush Niagara Gold, *162*
  recipe for, 233
Rio Grande, 24
Roadkill Coon Grizzly, *204*
  recipe for, 250
Rob's Black and Yellow Templedog, *204*
  recipe for, 251
Rob's Black Shrimp, *204*
  recipe for, 251
Rob's Orange Shrimp, *204*
  recipe for, 251
Rob's Raider, *204*
  recipe for, 251
Rob's Willie Gunn Templedog, *200, 204*
  recipes for, 200, 252
Rocky River, 133–134
Rogue River, 242
Roman Moser Traun River Stone, *93*
  recipe for, 218
Royal Coachman, 87
Royal Coachman Wulff, *175, 202*
  recipe for, 249
Royal Wulff, 60
Ruedi Dam, 47–48
Rusty Bronze Spinner, *84*
  recipe for, 207
Rusty Spinner, *86*
  recipe for, 209

Sacramento River, 139–140
Salar Root Beer Pupa, *90*
  recipe for, 212
salmon, *100,* 126, 128, *130, 132,* 141, *144,*
  159, 167
salmon, Atlantic, *10,* 14, 19–20, *20,* 24, 35,
  74, 104, 109, 118, 124, *124,* 130, 131,
  136, *140,* 142–143, 145–146, 150, 161,
  173, 174, 175, 178, 179, 181, 183, 184,
  186, 188, 190, 191, 194, 196, 197, 198
  See also salmon flies
  A/A phase and, 9, 11, 78, 141, *171,171,*
    172, 174, 177, *177,* 179–182, *182,* 189,
    193–194, *193,* 196–200, 203, 252
  catch-and-release waters and, 2, 15–16,
    195
  freestone streams and, 74
  landlocked, 198–199, *199,* 229
  overview of, 171–179
  P/D phase and, 15–17, *16, 17,*172, 178,
    179, 182, 185, 192–198, *193,* 200, 203,
    205, 250
  spring creeks and, 186
  S/R phase and, 12–15, 64, 65, 79, 172,
    174, 179, 182–192, *189,* 205, 245, 247
salmon, Pacific, 26, 28–30, 130, 140
  chinook, 24, *125,* 147, 149, 165, 234
  coho, 24
  sockeye, 29
salmon flies
  dry / subsurface wet patterns, array of,
    202
  dry / subsurface wet recipes, *247–250*